YALI'S
QUESTION

THE LEWIS HENRY MORGAN LECTURES / 2002

Presented at

THE UNIVERSITY OF ROCHESTER
Rochester, New York

YALI'S QUESTION

Sugar, Culture, and History

Frederick Errington
& Deborah Gewertz

WITH A FOREWORD BY ANTHONY T. CARTER

The University of Chicago Press   •   Chicago and London

FREDERICK ERRINGTON is Distinguished Professor of Anthropology at Trinity College. DEBORAH GEWERTZ is the G. Henry Whitcomb Professor of Anthropology at Amherst College. They are authors of four previous books together, most recently *Emerging Class in Papua New Guinea*.

The University of Chicago Press, Chicago 60637
The University of Chicago Press, Ltd., London
© 2004 by The University of Chicago
All rights reserved. Published 2004
Printed in the United States of America

13 12 11 10 09 08 07 06 05 04   5 4 3 2 1

ISBN (cloth): 0-226-21745-0
ISBN (paper): 0-226-21746-9

Library of Congress Cataloging-in-Publication Data

Errington, Frederick Karl.
    Yali's question : sugar, culture, and history / Frederick Errington &
Deborah Gewertz ; with a foreword by Anthony T. Carter.
        p.   cm. — (The Lewis Henry Morgan lectures ; 2002)
    Includes bibliographical references and index.
    ISBN 0-226-21745-0 (cloth : alk. paper) — ISBN 0-226-21746-9 (pbk. :
alk. paper)
    1. Ramu Sugar Limited.   2. Sugarcane industry—Papua New Guinea.
3. Social responsibility of business—Papua New Guinea—Case studies.
I. Gewertz, Deborah B., 1948– II. Title.   III. Series.
    HD9116.P264R353   2004
    338.7′63361′099573—dc22

                                                          2004003606

Contents

Illustrations

Foreword

Frederick Errington and Deborah Gewertz delivered the Lewis Henry Morgan Lectures on which *Yali's Question: Sugar, Culture, and History* is based at the University of Rochester in October 2002. Their lectures were the fortieth in a series offered annually to the public and to students and faculty at the University of Rochester by the Department of Anthropology. The forty-first lectures were presented in 2003 by Elinore Ochs. Paul Farmer will give the forty-second Morgan Lectures in 2004.

The lectures honor Lewis Henry Morgan. In addition to playing a signal role in the creation of modern anthropology, Morgan was a prominent Rochester attorney and a benefactor of the University of Rochester from its beginning. At the end of his life, he left the University money for a women's college as well as his manuscripts and library.

Yali's Question is, in the first instance, the story of Ramu Sugar Limited (RSL), a sugar estate and development project in Papua New Guinea (PNG). RSL was established in the late 1970s and early 1980s at the behest of the PNG government and with assistance from the global agricultural management firm, Booker Agricultural International, subsequently Booker Tate Limited (BTL). With somewhat more than 7,000 hectares in sugar cane and a factory with the capacity to produce 30,000 tons of "high-quality" refined sugar annually, RSL is a modest estate from a global perspective, but it is an enormous project in postcolonial PNG.

Errington and Gewertz follow the story of Ramu Sugar Limited through the intersecting local, national, and global narratives that have given the project its complex and always contested shape. Importantly, RSL might never have happened. The land might have been left in the hands of its native "owners" or, once it had been "purchased" by the government, leased to one or more privately owned cattle ranches. When it was determined that PNG should have a sugar industry, it might have taken the form of a series of small-scale facilities for producing raw sugar or a cooperative sugar factory, both common in India where the PNG government looked for models.

As Errington and Gewertz tell it, the story begins with the activities of Yali, the famous cargo cult leader, and other Papua New Guineans in Allied military intelligence during the Second World War. After the war, Yali became a strong advocate of racial equality who, the authors argue, would have embraced RSL as a means to this equality.

The story of RSL continues with the patrol reports of Australian colonial officials who toured the Ramu Valley in 1951 and 1960 and the planning guidelines and memoranda of the United Nations Development Program and of variously situated members of the government of PNG in the years leading up to and following independence in 1975.

Once the project is approved, the focus of the story shifts to the personal narratives of the expatriates—citizens of the United Kingdom and other developed countries—in charge of the construction and management of the estate, of the Papua New Guineans who are employed on it, and of the other Papua New Guineans living in the area who make claims on the land, sell sugar cane to the factory, or hope to benefit from its activities.

The RSL story threatens to come to an end in 2000 with the reports and documents produced by RSL and PNG government officials, by World Bank missions, and by academic critics of "free trade" as international advocates of globalization turned their attention to PNG. The tariff reductions advocated in the name of "free trade" would very likely put RSL out of business. At the outset, one might well have preferred to see PNG invest in a number of small-scale raw sugar projects. This was a direction the government considered and that appeared to fit the agriculture- and employment-based development strategy advocated by at least some officials and academic observers.[1] Twenty years later, however, with vast amounts of human effort

1. See, e.g., John W. Mellor, *The New Economics of Growth* (Ithaca, NY: Cornell University Press, 1976).

and tens of millions of dollars invested, Errington and Gewertz argue persuasively that the collapse of RSL will work enormous hardship with little plausible prospect for gain elsewhere in PNG's frail economy.

Informed by Errington and Gewertz's long involvement in PNG and gripping in its own right, the story of RSL also is a version of the stories of development projects around the world: from the Bhilai Steel Plant, the massive steel mill in Chhattisgarh, India, now being studied by the former Morgan lecturer Jonathan Parry, to proposals to build a "mixed-use complex," including a Frank Gehrey–designed arena for the Nets basketball team, in downtown Brooklyn. Like many colonial governments and most governments of newly independent states, the government of Papua New Guinea saw itself as using modern global knowledge to understand, transform, and improve local resources, human and material. Booker Tate Limited is one of a great many multinational companies operating in this milieu by providing management services and scientific knowledge to new enterprises in developing countries. The story of RSL thus speaks to wider issues involved in development efforts and their consequences in the landscape of nation-states that formed in the last half of the twentieth century. It forces us to ask how it happens that such efforts alleviate or exacerbate the systems of structural violence that rend human communities.

Errington and Gewertz also urge that the story of RSL is a piece of the story of how it came to be that "we"—the makers and readers of books in the developed world—have so very much while "they"—Yali, the inhabitants of the Ramu valley, and folks in the developing world generally—have so very little. Indeed, they argue that the story of RSL *is* this larger story in a nutshell. Here they engage with Jared Diamond's Pulitzer Prize–winning book, *Guns, Germs and Steel*, noting that Yali, the mid-twentieth-century PNG activitist, also was Diamond's interlocutor, that Diamond was endeavoring to answer what he took to be Yali's question: Why do black people have so little and white people so much?

In Errington and Gewertz's account, Diamond argues that the privileged position of those of us who are "developed" is not the result of our merits, but instead is a consequence of impersonal processes of cultural evolution. Human beings who lived in parts of the world favorable to the development of agriculture and the domestication of animals were more likely to engage in warfare and develop superior weapons, be exposed to infectious diseases and acquire immunity to them, and ultimately to develop large and complex industrial organizations. People with these attributes have the capacity to dominate others and, responding to compulsions inherent in human nature, they inevitably do so, all too often with unabashed brutality as in Tasmania[2] or King Leopold's Congo.[3]

Diamond is not, of course, alone in making arguments of this sort. Nearly a hundred years ago, Franz Boas, the founding figure of American anthropology, offered a not dissimilar account of why "the European race" had developed such a "high" civilization.[4]

Though they recognize that such accounts have the merit of being anti-racist, Errington and Gewertz argue that they are empirically and morally false. Empirically false because, as the case of RSL demonstrates, the people who plan and create development projects do not unthinkingly act out the compulsions of human nature but instead make choices. The government of PNG might have invested in dispersed raw sugar production or a cooperative sugar factory. Coca-Cola Amatil, the PNG producer of Coca-Cola products, could continue to produce soft drinks with less refined sugar. The World Bank is not required to "encourage" the government of PNG to eliminate tariff protections for the miniscule PNG sugar industry. Morally wrong because they serve as ideologies that enable us to overlook the choices we make and justify our privileged positions: we did not will it to be this way; it could not be otherwise.

To get it empirically and morally right, Errington and Gewertz suggest, we must understand Yali's question in a different way. In their view, Yali was not centrally concerned with the "goods" possessed by persons from "developed" societies—as if "goods" were inherently good. Rather, he was concerned with the unwillingness of those persons to accord moral worth to Papua New Guineans—to engage them as full human beings. Treating others as objects is, alas, all too common, but it is worth reiterating that recognizing others as persons like oneself makes it much harder to treat them violently.

Anthony T. Carter, Editor
The Lewis Henry Morgan Lectures

2. Robert Brain, *Into the Primitive Environment* (Englewood Cliffs, NJ: Prentice-Hall, 1972).

3. Adam Hochschild, *King Leopold's Ghost* (London: Pan Macmillan, 2002).

4. Franz Boas, *The Mind of Primitive Man* [1911] (New York: Collier Books, 1963).

Acknowledgments

MANY PEOPLE at Ramu Sugar Limited and elsewhere participated in this project. Without some of you, we would never have been welcomed to RSL. Without others, we would never have understood the complexities of our subject—the history of development projects in Papua New Guinea, the nature of sugar-based lives, the intricacies of field and factory coordination. We would also have been very lonely, and we would have produced a far less lucid manuscript. Each of you has given us important assistance. We hope that our book does justice to your help—our friends, colleagues, and teachers.

We wish we could thank you individually, but the list of your names would be lengthy indeed. There are those, however, whom we must single out for their special encouragement and assistance. First, there is Carolyn Errington, our extraordinary editor. Then there are David Brent, Peter Colton, Bryan Dyer, Paul Emmanuel, Peter Errington, Martin Evans, Wilson Gagas, Elizabeth Garland, Di and Stuart Hayes, Joe Herman, Robin Hide, Hartmut and Susanne Holzknecht, Kenzy Kamdan, Saking Kiruak, Lastus Kuniata, Ella Kusnetz, Yalibu Mangai, Sidney Mintz, Emmanuel Moba, Jack Morris, Nabua Morissa, Annamale Naicker, Michael Quenby, Carlisle Rex-Waller, Ed Robinson, Marilyn Strathern, Sidney Suma, Steve Vaux, Robin Wilson, and the anonymous reviewers for the University of Chicago Press.

In addition, we must mention the members of the Department of Anthropology at the University of Rochester, who not only invited us to give the 2002 Lewis Henry Morgan Lectures based upon our Ramu Sugar research, but also provided valuable criticism of an early manuscript. Thanks to Anthony Carter, Ayala Emmett, Signitia Fordham, Robert Foster, and Thomas Gibson.

Moreover, we gratefully acknowledge those who sustained us financially. We both received faculty research grants, Deborah from Amherst College and Fred from Trinity College. The Axel Schupf Research Fund at Amherst College deserves special mention. In addition, the work was supported through an International Award, jointly conferred by the American Council of Learned Societies, the Social Science Research Council, and the National Endowment for the Humanities.

We must also stress that, although those at Ramu Sugar Limited and Booker Tate Limited helped us greatly with our research, this book should in no way be regarded as reflecting the official positions of these companies.

Finally, and as always, we each thank the other.

.　.　.

We thank Booker Tate Limited for permission to reprint figures 1, 3, 7, and 11; Di Hayes for permission to reprint figures 6 and 13; the Australian War Memorial for permission to reprint figure 5 (negative P01090.001); the Victoria and Albert Museum for permission to reprint figure 20; figure 14, RSL for permission to reprint an advertisement displayed in Papua New Guinea. All other figures are our own.

Introduction: On Avoiding a History of the Self-Evident and the Self-Interested

WE WERE IMPRESSED AND AMAZED. Ramu Sugar Limited (RSL) is big and startling. Though we had been coming to Papua New Guinea for more than thirty years to do anthropological field research, we had never before visited, much less worked, at a place like RSL. Brought into existence in a remote part of Papua New Guinea's Upper Ramu Valley (see fig. 1), RSL is an embodiment of imported industrial production. Its Dickensian, smoke-belching, steam-shrieking factory and vast fields of carefully tended sugarcane contrast sharply with the surrounding grass-land, punctuated only by an occasional village (fig. 2). We soon learned that RSL is not only an immense physical fact, but also an immense social fact: it not only dominates and organizes the landscape, it also shapes, and is shaped by, the consciousness of those culturally diverse thousands who left their homes to live and work there. How was such a big and startling—and transforming—place established? And how does it work? Where is it going?

The world is filled with big, startling, and transforming places (and smaller but no less interesting and significant ones)—Cape Canaveral, Walt Disney World, the Eiffel Tower, Malaysia's Petronas Towers. These places are brought into being. They, in turn, bring people together to plan, to build, to work, to play. They sometimes flourish, are expanded, renovated, resurrected; they sometimes deteriorate, are diminished,

MAP 1

Papua New Guinea

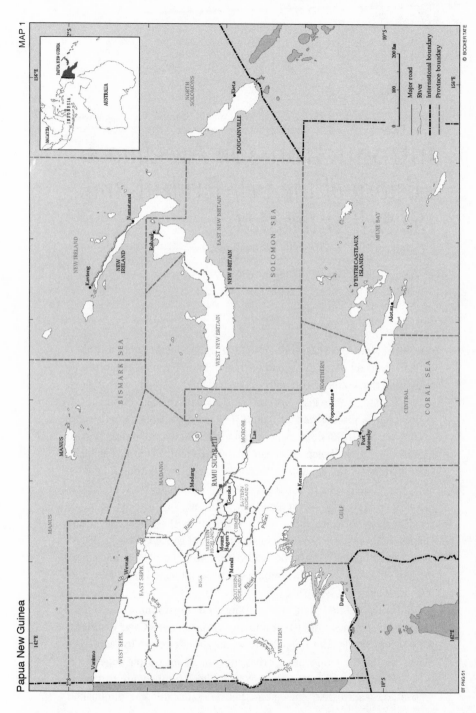

Figure 1. Ramu Sugar Limited within Papua New Guinea

imperiled, bombed. This book is an anthropological effort to tell the story—the history—of one such place. By extension, it is an anthropological effort to understand all such places as they are: to see them as the complex products of people located in specific times and places mobilizing (or being mobilized); to see them as the products of people with particular ideas about the desirable and the feasible. To understand such places requires that we actually investigate what historically and culturally located people want and seek.

Such an investigation demands that we scrutinize our own understandings, our own (often early) impressions. It requires that we problematize our own taken-for-granted ideas about why and how people act: our ideas about human nature, about the causes and objectives of human action, about the ways people intend one thing to follow from another, about how and why people engage in collective action. This course demands the recognition that not everyone in the world has the same objectives as contemporary Americans, wanting and seeking the same sorts of things as we do. Correspondingly, we must recognize that our own desires and lives, like the desires and lives of others elsewhere, are historically and culturally constructed. To think about such things, which is to say, to think not only about how differently located others think and live, but also about how we think and live, can be a sobering, if not a daunting, experience. However, working hard—taking care—to get such matters relatively right can be very worth doing, both intellectually liberating and politically significant.

Therefore, in telling the story of how a sugar plantation became such a transformative presence in Papua New Guinea, we take care to avoid assuming that we already largely know why and how it came to be. We take care to avoid wrapping up the whole complex process in any taken-for-granted package—labeled, for instance, with such apparently self-evident words as "progress" or "modernization." We take care to show, instead, that RSL was made to happen by often diversely positioned people conducting themselves according to a range of culturally grounded ideas about what life is and might become.

Such visions about life and its possibilities are embodied in the accounts—the narratives—that people convey about what is worth seeking and why.[1] As we use the term, narratives are a critically important aspect of culture: they organize desire and compel action by providing statements or images of, for example, lives well-lived or business unfinished, chances taken or opportunities missed, glory days or dark nights of the soul, overwhelming victory or humiliating defeat, salvation or

Figure 2. RSL's smoke-belching factory

damnation. Taking a range of forms, appearing in a range of contexts, and existing on a range of scales, narratives anchor people in their pasts, situate them in their presents, and—of even more importance—project them into their futures. Depending on the cultural circumstance, such narrative forms, contexts, and scales include spontaneous reminiscences and meditations on the meaning of life, family photo albums and formal biographies and histories, interviewing tips and structured career training programs, family budgets and corporate prospectuses, tearful memorial testimonies and funeral orations, just-so stories and clan origin myths, parental injunctions and initiation rituals, advertisements for lifestyle enhancement and national development projects.[2]

As we shall see, such narratives are far from static. As with other aspects of culture, they are worked through in various ways: they are thought about, commented upon, contested, borrowed, changed, and amalgamated as people deal with each other and with what has happened. In addition, we must recognize that, in their narratives (as they envision the desirable and the feasible, as they think about the way the world works), people must always, of course, accept the existence of material constraints. Not everything is possible: houses have to be built on reasonably stable foundations; neighboring groups with their own agendas have to be dealt with; illness, injury, and death have to be coped with. But such material constraints still leave considerable latitude for cultural shaping. Thus houses can be massive structures in nucleated villages or slapped-together shelters in dispersed hamlets; neighbors can be allies and trading partners or enemies and competitors; illness, injury, and death can be accepted as the lot of humankind or retaliated against as an unconscionable assault by malevolent forces. Correspondingly, big and startling RSL is the product of both practical and cultural appraisals. It could not have been built on a cloud—or even in a swamp. It could not have been built without international capital. But its existence reflects narratives that concern not only the practical feasibility of commercial sugar production in the Upper Ramu Valley but also a range of cultural perspectives about why such production might be desirable—and for whom.

To do justice to the complexity of RSL, all of these narratives must enter into our story. Some will be more familiar than others to readers with contemporary Western sensibilities. But unless we stretch our imaginations to take seriously perspectives and responses not necessarily our own, we will likely misread events as they have played and often continue to play out. Such a misreading, as we shall see, leads to an inaccurate history, a history written according to one's familiar perspectives and according to one's comfortable responses. Such a history is, ultimately, both intellectually and politically flawed. It is likely to be both a history of the self-evident and the self-interested.

In this book, we not only try to avoid a history of the self-evident and the self-interested. We also continue to argue actively against it. We will insist that it is not enough to say, for instance, that given certain familiar understandings of power and its uses, "of course" industrially organized RSL came to dominate physically and socially over the Upper Ramu Valley, or that "of course" RSL eventually came to be dominated by the free-trade policies of the World Bank and World Trade Organization. (Nor, clearly, is it enough to say that, given a particular distribution of power in the early twenty-first-century United States, "of course" the "Bush Doctrine" came into being and led to the invasion of Iraq.) Such a view does not consider that power and its uses are understood in historically and culturally variable ways, subject to a range of perspectives about the desirable and the feasible. Such a view, as we shall see, also leaves out issues of responsibility for making decisions, for choosing among the alternatives that are always available at any historical time. That power is reflected in historical outcomes is obvious. Less obvious is how to think about such outcomes, especially those that are historically or culturally distant: to understand how objectives and alternatives have been framed and pursued, to understand how choices have been made among them.

To comprehend, thus, how RSL was brought into existence, we must explore a range of different visions and alternatives. Australian colonists, British sugar experts, Papua New Guinean nationalists, ethnically diverse villagers, and others had sought to enact their different perspectives about what the sugar plantation was to be and why: What did development mean and for whom? How might land in the Upper Ramu Valley best be used? Was that land a commodity that could be bought and sold? How should ancestral presences in the land be appeased? Could sugar production actually help Papua New Guineans establish an independent nation, the equivalent of other nations in the world? Was white sugar better than dark sugar? Was one big project better than several small projects? How should labor be recruited, organized, and disciplined? How could people from all over the country and from many parts of the world live together? Who would be in charge? How and under what conditions would Papua New Guineans acquire European technical skills? Who owed what to whom?

Among those who would have had a particular view on all of these questions was Yali, a Papua New Guinean political leader who was active in RSL's sphere of influence. And Yali, it just so happens, features not only in our story about historical outcomes, but also in the story told by an especially interesting representative of the position we wish to contrast with our own. To clarify both the content and the political importance of our anthropological perspective, we consider the ideas of Jared Diamond, who less by default than by design, denies significance to cultural differences—denies relevance to particular, historically located visions of the desirable and the feasible. Diamond, a biologist who has long studied birds in Papua New Guinea and elsewhere,[3] wrote a Pulitzer-prize winning analysis of thirteen thousand years of world history, *Guns, Germs, and Steel* (1997). Although his book is certainly impressive—both compelling and sophisticated—we find it problematic in its view that history's grand course can be adequately understood without considering culturally grounded ideas about what life is and might become—without considering the ways in which various people understand the desirable and the feasible. Our disagreement with Diamond is not, we think, simply a reflection of the generality of his focus on history's sweep worldwide versus the specificity of our focus on history's swoop into the Upper Ramu Valley: our disagreement does not stem from our differences in scale, but from our differences on how history gets made.[4]

Diamond begins his book with reference to a 1972 conversation he had in Papua New Guinea with Yali. We knew about Yali well before both our RSL research and our reading of Diamond's book. Yali had become famous in the anthropology of Papua New Guinea as a "cargo cultist": Peter Lawrence (1964) writes about Yali's attempts, partially through magic and ritual, to bring Western commodities, or "cargo," to his people. Diamond reports that Yali wanted him to explain the discrepancies he was seeing: "Why is it that you white people developed so much cargo and brought it to New Guinea, but we black people had little cargo of our own?" (Diamond 1997: 14). Diamond's understanding of Yali's question leads to an extended answer, indeed to his book. *Guns, Germs, and Steel* is a discussion of the unfolding of the global patterns, as he understands them, that have accounted for "history's haves and have-nots" (93): it is a discussion of the geographical differences that allowed certain people to have the power of guns, germs, and steel on their side. Conversely, our anthropological understanding of Yali's question leads to a very different response, which we articulate in the form of this history of RSL.

In effect, from our anthropological perspective, Diamond gets Yali's question wrong. As we show in some detail in chapter 1, whereas Diamond understands Yali to be asking about "things," about Western "goods," Yali was actually asking about social equality. Whereas Diamond thinks Yali coveted nifty Western stuff, Yali actually resented the not-so-nifty Western condescension that allowed Europeans to deny Papua New Guineans fundamental worth. The misunderstanding matters, we think, as more than an issue of factual error. That Diamond does not stretch his imagination to understand Yali's cultural views of the desirable and the feasible is consistent with the history he presents. This is a history that he believes happened for reasons that we in the contemporary West already believe in. It is a history that accords with our view of how the world works. Because this history conveys the perspectives of the "haves," it not only hinges on the seemingly self-evident, it also sustains the self-interested.

In outline, this is the answer, the history, that Diamond sets out in response to Yali's question: Human beings evolved and eventually dispersed themselves throughout the earth. There were some who lived in geographical areas conducive to the development of agriculture and the domestication of animals, complex processes that were in no way beyond the intellectual capacities of any human group. All people everywhere were equally intelligent, and members of any group, living in appropriate areas, would have developed agriculture and domesticated animals. However, once certain people did develop agriculture and domesticate animals, they had distinct evolutionary advantages deriving from the population expansion these new forms of food production allowed: the more food available, the more people who could be supported, and the greater the number of specialists (including soldiers) who could be maintained. And significantly, the more people there were, the more necessary arable land became and the more likely people were to go to war to get it. Warfare, in turn, brought about the need for effective weaponry. Therefore, over time, those with certain mineral resources and with skilled craft specialists fashioned and employed superior weapons (eventually made of steel) to vanquish their neighbors. Moreover, those who could utilize metal and support craft specialists had other advantages as well. First, as agriculturalists with high population densities, they had developed hierarchically organized social organizations. Second, as people living around others and around animals, they had developed immunities to certain germs. Superior weapons and organizational skills (technologies and techniques), along with immunological resistances, enabled such groups, or apparently impelled them, to embark on ambitious programs of expansion, leading, repeatedly, to the conquest and exploitation of others. Especially vulnerable were those geographically cut off from such centers of innovation. Thus, eventually and inevitably, the native peoples of the New World (and elsewhere) were easily subjugated by a combination of guns, germs, and steel.

As Diamond brings this argument back to Yali and Yali's question, he stresses—and, of course, we agree—that Yali's circumstances did not reflect any lack either in his intelligence or in that of other Papua New Guineans. Rather, we learn that Yali was poor and relatively powerless in his own domain because his ancestors lacked access to the mineral resources, domesticable animals, and the other advantages that allowed some to conquer others. He was born, in terms of the luck-of-the-environmental draw, on the wrong side of the great geographical divide.

Yet neither Yali nor most of the other Papua New Guineans we have known over our years at RSL and elsewhere in the country would be satisfied with the inexorability of Diamond's luck-of-the-draw answer, with the implications of his that's-just-the-way-things-were-and-hence-must-be response. Such an answer would strike them as a perverse justification of colonial forms of inequality, part of a narrative that denied them moral worth in the past, to say nothing of the future. Indeed, as we shall soon see, the founding and development of RSL became part of a pressing narrative for reclaiming rightful worth in Papua New Guinea.

However, it is just Diamond's sort of answer, just this sort of invocation of historical inevitability, that tends to satisfy those who are already the haves. In this regard, the ideology inherent in Diamond's reasoning goes well beyond the particulars of the history he presents. This ideology supports the status quo, the interests of the already powerful. In fact, as we shall see in chapter 9, it is just this ideology that RSL has to confront in dealing with the interests of such haves as the World Trade Organization, the World Bank, and Coca-Cola Amatil in Papua New Guinea: organizations, it so happens, that express imperatives concerning free trade and comparative advantage in language remarkably akin to Diamond's. For all of them, in other words, the inevitable and the inexorable are handily synonymous with the interests of the haves over the have-nots.

More broadly, the ideology inherent in Diamond's reasoning is one we confront as teachers and scholars dealing primarily with the haves. Students tell us that their parents encourage them to read Diamond's book, finding it invigorating. The former president of Fred's college urged his faculty to read it. In fact, he sent copies of *Guns, Germs, and Steel* to members of the faculty as a model of the kind of book he admired. All over the United States, we learned, deans and presidents of other pricey institutions applaud the book. At Cornell, it became assigned reading for all freshmen. Moreover, many institutions pay Diamond generously to summarize his views in person, generally in packed lecture halls.

We think educated haves like the book so well because it resonates deeply with their own concerns—in effect, because it so readily sustains them. They come away from the book or lecture feeling pretty good about themselves—both enlightened and open-minded. They come away seeing the world without racial prejudice and having learned some important new facts and connections.[5] Furthermore, and significantly, they come away comfortably convinced that they have their cargo (unlike Yali and his people) for inevitable and impersonal geographic reasons. No one is to blame for the fact that some people are, and no doubt will continue to be, the haves and that others are, and will continue to be, the have-nots. Thus, Diamond's history is not only the delineation of an inexorable and inevitable trajectory. It is, as well, both retrospective and prospective. His depiction of the past provides a far from disinterested model for understanding the present and for shaping the future. This is to say, he presents the world as one in which the have-nots, whether in Papua New Guinea or elsewhere, must (seemingly) forever deal with the haves under conditions of fundamental disadvantage.

But what exactly is wrong with this history? Didn't the events Diamond relates really happen? Must a history necessarily be disqualified because it conveys the perspectives and interests of the victors, of the haves? Isn't Diamond's view simply informed by hardheaded realism about the way the world works?

We certainly do not deny that certain forms of power had a significant role in effecting the kinds of historical events that Diamond delineates. Diamond's depiction of the role that guns, germs, and steel played is plausible—indeed, as we said, it is compelling and sophisticated. What we do challenge is his conflation of the necessary with the sufficient. This is to say, just because guns, germs, and steel were necessary to make certain historical outcomes possible, including those so upsetting to Yali, we do not have to assume that their possession was sufficient to explain these outcomes. Just because sources of power are available, we cannot conclude that the power will be used for certain ends, or even that it will be used at all. And simply because European colonists had the power to pursue their interests at the expense of Yali and other Papua New

Guineans, we cannot automatically understand the nature and consequences of their varied encounters in terms of inevitable universal
patterns.

This conflation of the necessary and the sufficient grows out of the link
between Diamond's interest in "history's broadest pattern" and his deter-
mination to develop "human history as a science, on a par with acknowledged historical sciences such as astronomy, geology, and evolutionary
biology" (1997: 420, 408). As he says, his book "attempts to provide a
short history of everybody for the last 13,000 years" and searches for "ultimate explanations" that push back "the chain of historical causation as
far as possible" (9). Crucial to this search for lawlike explanations that will
generate long chains of causation back to first causes (chains of causation that even link mountain range formation to Yali's quandary) is
Diamond's distinction between ultimate and proximate causes. Ultimate
causes are those broadly applicable and pervasive forces, which led to
the possession of such advantages as guns, germs, and steel. Diamond is
interested in these causes because he thinks they are the ones that really
drive history. These ultimate causes shape derivative and more immediate occurrences, such as particular battles, conquests, economic systems. The effects of these more immediate occurrences, in turn, become
proximate causes of yet other events.[6]

Diamond's view of the relentless course of human history, driven by
the operation of ultimate causes over its thirteen-thousand-year span,
seems to rest on an implicit view of human nature as aggressive, acquis-
itive, and selfish.[7] It is this nature that, in Diamond's vision, keeps ultimate causes consequential throughout history. In short, human beings
necessarily lead their lives so as to extract maximum advantage over others: give a guy—any guy—half a chance and he will conquer the world;
give a guy a piece of appropriate metal and he will inevitably fashion a
sword to cut you down or a chain to enslave you within the hold of a ship
bound for a New World sugar plantation.[8] In a way that we in the contemporary West appear to find self-evident—once again, in a way that
does not problematize our understanding of how the world works—
Diamond suggests that people everywhere and at all times, if they had
sufficient power, would use it to maximize their own advantage through
the domination of others. This implicit view of a transhistorical and transcultural human nature is consistent with Diamond's explicit rendering of
both historical context and cultural perspective as irrelevant. In fact,
Diamond works hard to exclude such perspective and context from his
scientific history.

Thus, cultural factors are introduced only as "wild cards," applicable only in the relatively rare circumstances when Diamond's environmental factors—as ultimate causes—cannot fully explain historical patterns. Indeed, cultural factors are treated as exceptions to prove the rule of environmental determinism, for Diamond sees them as significant only to the degree that they work like geographical factors in facilitating or blocking the availability and effectiveness of guns, germs, steel, and similar resources. Hence, in his primary example, the happenstance of the homophonic nature of the Chinese language has the geographical effect of making China "a gigantic virtual island within a continent" (416).[9]

Correspondingly, Diamond describes the rise of mercantilism and capitalism as only "proximate forces" in the course of world history (10). From his perspective, mercantilism and capitalism are just epiphenomena—passing examples of history's general law. From our perspective, however, mercantilism and capitalism provide particular historical contexts in which (and in different though related ways) expansionism appears as an especially desirable activity—one made especially feasible by the availability of guns, germs, and steel. This is to say, rather than merely proximate causes of lives more fundamentally and inexorably determined, mercantilism and capitalism foster narratives in which guns, germs, and steel are employed in particular manners for particular ends.

These narratives of mercantilism and of capitalism have spurred people to be bold—to go to the ends of the earth if necessary—in a search for ever greater profits.[10] They have justified the subjugation of the New World as well as parts of Africa. They have also authorized the creation of lucrative, slave-run plantations in the Caribbean, whose profits sustained the lavish lifestyles of absentee planters and whose sugar sustained (in nutritionally imbalanced sweet tea and treacle-smeared bread) the impoverished lives of British workers—those who manufactured the guns, chains, and instruments of torture. (See Mintz 1985 for an elaboration of these conjunctions.) And, in a transformed, twentieth-century rendition, the narratives prompted the creation of RSL as a for-profit (yet enlightened) sugar enterprise, which, by bringing prosperity and autonomy, would help end colonial dependency.

Thus, although in our view such individual lives and historical outcomes may have been made possible by all sorts of material and physical resources or advantages, they were propelled and shaped by cultural visions of the desirable and the feasible, of what was worth pursuing and at what cost: winning favor from God and King, acquiring gold and silver, attaining certain lifestyles, or achieving national strength. However, where we see the likes of guns, germs, and steel as necessary but not sufficient causes of particular outcomes and lives, Diamond sees such lives—apparently all lives—as inevitably seeking as much conquest and domination as possible. For Diamond, in other words, the necessary is the sufficient. To have power is to express power; to have the power to dominate is to use it to dominate in the maximal way possible. Where we see human activities as propelled and shaped by historically located visions of what is wanted and what is possible, Diamond sees these activities as determined (presumably) by our hard wiring—as part of the biological nature of the human animal.[11] In these regards, activities of conquest and domination are simply in the nature of things—just as, for instance, lions by virtue of their size and armature will inevitably slaughter lambs.[12]

Raymond Kelly's recent comprehensive analysis of the origins of human warfare provides a relevant and contrasting view of human nature and of inevitability. In this critique of the Hobbesian notion that there is a "trinity of interrelationship between human nature, war and the constitution of society," he writes:

Warfare is an episodic feature of human history and prehistory observed at certain times and places but not others. Moreover, the vast majority of societies in which warfare does occur are characterized by the alteration of war and peace; there are relatively few societies—only about 6 percent—in which warfare is continual and peace almost unknown. It is only in this relatively small percentage of cases that something approaching a Hobbesian social condition of pervasive and unending warfare can be found. It might thus be said that it is "the nature of man" (or humankind) to conclude episodes of armed conflict between neighboring social groups by breaking off hostilities, by truce, and/or by reestablishing peaceful relations. (Kelly 2000: 121, 124)

Indeed, Kelly concludes, "The human propensity to peacemaking, so strikingly evident from the characteristic alteration between war and peace, is central to the nexus of interrelationships between human nature, war and society—and this bodes well for the future" (161).

It is certainly the case, to return to our primary example, that Yali was poor and that the people of the New World were brutally conquered by representatives of the Old. It is also the case that those who beat up other people have the capacity to do so.[13] But are these facts inevitable by virtue either of the nature of history or the nature of humans? As Kelly indicates, human beings always are capable of a range of behaviors and they always are capable of engaging with each other and their neighbors in a range of ways. They might make war, but they also might make peace. Whether they choose one or the other is powerfully affected by particular narratives of the desirable and the feasible.

To our position concerning history's rootedness in human culture rather than in human nature, we would add an emphatic stipulation. Since it has become clear to anthropologists that cultures contain multiple perspectives about alternatives and how they might be pursued and otherwise dealt with, it follows that human beings have a measure of choice about how to act.[14] Thus, for instance, from American ideas of the worth of the individual, one can generate political perspectives as diverse as libertarianism and welfare statism, the first position holding that no individual should be interfered with or regulated, the other, that no individual should be neglected or deprived. The existence of such alternatives means that human beings may, realistically, be held accountable for the choices they make. We find this stipulation important both in combating Diamond's general world history and in constructing an aspect of Papua New Guinea's more particular one. Pizarro, for example, had the capacity and resources to behave with remarkable brutality in the New World—he had both the technology and will to conquer. But the mere capacity to behave brutally does not absolve him from having done so.[15] Likewise, Europeans had the resources and inclination to treat Yali and other Papua New Guineans with contempt. But that position should not absolve them from having done so. Such considerations, we argue, are important in rethinking historical outcomes. Indeed, the haves may be prompted to do such rethinking themselves by recognizing that the have-nots may already have come to their own conclusions.

Earlier in this chapter we said that understanding a place like RSL demands investigating how historically and culturally located people—people like Yali, no less than the Europeans who built RSL—mobilize so as to pursue their visions of the desirable and the feasible. Correspondingly, a more complete understanding requires rejection of taken-for-granted ideas about human nature, taken-for-granted ideas about what people want and why. Although it is difficult to think against the grain of the familiar, we must stretch our imaginations if we want to understand whose perspectives are projected at whose expense—if we want to replace a history of apparent inevitability with one of potential accountability.

· · ·

We come to tell of RSL in Papua New Guinea's particular history because of our own history. First arriving when Papua New Guinea was still, in effect, a colony of Australia (Fred in the late 1960s, and Deborah in the early 1970s), we have made many subsequent field trips over the past thirty years. These field trips led to projects about a range of subjects, many of them focused on change: traditional ritual as well as evangelical Christianity; clan organization as well as class formation; male initiation through skin cutting as well as university graduation through test taking; barter markets as well as supermarkets. Throughout all of these projects, we were interested in the intersection between different narratives of the desirable and the feasible, narratives held by local people, by government representatives, by a social class of the newly elite, by international advisors.

Many of these projects concerned the frequent movement of Papua New Guineans from their villages to urban settlements. In exploring this movement, we became specifically interested in changes in food systems and the ways that these changes featured in people's visions about what life should offer. For instance, members of the new urban elite often told us that they would never return to their home villages where there was no assured access to "the little bags of sugar" to which they were accustomed. Or they told us, sometimes boasting, sometimes lamenting, that their children insisted on store-bought food when visiting their grandparents back in the village. In addition, our less affluent urban friends often told us, as a demonstration of their capacity for sophisticated coping, that they knew which trade store had the best prices on urban stables such as rice, canned fish, and Ramu Sugar. They also seemed to appraise the quality of their squatter settlement life, both its transformed modernity and its persisting traditionality, in terms of opportunities to share an occasional beer or Coke with a kinsmen.

In pursuing these interests, we taught courses at our respective colleges on the anthropology of food. In one course, we showed the film *Hungry for Profit* (Richter 1985), which describes the effects of "agribusiness" on much of the "third world." In its castigation of many multinational corporations for their aggressive third-world depredations, the film exempts one company, Booker Tate Limited (BTL). In fact, BTL is depicted as unique in its assistance, significantly improving the lives of local people through its management of sugar operations in Kenya. We thus became interested in this company—and our interest was further aroused when we learned that it was a subsidiary of Booker PLC, sponsor of the prestigious Booker Prize for literature. As we learned more, we found these intersections increasingly fascinating.[16] The parent company also had an important connection to sugar—indeed, with its origins as a slaveholding enterprise in early-nineteenth-century Guyana, to sugar's brutal history. In time, Booker PLC came to confront its past. Besides substantially revising its sugar operations, it has awarded its literary prize to books like Barry Unsworth's *Sacred Hunger* (1992), an unblinking indictment of colonial and capitalist expansion.[17] Finally, of great importance to us as anthropologists, we discovered that BTL developed and managed the sugar operation at RSL, which provided the "little bags" of such significance to our Papua New Guinean friends.

Thus, our multiply converging interests led us to RSL, built to be a centerpiece in newly independent Papua New Guinea's development efforts. Achieving independence in 1975, relatively late in world history, Papua New Guinea urgently wanted to develop and to avoid the mistakes in development made by other former colonies.[18] It wanted to catch up to and to learn from the errors of the rest. Created as both a grand project and a private, for-profit enterprise, RSL became a major—although often contested—component of these endeavors. Significantly, it was to be unlike sugar operations elsewhere, rooted as most of them were in a grim colonial past.[19] RSL was instead supposed to bring enlightened capitalist prosperity—good wages, technical skills, and a modern infrastructure—to transform a region deemed remote, underpopulated, and underutilized (fig. 3). Furthermore, this transformation would benefit the entire country.

RSL was also seen as bringing national self-sufficiency in a major commodity. Sugar, with such other imports as rice and canned mackerel, was already becoming central to the diet of Papua New Guinea's swelling urban population. Moreover, self-sufficiency in sugar would have important symbolic value: it would be a particularly appropriate assertion of national will. After all, sugar was originally domesticated in Papua New Guinea some eight thousand years ago. Furthermore, sugar was a major export of Australia, and Australia, it was thought, had protected its overseas market by stifling the development of a sugar industry in its de facto Papua New Guinea colony. It was not surprising, therefore, that for advice concerning the creation of its sugar industry, Papua New Guinea sought out, not an Australian-based firm, but a British-based one. They chose BTL's predecessor, Booker Agriculture International (BAI), a company with much experience in establishing sugar plantations in developing countries, to help establish RSL and provide its corporate managers.[20]

Figure 3. RSL transformed the Upper Ramu Valley

RSL, now an enormous agroindustrial sugar complex, is staffed by thousands of Papua New Guinean "nationals" from all over the country as well as by "expatriates" from many parts of the world.[21] At RSL, culturally diverse Papua New Guineans, with their nuclear families and neighbors, live in a secure, comfortable, and regulated company town. It is a gated residential community provided with the physical amenities of electricity, water, and sewerage as well as with the social amenities of schools, churches, recreational facilities, and medical posts. There, with their varied workmates and to the sound of factory sirens and the regulation of time clocks, they perform the highly coordinated tasks that have evolved worldwide over four centuries of sugar field and factory management.[22]

As at modern sugar plantations elsewhere, RSL's workers tend a grid of fields containing sugarcane varieties carefully selected to maximize productivity under local growing conditions. Following a scientifically determined schedule, they plant, fertilize, spray, and harvest thousands of hectares of carefully monitored cane, all with highly specialized machinery. And at the RSL complex, as at other sugar plantations, cane is not only harvested but processed (fig. 4). Implementing continual quality-control adjustments at the RSL factory, workers crush cane through massive rollers, concentrating, clarifying, crystallizing, and purifying the juice through evaporators, filters, vacuum pans, and centrifuges. Finally, they package the double-sulfated, mill-white sugar for sale to Papua New Guinea's domestic retail and industrial market—a market that was once a monopoly and is now tariff protected.

RSL is one of Papua New Guinea's most ambitious development projects. Its history therefore seems especially pertinent to detailed discussions about the basis and nature of such projects. In this regard, we think we provide the ethnographically informed study of a development project that Arce and Long call for as desperately needed: an inquiry that considers "how different discourses, values and practices . . . intersect and are intertwined in the everyday encounters and experiences of people from diverse socio-cultural backgrounds" (2000, 2–3).[23] However, our principal concerns in this book about how RSL was built and has come to operate are larger and more general: concerns about how history actually is made to happen, how outcomes may be understood and appraised.

RSL is the most diverse social context we have ever studied, and its story is necessarily complex: intertwined there are the lives of Papua New Guinean agronomic scientists, British agricultural economists, Australian factory engineers, Papua New Guinean agricultural workers, Australian and British development experts, and American anthropologists—and all are involved with a remarkable project that expresses a whole range of aspirations playing out against the world history of sugar production.

Conversely, working with so many differently located people presents us with a very diverse audience. In addition to addressing people who are interested in sugar production, Papua New Guinea, or development in general, we hope to engage a general audience of those who are interested in historical process, including those who may have met Yali in Diamond's book. Thus we try to keep our discussion as accessible as possible, relegating much academic debate to the notes, and we try to cover topics of broad interest. Our story encompasses, after all, a range of people who have at various times in their lives experienced a range of historically significant contexts. Correspondingly, they embraced, developed, contested, discarded, and synthesized a range of narratives about what these contexts might mean and might offer.

Figure 4. Cane-processing at the RSL factory

At times parochial and at times metropolitan, the people in our story burned grasslands to hunt wild pigs and fed factory boilers to produce sugar; they lined up for colonial censuses and voted in national elections; they defended their worth against all comers and submitted to hierarchical industrial controls; they maintained local identities and established regional, national, and international commitments; they were advised by expatriates and golfed with elite Papua New Guineans; they transacted in shell money or other traditional valuables and bought goods with a national currency responsive to International Monetary Fund policies; they grew crops for their own subsistence and produced commodities for national and world markets; they consumed coconuts with kin and shared soft drinks with shift workers—and we speak here only of the Papua New Guineans. Moreover, all of these experiences—including the contrasts between them—were appraised according to ideas of what life was, is, and could become.[24]

In essence our book is meant to stand as an anthropological answer to Yali's question. Our answer provides a particular kind of understanding of the relationship between his life as a have-not and ours, as haves. It is, we think, historically accurate and politically defensible because it is anthropologically nuanced.[25] In short, our book is an illustration of the desirability and feasibility of an anthropological narrative, a narrative that tries to avoid the self-evident and self-interested by striving to understand what various people at various times have wanted for themselves and for others.

1

What Do They (Should They) Want?

SOME THEORISTS ARGUE THAT all human desire derives from a primal, preverbal "wanting" for something that, once named (for example, the breast, a sugary confection, or even a BMW), becomes inadequate. But even such essentialists of desire agree that what people want, beyond their preverbal desiring, is socially constructed.[1] In particular, they argue that what people ask for is shaped by their history and in turn shapes their history. This is to say, what people want is formed in the context of the stories they are told and the stories they tell about the way the world works or might work—stories about what human beings might plausibly hope for.

Strathern (1992) illustrates well this social construction of desire in her discussion of the Papua New Guineans who first encountered Australian explorers in the Highlands of the country's interior in the 1930s. The Australians assumed that the Papua New Guineans were impressed with their complex technology—their guns and steel. Yet in Strathern's view, possession of novel technology initially marked the explorers as spirits, and from the perspective of the Highlanders, the appearance of spirits among the living was extraordinary but ultimately not very consequential. Spirits, after all, would likely disappear without much effect. Only when the Highlanders discovered that the strangers had large quantities of pearl shells and wished to trade with them did the Australians become plausibly human. Pearl shells, traded up from the Coast, were for a long time central in the Highland exchanges through which marriages were contracted, compensation for death or injury was paid, and alliances were cemented within and between groups. In other words, only when the Australians showed that they apparently valued what the Highlanders already valued and desired did the Highlanders regard them as interesting and socially significant. Only then could the Highlanders fit these strange but fundamentally peripheral beings into their own narratives as full human beings: they became persons with whom the Papua New Guineans could, and would want to, engage. Only at this point did these whites appear to enter history— Highlands' style—as people who were and would continue to be social players. This is to say, the way Highlanders understood what was happening around them and the way that they reacted to what happened depended, in significant part, upon their expectations for the future— expectations shaped by local narrative conventions, by the stories they told about the past, present, and future (see Donham 1999: 10).

To be sure, Yali's people and other Coastal groups had a much longer history of European contact (often dating from the latter part of the nineteenth century). Yali himself had especially extensive contact with Europeans. He served as a policeman in New Guinea's colonial administration before World War Two and as a member of the Allied Intelligence Service during the war. In fact, there is a photograph taken in 1944 in the Australian War Memorial Archives commemorating his military service (fig. 5). The image shows Yali inside the *Dace*, an American submarine, together with other members of his company of intelligence-gathering "Coastwatchers."[2] In advance of a major Allied landing, Yali's group of twelve—seven Europeans, one Indonesian translator, and four Papua New Guineans—had been sent to Hollandia, then Dutch New Guinea, on a hazardous mission to gather strategic information. In the picture, Yali and the other men are posed next to their weapons in cramped, machinery-packed quarters. After the war, as a distinguished veteran, Yali embarked on a controversial political career, one that kept him in close association with Europeans.

Yet, like the Highlanders Strathern describes, Yali's life and aspirations followed a largely Papua New Guinean historical narrative. In outline, this narrative focuses less on the material attributes of things themselves than on the social uses to which things are put (see Appadurai 1986; Sahlins 1988 and 1992; Thomas 1991). Things have value because they can be used in transactions to establish relationships of recognition

Figure 5. Group portrait of Coastwatchers on the submarine *Dace*. Sergeant Yali is second from the left in the front row.

and respect. Things are more like gifts than commodities, establishing qualitative relationships between the people exchanging them rather than quantitative ones between the items exchanged (see Gregory 1982). The major point of these transactions is thus to establish relationships of obligation, alliance, and friendship rather than to get "good deals." Therefore, when Highlanders desired pearl shells, and they did desire them with a passionate intensity, it was not for the sake of the shells alone. Indeed, as Malinowski (1922) points out about Coastal Papua New Guineans, men acquired coveted shells so as to be able to give them away at a later time.

Because the Highlanders were relatively inexperienced in European ways, they apparently thought that the explorers were generous in offering them the pearl shells that affirmed their fundamental worth—their shared humanity. In contrast, the Coastal peoples had long before learned that the colonists were stingy, offering them only meager wages that denied a common humanity. Moreover, exacerbating raw feelings was local recognition that whites had real and intrusive power. Certainly colonial administrators sought to bring many aspects of native life under their discipline, and they could, in fact, punish those who, by flouting their directives, challenged their power. Indeed, as we shall see later, Yali was to spend nearly six years in jail during the 1950s for his recalcitrance.

Yali and many other Papua New Guineans became preoccupied with the reluctance, if not refusal, of many whites to recognize their full humanness—to make blacks and whites equal players in the same history. In their efforts to establish the transactions, the exchanges, on which the elusive equality would be based, many Papua New Guineans sought, often through magical and ritual means, the European things—the "cargo"—that whites so evidently valued. It would be an error, however, to believe that it was the things alone that interested them. Rather, with these things, they hoped to become interesting and socially significant (exchange-worthy) to the Europeans. In *Road Belong Cargo*, Lawrence describes the attempts of Yali and his neighbors, including those in the Upper Ramu Valley, to acquire this cargo through what is now known as the cargo cult:

> It is based on the natives' belief that European goods (cargo)—ships, aircraft, trade articles, and military equipment—are not man-made but have to be obtained from a non-human or divine source. It expresses the followers' dissatisfaction with their status in colonial society, which is to be improved imminently or eventually by the acquisition of new wealth. It has, therefore, a disruptive influence and is regarded by the . . . Australian Administration . . . as one of [its] most serious problems. (1964: 1)

Deeply resenting their inferiority in colonial society, Papua New Guineans sought for decades to improve their status by gaining access to cargo. In fact, during Fred's early Papua New Guinea research on the island of Karavar (in 1968 and 1972), local people remained preoccupied with gaining long-denied respect from Europeans. In discussing their contemporary cargo activities (which focused on learning how to place an order such that a small payment would elicit a shipload of manufactured items), they described a history of their efforts to compel Europeans to recognize mutual humanness. In particular, they referred to the "dog movement," a series of meetings they held during the 1930s. The question addressed with perplexity and anger at these meetings was why the Europeans persisted in treating them with contempt—driving them away, telling them to get out, as if they were unwelcome dogs. Through obtaining cargo, they sought to win European respect by possessing what Europeans so obviously valued.[3]

Over a considerable period of time, hence, Papua New Guineans frequently sought to acquire and master the ritual techniques by which

Europeans accessed cargo. Influenced by Yali or other cargo-cult leaders, they tried a combination of recalcitrance and ritual experimentation. They interrupted and transformed normal routines: they refused to pay taxes, repudiated the directions of colonial administrators, established alternative governments, wrested theological control from missionaries, and mobilized villages, if not whole regions, in fervent invocation and prophesy. In their choice of such means, Papua New Guineans often became interesting and socially significant in ways the Europeans considered undesirable—ways that provoked greater exercise of European power and made recognition of mutual equality even less likely.

Diamond therefore misunderstands what many Papua New Guineans desired when he explains the background to Yali's question about the differences between white and black people. In Diamond's words: " [W]hites had arrived, imposed centralized government, and brought material goods whose value New Guineans instantly recognized, ranging from steel axes, matches, and medicines to clothing, soft drinks, and umbrellas. In New Guinea all these goods were referred to collectively as 'cargo'" (1999: 14). Because Diamond does not understand that Yali really was asking less about cargo per se than about colonial relationships between white and black people, he describes the introduction of centralized government as almost parenthetical to the indisputable fact that whites and their goods had arrived. Thus, he presents local resentment as directed not so much at the nature and use of concerted colonial power as at the differential access to goods. We might also note here that in using the term "goods" Diamond implies that such items were inherently desirable, instantly recognizable as worth acquiring. Yet, as we all know from advertising, things become desirable only when they are caught up in narratives that define them as such. In some cases, things may fit easily into a range of narratives—steel axes, for example. But as Sharp shows in his classic essay (1952) about the introduction of steel axes among the Yir Yoront, "Stone Age" Australian Aborigines, their significance—their meaning and use—is no simple product of any immediately obvious technological superiority. Indeed, for major segments of Yir Yoront society, such axes were far from goods, undercutting as they did indigenous trade networks and power relationships.

Moreover, in defining cargo as goods, Diamond provides a narrative in which local people will do whatever it takes to get such things. This kind of narrative, as Thomas (1991) points out, implies that, in their desire for these goods, local people are the agents of their own domination. Such a narrative, we think, serves to displace attention from the nature of colonial power relations. These relationships are not vested in the "nature of things." They are not inevitable because of the instantly recognized value of manufactured items. Instead, colonial relationships have been imposed, often to the resentment and resistance of local people. Papua New Guineans such as Yali wanted cargo not because of its inherent and instantly recognizable value, but because of a desire to transform the relations of inequality between whites and blacks that were pervasive in colonialism. They wanted cargo primarily because they objected to the ways in which the centralized, colonial government used power and, correspondingly, diminished their relative worth.

This sense of being ill-appreciated and ill-used was elaborated in various stories that presented Papua New Guineans and Europeans as sharing a prior history of social obligations. These stories were, in effect, arguments designed to demonstrate European immorality in denying this history and in behaving in ways that were inappropriately, almost inhumanly, asocial. As Lawrence demonstrates in *Road Belong Cargo*, Papua New Guineans often understood and represented this prior history in a range of changing forms. For Yali and others of his region, the history of social obligation was conveyed through myths, Christian beliefs, and accounts of wartime service. Whether the stories focused on a mythic brother who, after teaching cargo secrets to Europeans abroad, was prevented from returning to instruct his brother remaining at home, or on the Christian beliefs about the kinship of blacks and whites as descendants of the same original parents, or on the wartime actions of Papua New Guineans who jeopardized their own safety by saving Australians from death and capture, these stories were all proofs that Australians should recognize them as equals. This history, in all its variations, showed that for reasons of fairness, kinship, and alliance, Papua New Guineans were not only worthy recipients of such recognition, but also were owed this acknowledgment and the transformed future that would flow from it.[4]

· · ·

In this chapter, we begin the stories of why and how many people from different cultural groups and social classes in Papua New Guinea's Upper Ramu Valley (some of whom, in fact, knew Yali well) came to want, or came to contribute to the desire for, a particular kind of transformation: the creation of a plantation that would produce mill-white sugar, one of the quintessential "goods" of modernity. Central among their stories was a narrative in which expectations—indeed, desires—came to be focused on the idea of "development." In the Upper Ramu Valley, a place directly influenced by Yali's teachings about how equality between whites and blacks might be achieved, this narrative of development was the best that the centralized colonial government and its agents could offer. As we shall see, this narrative of development was designed so that local people could formulate "realistic" (non-cargoistic) desires and eventually realize a productive and satisfying future.

Place and Certain People

The Upper Ramu Valley had long been a place of confluence and contention for people of at least three different language groups. Now calling themselves the Mari, the Raikos (or Nahu-Rawa), and the Kafe, these people converged from different directions.[5] The Mari came up the valley from the plains to the east (originally from the contiguous Markham Valley); the Raikos came down into the valley from the coastal range to the north; and the Kafe came down into the valley from the high ranges to the south. Divided into small settlements, the members of these different language groups intermarried, traded, and fought with each other. More recently, all claim to have lived in the foothills on either side of the valley, where they gardened along the waterways flowing down from the mountains. All say that they ventured into the valley itself primarily for hunting, fishing, trading, and fighting. Specifically, they drove game by burning the grasslands, they fished in the Ramu River, and they met up with each other, sometimes peacefully, sometimes not.

This valley land, seen by colonial officers as remote, underpopulated, and underutilized, was purchased in 1956 by two Australian patrol officers, Douglas Parrish and Neil McNamara, on behalf of the Territory of Papua New Guinea. The land was to be offered to Australian settlers in the form of pastoral leases. Although, technically, no part of what became the nation of Papua New Guinea was a colony of Australia, practically speaking, Australia administered it as a colony. This was an era in which colonial development policy was generally one of noninterference, or "laissez faire," as it had been pre–World War Two. With the government primarily occupied with repairing the considerable amount of war damage and regaining political control over the entire Territory, it could, through offering these leases, pursue its modest development objectives. Furthermore, expatriate-owned ranching operations, it was thought, would provide beef for domestic consumption and would thus lessen the external drain on Territory resources by reducing the need for imported beef. In addition, these operations might also eventually incorporate Papua New Guinean smallholders in peripheral and subsidiary enterprises (Connell 1997: 20, 69–71).

However, although the Parrish and McNamara purchase was consistent with the objectives and the procedures of the day, the circumstances of the acquisition generated great and ongoing controversies: The Mari, who at the time of the purchase occupied the valley, today claim that their land was acquired for a pittance. The Raikos and the Kafe likewise claim to be the rightful owners, and each of the three groups claims that the government and, subsequently, RSL have unfairly benefited from a transaction between those who knew what money was and what land was worth and those who did not. Indeed, as we discuss at length in chapter 7, the justification for the original purchase, that the land was remote, underpopulated, underutilized, is now interpreted by local people as evidence that the transaction was inherently unfair: they contend that their ancestors, living under these circumstances, were so ignorant that they did not and could not give informed consent as to the permanent alienation of land that subsequently proved to be of great value.

In the course of our research into this land, in trying to discover what people have wanted of it and why, we collected many accounts and examined many documents. The three interviews we cite and paraphrase below illustrate well the perspectives of those Europeans who were instrumental in the land's transfer and transformation. As we shall see, these interviews all narrate and normalize what happened in a similar manner.

The first of the interviews we present, with Peter Colton, the chairman of the board of RSL, took place on the verandah of the general manager's house at RSL in February of 2000. The second, with Douglas Parrish, the senior of the two patrol officers who purchased the Upper Ramu Valley, took place in the foyer of a hotel in Sydney, Australia, in July of 2000. The third, with Barbara Jephcott, the owner of the ranch directly adjacent to RSL at Dumpu, took place in the dining room of her home in January of 2000. We had not talked to these people at any length before. We began by introducing our project, a history of RSL, and ourselves as anthropologists who, like them, had long worked in Papua New Guinea. Not surprisingly, we all knew, and could reminisce about, many of the same people and places. We also told them that we were collecting as many stories as possible and that our job was to speak not only to expatriates, but also to nationals. This did not distress any of them. (In fact, Jephcott suggested the names of several villages she thought we should visit for interviews.)

Our conversation with Peter Colton focused largely on the history of RSL once it came into being. However, because he had also been a colonial patrol officer and had himself acquired land on behalf of the Territory of Papua New Guinea, he was able to tell us about such earlier procedures and practices: At the time of the RSL purchase, the only way that land could be transferred from native to foreign ownership was for the government to buy it. This was "a paternalistic system," he said, meant to protect natives against "unscrupulous traders." RSL land must have been acquired by the government in "the normal way." The procedure was, first, to determine what the land would be used for—cattle ranching, for example. Then the patrol officer would walk around the area with the native owners in order to prepare genealogies reaching as far back as possible. In the process, he would discover what kinds of rights owners had to the land (disposal rights, gardening rights, hunting rights) and how these rights were transmitted (as from father to son). It was quite a complicated process, taking a long time. The officer would determine how much land a group owned and then try to figure out what percentage could be taken away and still leave enough for subsistence. He would submit his land investigation report, along with other information, such as census reports of native population growth, and he would make a recommendation as to whether the land should be acquired or not. If he thought the land might be under dispute, he probably would recommend that it should be left alone, or perhaps that a land court magistrate should decide. Colton thought that the land acquisition report about RSL's land might still exist in the Department of Lands. But since the land now used by RSL was sparsely populated at the time it was surveyed, used only for hunting small game, the report was bound to indicate that the patrol officers thought there was plenty of it for development.

Douglas Parrish, who was president of the Retired Patrol Officer's Association when we conversed with him, agreed with Colton's description of the procedure followed in the purchase that eventually led to RSL. Parrish's job had been to "establish the parcel"—"to ascertain if [the people] would be willing to sell." He found them "agreeable" to such a sale: their only concerns were that they would have sufficient agricultural land to grow their crops and sufficient grassland to burn for their small game hunting. The valley was practically empty. Some people from the hills had hunting rights there, and others hunted there regardless of whether they had rights or not. He walked up and down that valley, making sure that he understood who owned the land. Surveying the land with only a chain and compass was a difficult, painstaking task, but he believes he did a reasonably accurate job. The tract of land he surveyed was meant for a cattle project—which made the people happy because they really liked "bulmakau" (Pidgin English for "bulls and cows," that is, cattle). And they were happy with the money he and Neil McNamara eventually paid them for it, a significant sum in those days. They were a very poor people, by and large, and they were very keen to get the money because they were too far away from anything to sell their produce. They wanted some of the payment in actual cash; it was heavy lifting patrol boxes full of fuses (rolls) of shillings. Parrish encouraged them to put the rest of the money in the bank and did all the paper work for these deposits. He thought he was a good Pidgin speaker—not like some patrol officers who just knew a few words. Nonetheless, it was hard for him to learn much about the locals' beliefs. Yet, as far as he could ascertain, they were happy with the deal.

Lady Barbara Jephcott and her husband, Bruce (who, with Papua New Guinea's independence, became a member of Parliament), took the government-acquired tract at Dumpu when it was offered for pastoral lease in 1958. The government had bought land throughout the country in areas where population was low: it bought tracts of land in the Highlands that became coffee plantations, in Popendetta that became oil palm plantations, and in the Markham Valley that became cattle ranches. The land was surveyed, divided into blocks, and then gazetted. The only people who found out about it were those who asked for the gazette register. People applied for the land, and if they were suitable, they were allowed to lease it. Since the government always intended that her parcel be developed for cattle, Jephcott and her husband were considered suitable recipients because they had ranching credentials. Initially, they had a thirty-year lease on over fifteen thousand acres, and they had to fulfill certain conditions concerning how many cattle they would bring to the area (now six thousand head) and how many fences they would establish. They then were able to change to a ninety-nine-year lease.

Jephcott remembers driving a Land Rover during the early 1960s through the sparsely populated area up the Ramu Valley; most of the people hadn't seen a vehicle since the war, but they didn't even raise their eyes. Partly because of chronic malaria, they had little interest in things. Moreover, they had no conception of a work ethic. They were simply subsistence farmers. When the Jephcotts first came, they wanted to employ valley inhabitants, but found that they didn't know how to work. So they had to bring in outsiders, mostly from the Highlands. Over the years, however, they were able to employ more and more local people.

Development works, Jephcott explained, because it improves people's lives: it matters if for no other reason than the health of the people. She and her husband, for example, provided accommodation for nurses who came up. And the natives needed to learn the benefits that only work can provide, which is why she thinks RSL makes a valuable contribution—although, as a sugar project, it isn't particularly successful. Its sugar costs too much and it hasn't made much money. But as an entity, for employing, training, and settling people, it is a great success. It also brought a whole mixture of people to Ramu who, by and large, have settled down pretty well.

•   •   •

These accounts, though focused on past occurrences and experiences, many of which dated back forty years, have an ease and fluency that required very little prompting from us. The speakers appear to be covering subjects kept familiar by repeated and ongoing conversations with interested and like-minded others—indeed, perhaps with each other. All present a similar, or at least consistent, picture of the Upper Ramu Valley: First, it was a place much in need of development initiatives. The valley was sparsely settled by malaria-ridden, lethargic people who subsisted on garden produce and on game they flushed out by burning the grasslands. Second, landowners were eager to sell, and the government was eager to develop the land, initially, as cattle ranches. Furthermore, those who purchased the land followed standard procedures, carefully determining that the landowners were legitimate and had a right to sell to the government. Third, the subsequent development has proved relatively successful. Certainly people are better off now than they were.

We see two related reasons that these speakers present similar accounts of development—of a certain kind of change—in the Upper Ramu Valley. Colton, Parrish, and Jephcott all see themselves in largely comparable historical relationships to local people. And of more importance, they all share and have conversationally rehearsed fairly comparable views of what constitutes history. More specifically, they all share comparable views about what a historical narrative should consist of, about what desirable historical process is and, correspondingly, about how it should be recounted. Thus they all generally agree on what constitute historical "events" (happenings that make a difference), how these events are related to each other, and how these events and their relationship to each other should be organized so as to form a convincing account.

Not surprisingly, their accounts follow the narrative conventions of modernism, a historical perspective fully established by the late nineteenth century. In the context of modernism, development is "progress" and is marked by the increasingly efficient use of time and resources. In the case of the Upper Ramu Valley, progress is synonymous with the salutary transformation through orderly procedures of a relatively empty place where nothing much happened.[6] Thus, the accounts all advocate a particular form of human activity within time and space: disciplined and directed humans are to act over linear time in a fashion that incrementally fills and orders space.[7] Within this modernist narrative, events become consequential—historically relevant—to the degree that they cause people to use their time and their space efficiently and productively in order to thrive physically, ensure further productivity, and, indeed, generate a surplus. This story is, of course, the broad narrative that has compelled most development exercises, not only in the Pacific (Hanlon 1998) but throughout the world (Ferguson 1990; Esteva 1992; Escobar 1995).[8] Significantly for our RSL account, those compelled by this story were likely to regard it as the antithesis of the narrative that motivated all cargo-cult activities.

It is important to recall that such narratives of history are consequential, not only because they are about action, but also because they impel action. As Donham suggests, such stories shape expectations for the future, and expectations in turn influence how people understand what has happened around them and how they act (1999: 10). Those who believe, for example, that the future holds something worth having and belongs to people who think and act in an expeditious and orderly fashion will welcome technological innovations that increase their productivity. Such people, in other words, will do modernist things, in a modernist fashion, so that their lives—and historical processes more generally—will unfold in a modernist manner.

Also, not only do stories generate consequential actions, but actions generate consequential stories. And in the modernist narrative, *particularly* consequential stories are those that serve as written and consultable records. These, as we shall see, generate actions, which generate more records, which generate more actions—an apparently endless linear progression.

On, About, and Through Patrol

The patrols by Australian officers and their ensuing reports were important in, and thoroughly consistent with, colonial practices of regulation (see Errington and Gewertz 1995c; McPherson 2001; Westermark 2001). In their effort to impose modernist standards, patrol officers concerned themselves with population statistics, sanitation, housing, health, and education. They also reported on certain political situations: the intellectual capacities of leaders and the local support for the administration as opposed to cargo cults. In short, these patrols and reports exempted virtually no aspect of native life from administrative scrutiny and description. In addition, the patrols and reports were central to a process by which the productivity of colonial officers—their efficiency, thoroughness, and overall judgment—was subject to a hierarchy of evaluation. Hence, patrols and reports constituted part of a highly ordered and ordering process of intrusion, appraisal, and control.

Both ordered and ordering, the patrol officers sought to create productive lives for themselves as well as for the people they visited. Productive lives, according to their narrative conventions about how life worked, would not follow from the highly emotional, if not irrational, and impractical magical and ritual practices of cargo cultists like Yali. The patrol officers therefore sought to promulgate, either by example or explicit instruction, standards of discipline and efficiency in local villages. But by attempting to bring the villages more into line with their own standards, the officers were actually attempting nothing less than a transformation of locally embodied experiences and life rhythms. In other words, in the effort to lay the basis for development, they sought to change fundamentally the nature of local lives: to create what was, in effect, a new and modernist "fusion of self, space and time" (Feld and Basso 1996: 9).[9]

Moreover, not only did the narrative conventions held by patrol officers strongly affect their activities on patrol—their imposition of standards of efficiency and discipline so as to create new kinds of native places and persons—these conventions also influenced the way they wrote about their activities and the places they visited in their patrol reports. In fact, patrols and patrol reports—the way that events unfolded and were talked about—were mutually determinative.[10] Hence, a hard-working and efficient patrol officer would likely make the same kind of meticulous time-space observations and engage in the same kind of productivity-encouraging encounters during his patrol that he had already read about in an exemplary report about a well-executed patrol.

We will focus on two reports covering the area that became RSL. These accounts bracket a crucial postwar decade: one report, from 1951, is the earliest we have been able to obtain; the other, from 1960, followed the acquisition of substantial land from native control. This decade began with a strenuous administrative effort to suppress Yali's influence. In 1950, Yali started serving his almost six-year jail sentence for advocating and then creating an alternative government in which he had police powers. With Yali's imprisonment, the Australians hoped that his cargo teachings and practices would be discredited and his influence diminished. Provided that the patrol officers remained vigilant and suppressed any persistence or recurrence of Yali's subversive cargoism (at least one extensive patrol was explicitly charged with investigating rumors of increased cargo-cult activity), the way seemed clear for the administration to promote its own narrative.[11] With Yali silenced, it was hoped that his road toward cargo could be supplanted by the administration's path toward development.

These patrols and patrol reports followed a well-established pattern. Each patrol was led by an Australian officer of junior rank. He, together with several native constables and a line of locally recruited carriers, was sent from a relatively centralized location—in this region, often from the Bundi Patrol Post—to a series of villages. There he was expected to perform certain tasks. He would record his journey in a "diary," giving date, time spent traveling between villages, and time spent at each particular village or at each of his tasks, which generally included physically lining up members of a village to take or update a census and to collect taxes. The officer was also to evaluate the efficiency of village officials in carrying out administrative directives focused on raising the basic standard of living.

Consider J. E. Norton's report from the early 1950s. We present the first page and then some of his diary entries and subsequent discussion of the "native situation" (Norton 1951, 1, 3). We select passages that refer in particular to the four villages, spelled variously in different reports, from which the RSL land was acquired: Bumbu, Sankian, Bopirumpun, and Kaigulan (later renamed Mushuan)—all in the Dumpu-Kaigulan Census Division.

TERRITORY OF PAPUA NEW GUINEA

District Office
MADANG CENTRAL
3rd April, 1951

Patrol Report No.: 5/1950–51.
Area Patrolled: Upper Ramu River and Rauwa Areas.

Officer Conducting Patrol: J. E. Norton, Cadet Patrol Officer.

Duration of Patrol: 5th March, 1951 to 28th March, 1951—24 days.

Last Patrolled: September, 1947.

October, 1950.

Personnel Accompanying Patrol: No. 3261   L/Cpl. YABUAN

No. 2590   Const. WILAPAU

No. 3887   Const. SANGONDI

No. 6354   Const. KUSPAT

Objects of Patrol: (1) Compilation of census.

(2) General Administration.

Diary

20.3.51. .... Proceeded to BOIPIRUMPUN village in the foothill bordering the Ramu valley (4 hours). The first sight of the sun for nine days. Tracks very poor to BOIPIRUMPUN. The usual trouble experienced in obtaining carriers. ...

21.3.51. Lined BOIPIRUMPUN. Remnants of BANTA village living here now. Continued to BUMBU village (11/2 hours) where patrol awaited Const. SANGONDI'S return from DUMPU.

Rest houses [where patrol officers and their constables slept] in good repair in this upper Ramu sector.

22.3.51. BUMBU village lined for new census. Continued to KAIGULAN (approximately two hours). A very drab village. Native complaints settled agreeably. Continued to SANKIAN village (1 hour) where met by Const. KUSPAT with additional supplies from MADANG. Census conducted. Tracks cleared through kunai [grassland].

Native Situation

In this [Ramu Valley] area, one notices a general apathy in conditions under which the natives live and work. It is a surprise to find the natives such fluent speakers of Pidgin English, for this suggests a degree of Administration influence, but their desultory life suggests a lack of it.

Living conditions are poor, many villages being made up of Kunai hovels with gaping holes in the walls or no walls at all, leaving the occupants open to the wind and rain. Little attempt had been made to clean the village areas. This is all so much more depressing when it is remembered that many of these natives lived on plantations and in towns where they are taught a degree of cleanliness, have medical treatment and where they are given clean quarters and then return to their sordid living conditions at their villages.

From DUMPU up the valley to BOIPIRUMPUN, all villages but KAIGU-LAN, are clean and have better housing conditions than the lower part of the valley. The officials have more respect paid them and, consequently, this shows in their improved living conditions.

Consider, as well, excerpts from the diary of patrol officer J. G. O'Brien (1960), submitted almost ten years later as part of "Bundi Patrol Report No. 4/1959–60":

Saturday, 6th February, 1960
Departed Airstrip . . . at 0800 to arrive at DUMPU 0850. Census revision. Inspection of village site, discussions re tax and gardens. Departed 1115 proceeding along cleared native track parallel to the RAMU River to arrive at the SULIMAM River at 1330 to arrive old site of SANKIAN village at 1500. Rested ten minutes and followed new track away from RAMU River to arrive at new SANKIAN village at 1535. Began census at 1615. Discussion on general administration and tax. Tax collected 1730 till 1900. Various civil complaints during evening.

Sunday, 7th February, 1960
. . . Departed SANKIAN at 0915 arriving old site near Ramu 0940 turned parallel along well cut track to arrive old site of KAIGULAN at 1045, crossing WARIUS Creek, track angling away from RAMU River towards FINISTERRE Foothills. Arrived BUMBU at 1205. 1300, Discussions on absentee labour, tax, etc. Inspection of village and bull and heifer cattle purchased from Lutheran Mission. Cattle in good condition but no calves. Discussions with V/O's [village officials] re duties and responsibilities.

The reports written by Norton and O'Brien are typical in conveying to their superiors their hard work, efficiency, and good judgment. For example, Norton, who was plagued by rain for days, walked four hours along a very poor track before he reached "BOIPIRUMPUN"; O'Brien, on his arrival at "SANKIAN," took only forty minutes, presumably to set up his camp, before he began taking a census, discussing general administration and taxation, collecting taxes, and adjudicating civil complaints. In other words, the patrol officers lived out narrative conventions that were manifest in the report and in the patrol. In the patrol, they moved right along in a purposeful, time-cognizant fashion, across the space of their jurisdiction.[12] And in so doing, they embodied the narrative of development.

Their objective, both by example and by direct instruction and influence, was to transform local people. Although some of these people had profited somewhat by European contact, others, despite their experience on plantations and in towns, were still leading desultory village lives under squalid and sordid conditions. All, to differing degrees, needed to be caught up in development.

But what was perhaps most important about the course of development envisioned and enacted by these patrol officers is well conveyed by their use of capital letters to demarcate places. Their typography epitomizes the process by which local people were rendered both comprehensible and controllable by the state—the process by which, to use Scott's term (1998), they were made "legible." These capitalizations allow readers (superiors, anthropologists) to scan a report quickly in order to find and readily monitor any particular place. Norton states that villagers once living at "BANTA" had moved to "BOIPIRUMPUN" and, in another section of his report (1951: 6), that "BUNOGUNA natives are still living at KOROPA village whilst ASASA and ISAREBA have moved back to their garden areas" and live in "bush hamlets rather than in a central camp." But fortunately, "[i]n the KESAWAI area . . . the patrol was able to regroup the natives, gathering them in from their bush hamlets and resettling them in their larger groups." O'Brien reports that "SANKIAN" and "KAIGULAN" villagers had moved from old village sites to new ones and that he had spoken to villagers about "absentee labour," which is to say, about those who had left their villages to work at other places. This information was codified in the census forms that were filled out during the patrol and later included in the report.

Obviously, for there to be an effective administration, people had to live in particular places: if they did not, there could be no adequate census and taxation. Conversely, the practices of collecting census information and tax money were ways of keeping people in particular places. During the patrols, locals were questioned closely about any absentees and patrol officers went to considerable pains to ensure that everyone in the area showed up. In a general sense, therefore, a primary function of the patrols and reports was to put both natives and patrol officers "in their places."

Natives were put in their places in other regards as well. When visited by a patrol, local people had to line up, standing attentively in front of the patrol officer so that he might inspect, question, and address them: he had his place and they had theirs. Native officials were informed about their duties and responsibilities and were evaluated according to how well they performed them. In addition, natives and village officials were put into place relative to other natives living in other villages—where, for example, the living areas were cleaner and the officials better respected. In this latter sense, they were put in their places along the path to development.[13]

To move from one place to the next along this path, local people had to be re-placed: selves were to become receptive to proper authority and instruction; bodies were to become clean and energetic; villages were to become orderly and stable; lives were to become productive and focused on a better future. In this process, a place like Bumbu changed its meaning: initially consolidated from dispersed bush hamlets, it became "BUMBU" on the time-space grid of the patrol. This transformed village came to be embodied by correspondingly transformed inhabitants. For instance, among other things, it became a place where residents had to ready themselves for the arrival of the patrol officer. They had, not only to line up, but to provide census information, pay taxes (with money derived from cash-generating labor), and they had to have gardens, latrines, and a guest house in inspectable condition. Furthermore, residents were evaluated relative to other villages and villagers as either cleaner or dirtier and with better or more poorly kept houses. This is to say, within the newly introduced rhythms and expectations of life that constituted the narrative of development, the people of Bumbu were expected to emerge as modern selves with a modern appreciation of the disciplines of time and space.[14]

Replacement and Displacement: The Filling of Empty Space

It is clear that the patrol officers, as exemplars, instructors, and enforcers, were agents of this transformation (see Stoler and Cooper 1997). They believed that the people of the Upper Ramu Valley would progress, would be shaken from their lethargy, only if they became interested in their transformed futures. Yet they knew that the colonial administration could not afford to patrol the valley very often and that even the most assiduous government-appointed village official would have difficulty enforcing government policies in the absence of more frequent visits. Indeed, the officers speculated on several occasions that some of the more remote people in this generally remote area might be slipping out of control because they were not regularly patrolled (see, in particular, Norton 1951: 7).

The solution to the problem this area presented seemed relatively simple: if the government could acquire inexpensively substantial tracts of underutilized land, it could offer leases that would attract Europeans and their enterprises. The Europeans could benefit both themselves and local people by becoming resident exemplars and purveyors of development. And this is what was done.

The first step in this process of land acquisition was for Parrish and McNamara to complete and submit the land investigation report. After their report was accepted by the administration, Parrish and McNamara drew up a formal sale document: "Transfer of Title from a Native/s to the Administration" (1956). In this document, they carefully describe, in accordance with the modernist technologies and techniques of space delineation, the "boundaries of the said land as follows:—Commencing at the point of the junction of the Gallial and Ramu Rivers whence by the centre line of the . . . River upstream generally northeasterly for approximately 24,500 links thence by a line bearing 310 degrees. . . . All bearings being magnetic and all corners marked by a cairn of stones or a mound of earth" (1956: 2). They then list the names of twelve natives—three from each of the four landowning villages (Bumbu, Sankian, Kaigulan, and Bopirumpun)—who received a total sum of A£8,412.12.0.[15] That the natives agreed to the sale is demonstrated by the X's placed next to their typed names. (That these X's are strikingly neat and uniform has become, as we shall see, a matter of considerable significance to contemporary Mari.) In addition, Parrish and McNamara affirm that "services of an interpreter were not required as the Vendors and purchasing Officers all speak and understand Pidgin English." Moreover, as "Officers in the Service of the Territory of New Guinea" they testify that

the Vendors named on the above transfer signed the above transfer at SANKIAN in the Territory of New Guinea on the twenty-sixth day of June 1956 in our presence. That previous to our signing the transfer did interpret the contents of the said transfer into the Pidgin English language which is understood by the Vendor and pointed out the Boundaries of the Land as shown on the above plan. (3)

And finally, to establish unambiguously that the sale was meant as a quitclaim, they state:

Approximately 40 acres of the land were occupied by Natives of KAIGULAN Village as village site and garden land and approximately 5 acres of the land were occupied by Natives of SANKIAN Village as village site at the time of the sale. Occupation by the Natives is to cease when the new villages outside the boundaries of this land are completed and when the present crop has been harvested but in any case no later than the thirty-first day of December in the year one thousand nine hundred and fifty-six. (4)

The land purchase was deemed a success. McNamara visited the area a year later, and according to his report:

Per head of population these would be some of the wealthiest people in the area patrolled due to the purchase last year of 40,000 acres of land for pastoral leases by the Administration. They are eagerly awaiting the establishment of the cattle stations. They are very happy about the sale of the land and the price they received and do not wish to touch the larger portion of the money received and which they banked. They wish to wait for the opportunity and guidance to start sound economic projects. (7)

Barbara Jephcott has already told us something of what happened next: the land was, according to plan, gazetted for pastoral use, and various Australians were granted leases to begin grazing cattle on it. And, also according to plan, this early European presence was seen as having a generally uplifting effect on the entire area. In O'Brien's words:

At the present time there is a two man survey party . . . at work in the area. As the work of this team is mainly concerned with the boundary survey for a grazing industry their continued presence in the area is creating a healthy and alive outlook in the Dumpu people. Admittedly from February to June of this year there has been almost A£600 paid to these people by the Administration [presumably for labor, perhaps on the airstrip or road]; however the increasing alertness and good will observed in these people . . . is a result of the presence of the survey team. . . .

. . . [T]he future of the DUMPU-KAIGULAN C/D [Census Division] as a centre of the beef cattle industry appears excellent. The availability of the flat, wide and well drained plain between DUMPU A/S [airstrip] and GUSAP has always been recognized for cattle. (1960: 5, 8)

And O'Brien's immediate supervisor, assistant district officer G. R. Keenan, concurs in his letter of evaluation of the patrol:

It is interesting to note the good effect on these people of the presence of a hard-working team of Europeans. The Patrol Officer feels that the presence of the Lands Department Survey team in the DUMPU area has assisted to induce the people to lose some of their apathy and take an interest in means to improve their circumstances. . . .

. . . It is to be hoped that when the pastoral project planned for the DUMPU area does eventually get under way it will provide not only a source of income to the natives of that area but also perhaps an incentive to undertake observation and sensible advice given to them by the people who will oversee the project, perhaps the cattle owning villagers of BUMBU might have more success with their cattle than they have to date. The establishment of this grazing industry may be an inducement for some of the young men to seek work near their homes rather than away from the village. (in O'Brien 1960: 1, 4)

Patrol officers and administrators believed that, with Yali and his teachings suppressed and discredited, only habitual apathy kept local people from advancing along the path toward development. But now that improvement was a real possibility, this lassitude was being replaced by a "healthy and alive outlook." Moreover, natives would be able to benefit, to cite G. R. Keenan's words, from "observation [of] and sensible advice" from the soon-to-be-resident Europeans. Their irrational cargo dreams and lethargy would be replaced by a rational work ethic.

• • •

Some of what we have discussed thus far seems in agreement with what Diamond writes in the chapter in *Guns, Germs, and Steel* entitled "Yali's People." In answer to the question of why "Europeans colonized New Guinea, rather than vice versa," he suggests: "Europeans were the ones that had the oceangoing ships and compasses to travel to New Guinea; the writing systems and printing presses to produce maps, descriptive accounts, and administrative paper work useful in establishing control over New Guinea; the political institutions to organize the ships, soldiers, and administration; and the guns to shoot New Guineans who resisted with bow and arrow and clubs" (1997: 317).

We have, of course, seen many of these tools and practices in action in the Upper Ramu Valley: mechanized means of transport, compasses, maps, descriptive accounts, administrative paperwork, and centralized political institutions. These institutions dispatched armed constables and patrol officers who had the capacity to deal effectively with at least certain forms of resistance. But this is only part of the story—and certainly not the end of it. Two additional things can be said here about why Diamond's necessary explanation is not a sufficient one.

First, if one considers European colonial history as a whole, one realizes that the expansionist uses to which the techniques and technologies of power were put have been shaped variously: the narrative that impelled and justified Pizarro's conquest of Peru was of a different kind than the one that impelled and justified the European colonization of Papua New Guinea. One saw the desirable and feasible in terms of mercantilist plunder of gold and silver; the other in terms of capitalist development of resources and markets. And, correspondingly, Caribbean slave-run plantations were considerably different from what RSL as a development project was to become—as workers could readily attest. Second, the fact that the means of control existed among those who colonized Papua New Guinea (or conquered Peru) does not mean that they had to be used as they were. Just because colonists had the guns to shoot Papua New Guineans does not mean that they had to do so. That few did, and most did not, can only be explained in terms of historically specific alternatives and the choices individuals made among these alternatives.

Thus, it is neither accurate nor fair to describe Papua New Guinea as merely the playing out of a world-historical process between those with "advanced" technologies and techniques and those without them. Such a "thin description" tells us little about the experiential and moral components of the changes that were not only wrought, but often resisted and reformulated.[16] It tells us little about human agency; it tells us little about both the strategic and the principled dimensions of being a human actor in the world. Even within the asymmetrical power relations of colonial control, lives, engagements, and outcomes were far from fully scripted. One could discover those local people—like Yali—who somehow found enough latitude to give colonists a run for their money and to voice moral imperatives and appraise historical outcomes in ways that, as we shall see, many Papua New Guineans still find compelling. And, while there were many Australians who fully believed in the inherent inferiority of Papua New Guineans, one could also find those—including Peter Colton and others—who very much wished local people well and did, in fact, help them overcome significant difficulties.

2

Factories in Fact and Fancy

THE DESIRE OF AUSTRALIAN patrol officers and administrators to bring a productive future to the Upper Ramu Valley was dramatically fulfilled. Virtually anyone approaching Ramu Sugar Limited is impressed by the difference between the still largely empty grasslands, scattered with hamlets and small gardens, and the vast, neatly rowed cane fields with a massive factory complex at the center. As Bryan Dyer, RSL's first agriculture manager and later general manager, told us, it was a formidable challenge to put "such a physical mass in place."[1]

Indeed, RSL, with more than seven thousand hectares under cultivation, occupies a major portion of the native lands originally acquired by the colonizers for pastoral leases. Moreover, RSL clearly depends on the same technologies and techniques that these men valued and utilized: mechanized means of transport, compasses, maps, descriptive accounts, administrative paperwork, and centralized political institutions. Thus, at RSL, a surveyed and divided landscape is plied by huge harvesters, cane sprayers, trucks, and tractors; observations are made of productivity, of pest densities, of sugar quality and quantity; records are kept of expenditures, benefits, and work performance; memos are circulated and reports tendered; and everyone, from apprentice to general manager, is part of a chain of command.

In all of these regards, RSL might well appear to address the question Diamond thinks Yali was asking—of why white people had so much cargo and black people had so little: Europeans were cargo-rich because they had (for longstanding historical reasons) the capacity to transform land and other resources through the organized processes of factory production. Interestingly, RSL might also seem to address the question we think Yali was asking—of what it would take for Europeans to treat Papua New Guineans as equals. In fact, as we shall see in this chapter, it was important to the creation of RSL that people holding a range of views, looking for a range of answers, could all embrace it as a desirable future in their varied, historical narratives.

A Bit More about Yali

Yali was posted to the submarine *Dace* after extensive military training. To prepare him for intelligence work behind enemy lines, he was sent to Queensland, Australia, in 1942, to be instructed in jungle warfare. There, as Lawrence tells us:

> Yali saw things which he had never before even imagined: the wide streets lined with great buildings, and crawling with motor vehicles and pedestrians; huge bridges built of steel; endless miles of motor road; and whole stretches of country carrying innumerable livestock or planted with sugar cane and other crops. He was taken on visits to a sugar mill, where he saw the cane processed, and a brewery. He listened to the descriptions of other natives who saw factories where meat and fish were tinned. (1964: 123)

Lawrence believes that Yali was profoundly impressed by these experiences (see also McCarthy 1963: 224–25). So also, it seems, were the many other locally influential Papua New Guineans sent to Australia both before the war and after. Christin Kocher Schmid reports, for example, that the charismatic leader Yulo Nuo was "particularly impressed by the factories with their never-ending noise, the shift work and the participation of women in the production process" and that he based his concept of "paua" (power) largely upon this experience (Schmid, personal communication; see also Schmid and Klappa 1999: 89–110).[2] The goal of such instructional tours was to combat cargo ideologies by showing prominent and emerging leaders the "real" basis of Australian power (Swatridge 1985).

But what was this lesson about the real basis of Australian power? Presumably it was a variant of Diamond's historical narrative about guns, germs, and steel: that factories—their disciplined workforces, complex machinery, and useful products—were the result of centuries of rational and incremental development that encompassed the industrial revolution and its precursors. Factories were thus material embodiments of an argument that justified, both economically and morally, the Australian colonial control of Papua New Guinea: Australians had the goods and Australians had worked long and hard for them. In essence, Yali and other Papua New Guineans were being told that they must be more gradualistic in their expectations for material advancement and more grounded in the empirical as opposed to the supernatural. They must accept that they had a long way to go and much work to do. They must follow Australian instructions and examples of step-by-step development without resentment or recalcitrance if they wanted to achieve realistic goals.

Indeed, Yali appeared, at least initially, to learn this lesson well. This was the conclusion of J. K. McCarthy, who met Yali after the war. McCarthy was district officer at Madang (and eventually head of the Department of Native Affairs, the position he held at the time he wrote the foreword to Lawrence's *Road Belong Cargo*). Reflecting on their many conversations, McCarthy writes: "As a soldier Yali had been to Australia, where he had been deeply impressed with the white man's civilization and saw in it the key to his people's advancement" (McCarthy 1963: 224); there, Yali had learned that it was "regular and hard work" rather than a "touch of a magic" (225) that would bring development to Papua New Guinea.

However, McCarthy and other administrators were eventually disappointed. Lawrence sums up their realization: It would be wrong, he writes, to view Yali as a native "who had really seen into [the European] world: who had grasped some of the essential concepts at the basis of their own culture—hygiene, organization, and hard work" (1964: 127). In fact, Lawrence thinks that Yali's "social and intellectual outlook was still that of a southern Madang District native" (128)—but that, because he "gave the impression of almost complete Western rationality . . . , it was very easy to put a purely Western construction on everything he said" (127).

For the Papua New Guineans, whether from the "southern Madang District" or elsewhere, the visit to Australia and to its factories must indeed have been an extraordinary experience. However, in our view, they were unlikely to assimilate the intended message about the industrial revolution, its precursors and concomitants. Rather, what they were more likely to learn would have been grounded in Melanesian perspectives, in Melanesian narratives. These Papua New Guineans would focus not only on the things they saw in Australia but also on the related question of why they were invited to Australia to see such things.

Concerning the things they saw: they would view factories both as sources of goods and as goods in themselves; and, as we suggested earlier, they would understand that to gain recognition of equality from Australians they would have to gain access to goods, including factories. Factories were thus revealed to Papua New Guineans as a kind of mega–pearl shell, driving Australian life and history and making desirable things happen. Concerning why they were invited to Australia to see such things: Papua New Guineans might speculate that, as men of substance, they were identified as potential exchange partners. Although not yet active participants, they were at least invited to the proceedings. To become full participants, they must be taught how to engage in the ritualized contexts that, in many Papua New Guinean societies, governed much significant production and distribution. Thus, their introduction to Australian factories probably seemed to these visitors to presage the gift of what was important to Australians. The acquisition of factories would offer an immediate future of potential equality to those Papua New Guineans who would be able—finally—to reciprocate, to play in the same game. After all, as a place for the production of additional exchange-worthy things, a factory was a gift that would keep on giving.[3]

Hence, from the perspective of the Australians, inviting Papua New Guineans into their factories was meant to silence their demands for immediate advancement; it conveyed that Papua New Guineans lacked the requisite rational technologies and techniques to make them significant historical players in the command of people and material resources. From the perspective of the visitors, however, being shown these factories was a gesture of prospective equality; it was taken as a promise that Papua New Guineans would be given the ritual materials and skills to make them significant transactors in the exchanges that afforded recognition of worth.

That knowledge about factories was given a particular Papua New Guinean inflection is well illustrated by a patrol report written by Peter Colton during his patrol-officer days. As an assistant district officer stationed at Madang, Colton was assigned to provide political education among some sixty-eight villages where "only one . . . did not have a YALI representative" and where a "cargo cult has been in the area for years and in all probability will be there for years to come yet" (Colton 1971: 10). In his report, Colton presents the following conversation with "a young cargo cult leader" (5–6):

Self: I have now talked to you about self-government [about which we
will hear more below]. Do you have any comments to make?

Cult Leader: Yes we want self-government now.

Self: Why do you want self-government now?

Cult Leader: Because we will get our own factories, banks, etc.

Self: Do you know the tobacco factory in Madang?

Cult Leader: Yes I have worked there as a labourer.

Self: What will happen to this factory after self-government?

Cult Leader: We will get it.

Self: Do you mean New Guinea as a whole will get it or Matepi
village?

Cult Leader: I personally will run it.

Self: How will you get it? Will the owner of the factory give it to you or
will you fight him for it?

Cult Leader: No I will buy it from him.

Self: Where will you get the money from?

Cult Leader: I will get the money from the sale of copra and cocoa.

Self: How many cocoa and copra trees do you have?

Cult Leader: I don't have any.

Self: When do you want self-government?

Cult Leader: I want it now.

Colton found such beliefs widespread throughout the area of his
patrol and believed they had to be countered by a "political education
programme" (6) to explain the concept of money and its purchasing
power, as well as the concept that a country's money was only as good as
the level of its economy. Yet it is unlikely that the cult leader benefited
from such political education. It is unlikely that he accepted Colton's
gradualist course of development, based on the acquisition of the skills
and resources necessary for careful planning and investment: first you
establish the source of your income by planting cocoa and copra trees,
then you save your money. The cult leader evidently felt that with self-
government, resources and skills would become unproblematically available for the purchase and operation of the "factories, banks, etc." Or,
perhaps more accurately, the cult leader simply felt that, with self-
government, existing inequalities would forthwith dissolve so that he
could become the equivalent of, and hence, the replacement for, the
expatriate factory manager. The cult leader evidently felt that the transi-
tion from white to black control would be complete and immediate as,
quite literally, blacks became interchangeable with whites.

Clearly factories and other resources featured significantly, though very differently, in these Australian and Papua New Guinean visions of how the world worked and how a desirable future might be shaped. Rather than silencing Papua New Guinean demands for equality, exposure to factories provided new visions of how their demands could be satisfied. Indeed, these visions influenced a broad range of Papua New Guineans in their efforts to create a transformed future. With the prospect of self-government, it was not only Colton's "young cargo leader" for whom a factory was central to a future framed in terms of equality, but it was also, as we shall see, well-educated Papua New Guineans who saw a factory as central to their aspirations for national equality.

On Shaping the Future

As Colton's patrol report makes clear with its focus on political education, by the early 1970s the colonial administration had shifted from a laissez-faire approach to a more active involvement in development programs. As might be expected, various policy studies and technical reports signaled this shift. Below, we briefly visit some of those that were important to the creation of RSL.

The report of a World Bank economic mission visit in 1963 proved especially significant. It summarizes the general economic potentialities of the Territory and recommends particular programs to expand the economy and raise the standard of living. According to this report, Papua New Guinea had to restrict the focus of its efforts if it was to succeed economically: in order to "obtain the maximum benefit from the development effort" it must concentrate "manpower and expenditures in areas and on activities where the prospective return [would be] highest" (World Bank 1965: 35). In 1963 the World Bank thought that prospective returns would be highest in agriculture (later, as we shall see, forestry and mining were seen as the most promising sectors). The report describes the "large areas of good land" that were "relatively accessible" and development "relatively easy," although there was the unfortunate "tendency of the indigene . . . to cling to the past, to traditions, to special beliefs that oppose the unknown" (37). Papua New Guineans would have to be advanced through education and vocational training, and they especially needed to be taught to accept greater responsibility for their futures. Under these circumstances, the World Bank thought, expatriates remained crucial to real progress in most development efforts.

The 1965 World Bank report was followed in 1968 by another assessment, entitled *Programmes and Policies for the Economic Development of Papua New Guinea*. This document was prepared under the direction of the Territory's administrator in an effort to build upon the "substantial progress" that has been made in the Territory "along the lines [the World Bank] recommended" (1968: 3). As it turned out, the report accepted most of the World Bank's suggestions about concentrating efforts on high-returning development programs—the ones primarily in "the agricultural industries" (104).[4] Interestingly, one of the specific references made in *Programmes and Policies*—a reference to which we will later return—is to sugarcane:

> *Sugar Cane* has a substantial potential, providing that an adequate local demand develops for sugar. The demand is at present about 13,000 tons per year but is rapidly increasing and a commercial industry could be warranted within the period of the five year programme. Agronomic research is continuing with a view to establishing some 15,000 acres of sugar cane, possibly in the Markham Valley. (31)

Where *Programmes and Policies* differs significantly from the World Bank report is in its insistence that these programs allow "the maximum participation of the indigenous people, as a means of progress towards greater self reliance and social advancement" (104). This insistence, as Connell points out (1997: 23), was probably meant to give public acknowledgment to the imminence of self-government.

By the time *Programmes and Policies* was written, it was, in fact, generally clear that self-government was impending and that independence was a virtual (if still somewhat future) likelihood. Indeed, in 1962, a United Nations mission recommended that Papua New Guinea become self-governing as soon as possible.[5] As a crucial initial step toward self-governance, all Papua New Guineans over age twenty-one became eligible to vote for members of the first House of Assembly in 1964.[6] This democratic election was followed, in 1968, by the formation of the "Pangu Pati" (Papua and New Guinea Union Party), which promptly called for home rule and speeded-up economic development. Also in 1968, Michael Somare, later to become the first prime minister of the independent country, was elected to the second House of Assembly. He was returned to the third House of Assembly in 1972, became leader of the House, and, together with his colleagues, achieved self-government for Papua New Guinea on December 1, 1973, scarcely three years after Colton's discussion with the cargo-cult leader. Independence followed on September 16, 1975, and with that the House of Assembly changed into the National Parliament.

In 1972, just before self-government, another study concerning development, with a report to follow, was conducted under the sponsorship of the United Nations Development Program and the Australian government. The team undertaking the study, headed by Mike Faber, was recruited through the Development Group of the University of East Anglia, "then the most radical centre for development studies in the UK" (Fitzpatrick 1985: 23). This team's assessment, known as the Faber Report, provides an entirely new and different vision of development in Papua New Guinea. For example, both the 1965 World Bank report and *Programmes and Policies*, despite the latter's call for "maximum participation of the indigenous people," emphasize "economic growth no matter who got the benefits and no matter that, specifically, foreigners were getting the great bulk of the benefits and their proportionate share was increasing" (Fitzpatrick 1985: 23). In contrast, the Faber Report lists as the first two among seven assumptions "that any future PNG Government will regard its prime responsibility as being the welfare of PNG nationals. It follows that the welfare of nationals of other countries residing within Papua New Guinea must be considered of less importance" and "that national and social cohesion are to be regarded as important aims of economic policy and that therefore, even on economic grounds, there is an argument for combining an approach which would concentrate resources in the areas of maximum financial returns with the need to distribute the benefits of government expenditure more evenly between districts and between different categories of indigenous inhabitants" (Faber et. al., 1973: 5).

Colonial officials found this report threatening, preferring the old World Bank program emphasizing economic growth for its own sake, regardless of the fact that foreigners would thereby continue to receive the greatest share of the benefits. Nonetheless, the Australian government, wishing by this time to disentangle itself from its colony, supported the Faber Report.[7] Indeed, since the government knew that the report "would be contrary to the prevailing orthodoxy in the colonial administration in Papua New Guinea" (Fitzpatrick 1985: 22), it was probably commissioned to give the government some leverage against its own administrators.

Michael Somare and his colleagues in the Pangu Pati embraced the report and transformed it into the "Eight Aims," which became the philosophical basis for the new independent government. The "Eight Aims," as we shall see, provided a charter for the creation of the factory-focused enterprise of Ramu Sugar Limited:

1. A rapid increase in the proportion of the economy under the control of Papua New Guinean individuals and groups and in the proportion of personal and property income that goes to Papua New Guineans;
2. More equal distribution of economic benefits, including movements towards equalisation of income among people and toward equalisation of services among different areas of the country;
3. Decentralisation of economic activity, planning and government spending, with emphasis on agricultural development, village industry, better internal trade and more spending channeled to local and area bodies;
4. An emphasis on small-scale artisan, service and business activity, relying where possible on typically Papua New Guinean forms of activity;
5. A more self-reliant economy, less dependent for its needs on imported goods and services and better able to meet the needs of its people through local production;
6. An increasing capacity for meeting government spending needs from locally raised revenue;
7. A rapid increase in the equal and active participation of women in all forms of economic and social activity;
8. Government control and involvement in those sectors of the economy where control is necessary to achieve the desired kinds of development.

Most commentators believe that these aims, given their generality and sometimes ambiguity, were never directly translated into policy (see King, Lee, and Waraki 1985; Connell 1997). However, they were important as a "form of nationalist self-assertion and as a means towards greater Papua New Guinean control politically and participation economically" (Fitzpatrick 1985: 25). Indeed, government meetings often began with reference to, if not recitation of, the "Eight Aims" as the point of departure for subsequent discussion (Barry Shaw, personal communication). And, as a "rhetorical device of long-term significance" (Connell 1997: 27), they figured centrally, with some fascinating political twists and turns, in the creation of RSL.

Toward a Sugar Industry in the Upper Ramu Valley

During its early years as an independent nation and in accordance with the fifth of the "Eight Aims" concerning a more self-reliant economy, Papua New Guinea advocated a policy known as "import substitution." The Faber Report, in fact, has specific recommendations about how import substitution would work for agricultural products. Under the head-ing, "Strategies for Agriculture," the report counsels that a "[d]evelopment strategy in the domestic food sector should concentrate on replacing imports and spreading on a wider basis than at present with indigenous farm systems the growing of rice, maize and legumes" (1973: 54). Indeed, rice, maize, and legumes appeared to be just the sorts of crops that could be readily introduced into existing systems of small-scale local agricultural production.

Sugar, on the other hand, was not an obvious candidate for import substitution. Unlike those other crops, sugar (even in relatively small-scale operations) generally depends on the careful coordination of field production with capital-intensive factory processing. That the Faber Report mentions rice, maize, and legumes, but not sugar—and certainly not sugar disengaged from indigenous farm systems—points to the complexity of negotiations leading to RSL, the complexity of negotiations justifying it as consistent with the goals of import substitution, in particular, and those of the Eight Aims, in general.

• • •

The first serious attempt at development of a Papua New Guinean sugar industry was at Sangara Sugar Estates, Ltd. Begun in Papua by several expatriates in 1929, this project ultimately was to be defeated by Australian sugar interests. However, a 1931 article in the *Pacific Islands Monthly* describes this venture as having genuine potential:

PAPUAN SUGAR

Big Scheme Afoot
Half Million for Enterprise Near Buna

The prospectus has been issued of the Sangara Sugar Estates, Ltd., a company with a nominal capital of £1,000,000. The company, which is registered in Papua is to acquire 19,973 acres of sugar land in that Territory from the vendor company and will plant sugar cane there on an extensive scale.

The projected scheme represents one of the biggest efforts to develop the Territory. . . . [I]t is known that Papua possesses lands ideal for sugar-growing—it is the home of the "Badila" variety, the richest cane known in the world and the new company is convinced that its market is assured. . . .

Papua sugar cannot enter Australia. The chief markets for the product

will be Great Britain and Canada, and, as Papua is a British possession,
the cane will have the advantage of a British Empire preference which
at the present is £4/5/- per ton.

It is pointed out by the company that while there is at present an
over-production of sugar in the world, it must be remembered that
there is actually no overproduction within the Empire.

Indeed, the British government did "possess" Papua at the time
(although Australia was administering it on Britain's behalf) and might
legally have granted Sangara Sugar Estates tariff protection. Certainly, in
numerous letters and cables sent throughout the 1930s, members of
Sangara's board of directors regularly requested that the British government
do so. But such communications were simply forwarded by their British
recipients to Australian counterparts, sometimes with notes that assured
the counterparts of continued British support.[8] It seems that Britain did not
wish to jeopardize, in this way at least, its relationship with Australia. It
knew that no Australian government would accept a Papuan sugar industry
that might threaten the markets of its own entrenched Queensland sugar
interests (see Lewis 1996). And, in fact, Australian growers had surplus
sugar, which they would gladly offer to Britain to fill any sugar deficits the
Empire experienced. Hence, although Sangara did report a flourishing crop
in its experimental plots, it remained undercapitalized and without a market, and by the decade's end it was bankrupt.

It was not until the years of initial self-government moving into independence that the creation of a domestic sugar industry became a high,
though still controversial, priority. To understand the heightened significance for Papua New Guinea of developing its own sugar industry, we
must keep in mind several related factors. There was, we think, a perception by Papua New Guinean officials that Australia was not eager for
Papua New Guinea to have its own sugar industry. There was, in addition,
a perception by Papua New Guineans, as well as by their expatriate advisors, that the Australian sugar industry ultimately owed its existence to
Papua New Guinea, the source of all commercially significant varieties of
sugarcane. As D. R. J. Densley, an expatriate working within Papua New
Guinea's Department of Primary Industry, states in his overview about the
development of a Papua New Guinean sugar industry:

Despite the fact that sugar cane is indigenous to Papua New Guinea
there is as yet no commercial sugar industry in the country. . . . Papua
New Guinea is recognized as an area of origin of "royal" canes (noble

canes of the variety Saccharum officinarum). There is some suggestion
that Portuguese traders collected canes at the mouth of the Markham
River as early as the 17th century. . . . Indigenous sugar cane varieties such as Badila (collected in 1896) have been extensively used
overseas in hybrid plant breeding programmes with other varieties
such as Saccharum spontaneum, often with the view of improving
disease resistance. . . . The Bureau of Sugar Experiment Stations of
Queensland |Australia| collected some 740 varieties between 1893 and
1951 for varietal selection for disease resistance purposes. (1977: 2)

The policy of import substitution presented in the Faber Report and in
the Eight Aims only added to the sense among Papua New Guineans that
Australia had already appropriated the sugar market that was rightfully
theirs. In addition and of importance, world sugar prices were very high
at this time.[9] It could be argued, therefore, that it made especially good
economic sense for the newly independent Papua New Guinea to produce its own sugar.[10] After all, along with rice and canned mackerel, sugar
was a major import, and hence a major drain on foreign reserves. The
price of imported sugar more than trebled from 1969–70 to 1975–76, with
a national market for sugar in 1977 of 23,000 tons (Booker Agriculture
International 1978a: 6). The World Bank projected, moreover, that the
price of sugar would continue to be high.

Under these related circumstances, to achieve self-sufficiency in sugar
was a wonderfully appealing prospect. And it would be all the more
appealing—all the more important as a statement and symbol of national
pride, autonomy, and effectiveness—because sugar self-sufficiency
would be *factory* focused, the culmination of the aspirations of a range
of Papua New Guineans.[11] But that these considerations, whether of
national pride or economic prudence, eventually resulted in a sugar project of the size and the expense of RSL, needs further, and more detailed,
explanation.

•   •   •

A crucial phase in the story of RSL began with self-government in 1973,
when imports of ever more expensive sugar had increased to nearly
20,000 tons and pressure to establish some sort of self-sufficiency was
mounting. Although the newly formulated Eight Aims justified import
substitution, the declaration also specified, or at least strongly implied
in points 2, 3, and 4, that the benefits of import substitution, in terms

both of the self-sufficiency and the domestic production that made self-sufficiency possible, should be spread as widely throughout the population as possible. In the case of sugarcane, however, the benefits that would come from widely dispersed and thus relatively small-scale growing and processing would not be easily realized.

This was partially so because a sugar field and a sugar mill must be in close proximity. Unless sugarcane is processed within twenty-four hours of being cut, it loses much of its yield through bacterial action. Thus, if sugar were to be grown in various parts of Papua New Guinea, it would be necessary to construct a number of proximate mills. A plurality of mills would be economically feasible only if they employed a relatively inexpensive—that is, relatively simple—technology. Correspondingly, use of simple technology might well mean that those mills could produce only a relatively low grade of sugar, and low-grade sugar is invariably dark sugar. This fact proved very important in the debates about what course to follow in establishing a national industry.

To pursue the possibility of an inexpensive mode of processing—again, the only one that would allow multiple sites of production in Papua New Guinea—a delegation was sent to India to investigate production of "gur" sugar using the "Khandsari" method. This molasses-rich, sticky brown sugar was produced in small mills where the cane was simply crushed and the juice boiled down in open "pans." The delegation returned with the recommendation that two of these small mills be established. This recommendation, however, immediately generated critical comment: the sugar produced would be of a low quality and of the sort that Papua New Guineans would not find acceptable; it would be entirely unsuitable for commercial use given its color, texture, and tendency to spoil quickly. John Guise, at the time minister of the interior and a Papua New Guinean of considerable political significance, wrote: "I will have no part of the Indian Khandsari open pan system for Papua New Guinea" (1975: 1).

Rejection of "gur" sugar led to the investigation of a more sophisticated technology, although one that might still be implemented on a relatively small scale and thus in several places. Sugar Consultants of Australia proposed the development of several small vacuum-pan sugar mills, which would produce 1,200 tons of relatively high quality sugar.[12] To pursue this idea, the Papua New Guinean government hired two consultants, one in engineering and the other in agriculture, from Australia's Bureau of Sugar Experiment Stations. They were to evaluate the feasibility of both the mill design and two possible Papua New Guinean sites for sugar production and processing. One of these sites, at the Kemp Welch River area, was in the Papuan home region of John Guise. The other was in the Markham Valley, where the government already owned considerable land, bought, as was the land in the directly adjacent Upper Ramu Valley, for development as pastoral leases. Overall, the engineering consultant found the proposal technically possible: "[T]he establishment of small mills . . . is feasible. Operational procedures should be reasonably simple; the mill will be capable of good control; performance should be able to be maintained at acceptably high standard . . . and sugar of a quality acceptable for home consumption should be able to be produced" (Atherton 1975: 12). The agricultural consultant found both areas suitable for cane growing, but regarded the Markham Valley as having "greater potential because of the greater area available" (Hurney 1975: 4).

In 1975, shortly after independence, the World Bank was approached to fund development of a sugar industry in Papua New Guinea. However, the Bank was skeptical about the economic future of small-scale milling (Doery 1977: 2). In 1976, John Natera, secretary for primary industry, initiated another meeting with the World Bank to discuss funding a feasibility study on sugar and to seek the Bank's view on how best to finance a domestic sugar industry. According to notes taken at the meeting by Richard Doery, assistant secretary for policy review and co-ordination: "Mr. Natera explained that current Government policy was to develop the industry around a number of small factories. It will be necessary to seek Cabinet approval in that it appears that this form of development is uneconomic. Papua New Guinea would like to clearly establish what the minimum viable unit is for a Sugar milling operation" (1976: 1).

In fact, it soon became clear that the World Bank would not help fund any mill producing less than 10,000 tons of sugar annually. And, given the cost of such a mill, Papua New Guinea could afford only one. Any sugar industry would consequently be of direct benefit to only a single area. Moreover, the World Bank's position effectively eliminated Kemp Welch as a possible site, for land there was too limited to provide cane for a mill of such size. This outcome greatly angered Guise, given his connections to (and probable interests in) the Kemp Welch area. Subsequently, we were told, Guise became actively opposed to the creation of any Papua New Guinean sugar industry. Thus, the support for a domestic sugar industry as a desirable expression of the policy of import substitution was losing momentum. For these and other reasons, it became a much more difficult political and economic "sell."

The whole project might have been dropped at this point if not for the continuing efforts of John Christensen, an Australian working for the Papua New Guinean government. (Much of what we know about the debates over sugar at the time comes from notes, memoranda, and reports found in Christensen's personal file labeled "Sugar.")[13] As chief agricultural development officer within the Department of Primary Industry, Christensen was long a forceful, but perhaps abrasive, proponent of a development policy based on "big projects," such as large oil palm estates (see Christensen and Densley 1977). Presumably, he concurred with the World Bank position that opposed small-scale sugar-milling operations. Big projects, Christensen felt, had two main advantages: they could be run efficiently and would act as catalysts for further development. In this latter regard, they would provide, he believed, not only centers for regional development, but also centers for national development of infrastructure, such as roads, that would come to link them with each other. From his perspective, and from the perspectives of others he influenced, Papua New Guinea should be creating two of these big projects each year—and sugar should be one of them.

Christensen certainly encountered opposition in his support for big projects in general and for a centralized domestic sugar industry in particular. According to a colleague, Christensen dismissed (and presumably antagonized) the academics he dealt with in government, whom he derogated as "L.S.E. wankers" (i.e., the London School of Economics). He "hated those who were in his opinion left wing, those who tended to favor the small holders." These included anthropologists and sociologists, who worried about matters such as social impact. In particular "he didn't like economists." Concerning the creation of the big project that became RSL, he had actively to combat many in the Department of Finance (with, it was stressed to us, the notable exceptions of Barry Holloway and Oliver Gunawardena). These opponents feared that, if world sugar prices fell, a big sugar mill would become more of an economic drain than an economic boon to the country. For his part, Christensen was impatient with those he regarded as more committed to theory and talk than to action. And it should be noted that he had his admirers in his focus on getting the job done.[14]

Especially crucial to Christensen's success in promoting his vision of a sugar industry was the strong support of one of Papua New Guinea's most influential leaders, Julius Chan. First as minister of finance, later as minister for primary industry, and finally as prime minister, Chan supported Christensen's commitment to sugar as a big project—even while many economists and others seriously challenged it. (Indeed, Chan told us that he thought he would never get the RSL project through.) One well-placed advisor to the government at the time described Chan and his role in the sugar debates to us thus:

> Chan was always in favor of the grand project. This was a time when people spoke about creating lots of big projects each year: some of these big projects would be a highway, or the new airport terminal about which Chan was especially pushy. Other people were trying to tone these grand project-makers down by, for example, defining the upgrading of schools as a grand project.[15] Chan, however, was interested in glory. It was his driving force and he defined glory as archetypal third-world monuments. At the same time there was the nationalist line of self-sufficiency in basic commodities. Also, John Christensen was the chief agriculture development officer then and was a large-scale "ag-man." He thought that smallholder activity was a waste of time; he had a vision and waxed lyrical about it and Chan bought it. . . . Chan thought: Big project, great glory, nationalist image, might be viable.[16]

As minister for primary industry, Chan gained approval to study the feasibility of a large sugar project. This approval came, however, with an important proviso: even if feasibility was established, the project must be a private enterprise. This meant that the government could hold no more than 49 percent of the stock; the other 51 percent must be raised from private sources. As predicted by many—and as we shall shortly see—raising the requisite amount of private funding proved difficult. In fact, the sugar advisory firm chosen to make the feasibility study was selected not only because of its experience in establishing sugar projects, but also because it was the only one of those firms approached willing to invest in the project itself, should it prove feasible. This was a British firm, Booker Agriculture International (BAI), later to become Booker Tate Limited (BTL) and known locally as "Bookers."[17]

Chan set out the state of play as well as his priorities in a letter to his permanent secretary in the Department of Primary Industry on November 14th, 1977:

Sugar Industry—Policy

Sugar is the second most important crop to Rice. A firm development policy is vital. I have decided to locate this industry initially in the

Markham Valley. Booker Agriculture International has been approved to proceed with feasibility study to be completed within 13 weeks. Thereafter, I want a very firm decision and timetable. Again I am convinced we can do it and should begin without delay.

My general views are:—

(1) A large scale mechanised project is warranted with nucleus estate type scheme.

(2) Small scale village growing be continued with special assistance to see viability of producing sugar cane juice and brown sugar for local consumption—we should help.

(3) Staff resource remobilised to give priority to Markham.

(4) Submit a study report as soon as it comes to hand with documents.

Again I am keen to see this project with speed. Keep me informed of progress.

Thus, with a nod toward small-scale, village-based sugar, Chan firmly committed to a big project. (One of our informants was certain that Christensen had drafted this letter, which may then have been minimally revised by Chan.)

The BAI feasibility study investigated projects of different sizes: one would produce 10,000 tons of high-quality sugar per year (the minimum size thought feasible by the World Bank); one 15,000 tons; and the last 30,000 tons. It also investigated locating the industry at Kemp Welch (favored by Guise), in the Markham Valley (favored by Chan), and, in addition, in the Ramu Valley. The study concluded in favor of the 30,000-ton installation because a large installation would have economies of scale. It also concluded in favor of the Ramu Valley, rather than the Markham Valley, because sugar could be grown there without irrigation. And so, after a positive vote in the National Executive Council (NEC) in 1978, the government decided to proceed with the development of RSL. (The NEC consisted of the prime minister, by this time, Chan, and his cabinet.)

But many in government still objected. Notable among these was Stephen Tago, minister of home affairs, whose opinions were widely reported in the press. Tago contended that sugar could be purchased more cheaply from Fiji than produced in Papua New Guinea; that expertise in sugar production could be obtained more readily from Fiji than from England; that a domestic sugar industry would increase sugar consumption, with attendant health risks. Furthermore, he contended that a range of small-scale Khandsari-type mills would fulfill Papua New Guinea's objectives better than a single large-scale mill producing more refined sugar. In fact, he described RSL as "a disease," suggesting that if the "project goes ahead, not only we will have perhaps the most expensive sugar in the world but we will have lost the chance to spend millions on more important National Public Expenditure projects" (Solomon 1979: 1).

Tago's opinions, published in the press, were countered by Roy Evara, member of the NEC and Chan's replacement as minister of primary industry. In a twenty-page "Information Paper," Evara argued that Fijian sugar, because of certain import-export fees, would actually cost more to import into Papua New Guinea than was realized; that the Fijian sugar was a raw, low-quality sugar; that Fiji itself used BAI to advise it concerning sugar plantations; that sugar was no more a poison than any of the Papua New Guinean staple carbohydrates, such as sweet potato; and that the Khandsari method wasted sugar, produced low-quality sugar, and was not tested on the Papua New Guinea market. Evara's "Information Paper" (1979: 19–20) concludes:

> Despite the concern of our colleague, the Minister for Home Affairs, and the genuine desire of all of us, including myself, to see benefits of economic development distributed as evenly as possible throughout the country, and despite the concerns and doubts about what we refer to as "large-scale, capital intensive industrial development," I recommend to and urge you to continue to support the Ramu Sugar Project as approved by NEC Decision No. 135/78 as the only way at this time to meet our objectives of:
>   (i) self-sufficiency in sugar;
> (ii) to forestall the undesirable and uncontrolled effects of imported inflation;
> (iii) to establish a sound and economically viable project which might appear large now but which may not be adequate in future years as our population grows and our requirements increase;
> (iv) increased employment opportunities in rural areas.

Thus, Evara explicitly recognized that, although RSL might fulfill the aspirations of the Eight Aims pertaining to self-sufficiency and rural employment, it clearly contradicted the Eight Aims in other regards. Obviously, it would be neither a decentralized nor a typically Papua New Guinean form of economic activity.

Nor, in the eyes of others at the time, was it obviously a contributor to truly enhanced self-sufficiency. It was, after all, a heavily capitalized industry in which virtually everything but the sugarcane had to be imported. In fact, to establish an industry as ambitious as RSL demanded large sums from overseas lenders. Thus, David Storey, an economist at the University of Papua New Guinea, thought that RSL's creation would not, in fact, further the national objectives of self-sufficiency: repaying large foreign loans as well as meeting BTL's substantial management fees would worsen rather than improve the balance of payments (1979: 5). Bryant Allen, a geographer and Papua New Guinea expert writing while RSL was under construction, had similar reservations: "[The] scheme appears to contradict almost all of the principles set out in the national development strategy only six years ago: it uses high technology, imported skills, overseas capital and increases the inequitable distribution of incomes, services and housing" (1983: 233).

Moreover, there were—as there have been throughout RSL's existence—fundamental questions about the cost of this exercise to Papua New Guinean consumers. If world sugar prices were to decline substantially, then sugar could likely be acquired less expensively from neighboring Australia than from an infant domestic industry. Indeed, Christensen's adversaries in the Department of Finance had anticipated this possibility. Hence a precondition for the establishment of a Papua New Guinean sugar industry—and an assertion of national control—was the guarantee of a substantial measure of protection against outside competition. And this protection, as it turned out, through an initial monopoly followed by tariffs, could well make sugar relatively expensive for Papua New Guineans.

Yet Evara's statement was sufficiently effective in dealing with critics for the project to continue. A prospectus was issued, and Gunawardena was given the task of seeking private funds. We discussed the raising of these funds with John Middleton, a significant shareholder and a charter member of RSL's board of directors. (A naturalized citizen of Papua New Guinea, Middleton was knighted in 2002.) In our conversation, he said that when pressed to make an investment in RSL, he had some spare cash around and he agreed. It was an investment in Papua New Guinea, and a reasonably good one. He also said that Carpenters, a major import-export company, had bought shares, as had Westpac Bank, but these were token amounts. Bookers itself had made an investment. However, really critical to the funding of RSL was the investment by the Public Service Superannuation Fund.

Roger Gilbanks, an expatriate also on the board of RSL (placed there, initially against his will, by Chan), told us how Christensen tried unsuccessfully to coerce him into investing. While visiting at Gilbanks's office in Lae (Gilbanks worked for Harrison and Crossfield, a British firm specializing in oil palm), Christensen said: "Of course you are going to invest in Ramu Sugar." Gilbanks answered that he thought the project "a bloody dodo" and would do no such thing. (Gilbanks told us that he reckoned that since sugar originated in Papua New Guinea, there were some very nasty bugs waiting around for it when it returned home. This possibility, also noted in the BAI feasibility study, did—as we shall see in later chapters—come to pass.) So Christensen threatened that if he didn't invest, the government would no longer buy any of his firm's agricultural chemicals. In his turn, Gilbanks replied that if the government refused to ask for quotes from his company, he would blow the whistle on Christensen. They were friends, but didn't speak to each other for quite a while after this. Yet, Gilbanks said, Christensen did get people to invest—and it ended up that the private sector had by a whisker more invested than the public sector, which was what Chan needed.

Once the shareholder subscriptions had been raised from both the government and from private sources—some K35.5 million—the company could seek loans for the remainder—some K52 million, as it turned out. (These figures appeared in RSL's 1991 annual report, the earliest we saw. According to the exchange rate when these funds were raised in 1979 [K1 = $U.S.1.36], the shareholder subscriptions amounted to $U.S.48.3 million and the loans amounted to $U.S.70.7 million for a total capitalization of $U.S.119 million.) The loans came from a cluster of offshore banks and had to be repaid in yen and U.S. dollars. Even with the guarantee of RSL's monopoly, these loans were difficult to arrange. And their repayment, especially before they were converted into onshore kina, was to prove a serious burden on RSL.

A Factory, by No Other Name, Would Be as Sweet

In the "Information Paper" that he submitted to members of the NEC, Evara chides his colleagues not only for misunderstanding the costs of importing sugar from Fiji, but also for contemplating the introduction into Papua New Guinea of inferior sugar. He expands this latter point in a way that suggests the multidimensional importance of sugar and sugar production in a newly independent Papua New Guinea. A domestic sugar industry is, to be sure, a matter of kina saved and earned. But it is also, he argues, a matter of equal or unequal worth:

As far as other consumers are concerned, I am not aware that Papua New Guineans, including Ministerial colleagues, like to use raw sugar, even if it is available in the shops. Why should we force Papua New Guineans to drink Fijian raw sugar when we ourselves can produce a good quality sugar at a comparable or a lower price? I have brought some samples of sugar to show you what our colleague, the Minister of Home Affairs, wants us to buy from Fiji, what we are buying now from Australia, and what we plan to produce in the Ramu sugar venture. (1979: 3)

In this statement, as Lévi-Strauss (1962) suggests is generally true for all foodstuffs, sugar seems to be not only good to eat, but good to think; not only metabolic but metaphoric; not only sucrose but symbol.[18] Evara's argument asserts certain premises as fundamental. No Papua New Guineans, certainly not the most illustrious among them, should have to consume inferior, brown sugar from Fiji, another Melanesian country. Nor should they have to import superior white sugar from Australia, their former colonial master. Instead, they should consume superior white sugar that they themselves have made in their grand new venture, one marking them as an independent nation. The force of this rhetoric rested on a set of at least implied meanings: white sugar was a more refined product, and those who consumed it, more advanced; brown (raw) sugar and those who consumed it, less so. For Papua New Guinea to continue to import white sugar from "white" Australia meant remaining colonially dependent. For it to start to import raw sugar from "brown" Fiji meant becoming colonially independent, but second-rate.[19] For Papua New Guineans to be both consumers and producers of high-quality sugar meant that they could take their rightful place, as equals, among other nations. This was particularly the case because their high-quality sugar would be produced in a first-rate, large-scale installation—a world-standard sugar *factory*.

• • •

In tracing the complex choices that led to the founding of RSL, it becomes clear that RSL was the product of the diverse perspectives of a variety of interested parties—from patrol officers to late-colonial administrators, from World Bank advisors to Mike Faber's team, from cargo cultist to Chan—about what was desirable and feasible for Papua New Guinea and its people. What was the nation to be? Who should select the nation's goals, using what principles? How might Papua New Guinea achieve equality among the other nations of the world? Should expatriates remain in charge so long as local people clung to their pasts? How might Papua New Guinea articulate within a world economic system where it might (or might not) need to borrow capital? Should economic development emphasize growth for its own sake or be targeted to benefit particular groups or areas? Might socialism rather than capitalism better fulfill the country's Eight Aims, including the more equal distribution of economic benefits to everyone in the nation? Could Christensen prevail over the L.S.E. wankers? Was big better when it came to development projects? Should Papua New Guinea sugar be dark or light? Thus the building of RSL, this huge physical and social fact producing mill-white sugar in the Upper Ramu Valley, did not simply take place.

To be sure, RSL was brought into being at a time when certain necessary techniques and technologies, including those for the efficient thickening of sugar juice by the careful application of heat, were already well established. But it was also brought into being at a time when certain futures were seen by certain people as desirable and feasible. These futures were drawn from a range of ideas—imported, indigenous, reworked, intersecting, conflicting—about the nation, the economy, development, social justice, and moral worth. Indeed, these ideas gave RSL its initial meaning and made its creation, as a possible answer to Yali's most general question about how to redefine the relationships between white and black, colonist and colonized, an outcome actually worth fighting for and against.

3

The Peopling
of a Place and the
Placing of People

HAVING EXPLORED THE complex and contested decision-making
process that led to the founding of RSL, we now turn to how RSL assumed
its physical and social shape: how, in the otherwise remote Upper Ramu
Valley, there emerged a vista of green cane fields, a traffic of heavy equipment, a rumble of cane-crushing rollers, and a community of thousands.
Our focus is, in other words, on how RSL came into being as a *place*: on
how (to make explicit the core connotation of the word) RSL became a
densely meaningful space. A space becomes most fully a place—acquires
a thickness of meaning—when it becomes the subject of narratives both
large and small about life and its possibilities.[1] It follows that because
contrasting narratives create contrasting places, there often is ongoing
contention about which narrative—which place—shall prevail.[2]

We begin our account of RSL's "emplacement" with two quite different
accounts about the building of the factory. As we shall see, these broad
narratives will continue to generate contention about what sort of place
RSL is and might become.

On Building the Factory

Below is an excerpt from a lengthy interview we conducted in July of 1999
with Wilson Gagas, a Mari living in Sankian Village. Gagas is an "outgrower,"

which means that RSL grows sugar on his land in a profit-sharing arrangement. In this interview, which was conducted in Pidgin English, he describes the building of RSL's factory:

I was a supervisor of the crew which began the factory. I knew Bryan Dyer, the first Englishman to work here, and I knew the Japanese from Kawasaki, who [won the bid and] built the factory. This was a time when the road, initially a small one, was greatly widened but not sealed. I worked with twelve local men, initially to build four bush-material houses: one in which some Japanese lived; one in which the workers lived; one in which the food was stored; and one in which the tools were kept. I also built three toilets. Workers were given beer in the morning so they would work hard. I convinced the Japanese to give me a truck to help transport the building materials—a red Nissan six-wheel. Though my father was a tractor driver, he never taught me to drive. The Japanese didn't speak English or Pidgin so they gave me very little instruction. I told everyone to go a long distance away as I engaged the clutch. My first try was very funny.

I also remember an early job I did for the factory. It was to get rid of the tall grass at the site. The Japanese demonstrated the use of back-pack sprayers, which shriveled the grass in no time, such that it could then be lit and would burn. We all found this very impressive.

By far the hardest job was digging twenty very large and very deep holes where the factory was going to go. The Japanese then filled a truck up with the soil from these holes and weighed the truck so as to determine what the soil was composed of. This was to see whether the ground was strong enough to support the factory. We dug and dug until we hit water. When the holes were dug, the Japanese then wired the holes together to determine who owned the ground. They used ear-phones and a screen (like a television) to find out the real owner.[3] They did this secretly at 2 A.M., but took me down to see it. They didn't want me to tell anyone. What I saw was Nahiyel, the [Mari] ancestor of Emmanuel Moba [about whom we will hear more later]. He was the king of this ground and told the Japanese that if they didn't make him happy, the factory would soon break down and water would cover it up. He felt sorry for the people of the area because they didn't have good trousers and shirts. And so the Japanese had to give him a present so that the factory would last. What they did was to throw 2.5 million kina into the various holes—which became part of RSL's debt—and then cemented it up twice. Dimas [a local man] told me that he was going to dig up the holes but I told him they were too well cemented. These became part of the foundation.

Once I became angry with the Japanese for not fixing my truck. I drove away to the Markham Valley and the Japanese called the police to chase after me. But I tricked the police at a roadblock, and then threw them off my trail by dodging into a side road. My in-law from Chimbu was with me; he was like my clerk. I told him to keep his face down in the bed of the truck lest he get too scared. But he ran away, frightened of the pursuit. Eventually I told my bosses that I was sorry, but that they were wrong for not helping me fix the truck.

Now I get a little money from selling sugarcane to the factory. My fields have just been cut, and in thirty days my money will come through, but it will be less than I should get. They will deduct for transport and loading, spraying, management, and labor. Why is the company, which took our land, charging us again? The company has our land and yet it charges us and that's unfair.

Next is an excerpt from an interview we conducted with Stuart Hayes, a BTL employee who was the first factory manager at RSL. In this interview, conducted in February of 2000, Hayes, too, describes the building of RSL's factory:

The contract for the supply and building of the factory was put out to international tender. Kawasaki's was the lowest price and it became the main contractor. They subcontracted the construction to Kerry Engineering out of Malaya, which imported a large workforce of Chinese Malays.

First the area was surveyed by BAI and the plans drawn up. Once they got the slope, they figured out where the factory would go—and then put a peg in the ground and said "that is the corner of the process house; we will measure from there." It was just a huge expanse of grassland then.

The factory has a cement foundation, which had to be especially heavy because this is a class A earthquake zone. The Japanese designed it; they are experienced at such things because their country is earthquake prone. We got New Zealand consultants to check the Japanese plans, since New Zealanders are good at such things, too. Both the foundation and the steel work had to be substantial and we put a lot of liquid storage on the ground floor so as to keep the center of gravity low. Imagine what it would be like to have thirty to forty tons of liquid sixty feet in the air and shaking around. We employed civil engineers including the man who built the "bridge on the River Kwai" for the film. We had a batching plant for making concrete. Stone came from the rivers: we looked at lots of riverbeds, for those that had hard granite, not slate—and then screened the dirt off.

The residences were of five types, A, B, C, D, and E. BAI designed the houses, Wewak Timbers [of Papua New Guinea] made them up in kit form, and a New Zealand company built them. There was only one "A" house, the GM's [general-manager's]; five "B" houses for the HODs [heads of departments]; about forty-five managers' "C" houses; then the supervisors' "D" houses and the laborers' "E" houses. We didn't want the conventional labor lines as on plantations in Africa. Here we put the houses into "villages," with about twenty houses in a complex with a green on which people could play football or engage in other leisure-type activities. We intended to avoid a company-town appearance. That type of design leads to ghettos, which are unattractive. Long labor lines of houses are also uncomfortable, especially if you are in a middle unit.

There was hardly a tree anywhere. You could look from where we are now right to the factory. The wind would whistle down the valley and it would whine through the louvers in the houses. People found this unpleasant. So Bryan Dyer, the ag[ricultural] manager, started a nursery where you could get plants free. The trees have moderated the wind, but the down side is that the wind doesn't cool. And in the early days there was no air conditioning—just in the GM's office and the boardroom.

We didn't have any serious problems with the factory. It's not like you start the factory all at once; there was a slow workup. It was officially opened in July 1982; Sir Julius Chan spoke. It was largely national pride that justified this project. It's too small to be a commercial success unless it had a protected market.[4] Yet the government was determined to have its own sugar industry. Chan was in power and stayed in power for a couple of years after it was built. So, as part of the feasibility study, we [BAI and then BTL] provided samples in jars of common kinds of direct-consumption sugars: raw sugar, several kinds of mill-white sugar, and refined sugar—all of different colors. And we said [to the government officials], what kind of sugar do you want, since that would determine the kind of factory. We said that to make this kind of sugar will cost you X millions, and to make another kind. . . . They decided on mill-white, not refined-white. Then we told them we would do a financial plan and get back to them so they could attract investors.

When it began, there were about fifty expatriates working here, in all departments. [Many of them came with their families.] There were sixteen in the factory alone. Most were British, although a few were Australian. The problem was what to do about middle management. There was no history of sugar production in this country, and thus no trained workers with experience for us to draw on. So we tried to find a somewhat comparable country with some experience to get the middle management. BAI had a relationship with Victorias Milling in the Philippines, so that is where we went to borrow middle management. We made it clear that we couldn't offer them long-term employment, so we had thirty-three Filipino foremen and supervisors reassigned. We started off with those, and at the same time we sent groups of Papua New Guineans to do training courses in the Philippines. We sent twenty for six months and then another twenty. This was all prior to the factory starting off. When it did start off, it was with a group of British who had worked in the industry for many years, with Filipino foremen, and with Papua New Guineans working along side of the Filipino foremen as trainees. We were also recruiting people with degrees at the same time. Papua New Guinea wasn't turning out all that many graduates, and we needed both chemical and mechanical engineers. But so did everyone else, and we were all competing for the same people. So we decided to sponsor people for training in Australia. But often they would get their training and then leave us. Some places use bonding, that is charging a fee if workers leave before a certain time after they receive training. But we found that bonding never pays because if a man doesn't want to work for you, he won't do a good job.

Gagas's account is of a still "pre-BUMBU" landscape, that is, a landscape that has not yet been transformed according to a modernist fusion of self, space, and time. Gagas's landscape is a place neither of survey nor of alienation; it is a place neither abstract nor empty, neither uniform nor anonymous. Rather, it is a place for the likes of the original ancestor, Nahiyel. As understood by Gagas, such a place carries with it moral and, indeed, political and legal claims. Just as Nahiyel has inherent rights to this place, so the Mari have enduring rights. Just as Nahiyel could compel powerful outsiders to recognize his priority and potency (just as he could compel reciprocity from them by eliciting presents), so the Mari should compel powerful others (like RSL) to recognize their efficacy and worth.

Significantly, Nahiyel, once acknowledged as a transactor who must be dealt with, consented for the RSL project to continue so his people would have good shirts and trousers. These would indicate equality so that Nahiyel and others would no longer feel sorry for them. And, once recognized as the proper and enduring landowners who must be dealt with, the Mari would also consent for the RSL operation to continue so that, and provided that, the Mari would have the signs and benefits of development.

In fact, all of the encounters Gagas describes were based on the assumption that these were interpersonal relationships in which recognition of Mari worth and centrality should provide the basis of reciprocity. And Gagas's account is typical of the kinds of arguments many other Mari make. This is the same assumption regarding Mari worth and centrality that caused Nahiyel to insist that the Japanese present him with gifts. It is also the same assumption that should lead RSL not to deduct for agricultural inputs. And it is the same assumption that should have compelled the Japanese contractors to take care of his truck. As we shall see, Gagas's statement that the factory site is occupied by the king of this ground is part of an ongoing Mari argument about what is rightfully due them.

In contrast, Hayes's account is of a "post-BUMBU" landscape, which is entirely alienated and rationalized because it is abstracted and impersonal. Surveyed, pegged, cemented, and planted, it is a landscape whose use is determined by studies of land suitability, factory design, market potential, and sound management.[5] Hayes takes pride in the fact that the project was well planned and executed, though he regrets that economies of scale could never be realized.

Indeed, Hayes's account focuses on the technologies and techniques that should appropriately organize both place and people. Because RSL exists for the efficient production of sugar, good business practices dictate that it be structured as a hierarchy based upon technical and managerial skills. These practices also dictate that, within this hierarchy, relationships and expectations be made as explicit as possible. The responsibilities and qualifications of the job, the duration of the contract (as with the seconding of the Filipinos), the remunerations and perquisites must all be contractual and unambiguous. Good business practices also take into account the assumption that satisfied workers produce well and, conversely, that dissatisfied workers, whether bonded or not, produce poorly. Both company interests and worker interests are served by worker training—as with the acquisition of enhanced technical and managerial skills. In addition, because RSL exists to produce sugar, the hierarchy of work, and its differential system of responsibilities and rewards, is pervasive, extending from workplace to residential space: it is, however, in the company's interests that all employees, whether in type "A" or type "E" houses, have recreational space and pleasant, quiet (if not air-conditioned) living conditions.

In discussing Gagas's and Hayes's perspectives, we might, of course, portray them as more parallel. Gagas, after all, knows about earthquakes and about how different skills lead to different fortnightly pay packets as well as different housing assignments. And Hayes speaks about the degree to which he greatly values informal relations and friendships with many on different occupational levels—both expatriates and nationals. Therefore, the differences between these accounts should not be taken as absolute and irreducible—as essentialist.[6] Nonetheless, their perspectives are significantly different in emphasis: Gagas insists that reciprocal relationships, including, explicitly, those stemming from particularist, inalienable ties to place, be fundamental to the operation of RSL; Hayes insists that rationalized, contractualized relationships and practices of production, including, implicitly, those based upon quitclaim land transactions, be fundamental to the operation. Indeed, from Hayes's point of view, to build a major installation such as RSL on land one does not control would be the height of irrationality.

As we shall see, for people like Hayes, a major problem in rationalizing production, including the relationships of production, is dealing with the expectations, if not the demands, of people like Gagas. Conversely, for people like Gagas, a major problem in transacting with a rationalized RSL is dealing with the expectations, if not the demands, of people like Hayes. In fact, people like Gagas and Hayes know about each other in a range of ways, both accurate and inaccurate. Gagas, for instance, has to be explicit and adamant about his claims for enduring land rights because he knows that RSL is premised on the assumption that land is already alienated.

From "Ples" to Place

People like Hayes learned about Papua New Guineans in a variety of formal and informal ways. As one source of formal information, BAI issued an instructive and generally accurate booklet.[7] Designed to teach Europeans (mostly British) bound for RSL what to expect, it provides a description of Papua New Guineans—including those they would hire and train:

Socially, the indigenous population is broadly split between the peoples of the highlands and those of the coastal areas. Within each division there are variations, not only in appearance but in lifestyle, custom and language. It is this differentiation between language groups which is most important. There are estimated to be over 700 different languages in PNG (although the local pidgin is the most widely used and English is the language of Government and commerce). The various clans or "wantok" (one talk) groups have very strong attachments to their place [in Pidgin English, "ples"], reinforced by kinship bonds and obligations. They view land and resources as exclusive possessions and in the past there was open hostility between "wantok" groups. Such disputes are less frequent today although the concept of "wantok" is still in evidence. A ruthless "payback" system still operates between clans and vengeance for inter-clan thefts, injuries or deaths is carried to extremes. (Booker Agriculture International 1981: 8)

Thus expatriates were explicitly taught that Papua New Guineans are people whose lives are oriented around place ("ples") and kinship obligations; and they are people whose social relationships are based upon both positive and negative reciprocities. A bit later in the pamphlet, expatriates would also learn that, for personal safety, they should avoid being drawn into these "paybacks." Moreover, they were told that for the efficient running of RSL, they should be alert for the influence of "wantok" ties.

In fact, because the RSL township was to be constructed on a seemingly empty plain, BAI could plan it to minimize these wantok ties and the paybacks such ties were thought to generate. But BAI wanted to do more than to avoid building a wantok-ridden town. It also wanted to avoid building a "company town." The BAI initial feasibility study for the project states both these objectives:

In the absence of a local community and of essential services, the development of a new township will be an integral part of the project. It is essential that the plan takes sociological, as well as physical, factors into account in order to create a balanced community [that is, avoiding a preponderance of people from any particular group] which is fully integrated into the normal economic, political and social life of the country as a whole. Whilst the wealth of the community, and indeed its very existence, will derive from the sugar project, great care should be taken to avoid the creation of a traditional "company town." (Booker Agriculture International 1978c, app. 5, 11)

The five-hundred-hectare township that came into being in the Upper Ramu Valley has indeed been carefully planned and controlled (figs. 6 and 7).

Figure 6. Early days at RSL: "There was hardly a tree anywhere."

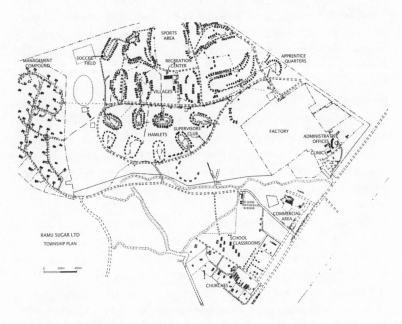

Figure 7. The layout of RSL housing

Its residential center, consisting of two adjacent gated communities, is surrounded by more than seven thousand hectares of RSL-owned sugarcane fields. RSL staff live in these two gated communities. All houses or apartments are provided with basic and free utilities, and most are reserved for the almost seven hundred permanent RSL employees and their immediate nuclear families. These families are defined in the *Employees Handbook* as "one husband or one wife and dependent children" (RSL 1993: 4). Any visitors, whether members of an extended family or of wantoks more generally, are to be registered and allowed to stay for no more than three weeks.

The more pleasant of these two communities is called either the "Management Compound" or the "Tarangau Compound." (The "tarangau," or eagle, we were jokingly told, is the top of the food chain.) The managers living there now include both Papua New Guineans and expatriates. In fact, all expatriate employees live there since all of them are managers. This community is farther from the factory than the other one: it is farther from its smoke and noise, including its shift-marking sirens. Entered through its own guarded gate, it is tightly secured not only by fences but also by the patrols of guard dogs and their handlers.[8]

The spacious houses of types A, B, and C that Hayes mentions are in this community. All are substantially elevated (at least eight feet off the ground), with shaded verandahs and well-planted and -tended yards. In addition, types A and B, for the general manager and heads of departments, overlook a nine-hole golf course (fig. 8). All of these houses have overhead fans (and, certainly by the time of our research in 1999–2001, the wiring for air conditioning), full kitchens, and cable television hookups. Also within this community there is the very pleasant and well-appointed Management Club, containing a bar, snooker table, swimming pool, tennis court, guest house and dining room, large multipurpose room (suitable for meetings, parties, or badminton), expansive porch for dining and drinking, and weight room (fig. 9). In addition, this community has an "international school" for managers' children in grades 1–6 and a relatively extensive library.[9]

The other community has no name. Although somewhat less secure, it is also gated and guarded. In it are houses of types D and E, for permanently employed supervisors and workers. Type D houses are detached, single-family dwellings with indoor plumbing, kitchen facilities, and electrification. Each is only a foot or so off the ground and has two bedrooms, a living room, a small front porch, and a back yard in which people often grow vegetables and erect bush-material shelters for out-

Figure 8. A "B" house, one of five set aside for heads of departments

Figure 9. The very pleasant and well-appointed Management Club

door cooking and relaxing. Type D houses are much smaller and much closer together than types A, B, and C, but still, depending of course on family size, they are relatively comfortable. Organized into horseshoe-shaped "hamlets" of about twenty houses each, they all front a green on which people can meet and children can play with their friends.

Type E houses, located closest to the factory, are the very modest duplexes assigned to workers and their families. Also slightly elevated and with small front porches, each unit has its own indoor plumbing and electricity for lighting, radios, and fans. Electricity is free to these occupants, as to everyone living in RSL houses. However, they, unlike others, are prohibited from using electrical appliances that consume more than one kilowatt of electricity (although this rule is often broken if families are able to buy refrigerators). These units are small and cramped, particularly given the often large size of workers' families. Organized into "villages" of about thirty houses each (with village names such as "Kaukau" or "Pukpuk"—"Sweet Potato" or "Crocodile"), the houses, like the others, front a green.

An assortment of others who are not permanent RSL employees also live within this second community: apprentices, contractors, teachers (for the community, not the international school), the district court magistrate, and anthropologists. (We lived during 1999 in one of the hamlets, during 2000 in a contractor's house—the only white people ever to have lived in this community once A, B, and C houses were completed—and during 2001 in the Management Club's guest house)

Although recreational facilities in this second community once included a supervisors' club and library, these are no longer operating. However, several large sports areas are actively used for the many RSL-authorized teams that include soccer, rugby, basketball, and volleyball. In addition, there is a large recreational hall for dances, prayer meetings, and other group activities. Finally, there is a union office.

Directly adjacent to this second community is the core of RSL's productive operation. It, too, is fenced in and patrolled (fig. 10). This area contains the factory, packing plant, workshops, warehouses, health clinic (for all employees, including managers), and administration office building for the general manager and the four heads of departments (agriculture, finance, human resources, and factory) and their staffs. Also in this area are additional offices (such as those devoted to managing the outgrowers and their accounts) as well as laboratories (such as those devoted to agronomy).

The rest of the township, known as Gusap, is not gated, but generally quite safe from criminal attack. On land also controlled by RSL, this portion of the township is a center for RSL people. In addition, as it is located approximately midway between the two major cities of Lae and Madang, Gusap is a center for those from a widespread area (see fig. 11). Indeed, buses and trucks frequently stop there to load and unload people

Figure 10. RSL's productive operation was fenced in and patrolled.

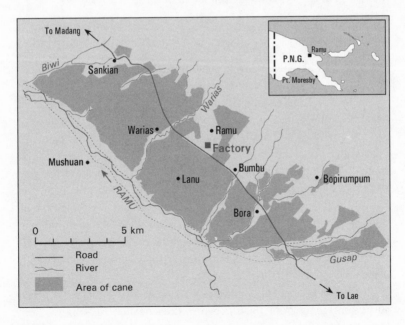

Figure 11. RSL and environs

and products. There is a district court office, a village court office, a police station with a jail, a health clinic for all the people in the area, a primary school through grade 8, a post office, and a shopping center comprising two mini-supermarkets, several small general stores, a convenience store, a gas station, and an open-air market at which people sell items ranging from garden produce to used clothes. There were banks once as well, but these closed after being robbed. There are houses for policemen, teachers, and health workers, barracks for RSL seasonal workers and for guard-dog handlers, and churches (Catholic, Assembly of God, United Church, Lutheran, the Evangelical Brotherhood Church, and various others, mostly Pentecostal).

Outside the township, RSL's influence is also obvious. There are, of course, the surrounding sugarcane fields. And in the midst of these are three more RSL-controlled villages, Warias, Lanu, and Bora. These house the mainly seasonal, agricultural workers. The houses here are small and the villages ungated. Finally, also surrounded by cane fields, there are the villages and gardens of the Mari outgrowers.[10]

Altogether, within a few years after it opened in 1982, RSL's presence had become immense. Indeed, by 1995 Peter Colton estimated that more than fifteen thousand men, women, and children either directly or indirectly earned a livelihood from Ramu Sugar (See Colton 1995).[11]

.   .   .

Not only did RSL strive to avoid creating a company town of uncomfortable and unattractive housing by providing everyone with convenient access to a reasonable number of amenities (although there were more benefits for the "Eagles" than for the "Sweet Potatoes"). It also wanted to avoid "wantokism" in both hiring practices and residential assignments. Concerning initial hiring practices, the expatriate officer who was in charge of the initial "manning exercise" told us that, to be sure, the goal was to find a competent pair of hands for every job. But RSL also "consciously decided not to hire just local people, but rather people from all over the country." It did "district-of-origin monitoring" and imposed quotas because it "did not want an overweighting of one people in any section of the company. What was to be avoided was any one section totally made up of Sepiks, Highlanders, or Tolai."[12]

Of the 668 permanent employees working at RSL during 2000, about 40 percent came from the three provinces nearest to RSL: 69 from Madang; 118 from Morobe; and 78 from Eastern Highlands. But there were permanent workers from all of the country's provinces, with the exception of Western.[13] In addition, there were 13 permanently employed expatriates: 4 Australians, 5 Britons, 2 Fijian-Indian-Australians, and 2 Indians. Finally, there were 789 seasonal employees, about whom we have incomplete information. However, we did learn the provinces of origin for about 300 of these workers, and they included all but Milne Bay and New Ireland.

Concerning residential assignments, the Papua New Guinean in charge of human resources during the time of our research, a man who has worked at RSL from its beginning, told us that you "don't put too many people from the same group into the same hamlet because employees must learn to see themselves in other employees." After all, "an important company value is unity." This means that there can be "none of this, 'I'm from Enga'; 'you're from the Sepik'; 'I'm from Central.' Everyone [at RSL] has to be a Papua New Guinean first. People have to become responsible for one another." Once this has happened, RSL has changed them "into something different and better." Certainly the neighborhood of permanent employees in which we lived during 1999 did have people from all over the country, and the same diversity could be found throughout the other hamlets and villages.

Thus Papua New Guinean workers are actively discouraged by recruitment and residence from establishing indigenous sorts of alliances (and oppositions). They are supposed to become a new sort of people, with a new sort of solidarity. The viability and very existence of this solidarity is to derive from the sugar project. The solidarity of the community is, in major respects, to be a product of a complex division of labor characterized not only by specialized occupational skills but also by their coordinated deployment. This solidarity, based on the division of labor, is described by Emile Durkheim ([1933] 1984) as "organic"—analogous to an organism with functionally integrated parts. Indeed, the specialized and coordinated system of organization by which RSL, as an integrated agro-industrial complex, produces sugar permeates everyday life, becoming something habitual, what Bourdieu (1977) calls "habitus."

The organization of work at RSL is unambiguously industrial, and that fact is explicitly conveyed (in English) through such widely available sources as the *Employees Handbook*. In the *Handbook* there are charts of organization, dubbed "organigrams," for RSL as a whole and for each of the departments. Scanning the chart for RSL as a whole (the first one presented) one can see immediately that the board of directors represents the highest authority, followed by general management, which supervises the various departments. The factory department is composed of the engineering and the production sections. The engineering section, at the fifth level down, comprises six categories of supervisory positions, including workers in process maintenance, mills/boilers, packinghouse maintenance, workshop, instruments, and electrical tasks.

The individuals who hold these positions are broadly categorized as managers, supervisors, and workers; and they are domiciled in corresponding houses. They also are subject to a fine-grained classification of grade and pay scale that reflects their skill and responsibility. Each grade has a "job profile." For example, the *Handbook* profiles grade 7 in these general terms: "In plant operation, capable of handling any item of plant/slash equipment to maximum performance consistently virtually unsupervised. A designated driver/instructor. A tradesman who has passed Class Trade Test." More specifically, in the factory such a grade 7 was a "Boiler Operator (level 2)," "Tradesmen Class 2 (fitter, mason, welder, electrician)," or "leading hand fugaller." In agriculture, such a grade 7 was an "Experienced mechanical harvester operator," or a "Tradesman Class 2 (mechanic, welder)."

Correspondingly, the organization of time by which work is regulated and coordinated is unambiguously industrial: shift changes are marked and recorded by siren and time clock. Some employees (clerks, groundskeepers, many maintenance personnel), work a forty-four-hour week as day staff, generally from 7:00 A.M. to 4:45 P.M., with an hour's lunch break. Others (agricultural and factory workers, in particular), especially during the annual harvest season, work shifts, beginning at 7:00 A.M., 3:00 P.M., or 11:00 P.M. For both kinds of workers, the factory siren is blown at 6:00, 6:45, and 7:00 A.M., to wake them up, to send then on their way to work from their different hamlets and villages, and to inform them when to clock in. Later it is blown to mark the day workers' lunch break, at noon, at 12:45 P.M., and at 1:00 P.M. (Shift workers do not get a lunch break.) Finally, it is blown at 3:00 P.M. and at 11:00 P.M. to mark the end of one shift and the beginning of another, and at 4:45 P.M. to mark the end of the day shift.

·   ·   ·

The pattern of spatial and social organization imposed by the patrol officers, at least provisionally, upon the Upper Ramu Valley and those who lived there (as described in chapter 1) has been repeated at RSL. The same narrative of development has been applied in each case: the

transformation of "Bumbu" into "ʙᴜᴍʙᴜ" by the application of the technologies and techniques of the patrol is realized at RSL in the organization of field, factory, and residence; the energized natives envisioned by
the patrol officers (a transformation of lethargic and disorder-prone villagers) is realized at RSL in the agroindustrial workers disciplined by the
organigram and the time clock.[14]

It is also important to realize that this same narrative of development
makes RSL a particularly apt manifestation of Papua New Guinea's independent status. Hence, in accord with the nationalist sentiments held
and expressed by many of the government's leaders and officials, RSL can
be regarded as especially important to the creation of the new nation. In
fact, because the township that constitutes RSL is organized according to
the narrative precepts of a modern nation, RSL can serve as a microcosm
of the new nation, illustrating what it can and should be.

By showing how ethnic conflict might yield to organic solidarity, and
how destructive payback might yield to productive cooperation, RSL
serves as a model of how divisive, primordial connections to particular
places (pleses) and peoples (wantoks) might give way advantageously to
more inclusive geographic ties and social allegiances. RSL is a model of
how more inclusive definitions of place and peoples can constitute a new
and desirable kind of place and people: RSL shows how place can
become nation and people can become its citizens.

In many regards, RSL serves as a model of an "imagined community,"
a concept introduced by Benedict Anderson in 1983 to convey the particular challenge involved in creating the modern nation. The challenge is to
convince somewhat dispersed and sometimes diverse people that they
have important commonalities and that they are all citizens of the same
place. The challenge is to dissolve, or at least to diminish, ties to people
one already knows and to create, or at least to enhance, ties to people one might never meet but only knows about. It is, in other words, to
create a community of fellow countrymen—by imagining, for example,
that people one will never meet are fundamentally like those in one's
local community.[15]

To be sure, RSL is not such a big project that it has to link people
who will never meet. It does, however, have to work hard to link people
who come from separate sociocultural universes. This is the explicit
objective of the Papua New Guinean in charge of human resources: for
employees to "see themselves in other employees" and for everyone at
RSL to be "a Papua New Guinean first." People have to "become responsible for one another," and once this happens, RSL has changed them

"into something different and better." RSL workers are thus to leave wantokism at their pleses and to develop a new culture and identity as Papua New Guineans.

RSL encourages people to see themselves in others partly by structuring life in a uniform way: all grade 7s, regardless of whether they work in agriculture, finance, or the factory, are comparable in skill, pay, and residence. Moreover, all grade 7s—like everyone else—have their work and leisure structured by the same sirens. All grade 7s are articulated at a particular skill level in an overall division of labor in which everyone knows his or her place as well as the places of all others. This is not only a thoroughly redundant organization, but it is also a redundant organization that permeates all aspects of life.

Correspondingly, because RSL's discipline and hierarchy cover so many aspects of life, they have a powerful effect in molding its workers. In these regards, RSL has many of the characteristics of "total institutions," organizations such as armies, mental hospitals, and monasteries, which are "the forcing houses for the changing of persons" (Goffman 1961: 12; cf. Smith 1967: 230). Grade 7 craftsmen, in other words, are themselves crafted, and in ways that go beyond any program directed at trade certification: they do not just happen. RSL is much as Smith describes sugar plantations in the Caribbean, "a peculiar kind of instrument for the re-socialization of those who fell within its sphere of influence" (1967: 232).

RSL's objective of transforming villagers into employees who are "Papua New Guineans first" corresponds to yet other aspects of the nationalist agenda that led to RSL's creation. Central to the project of "nation making" (to refer to the title of Foster's 1995 book) is a set of precepts to which all people must subscribe. Consistent with defining themselves as related to others in an "imagined community," they must also subscribe to a certain narrative—one creating a distinctive national past, present, and future. In this narrative, they are fundamentally linked to each other and to a place by virtue of a shared, yet special (if often imagined) history.[16] This indissoluble link between a group of people and a particular place—their place—should reveal and create a common, yet singular, identity.[17] And this identity, in turn, enables a nation to take its sovereign and rightful place as both distinctive from and equal to the other nations of the world.

For Papua New Guineans, the past that could link and ground all of them together could be only a rather generalized one: Papua New

Guinea's *national* roots could not be specific to any of their myriad cultures and any of their local pleses. Hence, any story linking all Papua New Guineans would have to be more embracing than the one, for instance, Gagas told about Japanese contractors discovering the Mari ancestor Nahiyel to be king of the ground.

We can now, even more clearly, understand RSL as an emblematic nationalist project. With RSL, Papua New Guineans have a modern factory (and big project). They are independent of Australia and its sugar interests. They do not have to accept substandard brown sugar from Fiji. And they can ostensibly pursue the Eight Aims. Moreover, with RSL, Papua New Guinea has a distinctive and embracing history that provides continuity and trajectory. Because sugar originated in Papua New Guinea, a modern domestic sugar industry can be read as grounded in Papua New Guinean history. This history, shared by Papua New Guineans generally, can contribute to Papua New Guinean destiny.

· · ·

We have seen three broad narratives of place in operation at RSL. First, there is Gagas's vision of what the creation of RSL should bring. From his perspective, RSL is meaningful as a place because the ancestor located underneath the factory will enable the Mari to receive due recognition of their social worth. Gagas's vision might be characterized as a micro-grounding, based as it is on a primordial connection to kin and ples. Second, there is Hayes's vision of what the creation of RSL should bring. From his perspective, RSL is meaningful as a place because the techniques and technologies of its organization will enable the workers there to produce sugar efficiently. Hayes's vision might be characterized as a macro-grounding, based as it is on universal standards of productivity. Finally, there is the nationalists' vision of what the creation of RSL should bring. From their perspective, RSL is meaningful as a place because it will enable "emplesed" Papua New Guineans there to emerge as citizen-workers. The nationalists' vision might be characterized as a synthetic grounding, based as it is on melding the primordial—the ples-centered "Gagases" and ur-sugar—with the forms of organization and production embraced by all modern and developed nations.

As we also see, those formally in charge of constructing and organizing RSL have to work hard to control, if not suppress, Gagas's vision of micro-grounding. In creating RSL, they displace and replace Papua New

Guineans from all over the country: moving them into mixed ethnic neighborhoods, they convert them into citizen-workers conjoined with their fellows into organic solidarity by employment grade and time clock. Yet the likes of Nahiyel are not forgotten, and Gagas and his peers are not easily silenced. As the subsequent history of RSL shows, all three visions of what to want and what to seek remain in active play.

4

Clansman, Family Man, and Family-of-Man Man at RSL

WITH THE CREATION OF RSL as an immense physical and social fact, the nationalists (at least those who embraced big projects) achieved their goal of a sugar factory to transform a primordial product into a modern one. And in a way consistent with the nationalists' objective of making citizen-workers, RSL was organized more according to "Hayes's" perspective than to "Gagas's": persons were to be evaluated as employees rather than as kinsmen; production was to be evaluated by its efficiency rather than by its enhancement of social relationships. Yet Gagas's ples-centered vision of the desirable and feasible continues to affect significantly social interactions at RSL. However, in so doing, this vision—this narrative—has shifted importantly, and in ways informative about how history actually happens. Narratives are far from homogeneous and static. They are thought and rethought as people negotiate with one another to deal with what has happened and to formulate and enact futures.

One such shift involves the meaning of ples itself. For many at RSL (and elsewhere in primarily urban contexts), the highly specific groundings provided by highly localized pleses are becoming increasingly diffuse and delocalized, more generalized and more broadly regionalized. This is to say that the groups formed among RSL workers sharing such a generalized and regionally based place are becoming more situational than ontological: they are the product of immediate interests rather than of fundamental essences (see Cohen 1974). Through reaggregation into such generalized groups, workers long away from home villages can still maintain a sense of ples, though a transformed one, to be sure. At the same time, they can use these broader commonalities to compensate for, if not partially subvert, some of the conditions of industrial labor—some of the hierarchical distinctions of workplace and residence at RSL.

From Fighting Tribalist to Supportive Neighbor

Most of the people who have become permanent employees of RSL (including those from BTL) are men.[1] Virtually all of those who work as seasonal employees—those hired for the annual six-to-seven month harvest season—are men. The number of seasonal, and hence male, employees was greatest (nearly three times the present number) during the early years of the company, when a large labor force was necessary to cut the cane by hand.[2] These cane-cutting "seasonals" lived primarily outside the main estate, in the three ungated villages within the sugarcane fields. According to Robin Wilson, a Tolai manager from East New Britain who once supervised one of these villages, about 60 percent of the seasonals were Highlanders and the rest were Raikos from nearby Madang Province villages. Since RSL is on the road from Lae to Madang and only a few miles from the point of intersection between this road and the Highlands Highway, both Highlanders and Raikos find it easy to come to RSL.

Everyone to whom we spoke, including expatriates, permanent employees of all grades, and seasonals themselves, describe those early days as full of "tribal" discord, indeed, of outright fighting, among the seasonal workers. Although the company policy has been to reduce ethnic conflict by avoiding residential concentration of wantoks, the fact that seasonals were coming from only a few areas made this policy difficult to implement in the ungated villages. Robin Wilson describes his days of supervising the seasonals:

> There were tribal concerns and I had some hard times. I was often called from my home to come and bring order—and was always surprised when people listened to me. I would shout: "Hey, you can't fight," and they would [sometimes] listen! There was always small infighting as you would expect with such a big crowd. Though the permanents were allowed to have their families, the seasonals were not. And this was hard to enforce. Moreover, people lived in two-room duplexes and there were four men in each room. So it was very

crowded, with a toilet and kitchen outside. They had to do their own cooking and provide their own firewood or kerosene. (But they did have free water and electricity.) If there was fighting, the "boss men" would try to calm things down first; but then they might radio me and I would contact Security and Personnel and, if the fight was really out of hand, the police as well. The Highlanders would really fight. I admired their dancing, but they were very dangerous people. It was frightening when Chimbu and Kafe [two Highlands groups] faced each other, throwing rocks. I was just missed by very big rocks on several occasions. Lucky.

During these early days, fighting also erupted in the gated areas of RSL, among both seasonal and permanent employees. Once, in fact, there was a major riot. This is how James Jacob, who was originally from the Madang Province and has been a long-time resident of the nonmanagement community, describes this period:

Particularly during the early years, the wantok system caused trouble, with [Highland] Wabags fighting [Highland] Taris, etc. There were many small social clubs then at RSL, but membership was primarily based on wantoks. These led to tribal fights and eventually to a riot. It was at Ramu Trading, which was the small [privately operated] trade store, now used as a church, right in this community. The riot began because the store didn't have enough food to supply the labor force, which was large; the store also made people wait in long lines, and the store was frequently closed so people had trouble buying what they needed. The word went around—including to all the [ungated] villages [within the cane fields]—that tomorrow would be a new year. This was the signal that the trade store would be attacked, which is what happened. But word had already gotten out to Cecilia Proud, who was half Kavieng [from New Ireland] and half Chinese. She managed the store and told people not to defend it. But one Sepik who worked for her had a shotgun and tried to disperse the [rioting] crowd. He fired two shots in the air and, with a third shot, killed a Wabag. The shotgun got taken away from him and he was beaten to death with it.

I was a recent arrival at RSL [in 1981] and was unaware of what was happening. I got up that morning and went to the store to get some breakfast. When I saw police vehicles there, I thought that they had come to control people during the New Year's holiday. As I walked to the store, I saw a can of meat and a shirt on the ground and wondered who had dropped them. Finally, somebody explained what was going on and warned me that everybody from "Momase" [that is, from the adjacent Morobe, Madang, and Sepik Provinces] should go to their home villages since the Highlanders were after the Sepiks [given that the Sepik shopkeeper had shot a Highlander from Wabag]. I only had K40 and couldn't afford to go home, but many others left. I just stayed in my house (no. 7) and hoped that, because the trouble had nothing to do with me, people would leave me alone. The next day, the mobile police came and rounded up everyone with a beard [Highlanders frequently were bearded]; they made them stand throughout the day looking into the sun as a punishment. Many of those responsible got three to six weeks in jail.

Stuart Hayes remembers these days as well. He said that, "during the riot, Clive Sabel, the [BTL] personnel manager, had a rock thrown at him and his jaw smashed." In his view, RSL "was something of a frontier town at the time. It took people a while to develop a sense of belonging and ownership of the place. . . . But then they were encouraged to develop village courts and become self-governing and they seem to have settled down."

· · ·

Developing a sense of belonging and ownership of the place, that is, settling down, is a complex process. It is, of course, more difficult for some at RSL than for others, depending on how long and under what circumstances workers are away from home. For many, there is the problem of accepting as normal the agroindustrial time and discipline—the terms and conditions of work. One worker who went to RSL immediately after leaving school writes of his experience in the *Sugar Valley News*, a magazine for RSL employees:

> I was required to start and finish work at a certain time of the day. This was probably the first time . . . I had to strictly go by the clock. I learned that to take some time off, to be absent from work and so forth, I had to first discuss it with my supervisor and manager, or else I was reprimanded. It was not all that easy wearing the heavy foot wear and overalls issued solely for protection at work. This was not to my liking especially during the hot sun. One very annoying case was when you failed to present your ID card to the security you were required to go and collect it before you entered the work place. (Pilato 1984: 7)

Another manager told us that, despite his experiences at school and at other jobs, the first two weeks were the hardest period for him because, sirens notwithstanding, he woke up late every morning and had to go to work without having eaten. Yet another worker said that as a farmer he was accustomed to working very hard, but not very hard day after day after day.

However, getting used to the work itself is not apparently the greatest difficulty workers face in settling down at RSL. Rather, it is learning to give greater priority to obligations to company, to nuclear family, and to workmates than to extended kin. Some of the pressures for such a shift of priorities come from the specific formal requirements of life and work at RSL. Some pressures come from a more diffuse recognition that life at RSL requires different kinds of strategies and alliances than in home villages. This shift in priorities gives rise at RSL, as it has elsewhere among Papua New Guinean wage-earners, to a range of compromises, denials, ambivalences, and adaptations.[3] However, throughout these changes, RSL employees are mindful that the arrangements they maintain while at RSL with kin and ples will likely have ramifications in the future.

Workers, as they soon realize, cannot just go home anytime their kin summon them, whether for a marriage exchange or for a fight. And even if workers do schedule clan business at home to coincide with annual vacations, they risk losing their jobs if they overstay their leaves to finish this business. Nor can they easily leave their posts when, for instance, wives flee back to their families, or take up with other men elsewhere.

An expatriate personnel manager, who worked at RSL off and on from the beginning, came to recognize the difficulty such circumstances created for workers. He said that he would like to be able to tell us that, when he first came, they motivated workers to accept the terms and conditions of employment with both "carrots and sticks," but the truth is that it was mostly with sticks. In fact, when we interviewed him in 2000, he thought RSL still too rigid and punitive in not being more sympathetic to workers caught up in the press of events at home. It is, in fact, often shortsighted to fire an otherwise good worker who has, for instance, not properly extended his leave. After all, someone in a remote area attending his father's funeral might well need to stay longer than anticipated and might well find it difficult to phone that information back to RSL.[4]

Not only are RSL employees unable to visit home whenever they might be called upon, but they are also prohibited from allowing wantoks to stay with them in their houses, except for brief visits—and, even then, only after they are "registered" with the housing office. Sometimes RSL stages house inspections to make sure this rule is upheld, and some-times it transports truckloads of illegally resident wantoks down the road to the intersection of the Highlands Highway. To some extent RSL's actions in these regards are appreciated by workers who find it difficult to support both their immediate families and visiting close and not-so-close kin. Space and money are usually short, and occasionally, we were told, overwhelmed householders might seek relief by privately requesting such a "raid." However, despite the rules and despite the strains, wantoks know that their kin at RSL will try to fulfill at least some of their requests. In fact, the township shopping area usually is filled on payday weekends with wantoks. Throngs of them can be seen waiting for their transport back home with mattresses, bags of rice, and cases of canned goods just purchased for them by their RSL-employed kin.

Some of the dilemmas RSL workers experience in dealing with kin stem from the company's retirement policy. Employees know that, upon retirement, they will have to leave RSL—and, likely, the Gusap area—and go elsewhere. They simply will have to find another place to live. The only housing available in the township is company-owned and reserved for current RSL employees and official others, such as the police. Since the usual age of retirement is fifty-five and it is often financially advanta-geous to leave before then (such as after fifteen years of service), workers do have to think about life after RSL.

Thinking about life after RSL makes many people distinctly nervous. Given that RSL has existed only since 1978, few have had occasion to retire after a full work-life there. Thus, most can only speculate about what retirement will be like. Certainly for many, the prospect of returning home in retirement is fraught with anxiety. In some cases, it has been dif-ficult while at RSL to fulfill kinship obligations more than minimally. Indeed, many have already encountered the pent-up claims of frustrated kin during visits home. For this reason, many—particularly those from provinces relatively remote from RSL—return home only infrequently, further attenuating kin relations. Many are afraid of further financial demands if they return home for good. Such appeals, they know, will make it difficult for them to build a house with the sorts of amenities that they and their families have become accustomed to at RSL. And, without such houses, they will have little to show for years of work at RSL. Their children, socialized at RSL, will find village conditions all too primitive, and their wives—especially those from other cultural traditions—will find themselves additionally out of place. Furthermore, when they con-sider the active tribal fighting and high levels of criminal activity they may

find when they return home, many fear for the safety of person and property.[5] And, finally, many—especially from places where land is in short
supply—suspect that they might not be welcome home at all by kin
whose claims they have previously sought to limit if not deny.

Hence, many workers discussed buying blocks of land on the outskirts
of urban areas for their retirement. Certainly, ethnically focused settlements—a ples away from the ples—are common in most of the country's
towns and cities.[6] However, criminality as well as financial demands by
kin are likely rife there, too. Moreover, the RSL workers, especially those
lacking high-demand skills, also realize that retirement benefits from the
company and their pension from a government-supervised fund will most
likely have to be augmented by cash and subsistence cropping on the
land they have best access to, the traditionally owned land back home.[7]

These ongoing concerns of RSL employees about how best to deal
with obligations at their various pleses are periodically accentuated when
someone dies at RSL. How and where someone is buried often highlights
the complexity of the link between life at RSL and life in a home village:
central to this complexity is the experience of non-kin acting in some
ways like kin and kin acting in some ways like non-kin.

That workers have to move from RSL at a rather young retirement
age means, to be sure, that relatively few actually die there. But fewer
still are buried at RSL. Although RSL has created a tranquil cemetery with
shade trees, ornamental plantings, and tended grounds, there are only a
handful of graves. Almost all of these are for young children. Remains of
those with more social weight—an older child, spouse, sibling—are sent
back home. Indeed, as a death benefit for workers and nuclear family
members, the company contributes to transporting the dead back to their
places of origin for burial.

In accord with this expectation, fellow workers—and other members
of the RSL community—not only comfort the bereaved with home prayer
vigils and church memorial services. They also donate money to help
meet funeral expenses back home. Thus workers—and not just the immediate workmates of the bereaved—sign payroll deduction forms that are
immediately posted on bulletin boards throughout the company. And
eventually thank-you notes from the recipients are posted in response.
Thus one factory manager, whose wife died unexpectedly while visiting
back home on Bougainville Island, posted copies of a "word of thanks and
appreciation" from his family. The note gives a breakdown of the money
he received from various sections and departments at the company:
K1,620 from management; K870 from the factory; K637 from agriculture;

K301 from finance; K619 from human resources; K100 from members of the Catholic women's group to which his wife had belonged; K157 from New Guinea Islands' Catholic Group, which included workers from Bougainville; and K260 from others. The total, K4,564, is also noted.

By contributing to a burial fund, fellow workers are simultaneously creating their community at RSL and acknowledging the complexity of relationships with home villages. Not only is there a clear recognition that the dead should be buried in the villages of their origin—that they should be grounded in these villages in order to become part of an ancestral presence—but there is also the recognition that the financial cost of maintaining this grounding is likely to be considerable, if not exorbitant. Just as wantoks, for instance, make demands on the resources of their kin at RSL on payday weekends, they also made demands on these resources when their RSL kin participate at home in customary ceremonies.[8]

In fact, RSL employees who return home for such ceremonies may find themselves distinctly disadvantaged. They will have to cope with the desires of neglected kin and they will have to deal with these desires in a context that demands the sort of ples-centered cultural knowledge they may have lost after their many years at RSL. Hence, RSL employees may discover that the ceremonies they are sponsoring are, in their barely fathomable complexity, far more expensive, with far more payments to far more sorts of people, than they initially understood. Indeed, as fellow RSL workers know when they make their payroll deductions, the customary obligations of burial at home can easily consume thousands of kina. Therefore, to help their workmates play out a scenario of enhanced, or at least sustained, social relationships as kinsmen at home, these industrial workers have themselves to act as neighbors, if not as quasi-kin at RSL.

In summary, Papua New Guineans, regardless of their formal education and regardless of the extent of their ples-centered cultural knowledge, still visualize themselves as having a primordial connection to a ples. Yet, while ples still provides a fundamental reference point, its meaning is, for many, shifting. For those who have settled down at RSL, their even occasional encounters with ples, perhaps during an annual leave or in the case of a death, are likely to make them realize that they lack local habits and knowledge. They are no longer fully at home in their "home." Moreover, since home villages themselves are also undergoing tremendous changes, what recollections and understandings of ples RSL employees do have are likely to be somewhat anachronistic. As a consequence, cultural "emplesment" is increasingly conceptualized in broadly sketched and nostalgic terms.[9] Importantly, such a shift in the nature of cultural grounding also lends itself to new forms of social life among Papua New Guineans living away from home at RSL (and elsewhere).

Community at RSL: All God's Children have Pleses of Equal Grade

If community at RSL is provisional, it is also real. Even though most employees understand that upon retirement they will likely not see their workmates and neighbors again, they nonetheless come together in mutual assistance and in sociability. But this sociability plays out with a particular twist as Papua New Guineans deal with RSL's cultural and occupational differentiation: as they deal with people from a range of pleses and with a range of hierarchically ranked skills.

To put it simply, three interrelated conditions have to be fulfilled for those at RSL to settle down into a community. First, for RSL workers to become friends and neighbors, industrial hierarchy has to be muted. This is to say, for grade 7 workers, grade 1 workers, and supervisors to engage as members of the same community, their differences in skill, pay, and housing have to be, at least sometimes, played down. Second, for RSL workers to maintain the groundings that will provide identity and life after RSL, their ties to specific pleses have to be at least minimally maintained and acknowledged; all Papua New Guinean employees have to be able to assert some measure of cultural distinction and difference. Third, for RSL workers with groundings to specific pleses to become friends and neighbors, their pleses have to be made comparable. Their differences have to be equally valid variations on common themes so as not to be too divisive. These three conditions are met simultaneously by the creation of generalized, regional cultures that link people of different grades, allow people to maintain ples, and render pleses equivalent.

Although people have long referred to themselves in such broadly regional terms as Highlanders, Sepiks, or even Momases, the meaning of these terms has significantly shifted from the time RSL was a frontier town. Such groups now operate in a vastly different way than in the early days of the venture, as described by Wilson and Jacob. Difference is still there, but it has become diffuse and defused. For example, at the local Catholic church, a different regional group will each Sunday choose the hymns, provide the music, and organize the processional. Sometimes the groups "cross-culture," as when Highlanders dress in Sepik-like grass skirts and join Sepik friends in playing Sepik-like hand-drums during the processional at a Sepik-run service. Likewise, the primarily intramural sports teams that occupy RSL workers on weekends are organized by broadly defined regions. The name of a team often denotes, with some well-recognized referent, the area of origin of most of its members: the Bismark Soccer Club, for the region adjoining the Bismark Sea; the Momase Soccer Club, for the region encompassing the adjacent provinces of Madang, Morobe, and Sepik; the Guria Soccer Club, for the region providing the "guria" pigeon habitat, namely, the Highlands. Even the soccer club called the "M Brothers," made up of "mixed brothers" from different home regions, calls attention to the regional norm.

We learned much about how such generally domesticated regional ties are constructed and how they operate in everyday life at RSL when, on a Saturday morning of a payday weekend, a neighbor, Anthony Satuhan, knocked on our door in Hamlet 1 (the supervisors' hamlet in which we lived during 1999). We had not yet met Satuhan, but he knew that we had lived in his home province, East Sepik, for many years while engaged in anthropological research. Thinking that we might be "lonely and bored," he invited us to his house for a small backyard gathering of fellow Sepiks. There, under an open-sided, bush-material shelter, we joined in convivial conversation and beer drinking with four other Sepiks. Although all came from the same province, their villages of origin were quite culturally, linguistically, and in three cases, ecologically distinct. No one knew anyone else before coming to RSL, whether in school or elsewhere. Moreover, they worked in different departments, lived in different neighborhoods within the township, and held differently ranked positions, from a seasonal worker to a supervisor. Yet at RSL they all knew each other as Sepiks and had bonded together as such.

Our conversation that morning ranged broadly. We spoke about national politics, discussed working conditions at RSL, and gossiped about other employees. But we also, as the beer continued to flow, began to wax nostalgic for the Sepik. In particular, our newfound Sepik friends praised the stringency of the initiation ceremonies practiced by their home groups—this despite the fact that, or perhaps because, none of them had been initiated. All their accounts were variations on a theme: One told that in his group, after scarifying initiates, the initiators throw them into a pool of water to intensify their pain. Another recounted that in his group, initiators beat initiates with lacerating canes. Yet another told that in his group, after subjecting secluded initiates to great, though unspecified, trials, initiators deny any parental claims for compensation for the mistreatment, even when an initiate dies. Finally, another told that in his group, if a young man dies during an initiation, the initiators hang his skull in the men's house and that was that. And, concerning death, all agreed that Sepik sorcery is very potent and each outlined variations practiced by their groups.

Despite the differences in their stories, there seemed to be a broadly drawn Sepik on our friends' minds that is largely essentialized and imaginary: a world generalized and homogenized as well as fixed and timeless. This Sepik is a place where men are formidable. It is a place of power, a place of strong traditions and traditions of strength. It is a place where sociability focuses on male gatherings in contexts of sometimes lethally potent ancestral practices. It is a place where young men, submitting to the collective wisdom and power of their elders (and ancestors), come of age through painful, but ultimately rewarding, ordeals.

Correspondingly, this Sepik of the imagination is not one where differences, often concerning knowledge of ritual minutia, provide the basis of considerable competition within and among groups. It is also not one where initiations, and social life more generally, have been transformed by missionization, labor migration, tourism, a cash economy, or the temporal constraints of formal employment and education. It is not a place where, for instance, initiations have to be scheduled during the Christmas holidays as the time many labor migrants as well as schoolboys are free to participate. It is not a place where initiations are scheduled to coordinate with the arrival of admission-paying tourists. Finally, it is not a Sepik where fewer and fewer men—like those who reminisced with us—are being initiated. Instead, it is a Sepik designed to be comparable to other essentialized places, say, for example, a Highlands where men exchange pigs and fight over land, but do not engage in arduous initiations or fearsome sorcery.

This regionalism certainly is not limited to RSL. It is developing throughout Papua New Guinea where people from various locales meet at boarding schools, universities, in urban work contexts, and in the military. In effect, this regionalism creates a cultural identity so diffuse that it is no longer based on a grounded way of life and, therefore, at least ordinarily, is not a source of significant discord. It is not really something to fight about or for. On the other hand, regionalism helps those who will have to return home eventually to maintain a cultural base. Indeed, it might help some as a means to rehearse their cultural base. Those, for example, who were not initiated might perform "Sepikness" through recalling the stories others have told them about initiation. Furthermore, as "tribalists" with primordial knowledge, interests, and commitments are transformed into regionalists, regionalists—certainly at places like

RSL—are defined in such a way as to undercut the inequality explicit in a hierarchical division of labor and house allotments. At RSL, as members of regionally oriented leisure gatherings, whether focused on sports or on sociable drinking and nostalgic reminiscences, men can readily regard themselves as comparable in fundamental masculine worth to others, whether Sepiks relative to Highlanders, or grade 4 workers relative to supervisors. Thus, as RSL has moved from frontier town to community, regionalism serves simultaneously to broaden commitments to RSL, to preserve a personally significant measure of cultural grounding, and to flatten hierarchical differences. Settling down at RSL has meant the transformation of the tribal discord and outright fighting between, for instance, Chimbu and Kafe cane-cutters into sociable beer drinking between men sharing an imaginary Sepik despite their different employment grades.

Not all informal, noninstitutionalized activities and gatherings at RSL are regionally exclusive. Certainly larger gatherings are not. That would be regarded as too overtly segregated. These larger gatherings, however, are regionally aware—but in the diffuse (generalized, homogenized, fixed, and timeless) way that characterizes an imagined Sepik world.

We were invited to one such gathering, a party, by Kenzy Kamdan, a man well known throughout the RSL community for his work as a magistrate at the village court. Kamdan is from the Highlands, specifically from Minj in Western Highlands Province. He has been working at RSL as a heavy-equipment driver since 1990, initially as a seasonal and eventually as a grade 5 permanent employee.

Planned and announced months in advance, Kamdan's party celebrated the first birthday of his only son (but tenth child). For this event, he invited a large group of Papua New Guineans, both from RSL and from the Highlands. Those attending from RSL included Kamdan's Lutheran pastor, friends, workmates, and supervisors. Many of the guests, as fellow RSL householders, arrived with wives and sometimes children. Those attending from the Highlands included his Chimbu in-laws (he married into a group not his own) and members of his own family.

When we arrived at 5:30, festivities were fully under way. Kamdan's sisters and daughters tended earth ovens in the backyard while men and women thronged in the front yard. After the four pigs, numerous chickens, and quantities of sweet potatoes, ears of corn, and greens were cooked, the food was heaped on a long table. Before approaching this generous buffet, each newly arriving guest placed a gift for the baby, a wrapped present or some money, in a washbasin provided for the purpose. And those of us already eating applauded.

At the height of the party, when about 150 people were there, Kamdan told us how pleased he was with the turnout: most of the tractor drivers with whom he worked had come, and also many of his friends and neighbors. He circulated throughout the crowd, greeting the men, and to a lesser extent their family members, by name, handing out soft drinks. Later, he provided groups of men with small bottles of liquor to mix with these drinks.

In addition to gifts for the baby, we brought a case of beer. One of Kamdan's workmates, a close friend and fellow Highlander, distributed these bottles to various guests, calling out: "Here's one for a man from Markham; here's one for a Sepik" (fig. 12). Then there were speeches. One man explained that he was, with Kamdan, a Highlander and a tractor driver. In addition, he described himself as always quick to sign up for payroll deductions when others were in need; and he was delighted to see so many of his workmates at the party. Another man called out the names of the "sixteen tractor drivers" present as well as the supervisors who were there. A third said that it was usual at RSL to give help when a worker's mother or father died, but Kamdan extended this good custom to include birthdays. Such parties, he continued, were common in the Highlands, but Kamdan decided to hold one at RSL. A fourth thanked Kamdan for working so hard to entertain his mates. Kamdan's brother-in-law, who was sitting next to us, mentioned privately that Kamdan liked working for the

Figure 12. Kamdan and his workmates at the birthday party

company and was something of a leader at RSL. In contrast, when he himself worked at RSL as a seasonal tractor driver, he never became used to the regimentation so he did not return.

Many guests began to drift away at about 7:30, as most of the food was already gone by then. Others stayed on to socialize throughout the night.

Kamdan's son's birthday party was understandable to everyone present. The Highland themes were sufficiently generalized and sufficiently widely known as to require no translation: pigs and other items were distributed by a "big man" who was mobilizing his own kin in a presentation to their in-laws; in addition, he was establishing and maintaining alliances and a rep-utation for masculine efficacy as measured by generosity. Yet, even if there was something "Minjish" or "Chimbuish" about this presentation early in his child's life, at RSL it was glossed as a birthday party that was somewhat like a payroll deduction. And as with birthday parties or payroll deductions, no one ended up in any real debt: no one ended up in a position of inequal-ity, either as a follower or as a potential defaulter. Equivalence, that is, self-respect, could be readily maintained in the normal course of events, as when men buy each other drinks. The exchanges at Kamdan's party gener-ated and affirmed the sociability of mateship. In so doing, they obscured and flattened the hierarchical differences that characterized RSL's formal social organization.[10] Although Kamdan's party was organized on a grand scale, it resembled Satuhan's gathering: both were occasions of nonhierar-chical inclusiveness, at least between men of nonmanagerial grades. Although Kamdan might have emerged as a big man (and he was consid-ering using an RSL constituency to stand for political office), he did not go up in RSL grade—getting neither more pay nor better housing.

Kamdan's party was correspondingly inclusive in establishing alliances and equivalences between people who had different regional identities. These broad identities were respectfully acknowledged and affirmed as comparable in the context of this general sociability: "Here's one for a man from Markham; here's one for a Sepik." As at Satuhan's, tribal discord and outright fighting were transformed into sociable beer drinking and the construction of a regionally focused cultural imaginary. However, at Kamdan's, the men collaborated in the construction and confirmation, not only of their own, but also of each other's, cultural imaginaries.

On Disputes: Mr. Du and Mr. Ku Come to Terms at RSL

The construction and confirmation of cultural imaginaries taking place at Satuhan's and Kamdan's were, of course, in contexts of amity rather than conflict. But even well past the turbulent early days of the company, all was not always so pacific at RSL. Indeed, one of the testimonies to the skill with which Kamdan managed his party was that the drinking remained good natured. One of the important forms of dispute settlement at RSL—and one that Hayes specifically believes helped RSL employees to settle down and govern themselves—is the village court system.

This system, as it works at multicultural RSL, invokes a form of regionalism in resolving conflicts. Indeed, it often goes further and invokes a form of transregionalism. Regional distinctions thus become doubly comparable: they are simultaneously different from (but equal to) each other and they are also variations on more fundamental common themes—Papua New Guinean themes. Thus, not only are initiation-preoccupied Sepiks seen as commensurate with pig-exchanging Highlanders, but both are shown as embracing such positive and general Papua New Guinean values as kinship commitments, cooperation, respect for elders, ples-centeredness. It is such comparable differences, based as they are on fundamental similarities, that establishes the basis of a multicultural community, whether of RSL or of the nation of Papua New Guinea. As we shall argue, these comparable differences and fundamental similarities establish Papua New Guinea's various regional branches of the "family of man."

For five days in August 1999, a concentrated lesson in the importance of regionalism and transregionalism in dispute resolution was conducted at RSL. Three instructors from the Madang provincial government came to give a "refresher" course to the magistrates, clerks, and bailiffs of the RSL village court. There were ten students in total, in addition to us. All were Papua New Guinean males; six were RSL employees; three were outgrowers; one was a local businessman. RSL provided free room and board to the instructors and released the RSL employees to attend the course. The RSL employees occupied different grades and were from various provinces: there was one grade 3 worker, from the Enga Province; two grade 5 workers (including Kamdan), from the Western Highlands and Enga Provinces; two seasonal employees, from the Madang and Enga Provinces; one manager, from the Morobe Province. Two of the outgrowers were from Bumbu, and one was from Bopirumpun. And the businessman, the owner of a trade store and snack bar located on RSL property, was from the Eastern Highlands Province. All the participants had been elected to the village court by their different RSL and Mari constituencies, although it should also be said that few such elections were contested.

These are the men who adjudicate cases brought to the village court by anyone living within the township and the immediately surrounding villages. Their cases concern a wide range of grievances that people want to settle through relatively informal procedures based upon "custom."[11] There is also a higher-level district court at Gusap, at which cases are heard by a provincial magistrate. Though he often does take "custom" into account in making his decisions, he is not obligated to do so; rather, his primary job is to enforce the laws of the land—those applying to all Papua New Guineans.

The refresher course was opened by Andrew Sagumai, provincial village court officer, who explained (in Pidgin English) about the village court system:

> The colonizers, when they applied their system of government to Papua New Guinea, used English and German and most locals didn't know these languages. Yet the colonizers also insisted that a man understand the law. Following African chieftain systems, it was decided, post-independence, to create village courts. [The Village Court Act was passed in 1975.] These would follow the traditional customs of local places; they would meet within small jurisdictions, use Pidgin English or local languages. . . . They would ensure that traditional customs wouldn't die. However, it was sometimes a problem when tradition conflicted with the law of the land. Nonetheless, village courts were much better than when patrol officers made decisions without explaining the reasons for them to local people: they acted as judges who said yes or no, although the people didn't understand why. . . . So now village courts use local languages so that people understand why they are being fined, why they are being asked to pay compensation and why they are being jailed.

Next, Yakasa Maniosa, the primary instructor during the course, spoke (in Pidgin English). He first introduced himself by stating his name and place of origin, Wabag, the capital of the Enga Province in the Highlands. Then he explained the operation of the village court at RSL:

> At Ramu Sugar there are people from the Highlands, Sepik, Papua, Kainantu [in the Eastern Highlands], Madang—and it is not clear which of their customs should be followed at the village court. Moreover, there are mixed marriages—a Sepik may be married to someone else, a Highlander to someone from Madang. If their marriage breaks up, one

side says that it wants K2,500, two pigs, and all the saucepans in compensation. The other side says, "That's not our custom." So the work of the village court is not easy because there are all sorts of people: some village courts have heard cases of people from Italy, from Rome, from New Zealand. So how do we know which customs we should use? Because we have "God-given intelligence" [English words used]. Whereas a monkey will try to get food out of a pipe with its mouth, a human will use a stick to do so. God has given humans the capacity to size things up and figure them out.

Maniosa was especially concerned that the RSL village court officials learn how to "mediate" during court sessions. Their job, he said, is not to make people afraid, but to help people achieve equanimity ("bel isi" in Pidgin). This is a prerequisite for all else: successful learning, productive business activities, and worthwhile social interactions. The magistrates should not believe, he continued, that the problems they adjudicate are unique to Papua New Guinea. Quite to the contrary, the kinds of difficulties found in Papua New Guinea occur all over the world—in Russia, America, and Australia. Consider Kosovo, where one group, claiming to be the rightful owner of the land, is fighting another, belonging to a different church. It is the same at Enga, where, if your pig ruins my garden, I will fight you because of it. All of us, everywhere, are prone to sin; we all have good and bad sides, but most of us would rather be good. Mediation helps us learn how to be good. To mediate is to use the law in a nonaggressive way.

Let me give the example of Mr. "Velevel" and Mr. "Hubaba" [made up names, he said, to avoid referring to anyone in particular]. Mr. Velevel is the defendant and Mr. Hubaba, the complainant. Mr. Hubaba has lost some betel nut, and Mr. Velevel has gained some. This is a case of theft. And magistrates can mediate such cases outside of court. First, the chairman of the village court should designate a certain number of magistrates—from one to three—to mediate. . . . They must not prejudge a case. They shouldn't judge by appearance as, for instance, when one guy stands up straight, with a shirt and tie on, and another, with his hair a mess and with only one betel-nut-blackened tooth in his head. Instead, magistrates must "listen, observe and think" [words he wrote on the blackboard in Pidgin English]. The point of mediation is to make both sides of any case feel satisfied. Mr. Hubaba said that Mr. Velevel stole his betel nut and should pay him K30 in compensation;

Mr. Velevel denied that he stole the betel nut and said that Mr. Hubaba only wanted the fine to pay school fees for his son. The magistrate should make each side listen to the claims of the other. He should say to Mr. Velevel: "I think you are a good man and have good heart. Mr. Hubaba is poor and you have to be generous to him. This is just a small difficulty and Mr. Hubaba is your cousin. You don't want to sever relations with him. Certainly, *if I were you*, I wouldn't want this. *If I were you*, I would say to Mr. Hubaba, "I guess I have a chicken to give you and can find K20 somewhere." I'd be sorry for him and would tell my wife to find a chicken and to get the K20. In other words, what a magistrate should do is to leave Mr. Velevel with a good impression of himself. He shouldn't be told that he is a thief, but that he has helped someone in need. He shouldn't be made into a worthless man, but into one who will want to be a good man from then on. (Emphasis added)

Maniosa also asked class members to provide problems from their daily lives. These were to be "real" problems, not "fake" ones, suitable only for "university lawyers." The businessman took up the challenge with the problem of "loans": What if someone lends K10 to a coworker and is not repaid? The case Maniosa created in response to this problem involved Mr. Ku, as defendant, and Mr. Du, as complainant. Ku borrowed K50 from Du, and two "fortnights" (paydays) passed without repayment. Ku had borrowed the money in order to buy a carton of beer to drink with his sister's husband, on the occasion of his nephew's (his sister's son's) birthday. Ku's defense was that the pay he received on Friday had already been spent by the time Du came for it on Sunday. To mediate this case, a magistrate should say to Ku:

Du has been a good friend to you and I doubt that you want to break the friendship, but would rather want to hang out with him and to have him call you "bro." You don't want to turn him into an enemy. Du says that you have promised twice to pay him back, but have failed to do so and now he wants his money. He has always helped you in the past and, if he takes this case to district court, he not only will win, but will continue to be angry with you. You will lose his friendship. So, *if I were you*, I would—while in mediation—give him a good answer. I would offer him K25 now and promise the rest later. I can't decide for you, but *if I were you*, I wouldn't want this friendship to be ruined. What do you think? Ku will probably accept this arrangement. (Emphasis added)

Once an agreement is reached, Maniosa said, the magistrate should ask the village court clerk to fill out form 2, which would describe the result of the mediation. The court should also advise Mr. Ku that if he failed to do as he promised, he would be fined an additional K200 or be sentenced to six months in jail. Remember, Maniosa summed up, "the key in mediation is not to dictate, but to give people suggestions—to say, 'if I were you, I would do such and such.'"

Then Maniosa asked his students to provide some more real-life examples of disputes and to adjudicate them. They were to divide into two groups, with one enacting the roles of claimant, defendant, and witnesses and the other acting as village court officials. One example the class provided was of particular interest to us because we already knew something of its real-life circumstances. The dispute concerned Emmanuel Moba, one of the students and a magistrate from Bumbu. (His ancestor was Nahiyel, the king, according to Gagas, of RSL's ground.) Moba was in conflict with his in-laws from Chimbu in the Highlands. Moba's son had met a Chimbu woman when her mother was teaching at Gusap. The couple lived at Bumbu and already had two children. Her family set her bride price, in both money and pigs, at a level Moba thought was unreasonably high—much higher than was usual among the Mari and among Coastal people more generally. Moreover, her family was putting increasing pressure upon him to pay, particularly because, as an out-grower, he had a regular income. However, Moba regarded much of this income as already entailed by the far more reasonable claims of immediate kin. What to do—particularly since Chimbu could be persistent in pursuing their interests?

The members of both groups decided which roles they would play. Moba, playing (as many knew) himself, was invited by the mediators (members of the other group) to describe his grievance. Sketching out the case, he said that the problem involved "a man of the Coast and a Chimbu woman." He said that the family of an in-marrying Chimbu woman wanted K6,000 and two pigs in bride price, but it was not the custom of his Coastal group to pay so much. Coastal people paid a maximum of K1,500. Could the court reduce the price? Then the man representing the Chimbu side of the case spoke. Interestingly, he was himself a Coastal from Madang. He said that it was usual Chimbu custom to charge much more than they had asked of this Coastal man, as much as K8–9,000 and ten to twelve pigs. The woman's family had already reduced the price to help Moba out, and had no intention of reducing it more. After all, there were two children born by this time. The girl's father, paternal uncle, and grandfather would not change their minds and the law had to straighten this all out now. Moba (obviously switching from a generic Coastal to himself) said that he only got paid for his sugarcane once a year. It wasn't the same as for those coffee-growing Highlanders whose money came in more often. Could he have a little more time?

The man playing the chief mediator of the village court first cautioned that it was not up to him to dictate a resolution. Nonetheless, he continued, if he were the Coastal man, he might agree to pay K3,000 and one pig the next Christmas and the same amount the year after. Moba and the "Chimbu" responded that this seemed fair. The mediator then said he would instruct the village court clerk to fill out the appropriate form and give a copy to each.

Finally, Maniosa asked what the class thought of this resolution. Pretty good, everyone agreed, because each side was treated equally and each could be seen as having a plausible case.

All of the other enactments we observed were comparable in their focus on real-life problems and in their insistence that people become advocates for the reasonability of cultural perspectives not their own. Significantly, in a way that addressed a major line of fission at RSL and elsewhere in Papua New Guinea, Coastals continued to play Highlanders and vice versa. In fact, Maniosa actively encourages such "cross-culturing" because he believes that for diverse Papua New Guineans to self-govern (and to settle down), they have to use their distinctively human intelligence—to listen, observe, and think—so as to make sense of each other and of each other's customs.

Overall, Maniosa's students found him an excellent teacher: dynamic, funny, ready with examples and sound advice. In particular, he was very helpful in suggesting specific ways that they might settle disputes at a place like RSL—ways that elicited the harmony of mutual forbearance and respect rather than the divisiveness of wantokism and tribalism. His lessons, whether through his examples of Hubaba versus Velevel and Du versus Ku or through the students' examples of Highlanders versus Coastals, all had the same objectives: through a set of overlapping approaches, they sought to render both individual Papua New Guineans and their wider cultures broadly intelligible and inherently reasonable to each other. Through typification of characters and of scenarios, as in the Du versus Ku example, it became feasible to take another's point of view, as in the respectful "if I were you" formulation. Through taking another's point of view—in fact, through taking multiple points of view—it became feasible to find the common ground necessary for a mutually acceptable solution. Through finding common ground, different cultural traditions could be understood as comparable, as equivalent. And, importantly, the reverse was also true: through understanding cultural traditions as comparable, it was possible to find common ground, take another's point of view, and render various cultures intelligible and reasonable.

The frequent smiles of recognition Maniosa evoked from the members of the class attested to his success in affirming broad patterns of understanding and acceptance. Indeed, his truths about Papua New Guineans were readily taken to apply not just regionally but also transregionally. In this latter regard, his students vicariously enacted the Papua New Guinean equivalent of the "family of man": of "everyman," engaging in compensation claims, borrowing to drink beer with in-laws, paying bride prices—all activities that would take place, not just in specific regions, but "everywhere" throughout the country.

Although Maniosa's lessons were exercises in finding common ground, he and the members of his class also recognized, as we have already seen at Satuhan's and Kamdan's, that Papua New Guineans (themselves included) have—or feel that they will be expected to have—particular ties to a local ples and its practices. This is to say, they knew that a Papua New Guinean everyman will—or will feel that he or she is expected to—emerge periodically as a highly parochial, intimately situated advocate of a distinctive cultural perspective. As such, he or she will worry about, for example, the culturally distinctive ways by which material goods may be transacted and sociability constructed: the ways in which redress may be most strategically effected, whether with pigs, pearl shells, money, fighting, or sorcery; the ways in which kinship and inheritance may be most judiciously formulated, whether through patrilineality, matrilineality, adoption, or affinity; and the ways in which marriages may be most usefully arranged, whether by cross-cousin marriage, sister exchange, or Christian choice.

But as we have seen, at RSL such parochialism can make harmonious social life difficult, and consequently, people often have to operate at higher levels of generality. They not only have to be able to associate their own particular culture with the cultures of others in a region (such as the Highlands, or the Sepik, or the Coast), embracing such comparabilities as the paying of high or low bride price or the coming-of-age through arduous initiations. They also have to be able to associate their own culture with all other cultures in Papua New Guinea (or even, in Melanesia), embracing such comparabilities as the importance of creating ties and resolving difficulties through gift giving and compensation. Depending on the individual with whom one is negotiating, an everyman would have to learn to pick the appropriate level of generality.

• • •

Kamdan is proud of the degree to which he helps make RSL a place where people from all over the country live together in harmony and the degree to which he can move comfortably through the various contexts of RSL. Once, when walking with us through the betel-nut market on the edge of the public shopping area, he volunteered his pleasure both at seeing Papua New Guineans of various sorts (but mostly Highlanders and Sepiks) "sit down well together" and at being respected by a whole range of folks. Indeed, he said, so well regarded is his judgment that the grass by his house has been worn down by people sitting with him as he mediates their conflicts. Just the previous evening, for example, he heard the case of a couple, married for only three weeks. The wife wanted to see a soccer game on Sunday between two RSL teams, but her husband, an evangelical Christian, thought this sacrilegious. In fact, marital difficulties are common at RSL. Many men have wives at home in their villages, but because they are wage earners, they can readily convince other women from elsewhere to live with them at RSL. These "Ramu marriages" often do not last because a woman's kin demands a bride price or compensation; in addition, the husband's existing wife or wives and kin also demand recompense (partly for the dilution of the husband's resources). Another recent case Kamdan had mediated involved a man who already had two wives but convinced a third woman to come from her village as his wife. It was only when she and her two children arrived that she discovered he was already married. She wanted to return home, particularly because his other wives were giving her a difficult time, but she had no money for her transport. Other common cases at RSL involve debts, like the situation in which a man borrowed K500 some five years ago and only repaid K300 of it. Fights are common, too, particularly when people drink. Last payday, for example, a man walking home was asked by a friend for a smoke and gave half of his cigarette to this person. An onlooker, for some reason misunderstanding what was going on, flattened the first man's nose with a punch. All of these were interesting cases and, Kamdan thought, God has given me the understanding to mediate them.

We asked him about his future. Where will he go after he leaves RSL? He seemed unusually optimistic about his prospects. He had, in fact, occupied himself variously at Minj before coming to RSL—as a farmer, tribal fighter, coffee buyer, mechanic. And, he replied, he has lots of land back home planted in coffee. At the moment, he is happy to have his brothers care for it. After all, coffee money comes in irregularly, and there are occasions— like a recent drought—when his relatives need the financial help his fortnightly pay can provide. And he keeps up good relations at home, visiting his village at least each Christmas. In fact, recently, he went home to participate in a big bride-price exchange of K5,000, fifteen pigs, and two cassowaries. He himself contributed K1,000 and two pigs. But he is happy that his daughters are being educated at RSL because then they can get good jobs at home, perhaps as teachers. He is even willing to have them choose their own husbands, so long as the husbands come from Minj. When he does retire from RSL to return home, he expects to open a small-vehicle repair business where he can use his RSL-honed skills. Eventually, his son can inherit his land and his daughters, with their educations and their Minj husbands, can help take care of him. He strongly wants to be buried at home so that his children can show their own children the resting places of their grandfather and ancestors.

• • •

When Stuart Hayes said the Papua New Guineans living at the frontier town of RSL developed a sense of belonging and ownership of the place, he implied, we think, what the expatriate personnel manager made explicit: that workers more or less have accepted the terms and conditions of industrial employment, faced as they were with both "carrots and sticks," but mostly sticks. Hayes implied that those long-term employees who choose to live their working lives at RSL adopt a vision of people and place somewhat like his own, wherein efficient employees settle down into a self-governing community, within a self-regulating agroindustrial complex, to make the new Papua New Guinean nation self-sufficient in an important commodity of practical and symbolic significance. And he implied that Papua New Guineans at RSL who do not fully adopt this vision are still retaining the ples-centered values of RSL's early fighting tribalists.

But such views ignore what many Papua New Guineans think makes life worth living. In contemporary Papua New Guinea, especially at a multicultural and hierarchically structured place like RSL, neither fully embracing "Hayes's" vision nor adhering to "Gagas's" vision will fulfill desire entirely or effect a satisfactory future. Thus, we have seen resourceful attempts by many Papua New Guineans to adapt to the new contingencies of life. In particular, we have seen how Papua New Guineans at RSL seek neither to be *fully* citizen-workers nor *fully* clansmen-wantoks. Rather, they seek a range of ways through which connections to each other (whether of commonality or diversity) are understood and enacted: this range of ways—still informed more by "Gagas's" vision, in its ongoing engagement with ples, than by "Hayes's"—allows them to be the various things they think they should be.

This range, in encapsulated form, includes clansman (kinsmen tightly linked in local communities with strong wantok solidarities); family man (householders closely linked through an agroindustrial division of labor with diffuse regional commonalities); "family-of-man" man (Papua New Guineans loosely linked through transregional similarities). Kamdan, after all, never ceases being a Minj (and, indeed, a Minj from a particular linguistic and clan group), although he also is a tractor driver and family man from the Highlands and a magistrate in search of common ground. Indeed, his birthday party was a graceful orchestration of all of these identities.[12]

5

The Life of Expatriates: Setting the Standards

WE HAVE BEEN EXPLORING how history is made, shaped by people with a range of ideas about the desirable and the feasible. To view history in this way also demands that we consider not only what people seek but what they are denied—or deny others. We need, in other words, to consider what Sontag calls "the determining weight of history—of genuine and historically embedded differences, injustices and conflicts" (1977: 33).[1] The burden of such differences itself becomes a consequential outcome of history. As differences, injustices, and conflicts are interpreted and acted on, they propel action. They define a past as one to be redeemed, a present as one to be resented, and a future as one to be struggled for. As unfinished business, this weight rankles and ramifies—as responsibility is assigned, accepted, denied, or discounted. Yali, as far as we can tell, had considerable unfinished business. He spent much of his life dealing in various ways with a bitter conviction that colonial inequalities had unfairly affected him and other Papua New Guineans. Europeans treated them with disdain, denying them fundamental social and moral worth: they refused to recognize the kindred ties and commonalities—whether as mythic brothers, as brothers in Christ, as brothers in combat—that would create meaningful social connections and reciprocal obligations.

RSL was designed in large part to help finish this business. Indeed, both the BTL-employed whites and RSL-employed blacks acknowledge that working free of colonialism's heavy legacy must be a priority. Thus, at RSL there is considerable effort by many to include expatriates and Papua New Guineans alike as full members of the RSL "family." Yet most expatriates socialize with other expatriates; most Papua New Guineans with other Papua New Guineans. The reasons are numerous and include important economic differences in perquisites and rates of pay. But they also include differences in how the standards for commonality are established. In part because the BTL expatriates are at RSL to help develop the country, they urge Papua New Guineans to take their point of view. Instead of, for instance, the leveling "if I were you" of Maniosa is the uplifting "if you were me" of BTL. Hence, the question of whose "family" it is remains very much the focus of social dynamics.

In this chapter and the next we explore social dynamics at RSL among and between expatriate and Papua New Guinean managers—those members of the "family" formally regarded as the most comparable.

Booker Tate Limited

As we have said, it has been Booker Tate Limited, a British firm, that has provided RSL with most of its expatriates. BTL's corporate headquarters are located at Masters Court in Thame, near Oxford. At least from an American perspective, the setting appears quintessentially English, if only because the Masters Court complex of buildings includes "the Old School House." Sketches and photographs of this handsome, stone, sixteenth-century building, once a grammar school, frequently appear in BTL literature. Although we conducted several interviews at these headquarters, our three visits there were comparatively brief, so that most of our information about BTL and what might be considered its culture comes from reading various BTL publications and from speaking to BTL employees working at RSL.

In its attractive promotional pamphlet, one that happens to have a picture of the green fields and surrounding mountains of RSL on its cover, BTL describes its "mission" as providing "a global agricultural management services business together with related engineering project management" (Booker Tate Limited n.d.: 1). On its Web site, the company states that it has engaged in sugarcane cultivation and processing for 160 years and currently has projects in ten countries (Barbados, Belize, Guyana, Jamaica, Kenya, Papua New Guinea, Saudi Arabia, Swaziland, Uganda, and Indonesia). Based on this experience, BTL offers a range of services that include industry reviews and feasibility studies, the implementation and management of new projects, the rehabilitation and expansion of existing estates and factories and the provision of technical support services to established sugar projects around the world. . . .

With our headquarters in the UK, we employ over 150 permanent staff, the majority of whom work overseas. . . .

While the particular requirements of a client and the conditions of a project vary greatly, we are committed to providing the highest standards of service to all our clients in the developing and developed world. . . .

Always aware of the need to meet economic and financial objectives, we are also conscious of the importance to stakeholders of social and environmental issues—the transfer of technology, the development of employee skills and the conservation of natural resources and the environment.

Where management is provided, we are responsible for the development of a total business plan including marketing, finance and human resources. In all cases the local management team is fully supported by staff from head office and by specialist staff, expert in their own disciplines, who regularly visit the project, review technical progress and advise on up-to-date technology and the most cost effective methods.[2]

To judge from our experience at RSL, BTL staff do, in fact, take pride in their professional competence, whether on long-term assignments as managers or department heads or on short-term visits as consultants. They have breadth and depth of experience and knowledge concerning the technical demands of running efficient and sustainable sugar operations in various parts of the world.[3] These demands may only be routine, as in maintaining the clarity of the sugar syrup and the size of the sugar crystals within certain parameters. They may also be extraordinary, as in confronting the potentially devastating outbreak of a previously unrecorded cane disease. To confirm the competence of BTL staff, a visiting consultant from the company who had himself worked at RSL for several years during the mid-1980s described BTL to us as follows: The company provides "great value for the money" since its staff members "are concerned and extremely able people who have more sugar expertise than anyone in the world and will work twenty-four hours a day on a problem." Indeed, he said, BTL employees will always go the extra mile. "[The staff] will really cover it with experts and will take full responsibility for a project's success."

Most BTL employees we met—and quite a number passed through RSL in consulting capacities—feel similarly. Many who worked for other agricultural consulting and management firms before coming to BTL believe that BTL is generally more concerned for its clients than are their previous employers. In addition, BTL staff members think they are able to work together in a particularly effective fashion. They take pleasure in sharing a common and apparently cordial work history, whether at the home office or on assignment elsewhere. This is not to say, of course, that BTL employees do not compete with each other in a range of ways—for favor and recognition on any particular assignment or for new assignments, especially as these involved promotion. Indeed, BTL employees share an understanding of what a desirable career trajectory is—such that the successful completion of an assignment in one part of the world will lead to (or, perhaps more accurately in the contemporary era of diminishing management opportunities, should lead to) a more responsible position in another part of the world.

BTL employees also share, we think, an "ethos," or "standardized system of emotional attitudes" (Bateson 1958: 111), that defines them as compatible, if sometimes competing, professionals: thus, as colleagues, they share not only sugar skills but also the felt consonances of easy sociability. These felt consonances—a shared and implicit sense of the appropriate—allow BTL employees to belong to a single community, regardless of whether working abroad or at the UK home office.[4] In other words, all BTL staff members have a comparable "sentimental education" (Geertz 1973: 449) concerning how and when to feel and say what is deemed suitable for a particular time and place. Conversely, as we shall see, because this ethos is not fully shared by Papua New Guineans at RSL, even highly skilled national managers find it difficult to feel that they fully belong to the same RSL community.

Bateson elaborates the concept of ethos with, for our purposes, an instructive reference to an aspect of English culture:

When a group of young intellectual English men or women are talking and joking together wittily and with a touch of light cynicism, there is established among them for the time being a definite tone of appropriate behaviour. Such specific tones of behaviour are in all cases indicative of an ethos. . . . In this case the men have temporarily adopted a definite set of sentiments towards the rest of the world, a definite attitude toward reality, and they will joke about subjects which at another time they would treat with seriousness. If one of the men suddenly intrudes a sincere or realist remark it will be received with no enthusiasm—perhaps with a moment's silence and a slight feeling that the sincere person has committed a solecism. (1958: 119)

Following Bateson's lead, let us look at comparable examples from "The Court Circular: The Weekly Newsletter of Booker Tate Limited." This two-page newsletter, which we read at RSL and saw BTL employees read there as well, is published at the home office and sent to all BTL operations around the world. It frequently includes humorous, often Anglocentric, material about the specific activities of employees. One, for example, rode a goat in what was dubbed the "Royal Ascot" of Kampala ("Court Circular," November 22, 1999). Another was offered "Mushroom with chicken bowel soup" and "Soup Tito"—not to mention "Abalone with pigs stomach soup" and "Chicken of crab soup with white wood ears" at a restaurant while on assignment in Indonesia. And all of this for "a mere £8 for three [people] including drinks." He concludes: "Although far away from Thame for an evening out I am sure they would do take-aways for those in search of an exotic eastern dining experience" ("Court Circular," November 15, 1999).

The newsletter also often includes humorous material about the general circumstances of the contemporary world. The following item from the issue of October 18, 1999, describes the different procedures "drawn up" for men and women wishing to withdraw money from drive-through cash dispensers. The "Male Procedure," taking a total of seven steps, is to

1. Drive up to the cash machine
2. Wind down your car window
3. Insert card into machine and enter PIN
4. Enter amount of cash required and withdraw
5. Retrieve card, cash and receipt
6. Wind up window
7. Drive off

The "Female Procedure," taking a total of twenty-seven steps, is (in part) to

4. Wind down the window
5. Find handbag, remove all contents on to passenger seat to locate card
6. Locate make-up bag and check make-up in rear view mirror
7. Attempt to insert card into machine. . . .

10. Re-insert card the right way up. . . .
11. Re-enter handbag to find diary with your PIN written on the inside
    back page. . . .

Whether for Bateson's English intellectuals to appreciate witty talk or
BTL's staff to enjoy the humor of the company newsletter, the joke must
not only be recognized as a form but its content must also be understood. In other words, one must not only know a joke is being made but
also get the joke. And this capacity involves considerable, and usually
semi-unconscious, learning. As Bourdieu says, "what is essential goes
without saying because it comes without saying" (1977: 167). Thus, to get
the joke about male and female procedures at cash dispensers, one has
to know about how cash dispensers work and about how gender is stereo-
typically depicted. Such culturally grounded knowledge requires a considerable familiarity with the habits of European, if not English, life, a
familiarity not easily acquired by, for instance, even a well-educated
Papua New Guinean. And not getting the joke means more than not
being familiar with cultural forms and contents, more than not sharing
the same common ground. It also means that one cannot engage in the
reciprocity of banter that often establishes the easy sociability of the collegial community: if one cannot get a joke, one cannot take a joke—or, for
that matter, provide a joke that someone else has to take.

By the same token, getting the joke but not finding it funny will also
disrupt the collegial community. Thus, if a woman suggests that the item
about male and female procedures at cash dispensers is at least as sexist as it is humorous, she will likely be seen as both unwilling to accept
the reciprocity of banter and as inappropriately spoiling the good-
natured fun of others. Indeed, as someone with the wrong ethos, she will
stand apart from the community. The only way she may register her
objections in an ethologically appropriate manner will be to create a deft
contrary example of male ineptitude. In other words, to remain appropriate, she will likely have to continue the banter to show her mastery and
acceptance of the ethos. Otherwise, she will have committed a gaffe.

To be sure, there may also be cases in which the ethos itself is such that
someone attempting to shift its dimensions will be seen as acting appropriately. Someone may break through convivial chat by, for example, calling a meeting to order. Someone may make a stand when the banter has
gone too far, as when a particular person has been too often the butt of
jokes.[5] Someone—especially someone with power—may display "sufficient force of personality" to swing "the group from one ethos to the other"

(Bateson 1958: 120). Yet, clearly, for such a person to be respected, rather than disparaged as simply foolish or out of place, will also require considerable cultural mastery of the contents and forms of talk.[6]

Interestingly, in the case of both Bateson's (presumably academic) intellectuals and BTL's sugar experts, the "lightly cynical" joking is juxtaposed with, and perhaps justified by, the hierarchical seriousness of everyday work. BTL employs people of different educational backgrounds and professional ranks and sends them to work and live together in different parts of the world. Some have doctorates, for instance, in agricultural economics or plant pathology; others have primarily on-the-job training, for example, in boiler maintenance or the mechanics of harvesting equipment. Some are "suits" and others are "rednecks," as one BTL manager at RSL describes his colleagues. Banter partly obscures these differences by precluding anyone from putting on too many airs. It partly transforms ranked coworkers into teammates and neighbors who will pitch in to get the job done or stand their round of drinks.

In this regard, the ways in which careers are presented in the "Court Circular" obituaries are revealing. Not surprisingly, in summarizing a professional career, work credentials and experience are stressed. Overseas assignments are delineated in chronological order, specifying when, where, and with whom the deceased worked. The obituaries include, for example, the names of the BTL sites, the general managers at these sites, and the "clutch of young hopefuls" who served as the deceased's "team" at a given time. (These "young hopefuls" subsequently, of course, have become very senior BTL staff.) The nature and value of such a life are well summed up in the final paragraph of an obituary that ran on April 1, 1999:

> Expatriate Life in general nurtures close ties between colleagues and also between families. The nature of engineering work in sugar factories also involves close co-operation with colleagues of all disciplines. For those of us who have known [the deceased] over the years we would like to say thank you for the friendship, thank you for the engineering advice and support that was so freely given, and thank you for the humour and banter that helped us through all of the problems. Our sympathies to his wife . . . and their sons.

Expatriate Lives: BTL at RSL

The writing about expatriates of European origin in Papua New Guinea, all done by expatriates, provides few of what Geertz (1973: 3–30) calls "thick descriptions," that is, little ethnographic contextualizing of lives.[7] Some are sketches of individuals deemed historically noteworthy (Griffin 1978; Sinclair 1995); others, correlations of variables deemed socially or psychologically significant (Feather 1981; Savery and Swain 1985); and yet others, interpretations of texts deemed politically revealing (Neumann 1997; Sturma 1997). Of the first sort are both humorous and hagiographic portraits—sometimes little more than vignettes—of magistrates, prospectors, educators, missionaries, and other colonial types. Thus, in one of many examples, Sinclair reports that "W. G. Johnson was known throughout PNG as 'Turkey.' He was a veteran prospector who was reputed to have purloined a large turkey, the property of the famed goldfield hotelier, Mrs. Flora Stewart. It was a brave man who attempted such a theft" (1995: 156).

Of the second sort are studies, frequently employing data gathered through surveys, that test hypotheses, often about troubling aspects of cultural contact. Thus, Feather (1981) determines, among other things, that on a scale of one to five, the longer white high school students live in Papua New Guinea, the more positive their attitudes become toward the country. And citing the surveys of others, Savery and Swain (1985) argue that conflicting leadership styles between white managers and Papua New Guinean workers account for worker dissatisfaction on a major mining project.

Of the third sort are analyses of texts that reveal the underlying themes and concerns of colonialism. In one instance it is argued that the film *South Pacific*, which depicts the ways soldiers and other expatriates engaged with natives on a generic island during World War Two, is more about race relations in the United States than about anything else (Sturma 1997). In another case it is argued that the nostalgic reminiscences in Australian newspapers by former white residents of the volcano-destroyed Papua New Guinean city of Rabaul are about the loss of a time-out-of-time wherein people drank, fished, and played golf, but rarely did any work (Neumann 1997).[8]

Nor is the thinness of such accounts of expatriate lives offset by in-depth anthropological studies. That anthropologists have come to Papua New Guinea for so many years without focusing on the expatriates there indicates something about both the conventions of anthropologists and the conventions of expatriates. In particular, it indicates there are certain compelling understandings about living far from "home," understandings which importantly affect virtually all expatriates, including expatriate anthropologists interested in studying expatriate lives. We will, therefore, introduce our "thickish" description of BTL employees at RSL with some discussion about the conventions as they influenced us and the RSL expatriates among whom we worked—as they influenced each of our senses of what the other was up to.

• • •

It is important, first of all, to recognize that white people in Papua New Guinea—expatriates of European descent—did not become a potential topic for anthropological field research until recently.[9] Certainly, most anthropologists who journey to Papua New Guinea, themselves often white and at least middle class, come to study people assumed to be substantially different from themselves. Why, after all, go to such a "remote" place to study those you can readily find at home, those you thereby feel you already largely know? Correspondingly, expatriates assume that the job of anthropologists is to study natives, not expatriates. This assumption, moreover, rests on pervasive understandings about who is appropriately studied by whom, who is scrutinized by whom, who is represented by whom, and who is gazed upon and objectified by whom.[10]

Furthermore, in a place like Papua New Guinea, anthropologists often rely on well-established expatriates for help and conviviality, if not hospitality, for logistic support and periodic infusions of the culturally familiar. Occasions of conviviality, moreover, whether at a club or a dinner party, are defined as leisure, not work. These are times when people can just relax and enjoy themselves in a relatively unguarded fashion. They are times for people to speak off the record, to let their hair down. For an anthropologist to be unduly serious, whether by overtly directing the conversation or by taking notes on what is being said, will be ethologically inappropriate and a betrayal of a presumed solidarity among the culturally and, generally, racially similar. It will be letting the side down in two regards: by making public what is conveyed privately, especially if remarks assumed to be off the record prove unbecoming in the light of public (published) scrutiny; and by betraying what is regarded as the common understanding of what anthropologists do, namely, study natives. Consequently, and paradoxically, anthropologists probably feel morally uneasy about using their best data concerning expatriate life. This moral uneasiness, finally, is compounded by the anticipation that expatriates can read—indeed, may well seek out, for example, in an Internet search—what anthropologists write about them.[11] And perhaps they may even take legal action for violation of privacy or for misrepresentation.[12]

We were not immune from these concerns. Nor were the expatriates with whom we spoke at RSL, both formally and socially, even though they knew that their lives were at least part of what we were trying to understand. Some, of course, were guarded. Indeed, one consultant warned his colleagues to watch what they said to us as he was once "burned" by talking too openly to a sociologist who then went on to describe him as a latter-day imperialist. And another employee took notes on the questions we asked and answers she gave during a prearranged interview. Most, though, seemed rather open and forthright during interviews and conversations, whether over coffee and tea in the workplace, or over drinks and dinner at the club or in their homes. They knew that our application to write the RSL story had been approved by the board of directors. And they knew that our work was gently monitored by the general manager during fortnightly "chats" about what we were learning. They knew, as well, that the general manager had asked people to cooperate with us, at least on material that was not commercially sensitive. Yet none of the expatriates at RSL was truly obliged to speak with us, much less be more than minimally polite. However, many—indeed almost all—seemed genuinely interested that we understand, in general, what their lives as "professional expatriates" were like and, in particular, what their lives were like at RSL.

There may have been additional and special reasons for them to welcome our ethnographic attentions. They were troubled by both the trajectory of BTL and of RSL. BTL was up for sale (and indeed in August 2000 would be acquired by a South African firm, Murray and Roberts Group, whose construction interests range from sugar factories to airport terminals). Moreover, management opportunities for BTL staff were clearly decreasing. Many of BTL's old projects had been "localized" (meaning that local people filled management positions), while new projects were increasingly scarce. Also, less expensive sugar-management experts from places like India, Fiji, and the Philippines were competing for what nonlocalized jobs there were. In fact, BTL could no longer afford to keep those of its people who were between assignments on the payroll until a new position might open up. Thus it was not at all clear to many of the expatriates we knew at RSL what their futures after RSL would be.

RSL's future was also not assured. Virtually from its inception as a "big project," it encountered serious and near-chronic financial pressures. It struggled, for instance, with a hitherto unknown and devastating sugar disease called "Ramu stunt," a weak domestic sugar market, and, most recently, a powerful attack on tariff protection led by the World Bank and supported by the World Trade Organization. Despite serious cost-cutting measures, it was forced to reschedule loan payments and was unable, except twice, to pay a dividend.

Not surprisingly, then, BTL expatriates at RSL, most of whom were middle-aged if not near retirement, had to come to terms with their professional lives. As employees of companies whose futures were uncertain, they felt nostalgia as they looked back to a time in which prospects seemed rosier.

• • •

That RSL is a rural enclave dedicated to the long-term production of a renewable resource makes expatriate life there somewhat distinctive. It is unlike the rural enclaves dedicated to short-term extraction of nonrenewable minerals where expatriates are a significant presence only during the relatively limited lifespan of the operation and, even then, on a fly-in and fly-out basis.[13] It is also unlike Papua New Guinea's larger towns, where expatriates can socialize with each other in a variety of clubs and other contexts (see Upton 1998). Thus, unlike the mining towns, RSL is not only a work site but also an enduring community; unlike the larger towns, RSL has only a very limited expatriate pool to draw on to form that community. Consequently, expatriates often describe the tenor of their lives at RSL—especially as it pertains to leisure and socializing— in terms of the fluctuating numbers of expatriates present at a particular time. And the key context necessitating a critical mass of expatriates is the Management Club, especially on weekends (fig. 13). Though most

Figure 13. The Management Club, social center for the expatriate community

national managers belong to the club and many often socialize there, expatriates and nationals alike regard the club as the core of expatriate social life. RSL thereby confirms Cohen's finding that such clubs constitute the "heart of the social life of expatriate communities" (1977: 41).

During our stay at RSL, the expatriates were keenly aware not only that their numbers varied considerably, but also that their numbers were, overall, on the decline. Most lived in the Management Compound at RSL and most socialized regularly at the Management Club. Over the period of our research, there were at most fifteen expatriate employees on long-term contracts: fourteen men and one woman. In addition, eight of these men had their wives with them, at least for most of the time. Only two of the expatriate couples had children regularly living with them. Two others had their wives and children visit them for extended vacations at least once a year. One expatriate woman was married to a Papua New Guinean national and had a young child.

Added to these expatriates on long-term contracts at RSL were others working there on short-term contracts. These included Stuart Hayes, a BTL employee, and his wife, who were there for about six months to upgrade the factory; a pilot, his wife, and their two small children, who were there for about three months for agricultural spraying; a supervisor with Guard Dogs, Inc., the firm employed by RSL to secure the estate; and many BTL consultants, who usually came for a week or two to confer about specific issues. There were, as well, four men employed by the European Union to supervise a road construction project in the immediate area and their wives. These people were living for the duration of the project in the Management Compound in houses built by the EU. In addition, several crews of expatriates came in for specialized tasks during the factory upgrade. All of them lived in the Management Compound. Most socialized regularly at the club, as did the two of us.

Also part of this pool of expatriates were a handful of workers living elsewhere, including several employed directly by the road construction company. Though they lived in a camp some twenty miles distant, they often came to the Club. Moreover, very occasionally expatriates such as Barbara Jephcott dropped by. There were special categories of club membership to cover those who were not affiliated with RSL, including "temporary members" like us and the expatriates working on the road, and the "country members" like Jephcott.

There were, to be sure, some differences among these expatriates. Even those on long-term contracts at RSL varied according to conditions of employment, to say nothing of nationality. Differences between

Britons and others, often Australians, frequently mirrored salary and other distinctions between those employed directly by BTL and seconded to RSL and those working for RSL directly. One non-British RSL employee sometimes referred to himself rather resentfully as a "kanaka"—a pejorative term for native—relative to BTL-employed staff. Yet most of the people we met were socially outgoing and thoroughly convivial at club gatherings.

And, indeed, if enough expatriates were around for a good Friday-night turnout, the club would positively jump. By the end of the 5:30–6:30 "Happy Hour," the tables would be packed with animated faces and the bar would be thronged. Everyone would be shouting to be heard and standing drinks for one another. Empty glasses and bottles would be everywhere, with trays of replenishments on the way. Sometimes a few of the group would briefly join the nationals, who tended to congregate in the snooker room adjacent to the bar, where the socializing, much of it involving joking in rapid-fire Pidgin, focused primarily on snooker competitions rather than on buying rounds. But most would remain with the rest their crowd. Eventually, one or two of the expatriate wives would arrive with the "nibbles" they had signed up to provide: the bite-size pizzas, barbecued chicken wings, crust-trimmed sandwiches, dips, and canapés.

Here, in summary form, are some of the conversations that occurred at a table around which ten expatriates, including ourselves, sat one Friday night over drinks and nibbles. Although most of this group were BTL staff, their conversations were consistent with those among the expatriates more generally—whether BTL or not. Their conversations were also consistent with—in fact, contributed to—the BTL ethos. They were, in other words, the stuff of the obituary in which thanks was given to a BTL colleague for his long-term friendship, technical advice, humor, and banter, all of which were part of what enabled expatriates to cope in their overseas postings. Aside from the relatively few instances of shoptalk, these were also conversations whose content and form would have been less than perfectly transparent to a national.

There were reminiscences about home and about other BTL assignments throughout the world, with humorous stories and witty interjections flowing into one another. For instance, in the course of an earlier conversation, the term "ha-ha" came up. One of the men then explained that the term referred to a kind of wall designed with a concealed face that would not interrupt the view from a manor house. He then continued with a story of the time he helped create a sort of "ha-ha" on a BTL-managed

Sri Lankan sugar plantation (a story from the time BTL still had major interests in what became a war-devastated country). Elephants, who loved sugarcane, had become a terrible pest on the plantation. For instance, the lead elephant would walk down the rows of freshly planted cane stalks, dragging a foot to uncover them so that the others, following behind, could eat them. To deal with this problem, someone suggested that a moat be dug around the entire plantation. But others thought that this would be too expensive. Finally, an old elephant-hand was consulted. He said that, for a fee, he could limit the elephants' operations. He observed the elephants for several days and then advised where to dig a pit. He covered the pit with mats over which he spread molasses. The lead elephant fell into the pit, and then the old elephant-hand sent several boys to build a fire near it. Elephants hate fire, and this elephant got very annoyed. Eventually, the elephant was allowed to escape from the pit. Then molasses-soaked mats were placed around the entire estate. The lead elephant allowed none of the rest to approach such a "ha-ha." The plantation managers were actually charged quite a bit for this advice, and it might have been cheaper to have dug the moat after all. This story led to several cautionary elephant tales: elephants, who hated threats even more than fire, might charge in rage if chased by Molotov cocktails; elephants, who loved oranges even more than sugarcane, might demolish a car if oranges were left inside.

There were conversations of a somewhat more personal nature. One woman mentioned that it was "expatriate lore" never to return to a place in which you once lived happily as you would always be disappointed. However, she was finding her return to Papua New Guinea better than she had expected. Another woman said that she would hate to risk disappointment by returning to Kenya. When she was first there, she was young, newly married, and in love with the world. When she first saw the flame trees, she thought she was the luckiest woman alive. This same woman, who together with her husband was about to leave RSL for home, said about a party to be held to "farewell" her that she would have preferred just to slip away.

And there were conversations about the current state of interethnic play at RSL, probably because we were present. One woman wondered whether we might be willing to take her into a native village. She had been living in Papua New Guinea for some time and had seen villages from the road, but had no idea what they were really like. Others wondered, and sought our insight, why so few Papua New Guineans came to the club to join in the conviviality. This, regardless of attempts to encourage them to do so, such as reducing the prices of drinks on Friday evenings, or offering a very inexpensive spaghetti dinner for the whole family. They wondered why, if national managers did come to the club, they remained on the periphery, in the snooker room, for example. Though these national managers seemed to be enjoying their own sociability, they should know that they were welcome to join the main group.[14]

On most Fridays, the food was finished by about 8:00 P.M. and then the games began—and the drinking continued. Under the direction of the club's social chairman, people were encouraged to play bingo, in-door bowls, or darts. Occasionally they were organized into teams to compete in a quiz, designed by one of the wives. The questions, like those on a moderately challenging television quiz show, usually tested general levels of expatriate knowledge about such topics as history, geography, current events, spelling, sports, and popular culture. Some of the prizes were free drinks from the bar. Others were money, which was invariably used to stand additional rounds. There was, as well, a weekly draw from a hat containing the names of all club members—both expatriate and national—and designed to encourage attendance. The winner had to be present to claim the cash prize, and as befit the conviviality and solidarity of the occasion, the winner generally left this money at the bar to provide free drinks to all comers as long as it lasted.

It was on these occasions that expatriates who knew RSL from its early days told us that this was almost the way it used to be.[15] And it was on these (and other) occasions that expatriates, anticipating, for instance, the completion of both the factory upgrade and the EU road project, commented that soon no one would be left.

An Effervescence of Expats: The Heydays Remembered

The significant reduction in expatriate numbers at RSL began some years before our time there. BTL has in fact been committed by its contract with RSL and by government law to train nationals to take over managerial and other positions. It was, however, a serious outbreak of Ramu stunt in the cane fields that vastly accelerated the process of expatriate replacement. This previously unknown disease so devastated the crop of 1986 that virtually the entire estate had to be replanted with more resistant varieties. And the replanting was almost ruinous, involving both direct expense and loss in production. BTL responded to this agronomic and fiscal crisis by sending in agricultural experts and cutting expenses, in particular, by reducing the number of expatriate managers on the payroll.[16]

What, then, were the heydays like, when expatriate numbers were at their peak. The textual versions of this past—both personal memoirs and descriptions created for general expatriate consumption—remind us of the newspaper articles Neumann analyzes concerning expatriates' remembrances of Rabaul, memories focused on "the New Guinea Club and golf course" (1997: 180). Central to the creation of such a desirable past is the evocation of good times, particularly a sort of conviviality that we already saw memorialized in BTL's "Court Circular" and enacted at the RSL Management Club.

We learned a great deal about these heydays from a memoir written by one expatriate wife who lived at RSL with her BTL-employed husband from 1980 until 1986. This memoir, written for her grandchildren in 2000 but kindly shared with us, was partly the story of a successful life lived abroad. Although from a modest background, during one of her husband's assignments she was even offered a butler (though she declined the offer). And at RSL, she had a houseboy and gardener. Like most of the self-designated "professional expats" with whom we spoke, this woman readily grants that she and her husband would never have left home but for the elevation in living standards that working abroad allowed. There was, to be sure, a downside to living abroad. There were the pains and sorrows of being far from family. She, in particular, could not return to England in time to be with her parents when they died. And it was a gamble as to whether the time away would pay off in retirement. Although her husband would have a good pension, she would not, since she had few opportunities for employment while abroad. But, overall, like many other expatriates, she describes herself as having had a "marvelous life":

> There were about 45 expat families on site and no television so everyone relied on the club and home entertainment for amusement. The men all worked very hard and played hard, too. Some of the functions during our time at Ramu included Christmas Dinners (for 100), New Years Eve Dances, Valentine's Dances, Pyjamma Party, Carol Concerts, Barn Dance, Pantomimes, Medieval Feast complete with Jesters in costume and stocks, Bunny Girl Calcutta Night (betting on who would win next day's golf), a Skit Night, Melbourne Cup Fashion Show Lunch, It's a Knockout afternoon in the pool, Horse Racing Night, countless BBQs, golf competitions and safari suppers. Every Sunday there was a Lunch at the Club and most Fridays there was food and dancing at the bar and often impromptu late swimming at the pool. . . . There was a dance

most months and a video shown on the large screen in the bar where we watched the Wedding of Charles and Diana. . . .

The Raft Race in 1983 saw me leading a team of Factory wives on the old raft that [my husband] and his crew had used the previous year. [Four of us women] wore matching tee shirts with blue hats and called ourselves the Factory Fillies aiming for a prize for the All Woman raft. I was swept off when we hit a tree and was flattened in swift but fairly shallow water. . . .

It had me scared and the next time I went down was with the men on [one man's] Monster Raft to compete for the prize for Most on a Raft. It had two enormous tractor tyre inner tubes lashed to a plywood platform and on top of that he had built a bar. This was staffed by [two women] dressed as Bunny Girls while the BBQ mounted on the prow was manned by the office cleaner who had begged to be aboard. . . .

[There was a] very popular General Manager team and when they left after six months they had a great send off. They used to entertain by having "drinks" with snacks [and once, the wife] came over to my house to show me how to make chicken liver pate. . . . We organized [for the sendoff] a Safari Supper. Drinks at [the home of one couple], starters at our house, fish [at another couple's house], main course at [another's], Baked Alaska for dessert at [yet another's]. . . . When they left, . . . [the wife] donated [a trophy in their name] for the ladies' golf section.

Of course, there was more to life at RSL than partying. The men worked hard, and the memoirist took her responsibilities to her national and expatriate friends very seriously. In fact, members of both groups mentioned that she had helped them in important ways. She was generous with her time and resources: she taught people skills and found them jobs; she provided people with solace. Yet, because RSL was an enclave some distance from any town of size, the expatriates did have to make their own entertainment—and much effort was expended in doing so.

To entertain guests in Papua New Guinea with delicacies like Baked Alaska was truly a feat.[17] Putting together a dinner party worthy of such a finale involved, on the one hand, clever coping—to pull it off one had to establish the networks to get, for instance, the best cuts of meat from the best butcher in the country. It also involved the use of the many resources available to help one cope cleverly—housecleaners, dishwashers, and servers, as well as drivers for the several-hour-long trip to Lae or Madang to purchases ingredients. Several wives also told us that they took advantage of BTL's generous shipping allowance by bringing sets of china and silver with them to various assignments. Baked Alaska served in Papua New Guinea, in other words, was a triumph and a perquisite. It was the proof of proficiency and privilege. It demonstrated deserved affluence, both in the fact of coping and in the fruits of coping. Moreover, in the not only convivial but also competitive world of BTL, it marked an achieving couple as an asset on some future assignment.

The story of expatriate conviviality come what may has been both memorialized in and reinforced by the video *The Spirit of Ramu* (Harvest Moon Productions). Made by the wife of the BTL-employed financial comptroller in 1996, after the heydays of the expatriate community at RSL, it operated, we think, much like the "Court Circular" in creating and conveying an ethos—indeed, a "metaethos" of expatriate life. Actually, it might be regarded as an "ethotic" consensus about ethos. So when the film debuted at the Management Club, people there, who were depicted as being in great spirits, all agreed (while being in great spirits) that this depiction truly characterized them. The people who watched it, while having a good time, watched themselves having a good time. Under such public circumstances, there was likely general agreement—thus establishing as a matter of record—that a good time was what was had, despite the fact that this was all taking place far from home under challenging circumstances.[18] Because the "evidence" was before them in the video, because it was being lived in the actual gathering, and because the ethos and metaethos were such that conviviality could neither be seriously challenged nor challenged by seriousness, this depiction of themselves as a pretty affable bunch who were still able to get the work done became, irrefutably, "the spirit of Ramu." And if they chose to purchase the video (as many expatriate managers did, the proceeds going to charity), they could experience this "spirit" over and over. The accompanying table of contents—listing segments, soundtracks, and length of the takes—provided an inventory of what RSL was like and a reference by which viewers could quickly find the segments they most wished to (re)view and relive once they returned home.

The Spirit of Ramu begins with an aerial view of the RSL installation and immediate area and covers (though not in this order) the amenities RSL provides (the golf course, swimming pool, club); the essentials it ensures (the preschool and the international school); the hobbies and interests it fosters (painting, gardening, soap making, sewing, trumpet playing, running, horseback riding); the collective expeditions it encourages (to the Goroka cultural show and through picturesque mountains in a caravan of sports utility vehicles to a very friendly native village—with the theme song from *Raiders of the Lost Ark* in the background). The few nationals occasionally appearing in the leisure activities (on the golf course, in the pool, or in the classroom) seem to subscribe completely to expatriate manners—to expatriate definitions of the situation—and to bring nothing indigenous to the scene. Conversely, there is no depiction of the most conspicuous context for fellowship among nationals, attendance at church. Indeed, in our experience, virtually no expatriates ever attended church at RSL. Significantly, there is relatively little in the video about actual sugarcane production and processing: except for the opening shots of cane fields, there is only a single segment showing cane being cut, conveyed into the factory, and then emerging, already processed, in packages; there is also a single sequence of a helicopter arriving with the fortnightly payroll. Also missing is any real consideration of the hierarchical relationships underlying expatriate life at RSL—there is nothing about jobs, salaries, houses, nature of contract (whether primarily with BTL or with RSL), country of origin, or competition for new assignments. The focus, in other words, is on leisure, as it was in the reminiscences of those Neumann chronicles (1997), fondly recalling the lost Rabaul.

It is taken for granted in the video that the expatriates are at RSL for work—because they are sugar experts. They have come all the way around the world, in the case of most of the BTL employees, to do a job at which they are presumably the best in the world. It is also taken for granted that, given the nature of sugar plantations, particularly in places like Papua New Guinea, the experts living there will form an enclave not only for working but also for relaxing in each other's company. In other words, for purposes of both work and leisure, they have to get on well together. This is presumably what the memoirist meant when she said that "the men all worked very hard and played hard, too." So, although hierarchy is present, it has to be muted and mellowed by conviviality in order that what results is a cooperative "team," including the "clutch of young hopefuls" (see also Barth 1966).

Thus, overall, the *The Spirit of Ramu* ensures that expatriates remember being convivial, valued, challenged, and on career track at RSL, rather than, perhaps, feeling alienated, exploited, bored, and marginalized at some out-of-the-way place. Moreover, in its positive depictions, the video shows expatriates at RSL as having experiences and perquisites that a range of folks back home, unless themselves quite privileged, could recognize as desirable, if not enviable. In fact, we were told that the video was used to recruit BTL employees for RSL assignments. Such commemorative accounts as the memoir and video, not to mention the obituary, are, of course, selective: they are constructed, as Neumann finds in his analysis of expatriate reminiscences of Rabaul prior to its destruction, "around conspicuous absences and silences. Those whose nostalgic sentiments inform the articles . . . yearn for something that can be filleted out of the colonial or post-colonial contexts" (1997: 180).

The conspicuous absences on which these nostalgic accounts rest are highlighted in a different kind of account offered to us in an interview by an expatriate physician. Although not a BTL employee, he worked at RSL between 1985 and 1990, when his contract was abruptly terminated. Among BTL expatriates, he still has a reputation for being impracticably committed to the social welfare of nationals, whether outgrowers or RSL employees; among these same nationals, he still is considered a good and honest man. His account of the past is, in essence, a counter-reminiscence:

> The expatriates were odd. I had never lived in a compound like this one before, with the management area filled with expats. Because of my work, I spent most of the day with local people talking Pidgin and did-n't spend much time with many of the expats, except when I saw them as patients. I had a friend who was a lecturer in history at U.P.N.G. [University of Papua New Guinea] at this time who visited and was shocked to find a compound like this still in contemporary P.N.G. with not one national at the club. There never had been much will on the part of either expats or nationals to mingle. Of course there were the young single guys who would go into the local community to screw the local ladies: they were frequently asked to leave because this was not one of BTL's standards. Many national women were religious and did-n't want their husbands drinking, nor did they want to be in a place where drinking went on. The expats would have liked them there, but only on expat terms. . . .
>
> My [mostly national] patients didn't talk much: the ag[ricultural] workers were not especially stressed because there was more flexibility in their jobs. But the factory workers were expected to conform to BTL industrial standards. And many snapped into anger and violence. Yet, in my experience, Papua New Guineans are not prone to neurotic types of illnesses and I rarely had to prescribe Valium-type drugs—unlike anytime I've practiced in Australia, where 50 percent of my prac-tice would involve drugs of that kind. . . . Psychiatric illnesses were more likely among the expats, as you would expect among the two

kinds of people at RSL. There were the workingmen with high standards, striving to achieve and stabbing each other in the back; and
there were the wives, who were bored. There was a lot of alcohol
all around and at least two wives with serious drinking and drug
problems—that everyone knew about.

Although the expatriate wife whose memoir we quote above told us
that she did not personally know about the wives with serious drinking
and drug problems, she was aware of scandals, backbiting, and internal
politics. At RSL, as in other communities and companies, there was
always gossip about who slept with whom, who drank too much, who
was transferred because of sexual indiscretion, who was effective as
head of department or general manager, who was fully up to BTL standards, who—from field or factory—was responsible for high or for low
production figures. She, like the other expatriates, heard plenty of talk.

However, while such talk could be readily evoked in memory, it was not
appropriate stuff for memorializing. Indeed, to say that "a good time was
not, in fact, had by all" would be ethologically dissonant. It would be as
dissonant as objecting to a joke in the "Court Circular" because it was
sexist. It would challenge the hard—because selective—work of nostalgia
in both commemorating and creating a community of those who can reminisce and who chose to reminisce about the same kind of things. It
would undermine the community of those who have given themselves
over to a certain vision of themselves as a community—a community syn-
thesizing work and leisure with the "spirit" of convivial teamwork.[19] To use
Durkheim's classic concepts ([1933] 1984, 1965), by enacting and recalling what were, in effect, occasions of collective "effervescence," which in
turn reenacted and recalled comparable other times, the "organic solidarity" of RSL's complex and hierarchical division of labor was annealed
with the "mechanical solidarity" of the shared values of the expatriate
community.

As we have said, by the time we came on the scene in 1999, most of
the BTL expatriates at RSL sensed that their days there, and perhaps
at BTL as well, were numbered. Indeed, there may even have been—
certainly there was for some—a nostalgia for nostalgia: a nostalgia for
the time in which a fond looking back was possible. This was a nostalgia
for a world in which an obituary (including their own?) could evoke and
create a history linking past, present, and future by reference to a "clutch
of young hopefuls." It was a nostalgia for a world in which yesterday's
young hopefuls were mentoring their own clutch of the up and coming,

whose members would memorialize them when the time came. Certainly, as numbers thinned and prospects dimmed, and when only a few showed up at the club, it was difficult to imagine a present, much less a future, as supporting a viable expatriate community—of supporting what might be termed an "effervescence of expats."

Sugar Valley News: In Place and Out of Place

From 1983 through 1991—during the efflorescence of expat society—RSL published twenty-three issues of *Sugar Valley News*, edited initially by Maureen Sabel, wife of the BTL-employed personnel and training manager. Sabel describes the purpose of this mimeographed booklet in the first edition: "Our aim will be to make it *your* newspaper which contains news of interest to *you*" (Sabel 1983a: 3). She and subsequent editors did publish articles of widespread interest, and the booklet, generously illustrated with photographs, eventually expanded from the eighteen pages of the first issue to some sixty pages.

The *Sugar Valley News* includes reports from national employees about work experiences and training trips abroad: Some articles concern adjusting to conditions at RSL. Others, like "My Three Month Course in England," concern an RSL-sponsored trip to Sussex to study "maintenance and management of agricultural plant and machinery" (Gagau 1985: 6–10). There are accounts from the various churches and sports associations at RSL, and always a big spread about the annual Raft Race.

There are news stories: Some concern visits of dignitaries, for example, the attendance of Pius Wingti, then prime minister (accompanied by John Christensen, the champion of big projects!), at the opening of the RSL distillery ("News around Ramu" 1983: 14–15). Others are about such matters as carvers from the Sepik completing the adornments on St. Luke's Catholic Church ("St. Luke's Catholic Church" 1985: 41). One piece describes fighting during the Independence Day celebrations (Masirere 1987: 25).

There are features from company officials: the general manager writes one for every issue. For example, A. W. MacGillivray warns that the "pests and disease which caused so much damage to the cane this year are still with us and are likely to be just as damaging again next year" (1990: 3). Heads of departments or of sections write from time to time. The agronomist G. Lee Lovick explains, "Agronomy is the research section of the Agricultural Department. Our aim is to advise the crop production and harvesting sections on the way to grow high yields of sugarcane as cheaply as possible" (1984: 9).

There are instructional and educational pieces: Some are in Pidgin English, like the one describing the safety measures to avoid electrical shock (Fred 1990: 14–15). Others are in English, on subjects such as heartworm in dogs (Garnsworthy 1985: 27) and the history of malaria (Cameron 1985: 24–25).

There are advisory and opinion essays: "Pride in Yourself Is Pride in Your Country" explains that "Papua New Guinea is a young country as far as being independent goes. As a result the people of Papua New Guinea are still in the process of finding their identity. . . . PNG Nationals have to stop thinking of themselves as Chimbus, Morobeans or Papuans for example and start thinking of themselves wholly and completely as Papua New Guineans" (Sabel 1983b: 8). "Ramu Should Be a 'Model' Community" stresses that "when someone does something it is counted for himself, his immediate family, his community and above all, his country. Whether good or bad, he has scored something which will bring him the type of an end that he deserves. If he has developed and improved himself to be a better citizen and do good things in his life, then he has a happy and peaceful ending" (Bego 1990: 16). "For Love of Bride-Price" describes a woman, a "Christian . . . not a Europeanized black," who appropriately wishes to convince her father to allow her to marry the man whom she loves rather than the man who can "offer the biggest bride-price" (Jerry 1987: 13–14).

There are interviews with important local people, such as the Jephcotts ("Dumpu and the Jephcott Family" 1985: 35–38) and Emmanuel Moba's father, a Mari leader especially committed to developing his people (Maino and Malein, 1988: 22–24). And there are poems, generally written by children, and traditional stories, such as "Why Dogs Cannot Talk" (Naiko 1990: 49–50), usually identified by region, but never further contextualized.

Finally, there are many textual and photographic "profiles" of employees and their families. Below we include two. Appearing in the same issue, one describes a newly arrived expatriate couple and the other, a national family:

Welcome to Ted and Joan Kaines

Ted joined Ramu Sugar on 22nd January, 1985 as Training Instructor. Prior to that he and Joan have enjoyed many years overseas working in several African countries. Like many of us with African experience, Ted and Joan are very attached to Africa with its unique flora and fauna. A move to the Pacific Region was a welcome change however, and they look forward to exploring the beauties of P.N.G.

Having completed the regulation national service in England and qualifying as a motor mechanic, Ted was able to emigrate to New Zealand in 1955 for a mere £10.00. It was there that he furthered his experience as a motor mechanic.

Soon after returning to England in 1961 Ted met Joan. In 1968 with their two sons they left England for Africa. After 10 years working for the Zambian and Malawian Governments Ted joined Bookers in 1978. He was seconded to Mumias in Kenya for 2 years. There he first gained experience in Instruction.

Joan, a qualified librarian, is a very keen gardener. She was delighted to find a fully established garden here at Ramu having created 5 from scratch over the last 17 years.

We wish them every happiness at Ramu. ("Welcome to Ted and Joan Kaines" 1985: 10).

Profile on Kevin Hecko

Kevin aged 29, comes from Kufar village Yangoru in the East Sepik Province. He is married and has a 5 year old daughter Judith. His wife Carolina is 26 years old.

Kevin attended primary School from 1962 to 1967 and High School from 1968 to 1971.

Soon after completing high school he joined the P.N.G. Electricity Supply Commission as an apprentice where he worked for ten years. During this time from 1973 to 1974, Kevin was sponsored to attend a Commerce Certificate course at the Lae Technical College. A year later he was again sponsored to go to U.P.N.G. but he decided against this, as he wanted to attend another course at the electricity Commission of Victoria at their staff training college for 1 year.

His first posting in P.N.G. was at the Ramu Hydro Electricity Scheme from 1976 to 1977 after which he was posted to the Elcom Headquarters at Hohola for one year.

At Elcom Headquarters he was in charge of the Costing and Investigations Department. He then resigned and joined Ok Tedi Mines as a senior Purchasing Superintendent. At Ok Tedi Kevin says he had to rise at 4.00 am and work until 8.00 pm from Monday to Saturday. This meant that there was very little free time and that was his reason for resigning, even though the pay was good. Also the Ok Tedi and Tabubil areas are amongst the wettest in the country.

Kevin says he is very happy at Ramu Sugar because here he has enough free time. The quiet and peaceful environment at Ramu also appeals to him and his family.

Kevin's sport is karate and he enjoys carpentry in his spare time. (Bego 1985: 9)

The *Sugar Valley News* provides a vision of community in which diverse peoples can learn to see themselves in others. There is an effort to include items of general interest. Furthermore, items of more specific interest to expatriates are balanced with those of more explicit interest to nationals. Indeed, the Kaines and Hecko profiles are carefully parallel to show that the new employees and their spouses are comparably qualified for work and leisure at RSL: they have appropriate educational and work experiences; they have left kin behind to establish nuclear families; they have hobbies and recreational interests. They will fit right into the RSL community depicted in and at least partly created by the *Sugar Valley News*. In this regard we might note that the *Sugar Valley News*, like RSL more generally, acts in support of the nation-state.[20] RSL nationals are enjoined in the *Sugar Valley News* to think of themselves "wholly and completely as Papua New Guineans" (Sabel 1983b: 8), as developing and improving themselves as better citizens (Bego 1990: 16).

Although we are not sure what RSL could have done differently through the *Sugar Valley News* to establish an actual sugar-producing community composed of both expatriates and a diversity of nationals, the relatively self-conscious representations it promotes are clearly expatriate orchestrated: the eyes through which both expatriates and nationals are encouraged to see one another are largely expatriate eyes.

Consider, as an instructive contrast, the following anomalous case, reported in the *Sugar Valley News* and presenting a Papua New Guinean vision of community, of conviviality, of equalization—of justice being served:

An extraordinary court case was tried a few months ago here at Ramu. Former . . . Manager, Mr. . . . , was arrested shortly before his departure from PNG to England. The arrest was seen by many as an attempt to keep [him] from leaving the country.

Village Court Magistrate, Mr. Veto Oraraka, had received a summons from one of Ramu's [female national employees] and the arrest took place shortly afterwards, outside RSL head office. Officers present at that time were RSL Security Guards, accompanied by "SingSing" [ceremonial] dancers led by Mr. Jim Wilson (in full SingSing costume) and the employees of Building, Estates and Housing. Most of RSL's clerical staff also witnessed the arrest.

At the trial, held at the "Rec" Hall, and at which Village Elder, Mr. Buka Atape, and others, were present, the defendant was accused of adultery. Mrs. . . . had brought along her baby boy, . . . , as testimony of the defendant's misdemeanor. . . .

[After reluctantly admitting guilt, a] compensation fine of K20.00 per fortnight maintenance fee for [the child] was set by the Magistrate. Furthermore, a special potion was prepared and drunk by [the defendant], in the presence of the court "to prevent him from committing any such further offenses." Magistrate Oraraka also ordered [the defendant] to pledge a good-behaviour bond for not less than 1 year, before finally dismissing the case.

To continue the good feelings resulting from this decision, the court defendant and witnesses retired to enjoy well-earned drinks and food prepared by Danice Wilson. ("RSL . . . Manager Arrested and Tried at Ramu" 1987: 32)

Significantly, the article includes a photograph of the court proceedings. In the center and looking at the camera is the glum-faced expatriate defendant. He is flanked by some thirty nationals who are either in security uniforms or in the shells, feathers, and leaves of native ceremonial finery. All are standing respectfully before—and subject to the authority of—the seated national judge.

In this case, it is Papua New Guineans who are promoting the relatively self-conscious representations: it is they who set the terms for comparison, define the nature of equalization. In so doing, they effect a set of reversals and transformations of the usual RSL patterns of authority and community. The orchestration of this paternity case provides Papua New Guineans with competence and legitimacy. The episode allows them to implement a vision of justice and redemption that joins national law with tradition through the presence of the magistrate and security officers as well as the singsing dancers. They make the expatriate progenitor into a Papua New Guinean father; they make him join a Papua New Guinean family; they make him become a "citizen" of a Papua New Guinean world; and they make him become, through the efficacy of the potion, a member of a newly constituted Papua New Guinean community, one in which his membership is as a chastened, rather than as an authoritative (and efflorescent), member. It is to their party, and on their terms, that he is "invited." The ethos at this party is thus significantly unlike that established by the essentially expatriate tone of the *Sugar Valley News*. It is also profoundly unlike that found in the banter-laden "Court Circular." At the "rec" hall on that day, the joke (as it were) is on the BTL expatriate. He is the odd man out. It is his gaffe that is the center of attention.

More on Setting the Terms

Many of the photographs accompanying the profiles in the *Sugar Valley News* make an attempt at equalization. There are, of course the portraits of people, such as those of the smiling Kaines and Hecko families as equal members of the RSL community. But there are not only the portraits of such nuclear families. There are also the beautified homes in which these RSL families are expected to live. In one issue, for example, we see portraits of four gardens and the houses they surround. Each is a winner in the RSL-wide competition for the best garden. Accompanying these portraits are descriptions that stress a European aesthetic of the domestic landscape:

> This carefully landscaped garden is the result of hard work and a love for beauty. Spreading trees shade a rich green lawn and a blaze of shrubs and annuals give colour.

> The most striking features [of two other of] the gardens . . . are the well cared for lawns. ("Health, Garden, and Home" 1985: 17, 18)

Interestingly, all the winners are nationals. More specifically, to judge from house type, all are supervisors. All, therefore, are living in detached, single-family houses in the complex of nonmanagement houses. As supervisors, they are nationals who have shown potential—who might appropriately strive to become managers. All, moreover, are awarded their prizes for plantings very different from those we found around the supervisor's house into which we moved during 1999: there we found the trenched, mounded, and scrupulously weeded sweet-potato gardens so pleasing to Highlanders' eyes and so central to Highlanders' subsistence.[21] Although vegetable gardening is not disqualifying in this RSL garden competition, subsistence is, evidently, to be distinguished from, and not dominate over, aesthetics. Thus one prize-winning housewife is described as spending "a lot of her time tending the vegetables and the flower beds" (17). Correspondingly, the national wife of a high-ranking national manager at RSL told us that her husband allows her to plant only ornamentals in her front garden. If she wants to plant Papua New Guinean subsistence crops, they have to be discreetly hidden in back of their house. Otherwise, expatriates might still think of them as "natives."

There were, of course, many expatriates, like Mrs. Kaines, who enjoyed gardening. Indeed the *The Spirit of Ramu* shows several beautifully landscaped expatriate homes. But, as managers, all these expatriates would have their lawns mowed by RSL and their shrubs and ornamental plantings tended by one or more nationals whom they hired and directed. And the vegetable gardens that some did have were intended primarily to provide the otherwise locally inaccessible ingredients, for instance, coriander and basil, for European-style dining and entertaining. That these expatriate gardens are apparently excluded from the *Sugar Valley News* competition suggests not only that expatriate beautifiers of home and garden would, by virtue of their outside help, have unfair competitive advantage over aspiring nationals; it also suggests that they are the exemplars, the standard setters. In this regard, it is important to note that national managers are also apparently excluded from the competition. To do otherwise might imply that they are still aspirants, and hence not fully up to managerial standard.

Thus the *Sugar Valley News* provides profiles and pictures of RSL families as well as portraits of the contexts in which these families should live: Westernized nuclear families (but, of course, no wantoks) are to live in homes beautified according to a Western aesthetic.[22] Indeed, as well as lacking traditional vegetable gardens, none of the prize-winning houses seems to have the Papua New Guinean–style of outdoor, native-material shelter for cooking and socializing often found throughout the nonmanagement areas. It was under such a shelter that we had relaxed with Satuhan and his Sepik friends.

•   •   •

As we have seen, the universalism promoted by RSL expatriates has often been significantly selective. Everyone at RSL—regardless of race, of geographical and cultural background, of relative affluence and power—can be included in the RSL "family." Indeed, provided that they meet what are perceived as inclusively universal standards, they will be welcomed. However, these standards for the definition of a common humanity—the standards for the affirmation of fundamental equality—have been less broadly universal than narrowly Western.

The terms of seemingly generous inclusion express an interested selection within the range of what human beings might legitimately be. Through the promotion of such a selective standard, diversely situated people are given a commonality that obscures the weight of history, that obscures the significant and consequential differences—those that make a difference—that actually exist among them. An ethos of inclusion under these terms, while often speaking to generous, if not liberal, impulses, nonetheless favors those already dominant. This is most obvious in the worldview of the "Court Circular," but also at the Management Club, in *The Spirit of Ramu*, and in the *Sugar Valley News*.

For expatriates to set the terms of inclusion in a less selective, less self-interested way would indeed be radical. Although RSL expatriates generally strive to say, "They are as good as we are," these same expatriates are unlikely to recognize, much less accept as meaningful, the reverse equation "We are as good as they are." It would be a rare RSL expatriate who would try to understand, much less participate in, the aesthetic pleasures of sweet-potato gardens, or the sociality of wantok networks, or the conviviality of indigenous forms of socializing, such as Kamdan's birthday party. In fact, virtually the only portrait we have of an expatriate accepting local standards of sociality and inclusion is that of the paternity case mentioned above: and in that instance, of course, his participation was involuntary.

6

Replacing Expatriates with Papua New Guineans

CONTINUING WITH OUR EXPLORATION of relations between expatriates and Papua New Guineans at RSL, we focus now on the ways in which RSL has sought to convey the techniques and technologies of the developed world, of the "haves," to promising "nationals." BTL is formally committed at RSL, as elsewhere in its worldwide operations, to a program of "training and localization." This program uses a broad narrative of development—one, in variant forms, advocated by the patrol officers, the "Hayeses," and the nationalists—that sets out how the "have-nots" can learn the elements of Western knowledge they need so as to serve both individual and national interests. More specifically within RSL, this narrative sets out how Papua New Guineans can assume the leadership roles they need so as to benefit both career and country (and move into the grade A, B, and C houses of the management complex). As we shall see, BTL's commitment at RSL to replace expatriates with nationals, and thus place Papua New Guinea on a new historical trajectory, reflects its efforts to learn from its own history, a history rooted in the oppressive labor practices of Caribbean sugar plantations. Yet many Papua New Guinean managers find BTL's commitment to training and localization disingenuous, compromised by its commitment to its own staff. Moreover, many of these managers are ambivalent about BTL's vision of what sort of leaders they could and should become—and at what sort of RSL. They seek to balance commitments to ples and kin with commitments to company and class (commitments to their particular "Gagases," including Gagases transformed by regionalism and neighborliness, with commitments to corporate objectives and managerial colleagues). And, hence, they often must tack back and forth between different alternatives about how life at RSL should be lived, between different visions of what is desirable and feasible.

Nationals Replacing Expatriates

Ed Robinson had worked for BTL and its predecessor, BAI, longer than anyone else we interviewed.[1] He wanted us to understand that BTL is uniquely qualified to manage a Papua New Guinean sugar plantation. Its uniqueness, Robinson told us when we interviewed him in London during 2001, derives not only from its long-term sugar expertise, but also from the "legacy" of Jock Campbell, a remarkable businessman with a "commitment not only to profit but to people." Consequently, BTL, with its expertise and its commitment, has "a special talent for fitting sugar operations to their national contexts in such a way that local people benefited."

We already knew something of Campbell. He had been chairman of Booker PLC (Bookers), BAI's parent company, and joint owner with Tate and Lyle of BTL. Eventually he became Lord Campbell of Eskan. He was also the most prominent businessman to back the Labour Party through the 1960s and 1970s. His philosophy, evidently the foundation of his commitment, is on record in an essay, "Private Enterprise and Public Morality," published in the *New Statesman* (1966). There he challenges as "dangerous nonsense" the beliefs of "a group of economics students in London [that] Britain's health, wealth, and happiness would be assured only if her businessmen would preoccupy themselves wholly with making the biggest possible profits":

> In 1934 I went out to work for my family's sugar business in British Guiana (now Guyana). The conditions in which past members of my family had pursued profits and made considerable fortunes came as a great shock to me. Conditions of employment were disgraceful; wages were abysmally low; housing was unspeakable; workers were treated with contempt—as chattels. Animals and machinery were, in fact, cared for better than the workers because they cost money to buy and replace. The plantocracy had great power in government: for instance—intent

on maximizing profits—they did all they could to prevent the establishment of other industries in order to maintain a surplus of labour.
There was bitter opposition to the formation of trade unions. The sugar
industry had been founded on slavery, continued on indenture and
maintained by exploitation, all in the pursuit of profit. (1966: 765)

After the war Campbell decided to make things right. This required
reaching certain decisions about a set of problems. The big sugar estates
were widely detested by the public and by their own employees. The
industry was disorganized and inefficient, with many sugar estates run
down. He contemplated various alternatives. If profit and responsibility
to shareholders had been the sole consideration, he and his board of
directors might well have decided to let the sugar industry slide into collapse while making and repatriating a considerable profit by selling the
company's assets. However, he also recognized obligations to employees,
"without whose skills and labour the company could not go forward and
to whom, moreover, shareholders owed a great deal." In addition, there
was an obligation owed to customers as well as to the people of British
Guiana. Thus, "fourfold responsibilities had to be recognized and balanced:
shareholders, employees, customers and community" (765). He acknowledged that "whereas Britain's economic performance, progress and prosperity still largely lie in the hands, and hearts and heads of businessmen
. . . the objectives and regulations of business should be formulated in a
way which is susceptible of general understanding and respect." The outcome he sought was not a bitter conflict between business and labor,
with each seeking maximum advantage. Rather, it was to strive for "a
sensible, pleasant, civilized society" for everyone (766).

It should be noted that Campbell, in formulating a society based on
such a cooperative commitment, must have understood that doing business in former colonies often demanded a change from past practices. It
had become good business for Bookers to stress the importance of uniting
commercial enterprise with public morality, whether the company stayed
on or returned to manage nationalized facilities.[2] Significantly, as Jonathan
Taylor, a subsequent chairman of Bookers, recognized, the pursuit of this
vision in Guyana led Campbell both "to modernise the sugar industry and
to train and develop Guyanese for the most senior positions within it." In
his obituary of Campbell, Taylor credits him for having articulated "a new
and exciting vision of business which encompassed the responsibility to
employees, to customers, and to the community as well as to shareholders"
(1994: 14; see also the *Times* obituary of December 28, 1994).

Consistent with this legacy stressing the synthesis of private enterprise and public morality, BTL has emphasized the training and development of indigenous personnel. Thus BTL's promotional pamphlet states:

> In support of line managers, Booker Tate has considerable training and development expertise gained from many years providing management, technical assistance and consultancy services to agro-industrial operations in many countries. This proven ability is reinforced by an understanding of the latest training techniques and appreciation for what is appropriate for differing cultures. . . .
>
> Firm dates for the replacement of expatriates by competent local staff are a requirement of many of our clients, and this has to be reconciled with the desire for high productivity and low operating costs. Booker Tate will identify potential management and will ensure that local staff are progressed as rapidly as possible, without jeopardising production targets and without subjecting individuals to undue career stress. (Booker Tate Limited, n.d.: 10–11)

The modern and enlightened sugar industry of Campbell and BTL is hence committed to training, localization, and recognition of cultural differences. All of these objectives are to be placed in the context of sound business practices—such as planning for succession, ensuring high productivity, and avoiding undue career stress. In these specific regards, as well as in its general policy of combining private enterprise and public morality, the modern sugar industry is explicitly designed to contrast sharply with the industry of the past, like that of Campbell's prewar family estates.

Indeed, no reputable writer would describe prewar sugar plantations as providing workers in field and factory with a sensible, pleasant, civilized society. Throughout the Caribbean—perhaps especially in British Guiana (eventually dubbed "Bookers' Guiana" given the company's control of the political economy)—labor was coerced through slavery, indenture (generally of workers from India), or through the destruction of other sources of paid labor, perhaps coupled with the stringent enforcement of vagrancy laws.[3] More generally, as the anthropologist Eric Wolf argues, sugar plantations typically effected pervasive and destructive transformations of local life:

> Wherever the plantation has arisen, or wherever it was imported from the outside, it always destroyed antecedent cultural norms and

imposed its own dictates, sometimes by persuasion, sometimes by compulsion, yet always in conflict with the cultural definitions of the affected population. The plantation, therefore, is also an instrument of force, wielded to create and to maintain a class-structure of workers and owners, connected hierarchically by a staff-line of overseers and managers. (1959: 136)

It is, of course, BTL's postwar, postcolonial vision of what the sugar industry should and could be, rather than what it is historically, that provides the narrative for RSL. In this narrative, RSL is to balance profit and morality in a way that has been configured to Papua New Guinean needs and in accord with the Eight Aims: it is to provide employment, training, and income for those in remote areas. Indeed, in this narrative, individual interests are merged with national interests as expatriate experts are replaced with fully trained Papua New Guineans.

Thus, of the thirty-three pages in the "Master Agreement" (MA) signed by Papua New Guinean government representatives and by RSL's board of directors (including BTL representatives) on April 24, 1979, four pages specify policy for "training and localisation." Crucially, this requires the submission of a "training and localisation programme" that will "(a) give details of the Group's foreign staff . . . ; (b) provide for the training of suitable Papua New Guinea employees for all levels of employment within the Group; and (c) provide for the progressive replacement of the Group's foreign staff, other than the Subsidiary's [RSL's] General Manager, Factory Manager, Chief Accountant, Ranch Manager, Agricultural Manager and Personnel Training Manager by suitably qualified and experienced Papua New Guineans as and to the extent that such persons become available" (Papua New Guinea and Ramu Sugar Limited 1979: 17–18).

In fact, in 1983 such a program was submitted to, and eventually approved by, the government—and it has been updated periodically through RSL's history, most recently in 2001. According to figures compiled in 2001 as part of RSL's performance review for its board of directors, localization appears to have been extremely successful. Between 1983 and April 2001, overall expatriate numbers declined from eighty-two (including fifty-five in management and twenty-seven in supervisory positions) to eleven (all in management positions).[4] Thus RSL can point to major accomplishments in fulfilling its commitments. As a sugar industry in newly independent Papua New Guinea, it has effected a particular kind of nationalist vision: through training and localization, in a way that merges individual and national interests, expatriates are being replaced with Papua New Guineans.[5]

As we shall see, central to RSL's nationalist narrative of training and localization is a particular kind of life trajectory—the idea of a career, and by implication, a sense of whether a particular life is on course or off course. In significant measure, many nationals at RSL, managers in particular, also define being on or off course in terms of training and localization, that is, in terms of their replacement of (generally BTL) expatriates.

On Careers

Permanent, nonmanagerial workers at RSL often find satisfaction in their jobs. To be sure, some, particularly those engaged in factory shift work during harvesting, describe their work as tedious and tiring. And many complain about the pay. In a faltering economy—with a deflated kina and an inflated cost of living—with large families at RSL to support and kin at home to placate, they often find it quite difficult to make ends meet. Moreover, these matters are not likely to improve soon despite the efforts of the Ramu Sugar National Employees Union. Aside from a major strike in 1983 and occasional walkouts, the union has not been able to flex much muscle. Thus, in response to union demands during 2000 for better pay and housing, the company yielded little ground, arguing that, though sympathetic to workers' circumstances, it was barely surviving as it was.[6]

Yet most workers are proud at having acquired the technical skills and interpersonal contacts necessary to do their jobs. Kamdan, for example, takes pride in his skill in operating the full range of RSL's agricultural machines. A clerk takes pride in his knowledge of office procedures and his good working relations with people on all levels of the operation. A mechanic takes pride in his ability to diagnose and repair anything that comes into the shop. A dispatcher for agricultural engineering takes pride in his capacity to allocate machinery with efficiency. But, though such workers may envision raises and promotions based on the acquisition of new or improved skills, they rarely speak of themselves as having a career. Having a career, in fact, seems to define what it is to be a manager, whether expatriate or national.

That national managers have a sense of career is at least partly the result of their long-term and successful experience in Western-modeled schools, where, extracted from ples and kin, they are taught some "underlying epistemological and ontological premises," including the notion, as LiPuma puts it, "that self-managing, self-contained individuals competed and cooperated in quest of the self-improvement of mind, body, and spirit" (2000: 294). Implicit in this vision of a person are ideas of ambition: ideas of making the best use of time to achieve worth, indeed to enhance class position, that are central to the concept of career.

The anthropologist Dorothy Lee, using modernist, American examples, has some astute observations about this concept of career, revealing it to be a narrative of a particular kind. Pertaining to the relatively elite, as her examples suggest, a career is the story of a life with a characteristic storyline:

> I tell you Sally is selling notions at Woolworth's, but this in itself means nothing. It acquires some meaning when I add that she has recently graduated from Vassar. However, I go on to tell you that she had been assistant editor of *Vogue*, next a nursemaid, a charwoman, a public school teacher. But this is a mere jumble; it makes no sense and has no meaning, because the series leads to nothing. . . . However, I now add that she is gathering material for a book on the working mother. Now all of this falls into line, it makes sense in terms of a career. Now her job is good and it makes her happy, because it is part of a planned climactic line leading to more pay, increased recognition, higher rank. There was a story in a magazine about the college girl who fell in love with the milkman one summer; the reader felt tense until it was discovered that this was just a summer job, that it was only a means for the continuation of the man's education in the Columbia Law School. Our evaluation of happiness and unhappiness is bound with this motion along an envisioned line leading to a desired end. . . . Our conception of freedom rests on the principle of non-interference with this moving line, non-interruption of the intended course of action. (1959: 118)

Indeed, RSL's national and expatriate managers tend to view their professional lives as journeys and their worth as significantly determined by their positions along a trajectory of professional challenges and accomplishments. More than nonmanagers, RSL managers are likely to describe themselves not only in terms of what they are doing, but in terms of their ambitions: what they might—or should—become.

In this latter regard, national managers often feel unfulfilled, faulting RSL's training and localization program for not facilitating career development. They describe what they view as their thwarted careers to us and each other in such related terms as "blocked," "passed-over," or "side-stepped." Their elaborations often take the same form: as blocked, they have not been promoted because they have not received proper training (perhaps, they think, because the company has favored another national, or because it has reserved the position for an expatriate); as passed-over, they have not been promoted despite their training (perhaps because the company has favored another national or has reserved the position for an expatriate); as side-stepped, they have been given another position, but one that is more a lateral move than an actual promotion (again, perhaps because the company has favored another national or has reserved the position they are in line to receive for an expatriate).

Contributing to the sense of many that their careers are not advancing is RSL's hierarchical structure. Not only does the MA specify that the top positions (the general manager and heads of departments) are to be reserved for BTL expatriates, but the charts of organization (the many broadly distributed "organigrams" described earlier) show that there is not much room near or at the top. Indeed, Peter Colton told us that he once asked a group of national managers how many of them aspired to become general manager. When about half raised their hands, he pointed out that all but maybe one would either have to leave the company or be satisfied with a lesser position.

Of course, not only is *having* ambition a prerequisite to the fulfillment of the career course, but *professing* ambition is a rhetorical form in the career narrative. Thus it is likely that some of the managers who complain that their careers are interrupted by the failure of the training and localization program, or who indicated to the chairman of the board that they aspire to become general manager, may simply be using this rhetorical form. Some may, in fact, be quite satisfied with the level of responsibility already achieved. Nonetheless, we are convinced that many are genuinely disturbed that they are not advancing more quickly. Some point to specific organizational flaws at RSL and have submitted proposals to reform the grading system so as to allow advancement within, not just between, management grades. Some want the company to "incentivize" so that those who do a good job can receive special recognition, not to mention bonuses. Many insist that a company genuinely committed to benefiting Papua New Guineans will provide the training to allow nationals to leave for jobs elsewhere, though they wouldn't necessarily choose to do so.

Significantly, most feel that RSL, as a private enterprise, is not upholding the public morality: there is, they think, a conflict of interests at the heart of the enterprise, in BTL itself. Their argument goes like this: Though BTL may be committed to the training of Papua New Guineans and to the localization of expatriate-held positions, it also has commitments to its own profitability and to its own staff. To be sure, it sells itself as a management company that, by training its own replacements, in effect works itself out of any particular sugar enterprise. But such a strategy is dependent on there being new overseas contracts, new career opportunities, for those it employs. And these are becoming scarcer. And so, in the views of many Papua New Guinean managers, BTL ultimately puts its own interests before those of the nationals. It denies Papua New Guineans the very top positions in the nationalist enterprise of RSL, and it refuses, past a certain point, to replace expatriates with Papua New Guineans.

Human Resources

BTL executives are aware of most, if not all, of the employee concerns about training and localization. While denying that BTL categorically reserves any positions except those necessary to exercise the corporate responsibility of its management contract (those such as general manager and financial controller), they readily admit that RSL training programs are not what they might be. This is the case, they say, because of a range of fiscal constraints and personnel difficulties. Training receives a lower priority than is desirable because RSL experiences chronic fiscal difficulties, if not crises, which divert funds and attention from training.

The BTL perspective on RSL's fiscal difficulties goes something like this: RSL has always been on the edge of disaster. In 1986, only a few years after it began to produce its first cane, a previously unknown disease, Ramu stunt, destroyed virtually its entire crop. Not only did this disease force RSL to incur the considerable costs of massive replanting, it also made the company import sugar at unfavorable prices so as to supply its market. Moreover, RSL's market has never been large, never large enough to provide economies of scale. Nor has this market expanded as hoped. In particular, the domestic retail market, RSL's most profitable sector, remains rather flat. Indeed, during the last several years of Papua New Guinea's general economic decline, this market has actually shrunk. Although RSL sells some raw sugar under a favorable quota to the United States, it does not have regular access to any other international markets, having been unsuccessful, for instance, at acquiring an EU preference. Its single area of increasing sales is to industrial customers, some of whom, primarily Coca-Cola, are hard bargainers concerning both price and quality. RSL has managed to clear itself of most of its debts, but it has been able to pay a dividend to stockholders only twice in its history. And its tariff protection has declined from full monopoly to 70 percent in 2001, slated to be reduced to 40 percent by 2005. Nonetheless, RSL has made substantial progress in both training and localization. Indeed, when costs had to be reduced after the Ramu stunt outbreak, many expatriates were replaced by nationals with lower salaries and less generous benefit packages. In addition, many people have, in fact, received training, ranging from on-site computer courses to overseas Ph.D. programs.

· · ·

Significantly, the area of training and localization in which BTL has invested the most effort, or at least the most conspicuous effort, is in the human resources department, that is, in the *administrative* division officially responsible for carrying out the functions of training and localization. Only twice in its history has RSL, under BTL's direction, selected a Papua New Guinean to be head of a department, and each time the appointee was head of human resources. Both of these appointments were strategic. As one expatriate told us, they were both "politically correct" and the appointees, BTL was confident, were up to the job.

Joe Herman, the first appointee, left RSL in 1995, some four years before our first visit, yet his name came up frequently in conversation. Everyone considered him exceptional, and it is obvious that much was expected of him. Certainly Ed Robinson, who interviewed him in New York for a position with RSL, thought that because of his background he was "an ideal appointee." He was born in Papua New Guinea, educated in Australia and America, married to an American, and wished to return to help develop his country. His own life and its trajectory—his career—appeared exemplary. From a traditional village background, he acquired those very skills and aspirations that BTL sought to instill through its training and localization program at RSL.

Indeed, after only a few years at RSL, Herman appeared especially well suited for promotion to head of human resources. There, he could contribute directly to the career development of fellow Papua New Guineans, and thus to the development of his nation. Moreover, as a national (and the sole national) head of department, he could shape the process of training and localization to Papua New Guinean conditions. At the same time he could attest to BTL's own commitment to that process. Herman could implement Campbell's "commitment not only to profit but to people" in a way that accorded, in Robinson's words, with BTL's "talent for fitting sugar operations to their national contexts in such a way that local people benefited." However, Herman's tenure at RSL did not realize either Campbell's commitment or BTL's talent. Such was the turmoil when he was head that a new general manager was appointed to regain control. The human resources department was dissolved and its responsibilities reduced and reallocated to the finance department. Herman left shortly thereafter.

As we shall see, nationals and expatriates alike came to express a range of strongly held opinions about Herman. We want to make it clear at this point that the opinions we cite are merely opinions. Herman is an exceptional person and became the focus of many conflicting expectations and perspectives. It is these expectations and perspectives we wish to examine. Because we were not there at the time of Herman's tenure at RSL, we cannot regard any of these opinions as authoritative.

Herman's life, as he and others narrate it, prompted contesting commentaries about the creation and shape of RSL as a society, including those about who is responsible for what. These commentaries address such overlapping questions as who owes what to whom, whether to particular people or to RSL in general; how shall the fulfillment or nonfulfillment of obligations, and obligations of what sort, be understood at RSL; what does doing a good job, especially a good job as a manager, consist of? Thus, the issue is not simply a matter of how Papua New Guineans might replace expatriates in a BTL localization and training program (operating, to be sure, under circumstances of economic constraint). Rather, it is an issue of what kinds of Papua New Guineans—acting in what sorts of ways, with what efficacy and intent, with what formulation of obligations and interests—should replace what kinds of expatriates. Moreover, these concerns were, of course, being debated in the context of a recently independent Papua New Guinea, a Papua New Guinea interested in developing its "ur-product" into a modern commodity through a big development project. But they were also being debated in response to, and reaction against, the debates of others—including those Campbell engaged in—concerning sugar industries elsewhere. Hence, in the Joe Herman story, we see with clarity the bewildering range of considerations, including the range of possible responsibilities, that have influenced the RSL project.

The Joe Herman Story

In his unpublished autobiography, a memoir written for his children, Joe Herman tells a story that we find both remarkable and typical. It is remarkable in that his experiences were extreme variants of the experiences of those he was to train and manage at RSL. It is typical in that his life, like theirs, was characterized by many attempts to balance responsibilities, to synthesize the often contradictory interests and objectives of different groups. Indeed, Herman's own story is, in effect, a narrative of training and localization as conceived both by the new nation of Papua New Guinea and by RSL. We shall quote and paraphrase his account (with his permission) as well as comment on it.[7]

Joe Herman was born in the Highlands, in the village of Kepelyam in Enga Province. His life was unexceptional until his mother gave him a dollar bill (sometime during the mid-1960s). The bill came from his sister's husband as part of a compensation payment, just one of an ongoing series of exchanges known among Engans as the "te," the "constant juggling of debts and credits" (Herman n.d. 20) that constituted much of Engan social life. He took the dollar to school, wanting to show it off to his school friends even though there was nothing to spend the money on. But once there, he was induced by his teacher into giving him the money to play "laki," a card game.

> Out of fear and respect I handed over the money to [my teacher] who bet and gambled with several people. . . . Watching my money change hands many times . . . I was tempted to grab and run with it, but was so scared of [my teacher] that I just sat there blinking back my tears. At dusk, the inevitable happened. . . . [A] young man from [an enemy clan] won my money and walked away with a great sense of satisfaction, singing humiliating songs. . . . If it had not been for the recent pacifying influence of the Catholic mission, these insulting songs would have led to clan retaliation. (24)

Herman was afraid that his older brother would punish him for having wasted the money, and so he decided to leave his village for a government station some fifteen kilometers away. He had relatives living there who would take him in. He began attending school, feeling at first both lonely and underprepared, particularly because he spoke no English and students were prohibited from speaking their local languages on the school premises. But he eventually settled in, winning "consistently respectable test scores" (56). He also began to recognize that, with his village background, he was different from the "station children," who had never been exposed to the "cultural norms of their village contemporaries. They were thus growing up in a cultural vacuum and, at the same time, they comprehended little of the new values promoted relentlessly by the [Australian-controlled] administration" (68).

Subsequently, after admission to St. Paul's Lutheran High School (also in the Highlands), his life took a most unexpected turn, a turn that eventually "alienated [him] from Kepelyam" (77). After a year at St. Paul's, Herman was invited by his former elementary school teacher to visit Australia. Although his family was stunned by the invitation—in fact, his brother was initially opposed to the trip—they agreed to let him go. The trip helped him unravel "some of the mysteries" (88) surrounding the white world. In particular, he was amazed that many white Australians actually did the tedious work expatriates in Papua New Guinea had natives do.

Upon returning to Papua New Guinea, Herman visited his village and was asked two questions by his father:

> First he wanted to know how long I planned on spending with him. I responded that I had to return to school the next day. . . . [Then he wanted to know] whether I was aware how long I had been away from the family. I knew precisely how long I had been away and how much schooling I wanted to pursue. He tried convincing me [to return] to Kepelyam to start launching my own identity. He felt it important for me to start planting my trees, building a house and set[ting] my mark on his vast land. However, I was not sure whether I wanted to stop my education. My trip to Australia in fact had reinforced my desire to pursue it further. (92)

Herman returned to St. Paul's, where he became aware that many of his Australian teachers doubted the capacities of their students. He recounts that when Papua New Guinea gained independence from Australia, these teachers were "skeptical about us ever performing tasks efficiently and effectively" (109). Nonetheless, he continued to excel. As the winner of the National Lions Youth of the Year competition, he visited Australia again, this time as a representative from Papua New Guinea. Upon graduation, he was "awarded the certificate for being the most outstanding student in academic leadership, sports and extra curricular activities. . . . [He was] the deux [first-in-class] of the year and . . .

was one of the very few students offered a place at the UPNG [University of Papua New Guinea] the following year" (111).

But his life took another unexpected turn. The Hermans, American Lutheran missionaries, offered to adopt and educate him at the same Australian boarding school attended by their two biological children. But first they had to win the approval of Herman's Kepelyam family: "[My parents] asked whether I will return someday. I replied that I really did not know what the future held for me. . . . Beyond the gallant control of emotions . . . , [my parents] were deeply hurt by the prospect of losing me. Children were very important to Enga families. . . . I felt so torn between two equal yet opposing forces that I was not sure what I wanted" (112–13).

The adoption took place, with Herman acquiring his adoptive parents' surname. He then completed two years of schooling in Australia. Returning to Papua New Guinea in 1978, he entered UPNG, intending to study law. But another opportunity came his way: he was invited to attend a small Lutheran college in Nebraska. When he informed his Kepelyam family that he had decided to accept this invitation, they told him that they doubted they would live to see him alive again, but promised to meet him in heaven.

Herman enjoyed the United States. He spoke to many Lutheran congregations in Nebraska about mission work in Papua New Guinea. He traveled with a college friend to Guatemala. And he met Linda, his wife-to-be, a young Californian student at his college. Initially he worried about the cultural and racial differences between Linda and himself.

> Ideally I would have preferred others accepting our relationship on face value as [between] two human beings. . . . This was an unrealistic [aspiration] because many [in America] were bound to have their reservations about interracial relationship[s]. . . . [But] my main concerns were [whether] the American relatives would proudly display our children's photographs and [if they would] accept their genetic composition. (131)

Fortunately, after Linda accepted Herman's proposal of marriage, her parents "accepted the inevitable gracefully" (133).

Shortly after the wedding, Herman received the distressing news that his mother had died. He relied on his "inner strength to overcome the painful grief." If he had been home at Kepelyam, he said, he would have found himself engulfed by "an army of wailing and crying relatives" (137).

Although Herman was tempted to pursue a career in the United States upon graduating from college, he felt a moral obligation to "make a modest contribution towards the development of PNG" (140). In addition, he wanted his wife to have a glimpse of his upbringing. He therefore applied to various concerns in PNG, including RSL.

In 1983, after his interview with Ed Robinson in New York, Herman accepted an offer to become RSL's community relations officer. And eventually, in 1986, he was made head of the personnel and training department. In both positions he was "the social shock absorber and the interface between the employees' expectations and the benefits offered by the Company" (155).

Herman found the work difficult. One difficulty involved the company's housing policy. Free housing was essential to recruit a skilled workforce to such an isolated, rural area. However, the types of houses offered were used by RSL to control, motivate, and highlight status in the company's hierarchy. This made workers helpless and dependent on RSL and further eroded their ability to rely on themselves. Moreover, family members were prohibited from visiting employees for extended periods of time, a policy "in direct clash with the local culture and the very fabric of PNG society" (156). Thus, employee morale was often low.

Another problem involved a general increase in criminal activity throughout the country. The company had to manage "a national project and . . . deal with the social breakdown in law and order with no easy solutions in hand." Unfortunately, Herman found the responses of BTL managers to such problems to be "autocratic" (157). Dominated as it was by expatriates, the management was either culturally insensitive or blatantly condescending to the expectations of the workforce. This meant that problems were exacerbated and workers' discontent was magnified:

Many [expatriates] enjoyed an artificial power and status beyond that which they would enjoy in their home countries. . . . [Many] belittled . . . locals [for not performing] as well as they could. They identified dozens of reasons why locals were incompetent or incapable of holding down management positions. . . . [They had lived] most of their working lives overseas, particularly in third world countries, and operated with the false sense that they could do just about anything without any [repercussions]. Some of the expatriates displayed some of the most admirable characteristics, yet equally many displayed cultural and racial arrogance. Although the expatriate staff represented less than 1% of the total work force, they [were responsible for] about

80% of the employees' grievances and morale problems. When it came to apportioning blame, however, [they usually did so to] someone further down the organizational hierarchy. . . . [But as] soon as local staff were appointed to managerial positions, they behaved [like] their expatriate counterparts, enjoying [being at] the helm of economic power while alienating themselves from social interactions with grassroots people. To the new elites, success meant playing golf, drinking at the exclusive bar and giving orders at the workplace. They used their position to maintain their position and effectively [enacted] the changes impose[d] by the [whites]. (159)

In addition, Herman faced problems with the Ramu Sugar National Employees Union, which on several occasions petitioned both BTL management and the Papua New Guinean government for his removal, once on the grounds that he was an American and therefore an illegal alien. Nonetheless, Herman tried to implement "a more balanced approach whereby the Company and the employees could work together as a team to share the Company's ultimate success." He tried pushing the employees toward "self-reliance, only to be accused of being an agent of expatriates" (162).

However, with immense efforts, the Company gradually gained respect from the work force. The vast majority of them began to view Ramu as their home, [not just a place where they would remain temporarily until returning permanently to their villages]. . . . They were better off with the social and community infrastructures we developed, including the biggest community school in the province, transportation and communication systems, a police station, health facilities, a vocational school, fresh food market, service station, and correspondence courses, and training facilities. . . . [W]ith my modest input, Ramu evolved into a self-sustaining community of over twelve thousand in what was the remotest part of PNG. (162)

Certainly, the company did more for the people of the area than the public servants whose job it was to work for the welfare of the country and to be "instrument[s] of development" (163). These public servants were lazy and corrupt, a fact that Herman attributed to the colonial government's creation of "a generation of beggars" who had moved "away from the self-reliant life" Papua New Guineans had "lived for centuries" (164).

Although Herman felt he was doing a very good job as "the social conscience of the Company, the custodian of good employment practice, the conduit for transplanting the strategic decisions of a distant board into local policies that embraced the trade union and others" (167), he and his wife eventually decided it was time to leave. They had the education of their children to think about, and would either have to put them in boarding school or leave Ramu. After thirteen years at RSL, Herman decided to return to the United States.

• • •

We have greatly abbreviated Herman's story, largely by eliminating some rich description of his engagements with people at home in Kepelyam. (His manuscript is 182 pages long.) However, the dimensions of contrast, and of synthesis, that we present pervade his entire account.

Herman sees his life as a journey from his mountain home across a range of social divides—of race, culture, and hierarchy. In a symbolically appropriate but noncoincidental manner, he is launched on his journey by the passage of a dollar bill both into and out of a social economy of often competitive reciprocity (see Meggitt 1972, 1974; Feil 1984). In many ways, like the dollar itself, Herman becomes a universal currency, a universal solvent: He can be embedded in, yet transcend, any particular social context—whether at his village, at school in Australia and America, or at RSL.[8] He can bridge and balance the interests of whites and blacks, villagers and urban or station dwellers, managers and workers, expatriates and Papua New Guineans. At RSL, in particular, he can become a shock absorber and an interface, able to mediate the objectives of all stakeholders in a complex social context. In a way that echoes BTL's commitment to Campbell's "sensible, pleasant, civilized society," Herman concludes his account of RSL: "After an emotional farewell to the employees and their families [with whom] we had worked side by side to develop a national project from its infant stage to . . . a respectable phase, we moved on to an uncharted destination" (179).

However, the more than fifty other accounts of Herman's time at RSL we heard—and people talked of him often—suggest that BTL's hope that he might effect a stable synthesis of RSL's disparate peoples and groups was never realized. Rather, during Herman's time at RSL, it became evident that fusion could also cause fracture, that compromise could also cause contradiction, that multiple facets could also cause multiple shards.

Below, we quote and paraphrase the range of comments differently located people made about Herman's years at RSL. Some statements were elicited by our questions, but many were volunteered. Again, we stress that our interest in providing this selection is not to get at any simple version of the truth, but rather to convey a portrait of a complex man and a somewhat turbulent time.

A Papua New Guinean manager said: "Joe couldn't work with the new general manager. But he built up a very strong political base in the ten years he was in the job. It was a mess. There was a real criminal element at work and a loss of discipline, trust, and respect. The problem was that Joe appointed all of his wantoks to managers and supervisors—and they had no discipline. There were bribes given and received. And there was a loss of standards and a general ethical breakdown, even criminal activities. Managers were sleeping with the wives of other employees. There were robberies. There were threats of violence. So a new general manager was brought in—an Australian—who was a real tough cookie. But he had a hard time: the managers had people break into his house and hold up his wife at night. And the internal security force was corrupt too. Eventually, to fix things, the company decided to dissolve the human resources department. It was the only way. And many senior managers—Joe's wantoks—were fired as well."

Yet the same manager painted a different picture on another occasion: "Joe got on well and easily with the expats—after all he had an American upbringing—but neglected his connections with nationals. Also, he had a very accelerated promotion within human resources, so he didn't know people at all levels and didn't encourage people lower down the hierarchy. He was being cultivated as the first national general manager. As head of human resources, he brought in a group of very capable national managers, including people in security, but was unable to control them. Also, the expatriate population was drastically shrinking, and so this base was lost for him. This was during an era when the expats insisted on people doing as they were told, so Joe spent his time pleasing them—as they expected him to do. I told him that this would be a mistake which would come back to haunt him. He was alienating the power base of nationals that he would eventually need. Also, with the new general manager, Joe didn't have a very sympathetic boss. Joe found himself in a no-win situation."

Another manager, also Papua New Guinean, commented simply: "Joe Herman was my best friend. I recently got a Christmas card from him which said that the children are well. He understood Papua New

Guineans since he was from here. He was approachable. In fact, he would drop by after work and play rugby on weekends. He would go out with the people. And thus if you knew that a stand-down or a strike was going to occur, you might tell Joe it was going to happen before it did. You would never tell an expatriate. Training has pretty much stopped since he left."

A third national manager weighed both views: "Joe was fired because the general manager hated him. However, Joe also had a hard time defining boundaries with his wantoks. Joe had too many friends and made *some* decisions in response to friendships. But, when he left, there was a big vacuum. There was no one to make personnel decisions. You had to arrange your own training, among other things. Joe left a hole from which the company has still not completely recovered."

Still another Papua New Guinean manager said: "In Joe Herman's day, the Supervisors Club used to be active, as well as the Staff Club [which was to say, not just the Management Club, as came to be the case]. There used to be music and dancing going on all night long during the entire weekend from six to six—with Joe there. For some of us it was a great relief when these stopped because they were so noisy."

A BTL expatriate reflected: "Many think that it's likely that Joe changed when his wife returned to the United States with the children before him [something not mentioned in Herman's autobiography]. Many think that Joe's wantoks were involved with various crimes and that there was some tribalism going on. However, people who knew Joe very well just can't believe he himself was involved. I liked Joe. He was very Westernized: he was recruited from America and interviewed in New York. A problem may have been that his head was above the parapet and attracted a lot of fire."

Two other expatriates, interviewed together, were less complimentary: "Joe was difficult. He was sometimes arbitrary. It reached a point where if he didn't leave, I would. There was, as well, a scam at 'Stores' in which it was rumored that some of Joe's wantoks were involved. Paperwork was rigged so that the company paid out more than it should have and the wantoks got this extra payout. This was a time of trouble."

A more recently arrived BTL expatriate gave his take: "Although Joe was before my time, I have heard some things. He was very well educated. Indeed, whenever I come across files that he wrote, I'm impressed with how very well written they are. This is what I think happened. Joe was well trained and very capable and came here with his American wife. At a certain point, she and the kids returned to the United States for schooling and he was left somewhat isolated here. At that point, he came under the influence of other Engans and got caught up in obligations to them that affected the way he was doing his job. At this same time, the Ramu security system [which was controlled by the human resources department] grew unreliable. Some security guards become enmeshed in crime and [were] compromised. Moreover, the company was concluding that the corporate structure needed reworking because it was top-heavy with a layer of national managers who weren't really necessary. These were fired and [human resources] was reorganized such that Joe was let go. And then there were paybacks after Joe left, including the holding of the GM's wife at knife point."

Another BTL expatriate observed: "Nothing has gone on with training since the human resources department was dismantled, and dismantling was the only way the company could get rid of Joe Herman. But Joe got a raw deal. He was definitely not a criminal. What's clear is that nationals like Joe need a power base. Joe was walking a thin line between his Papua New Guinean and his American identities. We expats can't possibly know about the political currents that affect the lives of people like Joe."

A Papua New Guinean supervisor told us: "I really liked Joe. Although he was accused by some of inconsistency, I think he just had less of an English management style. I've heard that he intends to come back to PNG and contest the parliamentary seat from Wabag [the capital of Enga Province]. He only left because of his family: his wife and kids went back to America when they got old enough for schooling to be an issue. He was highly respected. He didn't just fire people. He sat down and interpreted what was wrong."

A second supervisor, a national, said: "There was controversy. But there wasn't serious crime. Joe just had a Highlands mentality. He wanted things done right away and his way. He was a nice guy."

A Papua New Guinean worker asserted: "I count Joe Herman as one of my family friends. We played rugby together. Joe would insist that, during working time, people must work; but, afterwards, he would drink beer and mix with people on a very informal basis."

An expatriate member of the RSL board of directors commented: "I could see that the problem with Joe was coming. All of a sudden, I looked around and everybody was a Wabag. There was a Wabag jam. It was practically a closed Wabag shop. Everybody who has ever employed labor in masses in Papua New Guinea knows that you can't just employ your wantoks. Sometimes you can't discipline your wantoks. And sometimes, if you do, they will get rid of you for being too strong."

· · ·

Everyone who spoke to us about Herman was addressing—indeed, debating—several intersecting and far-from-dead questions. What had happened to cause Herman to leave RSL? What, if anything, had interfered with Herman's "moving line," his "intended course of action," to refer back to Dorothy Lee's language? According to Herman, it was his nuclear family and the future prospects of his children that pulled him away into the new challenges of an uncharted destination. According to most other accounts, it was assumed that something had gone wrong with his career at RSL.

Significantly, such statements of what had gone wrong for Herman at RSL are also at least implied statements of what it would have taken for things to have gone right for him. Hence, these appraisals about Herman are appraisals of RSL, of what kind of society it is and what kind of society it can become. As such, they are also appraisals of how BTL has succeeded with training and localization in Papua New Guinea.

Virtually all of these appraisals ultimately concern what sorts of Papua New Guineans should replace what sorts of expatriates in a developing Papua New Guinea. Focusing on the ongoing and touchy issue of training and localization, our respondents are pondering Herman's career and its RSL contexts: How should what happened to Herman, not only the first Papua New Guinean department head at RSL, but the department head in charge of training and localization, be understood? Was he a Papua New Guinean of the right kind? Did he have the right sort of standards and objectives? Was he effective? Whose interests did he uphold? What obligations did he accept? The portrait of Herman that emerges from these stories—with his undoubted capacities and complex purposes, his deep loyalties and contradictory objectives—is instructive.

The Herman described here was (1) too much a Papua New Guinean *and* too much an expatriate *and* too much a Wabag; (2) attuned to Papua New Guinean workers *and* inattentive to Papua New Guinean workers; (3) a best friend who could be counted on for support *and* a difficult boss who sometimes used power arbitrarily; (4) manipulated into an impossible position *and* too trusting of unreliable wantoks; (5) a family man *and* a party guy; (6) able to balance the formality of work relationships with the informality of recreational relationships *and* likely to let friendships influence his decisions.

It would be wrong to assume, however, that Herman was, in fact, either a good friend or too much or too little a Papua New Guinean. Rather, we think it likely that much of what Herman did was evaluated selectively. Herman was expected to be all of these things, some of the time. Indeed, we think that virtually all national managers at RSL are, or are expected to be, all of these things, some of the time. The range and shifting nature of the contexts within which Herman operated are inherent in life for nationals at RSL: it is a multiethnic, hierarchical, agroindustrial complex; it is one in which work and workplace are not clearly separated from leisure and residence; it is one from which, upon retirement, everyone eventually has to leave.

Thus, as we saw earlier, all national employees are, and know they are, periodically impelled to act too much like Papua New Guineans in order to maintain the wantok relationships necessary for their well-being after they depart RSL. They also know that they are subject to criticism by BTL expatriates and others for such relationships. Correspondingly, Papua New Guineans frequently note in their turn that all BTL expatriates are periodically impelled to act too much like expatriates (or is it too much like Papua New Guineans?) in order to maintain the wantok-like relationships with other expatriates necessary for their well-being upon leaving RSL. These relationships might be important if they are looking ahead to consultancies after retirement.

National managers also are, and know they are, periodically impelled to act too much like expatriate managers—to be too little committed, too inattentive, to wantoks: in order to justify, and of course to savor, the privileges they have earned, they sometimes let hierarchically based class interests overcome ethnic interests. In fact, at RSL, giving orders at the workplace means not only assignment to a particular house in the exclusive Management Compound, but also the enjoyment of other perks, for instance, the facilities at the Management Club. Recall that Herman himself castigated the new elites for their lack of grassroots connections.

Correspondingly, some expatriate managers are, some of the time, more attentive than national managers to the interests of Papua New Guinean workers. Indeed, whereas most of the expatriates distance themselves from a past of caste-based prerogatives, like those so infuriating to Yali, many of the national managers embrace a future of class-based opportunities for them and their children—a future of modernist well-being evoked by a ubiquitous Ramu Sugar advertisement (fig. 14).[9] For instance, at a meeting during 2000 of the members of the Management Club, there was discussion of whether nonmanagerial golfers, whose numbers were growing, might use any club facilities. This subject came up because the golf course is directly adjacent to the clubhouse—with its swimming pool, pool table, bar, and toilets. The expatriates saw nothing wrong with nonmanagerial golfers, all official members of the Golf Club,

Put some Ramu in it...

RAMU SUGAR *"Natural as Life"*

Figure 14. An advertisement for Ramu Sugar

occasionally using these facilities, arguing, "Let's all live together." In a rejoinder, unanticipated by most expatriates, many of the national managers insisted that the Management Club facilities be kept exclusive: they felt that nonmanagerial golfers should be categorically prohibited from using any of the club facilities, except for the toilets—and these only until the Golf Club had built its own separate toilets, outside of the fence enclosing the Management Club premises.[10]

Moreover, it is common knowledge that these national managers are in competition with each other for career advancement. Aside from blaming BTL for reserving certain positions for expatriates, they have to deal with each other's relative successes or failures. As with Joe Herman's career, these perceived advances and setbacks can be variously understood. Training opportunities and promotions can be interpreted as the product of the hard-won respect of bosses and colleagues, or of the favoritism of cronies or wantoks; they can be the product of meeting the professional standards of BTL and other expatriates, or of the successful catering to these expatriates. On the other hand, national managers, whose careers have lost trajectory, can gratefully duck certain professional responsibilities, avoiding Herman's predicament: if their heads are below the parapet, they won't attract fire. And, at the same time, they might ally themselves with the expatriates to ensure that the hierarchy they all enjoy is maintained, at least in its general parameters, if not in preventing certain golfers from using the toilet.

Finally, as an added complexity, all national managers know about and have to come to terms with certain at least implied expatriate criticisms: that Papua New Guineans are too tribal and too wantok-oriented to hold top jobs; that they do not actually want to advance in their careers because they are afraid to stand out unduly; and that national managers simply stop working hard once they get the promotion into the Management Compound.

As these examples illustrate and as Herman's case attests, national managers at RSL deal with many shifting considerations. How they should act, what they should seek to accomplish, what obligations, interests, and standards they should accept and pursue—all lead to decisions that will be praised by some and criticized by others. Correspondingly, RSL's political atmosphere is charged: it is one in which people are often, and sometimes simultaneously, facilitated and thwarted, chuffed and aggrieved, vindicated and vulnerable. Nationals continually juggle their obligations and interests.[11] Sometimes they are able to balance a few elements, at least for a while. For instance, one national manager balances obligation to kin with obligation to the company by hiring a number of his kinsmen and then firing those who are chronically late to work. However, for every balance achieved, other offsetting complications likely remain or emerge. Thus a delicate balance between kinship and company may be upset by complexities of national origin and class. For example, because the wantoks this national manager hires are (nonmanagerial) workers, he excludes them from his high-status house; although this decision is alienating to them, to welcome them would alienate him from other managers—both nationals and expatriates. And, of course, some of these other national managers he regards as having been either appropriately or inappropriately promoted, fairly or unfairly passed over, mirroring their shifting views of him.

As Herman's case suggests, any balance between conflicting interests and obligations is difficult to achieve and is itself frequently in conflict with other balances. And this means that virtually all national managers are often delinquent, off-balance: they are susceptible to criticism, if not attack, and uncertain about how to proceed. Partly for these reasons, and partly because work and nonwork lives at RSL are so tightly linked, gossip—much of it about hypocrisy, favoritism, wantokism, double standards, and currying favor—is rampant.[12] However, since balances sometimes can be achieved, at least temporarily, virtually all the national managers are sometimes virtuous and assured: deserving of reward, they rest, for the moment, content.

At least at the present time, there seems to be overall a mutual muddling along among the different types and ranks of those employed at RSL, an oscillation between an assortment of obligations and interests. The resulting life at RSL for most of these managers is by no means a bad one, and it is certainly an interesting one. It is, perhaps, the Papua New Guinean expression of Jock Campbell's "sensible, pleasant, civilized" life.

With Herman, at least in retrospect, instead of mutual muddling, there was divisive disarray. In the perception of many people (national managers, expatriates, supervisors, and workers), he had gotten the balances wrong. Many, though far from all, thought that (1) in seeking to effect a compromise between obligations to the company and to wantoks, he was contradicting the fundamental values of each; (2) in seeking to fuse Papua New Guinean values and Western ones, he was himself fractured—and was fracturing others—into stark oppositions; and (3) in seeking to exemplify and create a multifaceted identity for those at RSL, he was bringing into acute relief the existence of multiple, and sometimes sharply discordant, worlds and obligations. Of these difficult-to-negotiate balances, Herman's greatest problem (in the view of most, but not all) was to find the appropriate level of obligation to wantoks. Perhaps because of his long absence from Papua New Guinea, Herman may have seemed too concerned with fulfilling his kinship responsibilities. It was one thing to hire a few wantoks in subordinate positions. But if he had hired many in senior positions, he would have shifted the system in a way that compromised all other balances.

But, since Herman's dilemmas remained those of all national managers, his difficulties can be understood as potentially those of all as well. And, comparably, his controversial position at RSL should certainly be seen as a result of his situation rather than his character.

· · ·

As Dorothy Lee suggests, careers can be understood as following a narrative form, as having a particular storyline with appropriate protagonists. Protagonists should see their lives as having a certain trajectory, one of concerted occupational pursuit. Protagonists should be relatively undistracted by considerations that would deflect them from that pursuit. They are owners of their labor, selling or withholding it as they choose, according to their own appraisal of occupational opportunity. To act effectively upon such appraisals, they must be largely self-interested and self-focused individuals. Relatively unencumbered by social entailments, their primary kin ties are likely focused on their nuclear families. And such minimal social units can, and will, readily leave any particular place to pursue economic advantage and career development, largely measured in terms of economic remuneration. They may even go to Papua New Guinea to run a sugar plantation. This storyline will, of course, be most plausible among the elite, or protoelite, in certain socioeconomic contexts—especially capitalism, centered as it is on a market-based economy (see LiPuma 2000: 128–52.) In other words, we see such careers, such individuals and their pursuits of economic maximization, not as some essential manifestation of human nature; rather, we see them as the product of human culture and history, as the product of certain views of the desirable and the feasible.

Several things must be said about this narrative of the largely unimpeded and unencumbered pursuit of self-interest as it relates to the lives of RSL national managers embarked on careers within the BTL training and localization program. As we have shown, national managers need to juxtapose, contextualize, and balance different interests and obligations: to themselves, to their immediate families, to the company, and to their kin. Their capacity to do so becomes a significant measure of their effectiveness, of their will and capacity to succeed. Therefore, the narrative of a career pursued in a single-minded way will be, for them, a story of partiality and incompletion. It will be a story of effectiveness curtailed rather than fulfilled. This is not to say that RSL national managers lack ambition or are cheerful if their careers appear thwarted—if they are "blocked," "passed-over," or "side-stepped." It is to say, however, that for them, the idea of a career trajectory is tempered by the need to balance sets of interests and obligations. Thus, careers, as Lee defines them, are less important and as a consequence are more likely to be compromised.

Though RSL is indeed in many ways "a sensible, pleasant, civilized society," the compromises and adjustments that make it so are somewhat different, somewhat more extensive, than those Jock Campbell had in mind. The balance he sought was formulated according to circumstances in which both individuals and companies were focused on maximizing economic self-interest under market conditions. Campbell sought a voluntary tempering of this self-interest or, perhaps more accurately, an expanded definition of self-interest: he had in mind an individual who believes that it is good business to recognize and balance responsibilities to shareholders, employees, customers, and community. BTL's job—its business—has been to adapt Campbell's vision of private enterprise and public morality to the situation in Papua New Guinea (and other places) and to do so in such a way as to implement his view of prosperity. Prosperity ultimately rests, Campbell believed, "in the hands, and hearts and heads of businessmen." The problem for BTL becomes, then, to formulate business—which, though moral, is still business as fundamentally defined by businessmen—in a way susceptible to "general understanding and respect" within Papua New Guinea. For prosperity to come to Papua New Guinea, BTL would have to replace expatriates—enlightened, though business-oriented—with Papua New Guineans. But, as Herman's story attests, BTL has found it easier to have Papua New Guineans replace expatriates than to have Papua New Guineans become like British managers: simply put, because Herman and other RSL managers do not readily accept the career storyline as Lee describes it, they also do not accept a British-style, market-generated, bottom line—its vision of the skills and focus necessary to do even enlightened business.

BTL's bottom line, its "bottom-line-ness," rests on the primacy of the narrative of career within the context of a market-based economy. But a bottom line need not only be about efficiencies that maximize profit in a strictly economic sense. There may be a range of views about what constitutes the bottom line. Thus, the bottom line may be as much about the point of doing business at all as about the necessary conditions of doing business. And for many national employees at RSL, we would venture, the point of doing business includes a certain character and quality of life that may be deemed inefficient: their bottom line would be a capacity to juggle, if not meet, a range of obligations and interests—from Hayes's to Gagas's, so to speak.[13] Without this character and quality of life, these managers may well find an insufficient point in doing either business or having a career.

BTL would respond, undoubtedly, that unless a certain bottom line is accepted, RSL managers are likely to have neither business or career for very long, strapped as the company is to make ends meet. Indeed, BTL's and Jock Campbell's vision of the bottom line would be challenged (as we shall see in chapter 9) by other contemporary visions of the nonnegotiable—those of the World Bank, the World Trade Organization, and of RSL's major client, Coca-Cola.[14]

7

On Landowners, Outgrowers—and Just a Little Respect

AS A BIG PROJECT, RSL is designed to benefit more than those brought to work for the company. It is, as well, to continue the program of local development in the Upper Ramu Valley begun by the patrol officers, those seeking to replace the irrational (sometimes Yali-inspired) cargo dreams and lassitude of local people with a commitment to a rational work ethic. Thus, the agreement between the Papua New Guinean government and RSL requires a program not only of training and localization for those working at RSL, but also one of economic opportunity for those living near RSL. Specifically, the "Master Agreement" states that the company shall "encourage the development of a smallholder area by interested customary landowners. . . . [W]here required and at the cost of the said landowners, [RSL] shall provide all necessary technical advice and supply necessary mechanical services for the Smallholder Scheme" (Papua New Guinea and Ramu Sugar Limited 1979: 22).

The smallholder scheme, or the "Outgrowers Program," that RSL implemented encourages the Mari, whose land borders RSL's holdings, to use their labor and their land to grow cane for sale to the company. The price is determined by formula and subject to periodic review by the Department of Primary Industry. RSL freely provides technical advice and encourages locals to participate as fully as possible in crop production. In this way, outgrowers can maximize their incomes by minimizing the charges RSL levies for the inputs it finds necessary to provide. Some of these charges are difficult for outgrowers to avoid—for fertilizers, pesticides, herbicides, mechanical planting, harvesting, and transportation of cane to the factory, for example (fig. 15). However, as far as weeding and other aspects of cultivation are concerned, outgrower labor can at least in theory minimize RSL inputs and subsequent charges. Eventually, Mari villagers from relatively close-by Bumbu, Sankian, and Bopirumpun put some two thousand hectares of their land into cane, supplementing the roughly seven thousand hectares grown on RSL's own estate. Unfortunately, Mari villagers from the more remote Mushuan are unable to participate—their land lies on the other side of the Ramu River and cannot be reached by agricultural machinery.

The Mari land given over to cane was further "BUMBU-ized" by RSL: it was mapped and divided into the same straight-sided, agriculturally efficient fields as on the RSL estate proper. (Straight-sided fields maximize the length of cane rows and, hence, the efficiency with which the cane can be mechanically planted, cultivated, and harvested.) Initially, these fields were clan owned, and the Mari were left to work out for themselves how the income from them would be distributed within the clan. Soon, however, disagreements about this distribution led most of these clans to allocate particular fields to family groups. These allocations, in turn, were sometimes further divided, with individual fields given to adult sons, or

Figure 15. Charges for mechanical harvesting can be a burden for outgrowers.

to more peripheral relatives, or, in a few cases, to individuals simply deemed deserving. The division of land was generally amicable, with disputes never (as far as we know) becoming bitter to the point of causing a breach.

In its dealings with the Mari outgrowers, BTL has attempted to adapt practices it uses in Africa. In fact, these practices are widely regarded as both economically successful and socially enlightened. Thus, in *Hungry for Profit* (Richter 1985), the film that first brought BTL to our attention, BTL is praised for balancing private enterprise with public morality. This is particularly so, according to the film, with the sugar company BTL manages in Mumias, Kenya. There, rather than alienating people from their land as is usual in agribusiness, BTL created a smallholders program that carefully balances cane cash-cropping with subsistence agriculture. A Harvard Business School study generally agrees that BTL's practices are working well:[1]

> The Outgrowers scheme has been extremely successful and, although copied elsewhere, had been revolutionary in the sugar industry when it was developed. . . . Locally, both the Mumias Sugar Company and the people in the township contributed toward building local schools, medical facilities, and roads, significantly improving the standard of living in the area. . . . Booker attributed this success to effective management of agriculture and factory operations, to strong training and development programs, and to a positive work attitude and working relationship with the Kenyan people. Booker had succeeded in developing pride and commitment toward the Mumias operation. (Shaner 1989: 6–8)

Yet, however successful BTL's outgrower arrangement at Mumias is, the Mumias model does not seem to be operating very well at RSL. In fact, BTL finds the Mari outgrowers troubling. Unlike the Kenyans at Mumias, the RSL outgrowers do not seem to have a "positive work attitude." They are apparently unwilling to invest the effort—to maximize the input—necessary to enhance their cash income. Indeed, one BTL executive told us in 2001 that BTL regards the RSL Outgrowers Program as something of a failure: the farmers refuse to farm, preferring instead to sit back and let the company do most, if not all, of the work. Another BTL employee, an agricultural economist who was sent out from the BTL home office during 2000 to consult concerning outgrower "malaise," explained matters to us this way:

The farmers are spoon fed and pretty reluctant to take any responsibility. Historically, they aren't really farmers. They are more accustomed
to sitting under coconut trees and complaining when things go wrong.
Indeed, they are among the most unmotivated farmers I know, simply
refusing to get involved in husbandry. It is true that they only get about
25 percent of the proceeds, but they do not put any of their own
resources [except land] into earning the proceeds, and they take little
risk. . . . Really, the system here is more like leasing than farming,
which is too bad.

Some at BTL are thus troubled by the apparent lack of initiative, lack
of a work ethic, among RSL outgrowers. In fact, their perception of local
malaise seems to echo the perception of lassitude by a previous generation of expatriates. Not only are outgrowers doing nothing for themselves, they are insisting that things be done for them: not only are they
waiting for bounty to descend, they are complaining when the bounty is
less, or other, than they expect. (It is important to note that not all
BTL executives share this analysis. As we shall see later, economist
Dr. Martin Evans has concluded that the Mari response is entirely
rational, fully consistent with the maximization of their most abundant
resource, land.)

As we became more knowledgeable about the Mari, BTL sometimes
sought our anthropological expertise on the outgrowers. Why haven't
they developed? Where have all the millions of kina from the sale of their
cane gone? Why don't they spend their money more wisely? Why don't
they invest more effort in their land? Why do they always seem to want
more? What do they really want? What, most generally, has gone wrong
with the Outgrowers Program?[2]

As we discovered, central to answering these intersecting questions is the Mari insistence that they are not just outgrowers. They
are the traditional landowners and therefore must receive appropriate recognition and compensation. Being a landowner, especially
the owner of land that is valuable (whether the site of such cash-
generating enterprises as RSL or the mineral-rich Porgera area of the
Highlands), is not only to possess assets. It is also to have an inherent
and inherited status, a worth and efficacy. Events should—must—
reflect, confirm, and flow from such status. If they do not, then being
a landowner provides a legitimate (inherent and inherited) right to
shut things down: it is a particular Papua New Guinean kind of bottom line.

The Mari

Although we did not attempt a full ethnography of the Mari (learning only a bit of their Markham language), we did work with them frequently. We visited in one or another of their four villages at least several times a week: we took formal life-histories; conducted interviews, especially about how RSL affects their lives and how sugar money is spent; conversed about goals and aspirations; and attended church services and other ceremonies. In addition, we censused all four of the villages with the help of members of each and hired research assistants from Bumbu and Mushuan to help us. With their assistance, we explored (largely through surveys) the nutritional, educational, health, and social differences between those Mari just down the road from RSL and those living across the Ramu River from RSL. In other words, we explored the differences between those with sugar income and easy access to services and those without such income and access. We also trained as magistrates and then worked closely with several Mari on the Gusap Village Court (hearing cases brought by Mari against one another and against others in the broader community). And, finally, we traveled with leaders from all four villages to Rabaul as participants in a "study tour" designed to inspire the Mari with the example of the industrious and disciplined Tolai people.

In the course of all of this, we learned many things about "traditional" Mari life. Indeed, Mari are very interested in rehearsing to each other, as well as to us, the details of this life before contact or in the early days of contact with outsiders. By providing a wealth of ethnographic "fact," they seek to muster evidence (which, they hope, we will corroborate in our book) that they have lived for a very long time where they currently live: if their recollections are clear and detailed about their past life in this area, then they, the Mari, can be irrefutably confirmed as local landowners. In other words, they seek to rehearse and establish that they have an unimpeachable ancestral claim to the land—land that provides its occupants with considerable outgrower income.

They told us they once lived in small, named, clan-focused groups of four or five families that shifted in membership and in location within the vicinity. They resided in hamlets, primarily in the foothills bordering the Upper Ramu Valley, and gardened along the streams and rivers flowing into the Ramu River, which ran the length of the valley. The gardens that grew long-lived bananas, pandanus, bamboo, betel nut, mangoes, coconuts, and ginger as well as sweet potatoes, yams, and tapioca, could be revisited for many years. Of current importance to the villagers, stands from these long-abandoned gardens are still visible in the contemporary landscape and thus are "handmarks," clearly indicating and proving former Mari occupation. Mari groups also periodically hunted together on the valley floor. The men would descend from the foothills to burn the tall grass so as to flush out the wild pigs and small game.

Correspondingly, Mari practiced both gardening and hunting magic. The latter involved men preparing for the hunt by practicing sexual abstinence as well as by ritually conjoining the points of their spears within the socket of an ancient stone mace-head. The treasured mace-head, which was shown to us, also serves as a handmark. In addition, Mari told us that they had pierced the septums of young male initiates, that sometimes they had worn ancestral jawbones around their necks, and that they had practiced sorcery widely.

In addition, Mari told us about a complexity of relationships—of marriage, trade, and fighting—with neighboring groups. These other groups were (other) Markham-speakers residing in the foothills farther up the Ramu Valley, Kafe-speakers in the foothills across the valley, and Raikos-speakers (the Nahu and Rawa) in the foothills on the same side of the valley as the Mari.[3] We heard that when Mari married other Mari, sisters were usually exchanged; when Mari married non-Mari, bride price in large cowrie shells, dogs' teeth, and clay pots—items often acquired through trade—would be expected. Though Mari fought frequently with non-Mari and ate their enemies, occasionally treaties were arranged: young boys (and sometimes, others) might be exchanged between warring groups as go-betweens and guarantors of good faith.

This life, Mari agreed, was significantly transformed by the expansion of administrative control and Christian missions shortly after World War One. Life was further transformed during World War Two. The Japanese occupied the entire area and were displaced only after heavy fighting; the Allied forces had a major airbase at Gusap (some fifteen miles from the present township of Gusap) just up the valley. Both sides conscripted Papua New Guineans. The Mari, like others, sought refuge back in the hills.

By the time the fighting was over and the Australians had resumed control of the Trust Territory, the Mari were resident on the valley floor itself: certainly, the earliest patrols—those that effected the process of "BUMBU-ization" described earlier—found the Mari living more or less where they have remained. And this was the situation at the time district officer Parrish and patrol officer McNamara purchased the land from the

Mari, a fact to which the Mari often refer with pleasure when validating their rights to sugar money. But, as we shall see, they also refer to it with resentment when arguing that their ancestors were paid too little for land that became so valuable.

Although the Mari, and their Kafe and Raikos neighbors, all had relations of trade, marriage, and warfare with each other, and all used the valley floor periodically for hunting, none, we think, lived there permanently prior to contact with outsiders. Perhaps as a consequence, none of these groups can make a fully convincing claim, based on ancestral occupancy, that it "owns" in any exclusive way the valley floor. To be sure, the Mari can demonstrate that they lived on the valley floor at the time of the Parrish and McNamara patrol and the purchase. But how long they had been there is the subject of ongoing court disputes. The Kafe and, especially, the Raikos (the latter being the more active in pursuing the case in court) argue that not only did the Mari come down into the valley only recently, but also that they did so at the invitation and the pleasure of the "real" landowners.

Concerning this controversy, we must stress that we are in no position to determine the relative truth of such claims and counterclaims. We did not try to decide who, in fact, once owned (occupied) what territory and when. Although we spoke to people from all of the groups now claiming the valley, our primary focus was on the Mari because they are, de facto, the outgrowers. However, just because our account here is Mari-centric does not mean that we endorse one set of claims over another.[4]

• • •

Because the Mari were hoping our book would allow them to secure their land as well as attain adequate compensation, from the start many of our discussions seemed orchestrated to these objectives. In 1999, during our first week at RSL, Robin Wilson, the outgrowers' manager, sent word that the three of us would arrive at the various villages on a particular morning so that Mari might meet us and hear about our interest in writing a history of RSL and its effects on the valley. Although we had interesting conversations first at Sankian and then at Bumbu, it was at Bopirumpun that we learned the most. There we met Yalibu Mangai. He is elderly, lively, and opinionated and has strong convictions. He is also one of the wealthiest of the cane growers because, unlike other senior men, he has retained control over all of his clan's land. In addition, and of much importance, he was alive when the land was first sold to the government—young Mari erroneously think that he was one of the signatories to the sale. Finally, he is valued for his "traditional" knowledge. (He once bragged that he is the only Mari alive still to sing traditional Mari songs when drinking!) Indeed, he is regarded by Mari as their most authoritative spokesperson—a "meta-handmark" in that he is not only knowledgeable about the evidence from the past but is also, by virtue of his age, a direct link to that past.

When we arrived at Bopirumpun, Yalibu and about thirty others were waiting for us. One man began by welcoming us. He wanted our history to be placed in all government offices and become the official history of the area. After all, the Raikos and Kafe peoples were challenging the Mari rights to land—and with our history, their challenges would be squashed. So it was good we had come. Moreover, though once a warring people, the Mari now knew how to welcome others. They were Christians who liked others, not just themselves.

Yalibu spoke next. He apologized that he and the other Mari hadn't had time to dress properly (traditionally) so as to enact their history for us. He wanted us to learn more than mere words: we had to see the history embodied. We had to come back soon so that he could show us the full story. But for now we must photograph him together with a particularly important handmark (fig. 16). Then, unwrapping a decorated human jawbone, he suspended it from his neck. It was, he explained, the jawbone of his grandfather, Saliwi, who had been killed and eaten by those (other Markham-speakers) from Watarais, the next group up the valley. His ancestors were able to recover the jawbone in a reprisal raid. Thus it should be clear that Yalibu wasn't merely searching around for stories. The stories and their handmarks came to him straight through his ancestral line, from grandfather, to father, to him.

In other words, this jawbone (as with handmarks generally) is material evidence of where ancestors lived. The jawbone establishes a direct tie between the present and the precontact era (the time of Yalibu's grandfather and of cannibalism). Moreover, this jawbone can place the Mari ancestors geographically as immediate neighbors of Watarais ancestors (those they undoubtedly would have fought). The Watarais ancestors can be assumed to have lived where their descendants now live—immediately up the valley from the Mari. (Because contemporary Watarais people are not directly engaged in the ongoing controversy between the Mari, the Kafe, and the Raikos, no one disputes that they are currently living on their ancestral land.) Therefore, contemporary Mari are living where ancestral Mari lived (with Watarais people as their neighbors all along) and are not relative newcomers to the area.

Figure 16.
Yalibu with a
particularly
important
handmark

We were to talk a number of times with Yalibu. In fact, he was eager that we return so that he could give us several key documents that his son would copy for us. These, we found, included a history of Bopirumpun and of the Mari more generally, as well as a history of Yalibu's own Bantik clan. The more general history contains lists (in Pidgin English) of significant events: "During 1942, Mr. Norton, a British Colonel, arrived at Kaigulan [a traditional name of Mushuan] and designated several spokesmen. For Bopirumpun, he designated Mr. Yambuangk of the Bantik Clan and Mr. Paias of the Sangang Clan, the former as Luluai and the latter as Tultul." (Luluais and Tultuls were, respectively, government-appointed village headmen and assistant headmen.) The more specific history of the Bantik clan also contains lists: twenty-six "clan leaders," forty-nine named territories located in the valley, seventy-five named territories located in the mountains, and six major handmarks (all groves of trees or other plantings—with the proviso that they "have many more"). As part of the more specific histories, there are stories, often handmark-focused, which fill in the details linking persons to places.

Most Mari clans, we soon discovered, have compiled similar histories, both general and specific, and they are sharing them with each other as part of a project to construct an overall Mari history. This project is coordinated by Saking Kiruak, a Mari from Mushuan. Forceful, articulate, and one of few Mari who completed grade 10 and speaks English, he often acts as the spokesman for Mari when they present evidence in court to prove that they are the true owners of the land they currently occupy.

We gained a sense of what was necessary for such a court case as we examined documents Yalibu and other Mari clan elders pressed upon us and as we talked with these elders and other Mari. We were also informed by the more guarded conversations with representatives from both the Raikos and Kafe. They sought us out on several occasions in order to probe our commitment to the Mari cause. At the same time, they hoped to convince us that they are the true landowners without revealing strategic details that we might pass on to the Mari. In addition, we had access to material in a large and ever-growing file kept by the RSL general manager on traditional land ownership. This file consists of letters and other documents submitted by claimants (and their lawyers) to compel RSL to recognize the rights of one group or another. From all of these sources, we learned much about the ways that the Mari and contesting others are rendering their rival histories so as best to make their particular claims.

In making their case as the traditional landowners, local people have to produce cultural detail that will make their account convincing not only to them and others like them, such as neighbors and rivals, but also to a Papua New Guinean land magistrate. Clearly, a magistrate will not be readily convinced of the self-evident truth of parochial knowledge. Both by reasons of his neutrality (as removed from the village lives of the litigants) and by circumstances of his education (as removed from the village lives of those of his own culture), the significance of cultural specifics may not be immediately apparent to him. These specifics will have to be translatable; they will have to fit a magistrate's general understanding of what traditional people in particular regions actually believe. Beyond that, detailed cultural knowledge will have to be shown to be linked to the "objective" evidence of the material world: it will have to correspond to and be verified by the handmarks.[5] Thus, land claims based on tradition are, in part, shaped by influences similar to those that form local identity at RSL. As we discussed, Highlanders, Coastals, Sepiks, and New Guinea Islanders at RSL craft their particular customs to fit a generalized pattern of regional tradition so that these customs will be credible to members of other groups they work and reside with. Likewise, local people shape the knowledge on which ancestral claims are based to fit a generalized pattern so that this knowledge will be credible to outside adjudicators.[6]

Below is a story, offered to us for inclusion in our official history, that the Mari may well use in court as proof of their long-term occupancy of the region. It was told to us by several senior men, with details added by others along the way, at a large, multigenerational public gathering at Mushuan. As the story was recounted, with its wealth of circumstantial detail (some of which we only allude to here), it was collectively rehearsed and absorbed. And it was performed and brought to life in a way that was visibly compelling to both the audience and the tellers.

Many generations ago, ancestors of the Sasaiya and Birua clans joined together to initiate young men in a [named] men's house at a [named] location. This men's house was near a grove of betel-nut trees [some still alive]. Initiation involved piercing the septums of the initiates [a once characteristic Mari tradition]. On this occasion, Sararginu, a female spirit [married to Irang, a male spirit], heard the [still remembered] ancestral songs of the initiators. She went to the men's house and said: "You have no pigs. You should have asked me for some. What time will you release the boys? Give me some tobacco." Santu, one of the initiators, answered her questions and gave her the tobacco.

Returning to her [named] house—a boulder [still existing]—she and her husband began preparing for the release of the initiates. They readied a huge bundle of tobacco—the size of a forty-four-gallon drum—and a horse-sized pig named Kwasing. In addition, they gathered coconuts [from a still remaining grove] and yams as big as posts. Finally, they assembled bamboo flutes, to be played in celebration of the initiates, and ancestral salt, to be used in cleansing the initiates' newly pierced septums. When all of this was ready, they carried it to the men's house with the help of their two [named] daughters, who were to marry two of the initiates. Once there, they cooked the pork and other food. This food proved inexhaustible.

The celebration finished, Sararginu gave the jaw of the pig to Santu, telling him to keep it in memory of her. Several of the tusks remain, together with some of the ancestral salt and one of the flutes.

Unfortunately, the last of the tobacco was consumed a few years ago by an old man hungry for a smoke. The pig's tusks are still used in garden magic. And the descendants of the two daughters remain in the village on their ancestral land. Moreover, Santu's now elderly granddaughter is still alive and would sometimes place one of the tusks through her pierced septum [as she did for us].

This story fits well the criteria Mari, their rivals, and other Papua New Guineans are developing in formulating claims based on tradition and ancestral precedent. The story can be told with deep conviction. It can be related on its own or be linked with other stories to form a saga, a general history of the Mari. It can be told with varying degrees of detail—our rendition is abbreviated—according to a judge's interest in cultural esoterica. The story can depict distinctive customs, events, persons, spirits, and landscapes that are indissolubly linked to a particular cultural group. That the Mari can provide such a wealth of circumstantial detail will convince a judge, regardless of whether the judge wants to listen to all of the detail, of their cultural authenticity: it will convince the judge that Mari are, in fact, culturally grounded in a past and in a place.

Insofar as judges are known to favor physical evidence, the story contains indigenous place names as well as references to material objects still in existence (the handmarks). These objects can be physically examined by the court. Some, such as trees marking where people have lived or boulders marking where powerful nonhuman spirits have dwelled, can be visited by the court. Some, such as pigs' tusks, perhaps diminished in size in the course of time, can be brought to the court, ideally by an old person who is their semiancestral keeper. Reference to these material objects nicely complements a story lacking a current tangible referent, such as the one about the inexhaustible supply of food that the horse-sized pig provided. Interestingly, one of our younger Mari friends told us that it is important to keep old people focused in presenting their court testimony: they are coached on giving enough but not too much cultural detail and on giving stories that can be materially confirmed. Otherwise, they often ramble, describing in great and obscure detail events that obviously strike the magistrate as confusing and unbelievable.

For best effect, such stories should be presented within the context of a broader case constructed by the more educated members of a group, perhaps in consultation with lawyers. The case should be conveyed through official-looking letters and documents, preferably typed on stationery with letterhead and logo. These logos are often a visual representation of several of the handmarks of significance to members of the group.[7] We saw many such letters and documents (indeed, hundreds) that were sent to RSL and kept by the general manager in his file of land matters. Prominent among this correspondence are missives from a Raikos landowners association, the Akiki Dumuna clan. This group is probably the most active of the various claimants for the land the Mari now occupy. We had several conversations with members of the clan, some of whom work for the company. Though reluctant to tell us much, they sketched out a few of their ancestral stories and referred to some of the handmarks that proved their ownership of land the Mari wrongfully occupy: this land includes both the land the Mari now hold and the land that became RSL. Among their handmarks are old trees in which the bodies of various named ancestors were placed. Some of these trees are located directly on the RSL grounds. One, in fact, was where the factory now stands. In addition, they have five generations of genealogies, which, they said, indicate continuous land tenure.

A good example of the Akiki Dumuna Landowners Association efforts to present a broader case is a letter from 1999 in the general manager's file entitled "A Short History of Ramu Sugar Limited and How Land Disputes Started." Addressed to the district administrator of the Upper Ramu District, it is meant to compel the government to convene a land court to determine the rightful owners of the land in question. This letter is carbon-copied to the officer in charge of the Madang Lands Department, to the district courthouse at Gusap, to the general manager of RSL, to Mr. Peter Colton, and to the legal firm of Gamoga and Company. Three single-spaced-pages long, it is signed by the association's chairman, vice chairman, treasurer, secretary, clan elder, and advisor. We quote a few passages below:

> The agreement [that] has been reached between the traditional land owners and the Ramu Sugar Company [has] been misconceived as follows:
>
> a) At the time of the official signing of the agreement between the traditional land owners and the Ramu Sugar company, the representatives who came on behalf of RSL failed to approach Mr. Anis Yoto who was the one responsible for bringing the project to his land, the Ramu Valley. . . .
>
> d) Mr. Tom Muliap from Bumpirupun Village just outside the Ramu Sugar Estate was the National Parliament Member for Usino-Bundi (Minister for Police) took control of everything between the company

and the traditional landowners without consulting Mr. Anis Yoto and the Akiki Dumuna Clan Members for their part as the landowners. Because of his position in the National Parliament from 1982–1986, he used the power to twist things around so that his people were recognized as the traditional landowners while the Akiki Dumuna Clan was left out with nothing.[8] . . .

We are very desperate about the above issue, tensions are building up when seeing other people claiming what is supposed to be ours.

Please could you make an effort to speed up on the above matter [by convening the land court] as soon as possible and let us know in due course.

In our conversations with the general manager about this letter, he said that he could indeed imagine that the Raikos people are desperate. He thought that it must be terrible for them to sit in their mountain villages, looking down at night on the lights of RSL and feeling that they are both peripheral and have been denied what they are certain is theirs. And he also recognized that a sugar plantation, with its extensive and flammable cane fields, is vulnerable as tensions build up. Yet whatever sympathies the general manager may have, he has also been careful that RSL should not find itself in a position of adjudicating land claims, much less providing compensation or other payments in response to those claims. The RSL policy, as determined by the board of directors and as expressed in RSL's responses to the letters and documents it receives, is that RSL merely leases the land from the government. Therefore, all claims and grievances concerning land ownership should be addressed to RSL's landlord, the government.

The company always tries to remain completely neutral concerning all land claims, whether brought by the Mari, Akiki Dumuna, or any of the myriad others. It does not profess any opinion about what might or might not have taken place in the purchase of the land, or about whether the land was purchased for a fair price or from its rightful owners. This policy is applied not only to the land that RSL directly controls but also to the land the Mari have in cane. In this latter regard, the company never officially refers to the Mari as "landowners," but only as "outgrowers."

Thus, when provincial officials, unable "to speed up on the above matter," have asked RSL's help in convening the land court, the company consistently insists that it not become involved. In 1999, for example, RSL received a letter dated October 8 requesting that it provide K7,176 (then some U.S.$2,814) for the stationing of five policemen for the twenty-one days anticipated for the court hearing. The letter also suggests that such a hearing is in the company's interest and that it should move promptly lest its operations be disrupted. Then, in a more explicit threat, the letter states: if the court hearing cannot be immediately scheduled, the Akiki Dumuna clan may be granted a restraining order preventing cane from being replanted on outgrowers' land. In a response dated October 29, the general manager, Michael Quenby, replied: "You obviously are aware that Ramu Sugar is not party to these disputes and therefore we have to seek legal advice from our Lawyers on this matter before replying." Endorsing RSL's existing policy, the forthcoming advice was that it is not consistent with RSL's pursuit of its business (not in accord with company rules and regulations) for it to become involved in the issue of the traditional ownership of land.

From the perspective of the Raikos, the Kafe, and still other claimants, however, the company's business makes it fully involved, because that business allows the Mari to live a sugar-based life, a life that all of the claimants desire.

A Sugar-Based Life

Outgrower villages do not look particularly prosperous. In fact, they look poor. Most houses are substantially, if not entirely, made of native materials; none has a water tank; there is no electrification. Even the main (Lutheran) church is of native materials and has a thatched roof and dirt floor. Yet by Papua New Guinean standards, the Mari outgrowers are very well positioned. Not only is their subsistence base intact, but at least once a year, after their cane is harvested, large amounts of money from RSL flow into their villages.[9] In addition, there may be other payments, for example, cane-price adjustments or production bonuses (see table 1).

That outgrowers have an assured annual income also provides them with the capacity to get credit: they can sometimes get advances from RSL or borrow from banks; they can always get high-interest loans (at rates of 100 percent) from private parties, even from many RSL employees. Consequently, they can, with little difficulty, cover school fees, buy clothing, supplement locally produced food, and pay for clinic visits. In addition, they have easy access to an excellent community school, shops, markets, and a health center.

They also have considerable leisure time. The men in particular, who are substantially freed from both subsistence and cash-generating work, hang around the market, the shops, and their villages and, as we shall

TABLE 1

OUTGROWERS' NET INCOME (IN KINA) FROM THE 1999 SUGAR CROP

	Hectares	Farmers (no.)	First payment	Adjustment payment (approx.)[a]	Total earnings	Earnings per farmer	Earnings per villager[b]
Bumpu	423.1	36	166,234.10	78,000	244,234.10	6,784.28	601.56
Bopirumpun	794.9	44	382,800.54	179,000	561,800.54	12,768.19	1,404.50
Sankian	822.7	67	306,955.37	143,000	449,955.37	6,715.75	837.91

Source: Data from the statistical printout "Outgrowers—Revised Credit and Debit Per Farmer," compiled by Ramu Sugar Limited in 1999, when the kina was worth approximately U.S.$0.3922.

a. The "Master Agreement" signed between RSL and the Papua New Guinea government specifies that the rate of payment per ton of cane will be yearly set by the Department of Primary Industry according to the following formula:

$$\text{Cane price in year X} = \text{cane price in } 1983 \times \frac{\text{ex-factory sugar price in year X}}{\text{ex-factory sugar price in 1983}}$$

This formula is intended to preserve the link between the price of RSL's output and the cost of its major input, the cost of cane being about two-thirds the cost of producing sugar.

The "first payment" indicated above was made in accordance with this formula. However, because 1999 was a year in which the company earned more on the domestic market per ton of cane than it anticipated, it decided to share its profits with the outgrowers as "an incentive to them." Thus, an "adjustment payment" of K400,000 was made in February 2000. We do not know precisely how much of this adjustment money each farmer received, but are confident that it was roughly proportionate to his first payment.

b. There are other sources of income. Some villagers sell garden produce at the market. Others work for RSL, either as seasonal labor, permanent employees, or contractors (hired, for instance, to use their tractors to cut grass on the margins of the cane or to provide a crew to weed outgrowers' fields). Thus, the actual income of the outgrowers is somewhat greater than this figure indicates.

see, regularly visit the Outgrowers Office concerning their fields. Then periodically, when the money comes in, the men and their families enjoy the highly public shopping and the socializing it allows.

Since many Mari do not have bank accounts (and the banks at Gusap have long closed owing to repeated robberies), outgrowers often cash the large checks they receive at Macates, one of two main shops in town. In return for this service, Macates requires that 10 percent of any check cashed be spent at the store. But this does not seem to faze many of the outgrowers, who readily spend more, obviously enjoying the display of collective affluence that shopping in a mob of Mari allows.

On February 19–20, 2000, a Friday and Saturday, immediately after "adjustment checks" were distributed (see table 1), we asked Paul Emmanuel, our research assistant from Bumbu, to station himself inside Macates General Store to observe his fellow Mari on their shopping spree.

Paul observed that they were not concerned if they ran up big bills. They bought videocassette players and televisions (in some cases, by those without generators, just to decorate the house), cartons of canned fish and meat, large bags of rice, soft drinks, and cigarettes. They bought radios, "stockman" shoes, trousers, shirts, sewing machines, bush knives, CD players, mattresses, pillows, fishing nets, saws, hammers, bicycles, and nails. And they continued their shopping elsewhere, buying beer for the big party that would last throughout the weekend.

A more specific breakdown of the way that two rather large adjustment checks were spent is informative of both Mari patterns of consumption and of redistribution. Redistribution is generally to family members and other kin who have no direct access to sugar fields. Lasala Rinkant's adjustment check was in the amount of K5,031.90, or about U.S.$1,823.[10] Cashing it at Macates, he spent K800 there on a bicycle, radio, rice, a saw, a hammer, shoes, and various clothes. He also spent K300 on school fees, K950 in cash gifts to his four sons, and K1,600 in repaying a debt. This left K1,381 for future use. Emmanuel Moba's adjustment check was for K4,797.86. Having a bank account, he deposited it and then withdrew K2,700. Of that, he spent K30 on beer and cigarettes, K20 on food, and K6.50 on a new cap. He also spent K100 on school fees, K300 in a cash gift to his son, K500 in a cash gift to his two sisters, K380 in a cash gift to his mother's sister's children, and K100 in a cash gift to the pastor. Also, he spent K680 in repaying a debt. This left K583.50 for future use.

Annual income among outgrowers does vary according to crop yield, measured by the number of tons of cane harvested from their fields. Factors such as weather and pests, of course, affect that yield. Although cane, a grass, regenerates after it is cut, the yield gradually diminishes after each harvesting: thus, a field is expected to produce its highest yield (the greatest number of tons per hectare) from cane that is newly planted. (The cane in such a field is called "plant"; the cane after subsequent cuttings is called "first ratoon," "second ratoon," and so forth.) However, if newly planted fields have the highest yields, they also have the highest costs—costs often as great as, if not greater than, crop income—because fields are taken out of production during a fallow period and then prepared and replanted. Indeed, during 1999, nine outgrowers from Bumbu, fourteen outgrowers from Sankian, and eleven outgrowers from Bopirumpun received no income at all from their fields.

Not surprisingly, outgrowers are often reluctant to allow their fields to be replanted, preferring instead the diminished income from an advanced ratoon to laying the expensive "ground work" for a future invigorated crop. In response, the company tries to enforce a policy that mandates replanting if the yield of a field falls below sixty tons of cane per hectare. This means that, in most cases, replanting takes place every five or six years after the fourth or fifth ratoon, although there are some exceptional fields that yield above this minimum into the eleventh or twelfth ratoon.

The other major variable affecting an outgrower's income is the cost of the agricultural services provided by the company: these are the costs of agricultural chemicals and their application, of planting, weeding, and harvesting. As services are performed, sometimes by RSL employees, but more frequently by contractors hired by the company for specific tasks, the costs are recorded and eventually deducted from the amounts owed to each outgrower for his crop. An outgrower can reduce his deductions by performing some of the services himself. He can, for example, weed his crop using a backpack sprayer. But most prefer to let the company do the work.

This is not to say that the outgrowers are reconciled to the amount they frequently pay in deductions. Indeed, central to the Mari understanding of being an outgrower is that they *not* perform services on their fields, that they not act as farmers. Rather, their understanding is that they act as landowners, monitoring the services of others on their fields and vigilant over the use of their property. So, on designated days, they congregate at the Outgrowers Building to consult the records of debts against their particular fields. Although this building was paid for with funds levied by RSL against outgrower sugar incomes, it is inside the company's main fence. It is, however, provided with its own separate gate to the outside, which is opened on Tuesdays and Thursdays. On these days, outgrowers go to the Outgrowers Building for the slips recording what has been done to their fields and at what cost. And then, against a background grumble of disagreement, exclamations of specific protest follow. As these Mari assert individual efficacy and affirm collective interests, as they make sure that their contributions as landowners are not undervalued, they seem gratified to be exercising due vigilance. Although the Mari assiduously avoid confrontation among themselves and are quick to apologize if they suspect that offense has been given, they nonetheless frequently complain vociferously that unnecessary services have been performed; that they have been charged twice for the same services; or that they have been charged for services that have not been performed. These complaints, if formalized, can be pursued with the various members of the RSL staff assigned to the outgrowers and headquartered in their building.

Most generally, the Mari feel that the company is profiting unduly at their expense and that if it weren't for them and their land, there wouldn't be a company. After all, not only do they, as outgrowers, provide more than two thousand hectares of cane fields, but they, as Mari, provide the land for the entire enterprise.[11]

For its part, RSL, as mentioned, is concerned about its outgrowers and their "malaise." The report by the BTL agricultural economist, from the study RSL commissioned, confirms that the outgrowers are not doing well: "In recent years the margin earned by the OGs [outgrowers] between revenue from sale of cane and the charges for services provided to them had been steadily declining" (Innes 2000: 1). We shall return to these concerns later in this chapter.

· · ·

Nonetheless, from the perspectives of most Papua New Guineans, the outgrowers are in an enviable position. They can afford the magnificent blowouts and they have a generally comfortable life. The Kafe and the Raikos peoples are particularly envious, claiming as they do to be the rightful owners of the land and hence the rightful recipients of the sugar payments. The position of the Mushuan villagers is more complex.[12] They strongly support Mari claims and, as mentioned, provide Kiruak as spokesperson for the defense of these claims. In turn, they are sometimes given money by their better-placed kin—and, in fact, Kiruak was given a small sugar field at Bumbu in recognition of his services. However, the Mushuans are as aware as anyone of the differences in lifestyle and prospects between those with sugar money and those without. We were able to pursue this intra-Mari comparison with the help of our two research assistants, Paul Emmanuel from Bumbu and Jack Morris from Mushuan. In informal conversations and more formal surveys, we explored both immediate and ramifying effects of having or not having an assured income in a single, rather small linguistic and cultural group.

We learned informally, for example, that Paul's school fees were always easily met, but Jack's were not. In fact, during the tenth grade Jack was sent home from school for nonpayment of fees. When his family finally got the necessary money together and he returned to school, he was so far behind that his exam scores did not win him a place in the national high school. Now, though one of the better-educated Mushuans, he makes his living as a subsistence farmer; consequently, he and his family are finding it staggeringly difficult to raise the K750 to send his younger brother to high school.

We learned more formally about these differences through a series of measures we designed or adapted. One was inspired by Pat Barker's novelistic portrayal of turn-of-the-century Pacific research by W. H. R. Rivers. Rivers, according to Barker (and we have been unable to ascertain the truth of her story), began his exploration of a social context by asking his informants, "[S]uppose you were lucky enough to find a guinea, with whom would you share it? This produced a list of names, names which he would then ask them to translate into kinship terms. And from there one could move to virtually any aspect of their society" (Barker 1995: 118).[13]

It took us a while to shape this exploratory exercise to Mari life. Working with our assistants, we first sought to determine the amount appropriate to engage Mari imagination and sense of responsibility. We suggested K100. Paul thought this amount would make good sense to the Bumbus. But Jack thought this amount would overwhelm the Mushuans. Instead, he suggested K10 and we agreed. Then we worked out with our assistants the origin of this money. While accepting that it should appear to arrive with no strings attached, so repayment would not be an issue, both thought that "lucky enough to find" would only puzzle and raise other questions. We suggested that it simply fall from the sky, dropped by a hawk out of the blue, a windfall. This was vetoed on the ground that such money would obviously have a miraculous origin and should go to the church. Finally we settled on a gift from a rich tourist who donated the money in thanks for being shown around the village and then left for the airport. However, Jack found that this formulation required further adjustment to be plausible to Mushuans. No tourist ever forded the Ramu River to visit them. In fact, only a few RSL officials ever made that trip. Moreover, they never received unentailed money—it seemed inconceivable. Thus, Jack simply decided to ask Mushuans to remember an occasion when they received money from someone and how they spent it.[14]

The initial discussion with Jack and Paul that suggested Bumbus can readily fantasize about windfalls, while Mushuans cannot, proved among the most interesting aspects of this comparison. It was consistent with material they subsequently recorded. Mushuans did tend to view money as short and hence as something to be conserved; Bumbus did tend to view it as easy come, easy go. Thus, an adult man from Mushuan, who actually received K100 from his in-laws from their sugar fields at Sankian, said he spent it on the following items: K10 on a ten-kilo bag of rice; K5 on kerosene and soap; K2 on betel nut; K3 on "lambflaps," a popular inexpensive and fatty cut; K50 on a cash gift to his wife; K10 on a cash gift to his younger brother; K20 on savings. In at least partial contrast, an adult sugar-field owner from Bumbu said he would spend his K100 on the following items: K40 on beer; K10 on a bush knife; K10 on rice, chicken pieces, and loose tobacco; K5 on a cap; K5 on a spade; K30 on savings, to be hidden in the house for later use. Moreover, and most strikingly, one middle-aged Bumbu man said that he would blow the entire K100 on a night of drinking, smoking, and playing snooker with his friends.[15]

We also asked our assistants to report what they and some of their fellow clan members ate for the first week of every month for five months (from February to June 2000). We asked them only to list the kinds of food each of the individuals (forty-three for Jack and twenty-five for Paul) reported consuming daily, as recording the quantities of the foodstuffs consumed would have been too major an undertaking. Although their data were somewhat skewed by the fact that both spent some of their wages from us on food, it was clear that Mushuans consumed store and market-bought food far less often than did Bumbus. Thus, Jack's Mushuan relatives ate some purchased food about once a week: rice, noodles, and canned fish. The rest of the time they ate food they themselves produced or collected: bananas, coconuts, sweet potatoes, yams, tapioca, native greens, peanuts, sugarcane, fish from the Ramu River, and occasional small game. Just once did a family treat itself to lambflaps bought in town. And only occasionally did a person who traveled to the market to sell, for example, peanuts or bananas, buy herself a soft drink or other snack. In comparison, Paul's Bumbu relatives frequently ate store-bought rice, canned corned beef, canned fish, lambflaps, and chicken pieces, in addition to market-bought spring onions, watercress, and carrots. These heavily supplemented the bananas, coconuts, sweet potatoes, yams, tapioca, and native greens from their gardens. Strikingly, all of Paul's informants ate some store-bought snacks, including popcorn, soft drinks, scones, and cookies, at least once a day.

Perhaps predictably, given the differences in nutrition (the diet of Bumbus included far more high-quality protein) and given the differences in medical access (Mushuans had to ford the often-flooded Ramu River to get to the health center), there were differences in the incidence of death: the 83 women living at Bumbu during March 1999 had borne 282 children, 24 of whom had died, indicating an overall loss of 8.5 percent; the 99 women living at Mushuan during March 1999 had borne 304 children, 66 of whom had died, indicating an overall loss of 22 percent.

Finally, an analysis of our census materials (tables 2–5) indicates that, in terms of both village size and rates of in- and out-marriage, Mushuan is the smallest and least desirable of the Mari villages. It also sends out the highest proportion of its population to other Mari villages and sends out substantially more than it gets in.

These differences notwithstanding, all Mari villages look poor to an outsider: a passerby cannot readily tell the difference between Mushuan and the other three, far wealthier Mari villages. All lack the outward signs of development, such as permanent-material houses with sheet-metal roofs and adjacent water tanks. Although millions of kina have passed through Mari hands over the years, these millions were divided among numerous kin and were spent on numerous items of consumption. The most striking example of consumption we encountered is provided by Yalibu. As mentioned, he is somewhat exceptional in maintaining control of most of his extended family's sugar holdings: he annually receives some K50,000 in sugar income. We learned about how some of his money was spent when he showed us the ancestral jawbone. Among the various documents he brought out for us to see was a list of sixteen vehicles: buses (from five- to thirty-seaters), trucks (from pick-ups to dump trucks),

TABLE 2
MUSHUAN CENSUS MATERIALS

Total population	286
Number of dwellings	89
Number of hamlets	5

In-married adults							
Males				Females			
Bumbu	Bopirumpun	Sankian	Elsewhere	Bumbu	Bopirumpun	Sankian	Elsewhere
2	0	1	4	5	3	4	8

Percentage of total population in-married from Mari villages	5.2
Percentage of total population in-married from elsewhere	4.2
Percentage of total population in-married	9.4

Number of adults sent to other Mari villages	22
Number of adults received from other Mari villages	15

TABLE 3
BUMPU CENSUS MATERIALS

Total population	406
Number of dwellings	74
Number of hamlets	3

In-married adults

Males				Females			
Mushuan	Bopirumpun	Sankian	Elsewhere	Mushuan	Bopirumpun	Sankian	Elsewhere
6	2	1	12	9	4	5	16

Percentage of total population in-married from Mari villages	6.7
Percentage of total population in-married from elsewhere	6.9
Percentage of total population in-married	13.6
Number of adults sent to other Mari villages	23
Number of adults received from other Mari villages	27

TABLE 4
BOPIRUMPUN CENSUS MATERIALS

Total population	400
Number of dwellings	110
Number of hamlets	4

In-married adults

Males				Females			
Mushuan	Bumpu	Sankian	Elsewhere	Mushuan	Bumpu	Sankian	Elsewhere
1	0	1	12	0	4	3	26

Percentage of total population in-married from Mari villages	2.2
Percentage of total population in-married from elsewhere	9.5
Percentage of total population in-married	11.7
Number of adults sent to other Mari villages	10
Number of adults received from other Mari villages	9

TABLE 5

SANKIAN CENSUS MATERIALS

Total population	537
Number of dwellings	117
Number of hamlets	5

In-married adults

Males				Females			
Mushuan	Bumpu	Bopirumpun	Elsewhere	Mushuan	Bumpu	Bopirumpun	Elsewhere
1	3	0	27	5	9	1	25

Percentage of total population in-married from Mari villages	3.5
Percentage of total population in-married from elsewhere	9.7
Percentage of total population in-married	13.2
Number of adults sent to other Mari villages	15
Number of adults received from other Mari villages	19

and tractors. When we asked him where all of these transports were, his response was gleeful: "They're all broken down!" he hooted. Clearly, his list is a record of his affluence and efficacy. In this regard, we are reminded of Highlanders whose necklaces indicate the number of pigs they have given away at ceremonial exchanges.

That most Mari spend their money on such items of transitory consumption as beer and even vehicles rather than on such items of long-term use as permanent-material houses and water tanks is not simply an indication that they enjoy spending it—although they surely do enjoy spending it! They spend their money as they do for two major reasons: one has to do with who they are as Mari and the other has to do with who they think they should be as landowners.

As Mari, who only relatively recently gave up the impermanence of lives as shifting horticulturalists, it makes only uncertain cultural sense for them to invest heavily in fixed structures. Indeed, the number of often dispersed hamlets that constitute a Mari village attests to the fact that Mari still find it easy to shift residence. Only a few years before our study, a sizable number of people left the main Bumbu village to establish a major settlement several miles away: they had become tired of the payday drinking of RSL workers at the village roadside beer store. As

Mari, who only recently gave up the solidarities of lives in clan-structured hamlets, they find that it makes only uncertain cultural sense for them to invest heavily in more nuclear households by sheltering income from the claims of less close kin. Indeed, the amount of sugar money that is redistributed to peripheral relatives attests to the fact that Mari are still inclined to maintain a breadth of kin ties. And a sizable number of Mari, perhaps all, still believe that to accumulate is to evoke jealousy: they are convinced that to rise above the rest attracts the attention of sorcerers. Thus, although virtually all Mari see development as a good thing, and virtually all agree that solid, permanent-material houses are an important aspect of development, few people are willing or able to build such houses.

Moreover, as landowners, they think permanent-material houses and other aspects of development should come, not from their sugar earnings, but from RSL directly, in recognition of the value of their land. Such an arrangement is eminently worth struggling for. If RSL does contribute in these significant ways, Mari can continue to spend their sugar earnings in highly gratifying, socially solidifying ways. And they can all rise together in a way that minimizes internal discord and differentiation. Furthermore, they can receive their due both in their own eyes and in the eyes of other Papua New Guineans. In this latter regard, Mari are heavily influenced by emerging Papua New Guinean definitions of what it means to be a landowner.

Throughout the country, landowners are increasingly militant. They are both challenging the government's ownership of what had been their land and demanding that the use of their land—however acquired—be generously compensated for. Thus, for example, a recent lead headline in the *National* (one of Papua New Guinea's two English-language daily newspapers) states "Landowners to Get K5m Compo." The article continues, "Goroka landowners will receive more than K5 million compensation, paving the way for the reopening of the Goroka University and other institutions today" (Per 2000b: 1) In addition to shutting down all academic activities on the Goroka campus, an earlier edition of the paper reports that landowners also closed "the Goroka Business College, Goroka Town Capital Town Authority Works, Goroka District Office Eastern Highlands Provincial commerce office and Eastern Highlands university study center" because "the landowners say they were not properly compensated when the State acquired the land from them during the colonial days" (Per 2000a: 1). Mari are well acquainted with issues of ownership and compensation, with such events being widely reported throughout Papua New Guinea. Indeed, events such as those at Goroka also are stimulating concern among BTL management at RSL, who fear that the government's capitulation in response to these takeovers encourages further takeovers.

Moreover, throughout Papua New Guinea, traditional owners of land where gold and copper mines and oil fields are located have, in fact, negotiated "Memoranda of Understanding" (MOU) such that they receive royalties as well as a range of amenities, including modern housing, running water, and electricity. If these are not satisfactorily forthcoming, landowners will, or will threaten to, shut the operation down. As we will see, Mari are very interested in converting RSL's MA with the government into an MOU with them. They are acutely aware of how their level of development compares with that, for example, of the landowners at the big Highland gold and copper mines of Porgera and Ok Tedi, as well as that of RSL employees, who have electricity and running water. And they hope that a new agreement with the company will provide them with the amenities to which they strongly feel entitled.

The Mari seek good houses, not only because they purportedly provide comfort and convenience, but also because they are signs of collective development. Without such signs, the Mari feel shame relative to others. Most specifically, they feel ineffective—and think therefore that others look down on them—compared to landowners elsewhere. They feel particularly ineffective in comparison to Highlanders, who not only seem able to get conspicuous benefits from the government and mining companies but are also, as we shall see, a very forceful presence at RSL and in Mari lives. To negotiate such benefits successfully will show that the Mari are taken seriously, that they are to be engaged with.

What the Mari especially want is to be able to compel the company, an obviously wealthy and powerful entity, to show them the respect they think they deserve as landowners. Given the social meaning of things, such respect would be substantially demonstrated by giving them, or by vigorously helping them to acquire, the appropriate markers of development, that is houses, water-supply systems, electricity. In effect, they desire the same kinds of things and for many of the same reasons as did Yali. However, at this historical juncture, the issues of respect and worth are becoming very complicated: points of reference are shifting from relations between white people and black people to relations between a range of postcolonial peoples, in Papua New Guinea and beyond. Thus, what is a reasonable expectation and what is not is, in fact, an appropriate subject of debate.

On the "Economizing" of Yeoman Farmers

BTL knows that the outgrowers are averse to putting more labor into their fields and also that they are unhappy with what they receive from RSL. Unlike the Kenyans with their positive work attitude, the Mari are troubling, both as a component of RSL's sugar operation and as a target of BTL's mission to put groups on the trajectory of development. In terms of BTL's business of conveying to the third-world "have-nots" the fundamentals of first-world success—the technologies and techniques, the concerns with economizing and maximizing—the Mari are not a great success. After all, if the Mari view the absence of permanent-material houses as a failure in development, so does BTL. Moreover, the Mari are not only troubling, they are trouble: they complain and clamor. What the company explicitly hopes is that the Mari will become more like yeoman farmers. But although some at BTL have not given up on hopes of development, if it is not to be, if the Mari are to remain rent takers, then perhaps they can at least learn to use their income more wisely.

To this more limited end, RSL has moved in two related ways. The first and more structural is to redefine its relationship to the Mari as outgrowers: RSL hopes that by making them into a corporate body, it will be better able to negotiate agreements with them. The second way is to transform the Mari themselves by providing them with a good example. If they can observe other Papua New Guineans taking responsibility for their own development, the Mari may learn to economize their expenditures and thus rely less on RSL for help.

· · ·

As the first aspect of its strategy, to effect structural change, RSL is encouraging the Mari to organize into an "Outgrowers Association."[16] According to the proposed constitution of the association, it will be "a legal body representing all sugarcane Outgrowers within the villages of Sankian, Mushuan, Bumbu and Bopirumpun, surrounding the Ramu Sugar Ltd. estate . . . [which will] liaise with Ramu Sugar Ltd., in all matters related to cane agronomy, varieties, Outgrower extension, provision, and supply of services and inputs by Ramu Sugar Ltd., for the Outgrowers" (Ramu Sugar Limited 2000: 3–4). As the general manager explained to us: it is very important for there to be a body, "an entity," with which the company can negotiate concerning many different outgrower-related matters. Such an association will be independent of RSL. Indeed, it will be housed in a building outside of the RSL estate. Significantly, it is also hoped that this building will prove to be a nucleus for Mari-generated development efforts.

Although outgrowers did express some interest in this association after the company first suggested it in 1999, one event in particular convinced them that this association might help them defend their interests in a more coordinated and effectual fashion.[17] This was when Emos Talabe began construction on a new service station and convenience store at Gusap's commercial center. Talabe was a former RSL factory manager and a Southern Highlander from Tari. He was successful both in obtaining a contract from RSL to use its government-leased land and in arranging his own financing from a bank loan and from his personal savings.

The outgrowers were incensed at his project and responded with intense alarm. They experienced it as a compound failure—indeed, as a massive humiliation. Mari thought that *they* should have enough influence on the company, enough understanding of business opportunity, and enough capacity to muster their collective resources to ensure that any new enterprise at Gusap be theirs. Moreover, that a Highlander succeeded where Mari had failed was additionally galling. They confronted Talabe, who responded that the Mari had plenty of opportunity—lots of time and income—to create such a business for themselves. Moreover, he told them, as a citizen of Papua New Guinea, he had as much right to government-owned land as they. There were scuffles and threats to burn the project down, but Talabe and his crew—all but one from Tari—were not intimidated. Work continued to the increasing frustration of the Mari.

The outgrowers did not give up. They called for a meeting with Roy Gagau, RSL's Papua New Guinean head of human relations, demanding to know why the company had allowed Talabe to build on RSL ground. While eventually addressing this point, Gagau took the opportunity to make explicit RSL's new strategy toward the outgrowers. On February 2, 2000, about thirty outgrowers heard him explain what services and other arrangements they could or could not expect from the company.

Consulting a piece of paper with a list of seven agenda items, Gagau explained (in Pidgin English) that the company found itself in serious trouble, as it had been hurt badly by the devaluation of the kina and had almost declared bankruptcy. It was only because it received payment for the quota of sugar it sold to the United States that it was able to pay the salary of its workers.[18] Gagau continued:

What you [Mari] have to understand is that RSL's primary goal is to grow sugar and its primary concern is to strengthen its business.

The company wants to survive forever. Yet, RSL also helps its outgrowers, workmen, and community. Thirty-three percent of our costs are social services. We pay for security, clinics, the school, and we provide free power and water—and none of this is necessary to the production of sugar. We would like the government to take over all of these costs so that we can concentrate on our business. After all, our business is not like the business of a mine [with massive infrastructure covering a range of social services, but commitment limited to the relatively few years of a mine's life]. We produce sugar, which is a resource that will be here forever. . . .

[Concerning the block of land on which Emos Talabe has been building his service station]: In 1998, Emos applied for it. The Board gave its commitment and put this on paper. . . . Emos did not get the land just because he was someone's wantok. . . .

You yourselves have to straighten your own houses. . . . The challenge to develop must be yours. We can help you in many ways. But whatever you do must be outside of company boundaries. . . . If you don't do things by yourselves, then RSL will get the credit. . . .

You need to unite and form an association that will coordinate the way in which you spend your money. . . . All too often, the government does not do what it should because it assumes that the company will take care of things. No longer. The Mari earned over K900,000 last year, and money like this should be spent on building independent enterprises. The company will support you, but you have to think in the long term, not only for yourselves, but for your children. . . . I know you have a lot of money. You should use it well.

The outgrowers were far from convinced. Although they told Gagau how pleased they were to see a Papua New Guinean in such an important job at RSL, they were disappointed that he had at least tacitly approved of Talabe's store. They could not understand how the company would allow Talabe, a non-Mari, the use of Mari land. Nor did they accept the company's delimitation of its responsibilities. Nonetheless, they thanked Gagau for his presentation and Gagau departed to cordial farewells.

In the general discussion following Gagau's departure, several Mari continued to affirm what has become almost a Mari creed. This is that the government purchased their land long ago, but for far too little money and from backward, uneducated, easily duped ancestors who knew nothing about what they were agreeing to. Specifically, "millions should have been paid, not just a few pounds"; that the company has been planting sugar as if this was "bastard ground without a father"; that someone other than the proper landowners must have "been claiming royalties over the past twenty years."

In this discussion it was evident that Bill Muliap had the clearest sense of what should be done. Bill had recently returned to his Mari home. (His father, Tom Muliap, had been a member of the National Parliament.) Bill was well educated, fluent in English, comfortable with Europeans, had worked in a bank in West New Britain, and was married to an educated Tolai woman, an accountant. It was apparent to all, including senior managers at RSL, that he was interested in becoming a leader of the Mari, the president of the new association, and perhaps a candidate for national office. Thus Muliap sharpened the discussion at strategic points. He argued, for instance, that the MA approved by Mari ancestors had been "illegally issued" and must be changed into an MOU, approved by the association; that this new MOU should guarantee the Mari first rights to everything and should ensure that they will be paid the "royalties" owed them for their land since RSL began production. The Mari must write a letter protesting the company's decision concerning Talabe and carbon copy the minister of lands, the general manager, the chairman of the board, and others. They must also "call an urgent meeting to create and register an association" so as to make sure that they get their due.

At several meetings that were held subsequently to discuss an Outgrowers Association, this rhetoric—especially as Muliap was shaping it—was repeated and refined. At the first of these meetings, Muliap began by setting forth the goals of the proposed association in a clear and compelling manner. After ample discussion, the sixty-eight outgrowers present unanimously decided that the Mari needed to establish a "legal body" that can take the government to court and force it to transform the MA into an MOU. This MOU will specify that RSL has to supply all of the Mari villages with a good water supply, electrification, roads, permanent-material houses, and a health center if it wishes to grow sugar on Mari land. Each outgrower agreed to contribute K100 to the association for its forthcoming work.

Consequently, though RSL and the Mari have clearly different ideas about what may be feasibly accomplished, at least the outgrowers have enthusiastically embraced the idea of forming an Outgrowers Association.

•　•　•

As the second aspect of its strategy, to effect attitudinal change so that the Mari will take more responsibility for their own development, RSL decided to subsidize the "Rabaul Study Tour" proposed by Robin Wilson, the RSL manager directly in charge of the outgrowers. Thus, as the Outgrowers Association was taking form, Wilson's plan—one he described to us as his "dream"—of escorting selected Mari to visit his own Tolai people in their home province of East New Britain was also materializing.[19]

Wilson was sure that the Tolai example would convince the Mari that Papua New Guineans can obtain the important signs and comforts of development, such as good houses, while also remaining significantly Papua New Guinean. In his view, the fact that Tolai are famous not only for their prosperity but also for their continued use of shell money in ceremonial and, to some extent, in market transactions shows them as successfully blending the modern and traditional.[20]

Mari enthusiastically embraced the idea of the study tour. Indeed, along with their Outgrowers Association, it became a significant component in their plans for dealing with RSL. Thus, as Muliap explained during one of the meetings held to discuss the association, not only would the association be able to change its relationship with the company for the better by replacing the MA with the MOU (and thus ensuring that the company fulfilled its responsibilities to them as landowners), but the study tour also would change the Mari people for the better by transforming their still backward, still ignorant lifestyle. Muliap elaborated:

> The reason that this is an important trip is because your lifestyle is not good: you spend your money on nothing; your wives and children are dirty and sick. You are just "kunai" [grasslands] people. The best thing to do would be to learn from other people. This trip will be like school where you will learn to change your customs. You will learn how to budget your money. You get a lot of money yet in seven months it is gone. I have worried about you because you are my people. The purpose of this trip is to change your customs, your lives. I am not interested in changing your ancestors, or your language. . . . There is not going to be any rest during this trip. It's not meant as a vacation. In one day we will see at least four different things. And everything will be videoed so that we can show the video and hold school at our villages when we come back.

Although there was some grumbling that only a few men would be going, the consensus was that the trip would be beneficial because it would help the Mari shape up their lives. As one man synoptically put it: "It's good that twelve men from our home villages will be going and wearing neckties all day long. They will have to shave every day; they will have to look clean." Such a transformation, all agreed, was necessary if Mari were to take their appropriate place in the world, as modern disciplined people, with an association of their own. Otherwise, people like Talabe would continue to get the better of them, RSL would continue to treat (and cheat) them, as they had cheated the Mari ancestors, and others would view them as backward and out-of-it.

· · ·

For RSL's part, both the Outgrowers Association and the Rabaul Study Tour represented a combined strategy to free the company from "unreasonable" Mari demands—demands that make it difficult for RSL to stay in business, much less generate shareholder profit. Many of these demands derive, RSL believes, from the negative aspects of Papua New Guinean custom. These include wantokism, jealousy, exorbitant landowner-claims, and a handout mentality. These customs take no account of, indeed are oblivious to, the world of business: they fail to accept what the bottom line is and must be. Thus RSL, in its dealings with its neighbors and especially with the Mari, is striving to insist that a good working relationship must be based on the consistent and evenhanded application of explicit and prudent policies. In this regard, RSL is careful to define the Mari with respect to a business relationship—not as landowners but as outgrowers. RSL is also committed to treating all citizens of the country with fairness. Theirs was a reasonable decision to allow Talabe to build his business at Gusap: to recognize his competence and industry and to encourage the development of Papua New Guinean enterprises. Their decision in this matter was not a handout, nor was it based on wantokism. Conversely, this decision, and Talabe's hard work and initiative, should not be blocked by Mari jealousy or by a hyperextension of their claims as landowners.

Through the Rabaul Study Tour, RSL was hoping that the Mari would both come to accept the world as defined by RSL's bottom line and also to succeed in that world. In both regards, Mari would have to learn how to adjust their culture. In this, the Tolai could be their mentors, teaching them how to preserve those aspects of their culture that are socially positive while relinquishing those that are negative—those that impede their doing business or that divert income from their own development.

For the Mari's part, by this time in their history, they have become eager to see what they might learn from the Tolai. Always sensitive to the idea that other Papua New Guineans view them as ineffectual grassland men, they are open to change because of the renewed pressure from RSL and also because of the immediate humiliation stemming from the Talabe incident. The Tolai—too distant to be immediate competitors—might help them take stock of themselves in the contemporary world. Perhaps they are still too much like their ancestors, too much like those who were duped or coerced by the government into selling land worth millions for just a few shillings. But if so, this does not mean that they should change in the ways that RSL is pressuring them to do: it does not mean that they should accept the bottom line as RSL is defining it. What RSL sees as wantokism, jealousy, exorbitant landowner claims, and a handout mentality the Mari insist is moral obligation, sensible fear of sorcery, and rightful insistence on their due as landowners. The question of whose bottom line will be accepted as such will outlast the Rabaul trip.

8

On the Road, Mari Style

THE "RABAUL STUDY TOUR" took place against a backdrop of trips designed to educate Papua New Guineans about modern life and its possibilities. Indeed, as we have seen, Yali and Papua New Guineans of his generation were taken to Australia on similar trips. Such trips were part of a series of massively self-validating attempts by Europeans to transform Papua New Guineans' worldview. Exposed to the omnipower of European practical reason as evidenced by its cities and factories, Papua New Guineans would, Australians hoped, abandon their own cultural (mis)understandings—their fundamental assumptions about both the physical and the social worlds, including how things are acquired, how relationships are constituted, and how worth is achieved.

The first step in this transformative effort, often described in anthropological and other literature as "first contact" (Connolly and Anderson 1987), generally involved European attempts to maximize their initial impact so as to change forever local perceptions of relative worth. Thus, on their gold-prospecting explorations into Papua New Guinea's Highlands, Michael Leahy and his brothers carefully orchestrated their first contacts to awe locals by strategic shows of technological power. For instance, they would buy a pig and then in front of a large crowd demonstrate the marvelous capacity of their rifles by shooting it. Indeed, it is obvious from Leahy's documentation of the expedition's exploits, excerpted in Connolly and Anderson's 1984 film, *First Contact*, that he especially savored his role as intrepid maker of history in the creation of such moments of sudden "enlightenment":

> The filmic record contains many examples of Australians demonstrating their technological wonders to suitably impressed onlookers. The highlanders watch planes land and cringe in terror; they start at demonstrated rifle fire; stare uncomprehendingly at record players; grin at mirrors. The pathos of their terror and mystification is certainly preserved for posterity, but the movie scenes and photographs reflect as well the Australians' confidence and pride in their own civilisation. It was an easy step for them to assume that the obvious material superiority of their culture was equaled by an intellectual and moral superiority as well. (Connolly and Anderson 1987: 116)

But as Leahy and others, whether explorers, evangelists, or patrol officers, were to discover, local people and local expectations were not so easily discredited, not so easily transformed by their first (and early) contact experiences. European intentions to engage in portentous and heroic action—to precipitate *events*—were frequently frustrated. The engagement between Europeans and Papua New Guineans—the "structure of the conjuncture," to use Sahlins's phrase (1985: xiv)—usually did not result in the shattering of indigenous social and cultural systems. Indeed, Europeans were to discover that it was not their world that was locally recognized as having a more fundamental reality as, quoting Sahlins again, "refractory," as "intractable" (145, 149). Instead, "traditional" meanings, albeit in shifted form, reasserted themselves in expectations that sought to entail and equalize these powerful arrivals. As Europeans found themselves held to local standards of sociability, they often became embroiled in complex and shifting relationships of negotiation, contention, critique, and resistance. Rather than capitulating to a superior European rationality, Papua New Guineans frequently proved recalcitrant and demanding, if not angry and "bloody-minded."[1] In fact, colonial literature, including the patrol reports mentioned earlier, is filled with references to locals as lethargic, lazy, superstitious, ignorant, sullen, difficult, and otherwise uncooperative or unreasonable. In this situation, emulation, if any, was likely to be conditional. To be white, European, and developed continued to be refracted through local perceptions of value and worth, through local perceptions of the desirable and the undesirable, of the moral and the immoral (see Bashkow 1999.)

In essence, Yali's trip to Australia could be regarded as a "first-contact refresher course," a trip to the home country to experience, through immersion, an entire way of life.[2] Central to the vision the Australians wished to convey was a particular bottom line. Money and associated commodities—cargo—did not "grow on trees," but instead were the products of hard work, technical training, skillful management, and capital investments (including factories). Significantly, this in turn meant that those who controlled (owned) them had in some way earned them and consequently deserved them. Furthermore, this meant that these items could not, and should not, just be "given away": to do so would be to reward the unearning and undeserving. Thus Yali and other Papua New Guineans should not expect Europeans just to hand over or otherwise share their power and privilege. Moreover, not only had Papua New Guineans not earned power or privilege, and thus had no right to them, but they also did not understand their true value and thus would just waste them. Indeed, to hand over or share power and privilege precipitously would only backfire: it would only fuel unreasonable expectations and thereby discourage Papua New Guineans from accepting the role of dutiful colonial subjects, the role of apprentices. Only through accepting such a role might Papua New Guineans eventually master the technologies and techniques upon which power and privilege, and the status that appropriately attended power and privilege, depended. Having learned this, Yali and others would finally accept that their relationship to Europeans could not yet be as full equals. And their conversion effected, their attitudes transformed, their desires made reasonable, they were expected to convey, indeed, to preach, these new truths to constituencies at home.

By the time of Papua New Guinea's independence and RSL's creation, first contacts and overseas "refresher courses" were largely in the past. Papua New Guineans continue to travel abroad for educational purposes, but this education is likely to be more narrowly defined, focused increasingly on individuals rather than on natives embedded in social contexts. Such study trips are no longer designed primarily for conversion and for subsequent broadcasting of newly realized truths to a home audience. Instead, they are meant to hone the professional and technical skills of selected individuals. Such skills, by their often specialized nature, are less suitably "broadcast" than "narrowcast" (Lindstrom 1990). To be sure, those so trained may share their augmented knowledge with coworkers and serve as examples to be emulated. However, the point of the training is not to transform an entire group, but to enhance the careers (including the future mobility) of individuals who are already substantially extracted from a ples-centered identity. These individuals have already been greatly influenced by a Western education, which, as LiPuma suggests, "is not concerned with collectivities, but with individuals" (2000: 293).

Thus, RSL often sends nationals, primarily supervisors and managers, for training abroad so that they can experience sugar production elsewhere, learn particular skills at workshops, or even earn advanced degrees.[3] RSL offers such opportunities to teach and reward promising employees. In so doing, it seeks to improve the quality of RSL staff in (tax deductible) ways that comply with government mandates for training and localization.

Such study trips often serve as reference points in employees' career narratives. In talking to us about their lives at RSL, national managers mention these trips as an indication of their career trajectories. The *Sugar Valley News* often features accounts by nationals of their trips abroad, frequently showing photographs of them in obviously foreign contexts (a snowy English setting, for example). Conversely, nationals, in speaking of being "blocked" or "passed over," mention crucial training they have missed out on when another was selected for a particular trip.

Thus, it was against a considerable backdrop of excursions that Robin Wilson proposed to take those under his charge, the Mari outgrowers, on the "Rabaul Study Tour." The trip was to provide the Mari with a variant of first contact—this would be contact with Wilson's own group, the Tolai. The Tolai were widely regarded as among the first in Papua New Guinea to have had dealings with outsiders, contacts dating from shortly after the 1875 arrival in the area of the Methodist missionary, George Brown.[4] Both despite and because of this early contact, the Tolai were known both to have retained (perhaps, more accurately, adapted) much of their tradition (including the use of shell money) and to be among the most industrious and developed groups in contemporary Papua New Guinea. From intensive exposure to the Tolai, in a complex reprise of first contact, the Mari, it was hoped, would become less troubling and less trouble to RSL.[5] Although RSL would like to see a relatively complete conversion, such as the Mari acquiring a work ethic comparable to that of the Kenyans at BTL's Mumias operation, RSL would settle for a change in Mari patterns of consumption. If the Mari could at least learn the necessary skills and discipline, the rational technologies and techniques, to invest their sugar income in the improvements that constituted development, they might be induced to give up their "unreasonable" expectations of RSL.

The study trip to Rabaul also was, and was intended to be, a reformulated narrative of Mari life that included the possible shapes such a life should take: it was a trip that followed from a sequence of events at home in which the Mari became acutely concerned about the future nature of their relationships with their neighbors and with RSL; it was a trip that conveyed selected Mari step by step into the context of Tolai life, a context offered as an image of the Mari's own future; and it was a trip that concluded with a narration of the trip itself in each of the four Mari villages (told in part through a videotape made of the tour).

Thus, the trip was and was intended to be an event. It became a reference point for the Mari as they engaged with, and thought about their engagement with, a range of encounters between themselves and various others, including variously positioned Tolai. Through these conjunctures, the Mari were able and in fact were eager to consider how they might lead satisfactory and far-from-static lives. By focusing on the aspects of present and future realities that most compelled them, they were taking stock of who they were and who they might become. They were, in other words, thinking carefully about what was, for them, the "bottom line," what was the most refractory, the most unyieldingly true and evident.

We provide an account here of a Mari venture into a possible future, a Mari exploration of how the world can work and what human beings might plausibly hope for. This was also, therefore, an exploration into what expectations about moral worth and responsibility might be regarded as "reasonable" or as "unreasonable." Indeed, this is an account of engagements between actors preoccupied with issues of moral worth and responsibility. As we shall see, such issues went well beyond the properties and ownership of things per se: they involved the socially determined meanings and uses of things in conveying worth and fulfilling responsibility. In these regards, our account concerns a contemporary Papua New Guinean repetition of Yali's question—indeed, of his quest.

To the Promised Land

On April 3, 2000, a party left on the "Rabaul Study Tour." The twelve Mari—four from Bumbu, four from Sankian, three from Bopirumpun, and one from Mushuan (Kiruak, the Mari spokesman)—were accompanied by the two of us, Wilson and his wife, Nerrie, and Tolu, a supervisor in the Outgrowers Office (who was to videotape the trip). Wilson planned the itinerary carefully to facilitate a shift of responsibility for Mari development from the company to the outgrowers themselves. In this regard, the itinerary was both a demonstration of and an argument for what an autonomous Outgrowers Association might accomplish. Wilson also selected the outgrowers carefully, choosing those who would be receptive to learning about new possibilities and effective in conveying these possibilities, both through personal example and more general influence. Some were already entrepreneurial; others were young, vigorous, and had potential; still others were respected elders.

It must also be said that Wilson was very proud of his Tolai people. Indeed, he was something of a Tolai-chauvinist, interested, for example, in having us help him acquire all of the ethnographies written about the Tolai. In effect, he believed, with Scarlet Epstein (1968), that Tolai traditions, particularly their possession of a shell currency with many of the attributes of Western money, predisposed them to success within a modern world.[6] Consequently, he rather relished the opportunity of impressing the Mari with Tolai success at conjoining the traditional and the modern—of impressing those who were often so troubling and troublesome, not only to RSL in general, but also to him in particular as the outgrowers' manager.[7]

On the morning of departure, the travelers were in high spirits, despite the fact that they were initially upset to discover that they would have to cover half of their airfares and other expenses. The costs would be deducted from their sugar income. Presumably, this reflected the company policy of weaning them from their dependence. All the men (except for one with a full beard) were clean-shaven. All took pains to dress neatly. Some wore ties. Others wore the RSL-monogrammed polo shirts that were issued to all of us. All wore shoes. This was a big occasion: it was to be filled with many remarkable, if not first-time, experiences. In fact, not counting us, only four of the participants had ever flown before and the majority had never been farther from home than the provincial capital of Lae, some 110 miles from Gusap.

Our first day in the Tolai home province of East New Britain was scheduled to begin with a talk from representatives of the provincial government. But our plane was delayed, and so we spent the day sightseeing in a small bus. As we drove through the countryside, videotape running, as it did throughout the trip, Wilson was careful to point out similarities between Tolai and Mari lifestyles: for instance, bananas were a garden staple in both places. He also pointed out the areas in which he had lived and worked as a young man, the home villages of Gagau (the RSL head of human relations), of the secretary of the Outgrowers Office, and of other RSL employees or their Tolai spouses. In addition, he showed sites of noteworthy events, such as the spot where the first Fijian missionary had been killed, cooked, and eaten in the early days. "Even his shoes were consumed," he told the outgrowers. "Wow," they said. "Yes," Wilson replied, "we were real primitives then." (It should be noted that virtually all conversations on this trip, including most among Mari themselves, were in Pidgin English.)

Wilson also pointed out differences between Tolai and Mari lifestyles, calling attention to an impressive level of Tolai development: most Tolai lived in permanent-material houses with water tanks; many of the remote villages were electrified, and most had schools and churches. "Wow," said the outgrowers. The outgrowers were also interested in the cars the Tolai drove. How did they acquire them? Did they finance them? Did they get together in families to buy them? Clearly, they concluded, Tolai invested in houses before anything else. They didn't spend their money on drink.

Our second day began with a visit to the East New Britain Savings and Loan Society Limited. Wilson had already explained that he had arranged this visit because the outgrowers might want their new association to provide such a banking service for its members. We were ushered into an air-conditioned boardroom with a seminar table, and Wilson introduced us to the managing director, explaining: "Every year at RSL there's a big cash flow to the outgrowers. But there is no commercial bank in the area. And it's hard for these people to hold back money. They receive it and are happy and then they spend it to make themselves happier. And then it is finished."

The manager responded by providing a brief history of the savings and loan society and then called for questions from the outgrowers. These he answered in a straightforward, noncondescending manner. Some of the questions had to do with the procedures of such a society: What was a minimal deposit? How much did one have to keep in savings before one could take out a loan? What happened if one's crop was less than expected and one could not repay the loan? Other questions involved how to establish such a society: How much money did you need? What kind of help did the government give you? Who could give them advice if they wanted to start a society at RSL? The outgrowers listened attentively and many took notes throughout. Toward the end of the session, the outgrowers felt both excited enough about what they were hearing and comfortable enough with the setting to express their enthusiasm about establishing a society of their own. "We came here to learn from you because we're new at this," said one, "and we're very happy with the information you have given us and with Robin Wilson for bringing us."

The afternoon was spent on a tour of the countryside, including a drive past Wilson's home village of Vunamami. We saw copra and cocoa plantations, schools, and a community of Tolai resettled from volcano-damaged areas. Outgrowers took notes as we drove, making sure that they had the names of the places we visited on their lists so that they could properly recount their travels to people back home. As one said to us, "Unless you have the names, no one will believe your stories."

Perhaps the most interesting part of the afternoon for the outgrowers was a stop at Bitapaka, the World War Two memorial and cemetery. There, next to the names engraved on memorial stones of Australian soldiers killed (whose bodies were never found), were names of some Papua New Guinean constables. One was Bigri. He, we were told excitedly, was a Mari who belonged to the Pulap clan of Sankian. Originally recruited to work on a coastal plantation at Salamoa, he became a constable and then was called for war duty. Many of the outgrowers wanted photographs of themselves pointing to his name. Who would have guessed, they said, that we would have found the name of one of us way out here? One joked that they should ask for compensation for the man's death, maybe K200.

Our next day began with a trip to the Coconut and Cocoa Research Institute, an industry-supported facility where research relevant to the production of these two tropical tree crops was carried on. The outgrowers, introduced as "Ramu Sugar men," were pleased with the tour of the impressive facilities, particularly when they got to help graft and pollinate cocoa and thereby, as one of the outgrowers put it, "leave Ramu's mark in East New Britain." Several outgrowers had tried to grow cocoa on their land, and they vowed to reapply themselves with renewed vigor to these projects. They also expressed regret at not having RSL-imprinted gifts, such as logo-decorated tee-shirts, to leave with those who showed them around and taught them new techniques.

The third day was, perhaps, the most fascinating of all. That day we visited with Daniel Torot, Wilson's old friend and colleague. Wilson wanted the outgrowers to meet Torot, whom he saw as an exemplar of how they might both develop and remain Papua New Guinean.

All the houses in Torot's village were of permanent materials. Torot's wife welcomed us, invited us to sit on mats, and then distributed betel nuts and their accompaniments for us to chew.[8] Wilson told us that he and Torot had been friends since the early 1970s, when Torot hired him to work for the company that Torot helped develop. It was a time of political upheavals in East New Britain: there was much racial discord, but Torot and Wilson advocated racial equality. They believed that white men,

Chinese, mixed-race people, and Papua New Guineans should work together. The company they ran, called New Guinea Island Products, was the largest one owned by Papua New Guineans, a cooperative that received no government funds but nonetheless grew to own plantations, trade stores, and fermentaries, in addition to buying copra and cocoa. It was such an extensive company that it took one full day to visit all of the cocoa fermentaries it owned. However, although Torot was an important businessman, he always remained a true Tolai, always active in the political and economic life of his people. As the outgrowers could see, Torot lived the simple life of a village man. Nonetheless, he had great influence throughout the region. If there was any trouble, Torot would be called in to resolve it. He also helped his children, but insisted that they build their own houses because he wanted them to be self-sufficient.

The outgrowers were obviously impressed. One gave a short speech thanking Torot for welcoming them to his village and saying that it was a pity the Mari had only Yalibu and a few other elders left alive. Torot spoke next, providing a short autobiography to which the Mari listened with interest:

I'm seventy-two years old and have four children and many grandchildren. I've worked for the government for thirty-two years, first as local government councilor [an elected representative authorized to allocate tax monies to locally significant projects, such as roads and aid posts]. . . . I didn't know English. I wasn't an educated man. . . . But I worked hard and was afraid of no one, not even of the premier [of the East New Britain Province]. . . . And I have worked with the mission too. In 1969, the mission sent me overseas . . . to visit six countries over a month and a half. My leadership was good and I helped bring productive ideas and industry—a good life—to my people. One important thing is prohibiting drinking alcohol, because this is the best way to lose money. It's important to understand this. A drink or two are fine, but too much drinking simply wastes money. I have always helped the people with such ideas. . . . And when I spoke, things happened. . . .

You should know that, in the past, we didn't have money, just shell money. When I was young, I journeyed to [the neighboring province of] West New Britain to get some shell money. When a high sea capsized my boat, I persevered and got there anyway because I knew that, if I didn't have shell money, I wouldn't be a man. If you don't have shell money, then your children cannot marry. You are a rootless man. You aren't a Tolai.

At this point various Mari began talking about the importance of custom, literally providing a chorus of agreement that one should hold one's custom dear and ensure its preservation.

Francis Gagas, Wilson Gagas's brother-in-law from Sankian, broke from the chorus to say:

> I want you to know that we of Ramu Sugar are always arguing with your son, Robin Wilson. But, he has given us strength. He has watched over us, even though we bicker with him. . . . He has been our good friend. He has put his heart with the people. Big man [referring to Torot], you should know that Wilson is not just an employee of Ramu Sugar. He has taken his strength from you. You are at its roots. . . . He doesn't just work for his fortnightly pay. He is full of fire. He is truly a son of the Tolai people. His Tolainess is hot. He is the same as you. He has left your house fire, but has remained your son.

Torot responded, saying that he hoped the Mari would, in the future, follow Wilson's advice. Yes, the Mari promised. But, as one Mari stressed, Torot must understand that they were new at development. In fact, this was the first time many were away from home. They hadn't had sugar money for long. Before, they had a "low standard of living and were men of the bush." But now they saw the good houses owned by Tolai and were determined to learn how to look after their money. After all, another said, missionaries came to the Mari far later than they had to the Tolai: the Mari were the last to be taught, but were now committed to progress. Torot agreed that they had a bright future so long as they remembered to work for themselves and not rely on the government for handouts. "The fire," he said, "is not with the government. The government is cold. You have to work for yourselves and have your own heat."

Wilson then returned to the earlier topic of shell money, explaining that having two kinds of money, kina and shell money, helped the Tolai to develop because it prevented jealousies between the poor and the rich. If a poor man hadn't any kina, he always had shell money with which to buy chickens, or garden produce, or pay bride price. He could still engage in the life of the people. He wasn't out of the game, but could still be a respected Tolai.

We were then invited into Torot's house to see his shell money. Nerrie Wilson announced that Torot was, in shell money, the richest man in East New Britain. At a rate that made ten fathoms equivalent to about K40, he owned more than enough to be a "millionaire."[9] But he was not interested in converting his shell money into kina—the former was much more important to him than the latter. Indeed, Torot's storeroom contained over twenty-five large rolls of shell money—thousands of fathoms of it. It was a most impressive display by both Tolai and non-Tolai standards, and many of the Mari asked to be photographed next to it.

Nerrie Wilson and Torot demonstrated how the shell money was distributed in fathom-lengths during various marriage and death ceremonies (fig. 17). Wilson told us that he had brought two hundred fathoms (worth about K800, he said) with him to Rabaul so that he could distribute it at the bride-price presentation we were all to attend later in the week. Francis Gagas asked more about bride price, telling Torot that, among the Mari, it had increased to between K1,500 and K2,000. High as this was, the kinsmen of in-marrying Highland women were demanding

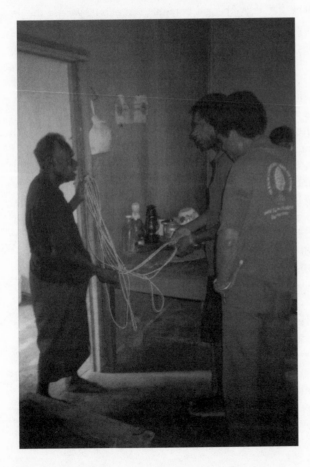

Figure 17.
Torot displaying
shell money in
fathom-lengths

much more. Nerrie Wilson responded that people who charge so much have lost their customs. Torot said that at his death ceremony, his kin would distribute all of his shell money—it would all be gone. This seemed to upset Wilson Gagas, who advised him: "Old man [a term of respect], sell half of it to enjoy life now and keep half of it to distribute at your funeral later."

Food (rice, corned beef, and greens) was brought out in individual banana-leaf packets. At this point, we were joined by several other senior Tolai men from Torot's community. As we ate together, most of the conversation concerned the political organization of Tolai communities. One man explained:

> We make plans for projects in our villages and then take these plans to both provincial and national representatives. But we rarely benefit from the government. Rather, we benefit from our own efforts: We use the money we earn from cocoa and copra sales to better our lives. We don't rely on others, just ourselves. Every once in a while we get a little help from the government, but not much.

After more discussion about village courts, the local government council and the mutual respect Tolai generally show each other, Torot wrapped the afternoon up: "There are things political and things economic. I don't believe in the political too much because it ruins the economic. So work, work, work. And, remember, if you don't, when I die, I'll come back to bother you."

That evening in conversation with others on the tour, we learned that the Mari were both impressed and instructed. They found Torot gracious and got some valuable ideas about the importance of self-reliance, respect for leaders, and pride in one's community. Development must come, they said, from the bottom up, and men must lead by example. However, they were somewhat ashamed that, relative to the Tolai, they were "ignorant, grassland men." Moreover and significantly, they knew that if they worked as hard as the Tolai to get ahead, they would expose themselves to sorcery by other Mari.

The next major event on our itinerary came a day later. It was a bride-price presentation and another example of the exemplary blend between the traditional and the modern in Tolai life. We were to accompany the groom's party to this presentation since Wilson was the groom's kinsman on the father's side. The Mari were excited to participate, not only because they had been designated fictive kin as part of Wilson's entourage, but also because they felt a connection to the groom: he was a tradesman at RSL, living in Village 5. Because his presence was not necessary, indeed not appropriate, at this presentation, he had remained at RSL.

The presentation took place at the impressive home of the bride's father. Some three hundred people gathered on the front lawn, divided about equally between the groom's side and the bride's side—the matrilineal and patrilateral kin of each. (Among the Tolai, inheritance is matrilineal, that is, inheritance is traced through a female line such that a child belongs to the family of his or her mother, with the mother's brother an important senior male kinsman. However, important ties are also maintained with patrilateral kin—with those on the father's side, including with the father himself.) Most of the Mari and the two of us were seated on chairs with Wilson on the groom's side. After we were welcomed with betel nut, a United Church pastor delivered a brief prayer in Tolai. Then the transactions in shell money began. The central presentation was of the bride price itself. This was the two hundred fathoms brought by Wilson.

After the bride-price payment, it was time for the groom's side to find the bride, who was sequestered in her father's house. Young men of the groom's side stripped off their shirts and started up the flight of stairs to the porch, where young men of the bride's side showered them with buckets of water reddened by betel-nut spit. The Mari whooped with delight and encouragement as Kiruak, the single Mushuan representative, took off his shirt to join enthusiastically the other men in their quest (fig. 18). A few minutes later, they emerged, half carrying the bride, who had been hidden in a darkened room under empty copra sacks. The abductors were beaten with fronds and nettles and again showered with reddish water as they descended the stairs with their prize.

The ceremony concluded with the distribution of additional shell money. The bride's kin responded with a counterpresentation to all of the groom's kin—including the RSL delegation—as well as to some selected others. The afternoon ended with a few speeches, given largely in Pidgin English rather than Tolai for the benefit, we were told, of the RSL delegation. A man from the groom's side said that custom was very important and could not be learned at school on a blackboard: it was something one must see and do at home. The local government councilor, a member of the bride's side, berated those Tolai who did not insist that their children attend such traditional events as these. He was worried that Western customs would ruin the Tolai completely unless they held strongly to their

Figure 18. Tolai wedding: the groom's men search for the bride.

customs. He believed, moreover, that the good things that were learned from the West—store-bought food, cars, good houses—would be lost if custom was lost. Custom was good because it involved and committed everyone in the community. In this case, everyone would sustain the marriage. Indeed, those from RSL, who received shell money, must now look after the bride when she came to Ramu.

After a concluding prayer, the crowd dispersed. The whole event, which lasted about two hours, was extremely well orchestrated, indeed, very classy. The Mari were impressed, telling us that nothing back home was done with such precision, in such a well-organized way. They repeated that the Tolai were strong and had good houses because they acted collectively in following their customs. They also congratulated Kiruak for having raised up the name of Ramu Sugar by joining the proceedings. Several reiterated that because they received shell money, they were obligated to look after the bride when she came to Ramu. One said that if they were to discover an argument between husband and wife, they must work hard to mediate it; another added that if such a circumstance arose, they should show the couple the shell money they were given as a warrant for such mediation.

The next day was Sunday, and while sightseeing we decided to stop at the ordination of Isikel Tioti, the new United Church bishop, at his home village of Takubar. This event genuinely overwhelmed the Mari. It was an all Papua New Guinean show (we were the only expatriates we saw). Thousands of parishioners, mostly Tolai, dressed in immaculate Sunday attire, came in cars, trucks, and buses. Vastly overflowing the small village church, they filled the surrounding grounds. A printed program was distributed and followed: there was a long and orderly procession of church and government dignitaries into the church; there were United Church choirs from all over the province, which, in their turn, stood up to perform hymns in multipart harmonies; there was a church service; there were speeches. Our Mari friends were somewhat diffident. The size of the crowd, the quality of the performances, and the coordination of the events were of a scale that no Mari had ever seen before—except, perhaps, when organized by BTL people at RSL. Moreover, they were somewhat embarrassed. Most of them were in travel-weary clothes because they did not know that they would be attending this event.

It was with some relief, we think, that the Mari spent most of the afternoon resting. Then came the farewell dinner that evening at Wilson's house, the house he planned to retire to upon leaving RSL. Wilson's house was built on land that had been transferred from traditional and collective to state-authorized and private ownership. He had purchased it from his father's matriline and registered it in his own name.[10] The Mari were obviously impressed. The house, comparable to the house of a manager at RSL (type C), was made of permanent materials, electrified, and elevated. It had a spacious porch and was flanked by large tanks to collect rainwater from the corrugated metal roof. There was another house on the land Wilson purchased. It, too, was made of permanent materials and now served as a trade store.

After we were welcomed with betel nut, Wilson introduced us to the several senior men and women of his matriline and explained to them that his job at RSL was to help "the farmers." To this end, he brought them to East New Britain to learn how the Tolai lived. He hoped his relatives could help by explaining a bit about their lives.

Several Tolai men spoke about "tradition"—about marriage, bride price, love magic. Several others, about the economy—about growing coconuts and cocoa for sale on the market and using the money earned to build good houses and the like. A Tolai woman spoke about family life. There must always be "two involved in a family, a man *and* a woman." Income should first be used for domestic well-being. It would be all right, of course, to invest income in a trade store if the money thereby generated would be for the use of all family members. The Mari must understand that women worked for the family: Women should go to school so as to help men earn money for the sake of their family. A husband and wife should jointly open a family bank account. Men should not look down on women. God made both men and women and meant both to work. Both must work to earn money for the family.

Francis Gagas was the first among the tour group to respond. His words were echoed by other Mari throughout the evening:

> These are good stories you are telling us. We have learned that your lives are good because your customs are strong. We have lost our customs. Once we had customs comparable to yours, but they are gone. Now a man will sleep with a young woman and the next thing his parents learn is that they have to pay K2,000 or K3,000 in bride price. With you, life is still good. We've seen this to be true and will carry the message home with us.

> But now I want to say a few things about this nephew of yours. He left for Ramu Sugar when he was just a boy. And I want to tell you that he has not just thought of himself, about filling his own pockets. He is paid by the company, but it is for us that he works. He's the "papa" of our fields and helps us with them day and night. He's done a big thing for us. He has worked hard and now we have cars and plenty of money. Yet he has seen that what we do with our money is wrong and so has brought us here to see your customs. He wants us to change. He is a good brother of ours. We've been cross with him, but he works for us nonetheless. God has given him the intelligence to do well in school and he has shared his knowledge with us. It wouldn't have been good if we came here and did not tell you his history. I want you to know.

Nabua Morissa, from Bumbu, spoke next:

> I would like to endorse Francis's statements. You Tolai people plan well and, with the little money you earn, have created a good life for yourselves. It's been eighteen years since we started planting sugar and, in this time, we have earned lots of money. But we've spent only a little of it on our families, and our lives in our villages aren't very good. Will we be able to make use of what we've learned here? We do not know. Wilson, our boss, manages our business. He brought us here so that we can learn new things and try to make use of them when we return to Ramu. We have come to learn how to budget our money. You have a little money, but you make good use of it. We have a lot of money, but we

waste it on whatever we want, on such things as cars and radios. We throw our money away and therefore don't have one little thing to show for it. So we want to thank our boss. We're happy to have come and learned from you. But who knows if we'll be able to make use of what we learned. We'll go home, speak to the rest of us, and try.

After several similar speeches, Wilson announced that it was time to eat. He asked one Mari to say grace, and then we all climbed the stairs to the porch of his house, where a feast of fried chicken legs, noodle chow mein, earth-oven-baked chicken, taro, various greens, bananas, rice, and soft drinks was set out. After dinner, conversation continued on a variety of subjects: the different kinds of fish available in rivers like the Ramu compared to fish in the ocean that edged East New Britain, the grass-lands of the Ramu Valley, the water shortages of East New Britain, the effects of World War Two on both areas.

The outgrowers concluded their study tour with a visit to the East New Britain provincial government headquarters in order to learn what help their own provincial government might be expected to provide. The two of us did not accompany them at this point, but when we met them back at RSL some five days later, they were still abuzz from the experience, chatting with everyone they met about what they saw and did. Meanwhile, the videotapes of the trip were being edited into about a two-hour version of the highlights, which was shown late in April at each of the four Mari villages. (The necessary generator, television, and speakers were even carried across the Ramu River for the showing at Mushuan.)

• • •

All four of these sessions were well attended by Mari of all ages. Those who were on the tour introduced and commented on the video, explain-ing, amplifying, and endorsing. The audience was interested and im-pressed with the level of Tolai development. Many remarked about mod-ern houses and good cars. Yalibu, Bopirumpun's wealthy, respected, and somewhat profligate elder, demanded that a savings and loan come immediately to the Mari. Indeed, virtually everyone embraced the idea, thinking (erroneously, of course) that a small deposit would make pos-sible a very large loan.

Viewers were also interested and impressed with the strength of Tolai custom. Everyone found Daniel Torot engaging. All agreed that he excelled in both business and tradition but remained accessible and generous. The older men, especially, were fascinated by his display of shell money. Somehow he won respect without provoking the ire (and sorcery) of others.[11] All were also engrossed, as had been the tour members, with the bride-price distribution. Many commented on the size of the gathering and the intricacies of the exchange. And they were pleased that the exchanges incorporated the Mari visitors. They hooted with delight at Kiruak's direct participation in the events. They were thoroughly pleased that the newlyweds would be living at RSL. And they were moved by the story of the Mari constable left behind in East New Britain.

Mari also lamented the loss of many of their own customs, such as those concerning sister-exchange and other forms of marriage. Yalibu immediately got out some old Mari shell valuables and began wearing them. In the course of this discussion, tour members stressed that it was because the Tolai had preserved their customs and because these customs emphasized the importance of mutual respect and cooperation that the Tolai were able to work together in a way that promoted development.

There were, of course, some grievances voiced at these presentations: Some women feared that Mari men would never heed the words of Tolai women about valuing the contributions of women. They said that they, too, would like to live in permanent-material houses, but the men who wasted so much money over such a long period of time would probably continue to do so. Some men also complained that their sugar fields were smaller than those of others and therefore the new savings and loan wouldn't benefit them as much. Some noted that it was obviously a wonderful trip and hence it was a shame that they were not able to go. Others worried that the cost of the trip would be deducted from the sugar income of all the Mari.

For his part, Wilson told us that he thought both the study tour itself and the subsequent video presentations went well. His mission, to convince the Mari that Papua New Guineans could develop through their own efforts, was likely successful. He could not be sure, of course, whether the Mari would truly change as a result of what they learned during the trip. Perhaps the way they used their next several sugar payments would provide an indication. He was optimistic, however, because a number of Mari expressed interest in his offer to draw up plans for permanent-material houses with adjacent water tanks, houses they might build with their sugar incomes. He was also strongly encouraged by their desire to establish their Outgrowers Association as soon as possible.

Indeed, Mari were already consulting with Wilson concerning where on their land the association's building would be best located. The plan was that this building would house a savings and loan facility (although security might be problem) and a women's center. Perhaps, as well, it might house several small businesses. Wilson assured the Mari that RSL would help them set all of this up. RSL would, for instance, help them register their association with the government, survey their building site, record it as association property, and organize and certify their savings and loan society. RSL would also instruct Mari in business skills and advise them about viable business enterprises. But, Wilson emphasized, the Mari must themselves assume full responsibility for the success or failure of the association and its enterprises and activities. RSL could not bail them out.[12]

· · ·

Wilson's escorting Mari to his East New Britain home on a study tour was both similar and dissimilar to Australians' taking Yali to their home country on a "first-contact refresher course." Like the Australians, who hoped that immersion in selected aspects of a developed way of life would effect a conversion among the Papua New Guineans, Wilson hoped that the immersion in selected aspects of a Tolai way of life would effect, if not a conversion, then at least a transformation. Significantly, it would be more feasible, and less demeaning to the Mari, for them to strive to become more like Tolai than it would be for Yali to strive to become more like Australians.

Certainly, the trip was designed to convince the Mari to accept the bottom line as defined by RSL and ostensibly by the Tolai, particularly the idea that business must be constituted in a particular way. Success in business necessitates hard work, discipline, and skill to produce income sufficient to cover costs, if not to make a profit. Correspondingly, this bottom line also holds that, since business success must be earned, the fruits of that success should go to those earning it. However, the trip was also structured to persuade the Mari that modern business success and traditional sociability—that a work ethic and a social ethic—need not be opposed. After all, Daniel Torot could claim the rewards of his own hard work while being a magnanimous host. Just as the Tolai could be hardworking while remaining culturally rich, so too the Mari can develop while maintaining and enhancing key aspects of their culture.

These key aspects, primarily those valuing connection and cooperation, were ones Wilson thought the Mari shared with the Tolai and, by extension, with many other Papua New Guineans. In a way that we think came easily to Wilson, given his personal generosity and his own background as a Tolai and a Papua New Guinean, throughout the trip he helped the Mari establish gratifying social ties. Defined on the study tour as affluent and as "Ramu Sugar men," it was with an enhanced sense of identity and worth that Mari forged new relationships with a range of Tolai, from Torot to the newlyweds and their kin. The Mari also thickened existing relationships with RSL's Tolai staff by, for instance, seeing their home villages. In addition, they were able to see Wilson embedded in his home contexts and to engage with him and his kin in these contexts.

Thus, unlike Papua New Guinean experiences of first contacts or first-contact refresher courses, the Mari's contact with the Tolai was not intended to shatter or discredit their culture. It was intended, instead, to suggest ways, based on the accumulated experience of the much earlier contacted Tolai (who once ate a missionary, shoes and all), in which Mari visions of relationship and worth might be adjusted and enhanced. It was intended to convey that mutual claims based on relationship might be tempered by the recognition that business had its own rationality, its own bottom line. It was also intended to convey that, through such recognition, the collective Mari sense of worth might be enhanced. They might truly become developed outgrowers rather than inefficacious grassland men.

All this being said, Wilson was also conveying to the Mari that they should stop complaining. They often gave him a hard time. They admitted as much to Torot and others. Thus, Wilson was pleased to be able to show them that he (unlike they) came from a place that maintained culture and achieved prosperity—and a place to which, his term of mentorship done, he would retire. Mari have, as we have said, given RSL a lot of trouble. This trip, among other things, would show them that if they do not develop, it will be their own fault. After all, the Tolai have developed and with fewer resources.

For their part, the Mari were greatly taken by what they saw and learned during the tour. Not only at the video shows after the tour, but also in their conversations for months to come, the trip served as a point of reference. They continued to be impressed with the Tolai, with the strength and complexity of their culture, and with their prosperity. They felt validated by the cordiality with which many Tolai welcomed them. Pledged to revive their own culture, they planned, for instance, to decorate the future headquarters of their Outgrowers Association with traditional Mari motifs and to open it with traditional dancing. Importantly, the building was to be located so as to be highly visible, even to someone just driving by on the main road. Moreover, the savings and loan society housed there would attest to Mari development as well as foster that development. With this banking facility, it would be easier, both practically and psychically, for outgrowers to save their money. As it was, if they wished to bank their money, instead of cashing their checks through local purchases, they had to travel several hours to either Lae or Kainantu. Depositing, rather than immediately spending, would be that much easier with, not just a local savings facility, but *their* local facility, one that all Mari would use. In addition, the deposited money could then be withdrawn for such widely approved projects as house building, perhaps according to the plans Wilson would be providing. Indeed, the outgrowers planned to join together to build such houses as collective projects. Though some Mari recognized that providing physical security as well as competent oversight for their savings and loan might be difficult, they nonetheless saw it as providing a possible way for them to "come up together," as they say—in a way that minimized jealousy and fear of sorcery.

Significantly, while the Mari were captivated with these tour-generated possibilities for self-help and were, for the moment at least, disinclined to give Wilson a hard time, they were not willing to release RSL from its purported responsibilities toward them. Continuing to insist that they were landowners, they refused in this particular area to accept RSL's version of the bottom line. Although they agreed with Wilson that an association could help them collectively take charge of their destiny, part of that destiny, they believed, was to become strong enough to compel RSL to provide them with what remained their due. Indeed, Mari outgrowers seemed to regard their association itself as part of a cluster of technologies and techniques that would enable them to assert *their* bottom line, to fulfill their quest. No longer ignorant, as were their ancestors and others of Yali's generation, they would act like other sophisticated Papua New Guineans and compel the company to replace the MA with an MOU specifying RSL's responsibilities to pay royalties and to provide roads, water, electrification, and the like—perhaps even good housing. After all, RSL had become rich over the years through the use of Mari land. Finally, all would see that the Mari must be taken seriously.

One Year Later

When we returned the following year to RSL, in June 2001, we caught up on what had happened with the outgrowers. The land for the association building had been surveyed and several possible architectural plans drawn up. Although the registration of the Outgrowers Association was nearly complete, there had been no serious move to change the MA into an MOU. This was, at least partly, in recognition that RSL remained strapped for cash. The crop had not been good and, because the Papua New Guinean economy was in disarray, consumer demand was down. Furthermore, because the outgrowers knew that RSL had told the union its demands for pay and benefit increases simply could not be met, they were limiting their actions against RSL to complaints about not earning enough. Although Mari told us that not much had changed, wryly admitting that they still spent their money—still, they said, far too little—much as before, they also conveyed to us that they remained poised for a transformed future.

For its part, RSL continued to insist that it could not afford the social services that many Mari were convinced should be theirs as landowners. Nevertheless, RSL had come to acknowledge that the outgrowers probably should be paid more for their cane. Indeed, based on the previous year's report by the BTL agricultural economist (Innes 2000), RSL did increase the rate of compensation. RSL was also coming to terms with the lack of the outgrowers' input into the cane crop, that is, their refusal to adopt a work ethic like that of the yeoman farmers in Kenya. Indeed, as mentioned in chapter 7, Dr. Martin Evans, a BTL economist, concluded that in fact the Mari preference to be rent-takers, rather than farmers, made good economic sense: after all, because they lacked capital and labor but had plenty of land, they were maximizing what they had in most abundance.[13] Thus, apparently relieved from the expectations of many at BTL and RSL that they labor unceasingly in stiflingly hot cane fields, the Mari could rationally give themselves over to monitoring the company's cultivation of their fields!

When we met with Wilson, he said that he was sympathetic to outgrower complaints that they were not earning enough. Though it was true that they were now getting more for their cane crop, the company was also deducting more for its services. In particular, it was charging more for the application of agricultural chemicals: these were imported and were costing more, given the decline in the kina's value. Nonetheless, the outgrowers were still impressed by the "Rabaul Study Tour." Although little looked changed in the villages, Wilson was sure that savings, budgeting, and development-focused investment (for example, in permanent-material houses) would begin once the outgrowers got their annual payments. And as soon as the savings and loan society was certified and in place (and Wilson was working hard toward this end), development could really take off. He certainly was going to work his hardest to make all of this happen. When he retired in three years, the project was bound to be completed. Certainly, he did not want to leave things unfinished. This was an exciting time for him.

Tragically, after work on the following day, Wilson suffered a heart attack and died.

• • •

The extended RSL community was deeply distressed. Hundreds mourned at Wilson's house throughout the night after his death, and dozens—including many outgrowers—accompanied his body the following morning to the morgue in Lae, where it rested for several days. Although Nerrie Wilson wanted her husband's body to be taken from Lae directly back to East New Britain, she was reminded that "he is not a son of the Tolai alone," but important to many at RSL. And so she agreed to a memorial service at Gusap.

When Wilson's body was returned to RSL about a week later, his hearse was accompanied by a procession of some twenty-five cars, trucks, and buses. The program, which was drawn up by a committee of kin and colleagues, called for his body to remain for a half hour or so at each of the outgrowers' villages, but time proved too short for that. Consequently, the principal stop was at Bumbu. There his coffin was welcomed by an honor guard of Seventh-Day Adventists from Bopirumpun and placed within a flower-bedecked enclosure (fig. 19). Hundreds of sobbing outgrowers and their families filed past the coffin, viewing the body and paying their respects.

After a brief speech by Kiruak attesting to the magnitude of Wilson's help to the outgrowers, the coffin continued its journey. It passed briefly through Sankian and was placed within Gusap's United Church, where Wilson had served as a respected elder. Although the factory was kept running by a skeleton crew, RSL had, in effect, closed for the day. Thousands of workmen, managers, outgrowers, and others crowded the lawn surrounding the church to hear speeches by clergy as well as by RSL's general manager, the chairman of the board and the head of the Department of Agriculture.

To a responsive audience, all the speakers praised Wilson's sincerity, wisdom, and commitment to his family, community, and work. But RSL's chairman, Peter Colton, truly captivated the crowd. Speaking in fluent

Figure 19. Wilson's coffin borne to a flower-bedecked enclosure at Bumbu

Pidgin English, he said that, during his many years in the country, he worked often with educated Papua New Guineans. But none was like Wilson. Wilson was the kind of person who was wise and never quick to anger. He dealt fairly with all, regardless of their race, language, ethnicity, occupation, or education. He was someone from whom everyone who knew him, including Colton himself, learned important lessons. How to memorialize such a man? In just one way: by following his example and working together for the good of all. "We may fail from time to time, but if we try sincerely, then Wilson will be watching and will be happy."

The Mari certainly sought to commemorate him. They pledged to name their association building for him. They sat with family, friends, and colleagues throughout the final night before Wilson's body was returned to East New Britain to be buried. They purchased cows, pigs, and chickens to contribute to the final feast. And, in addition, the outgrowers quickly agreed to donate K100 each—some K14,000 altogether—as a collective gift to Wilson's wife. RSL readily consented to advance them this money from their respective sugar incomes.

Moreover, many of those who had gone on the study tour decided to return to Rabaul for the funeral. And RSL, easing at least somewhat its concern with the bottom line, contributed K18,000 toward their airfares and other expenses. Some, including Yalibu, bedecked with his Mari shells, paid their own way to travel by boat. Those from the study tour took the shell money from their earlier trip to give back at Wilson's funeral. The quintessence of the desirable and feasible, this was how life should be conducted.

9

Hewers of Wood
and Drawers of Water

EARLIER, WE ARGUED THAT the complex and far from static social context that became RSL is the product of a negotiation between three general narratives. Each is a different story about what is desirable and feasible; each is about how people should act and about what the future, including a future of factory-focused development, might bring. The first, broadly exemplified by Wilson Gagas's position that the Mari have inherent worth and corresponding rights, derives from a primordial connection to ples. The second, broadly exemplified by Stuart Hayes's concern that sugar be produced efficiently, derives from a rational evaluation of the technologies and techniques most appropriate to solving the problems set by a particular, developing place. The third, broadly exemplified by nationalists' interests in equality and distinctiveness, derives from the postcolonial desire to forge, from the many different pleses in the country, a modern Papua New Guinea that can take its place among the developed nations of the world.

Here we must introduce a fourth narrative—one that grows out of and continues, yet also undermines and even contradicts, the other three. This is a narrative of global capitalism told to both RSL and the Papua New Guinean government by such institutions as the World Trade Organization and the World Bank. It is a narrative, moreover, which materializes in the operations of such corporations as Coca-Cola Amatil

(CCA), producer of the Coca-Cola line of products in Papua New Guinea and Australia. As we shall see, this is a narrative about the pervasive and ubiquitous. It is a narrative about the fundamental nature of the world, and it has many dimensions in common with the seemingly inexorable process characteristic of Diamond's answer to Yali's question.

Coke Ples

During 2000 and 2001, an advertisement for Coca-Cola frequently was broadcast on EMTV, Papua New Guinea's sole domestic television station, showing a group of unsmiling, uncommunicative, ostensibly unrelated Papua New Guinean adults—men and women, young and old—traveling in the back of a pick-up truck. It is not clear from the advertisement who they are, where they have come from, or where they are going. The truck stops, and another passenger, a young man who has been standing by the side of the road, gets on. Despite the looks of the other passengers, registering indifference, if not distrust, the new arrival reaches into his knapsack and offers to share a liter of Coke. This immediately prompts one of the older men to open his cooler filled with Coke and to pass bottles around. A festive atmosphere immediately prevails: everyone begins to smile, laugh, and converse.

In our experience, such sharing is the sort of thing that virtually any Papua New Guinean will do with wantoks. Indeed, sharing of such items as betel nut, tobacco, and soft drinks, including Coca-Cola, is central to the easy sociability of kin and community. Thus the message of this advertisement, at least as we understand it, is that Coke can be a catalyst for transforming delocalized and often suspicious strangers into people fully at home with one other, able to interact as if they have known one another all of their lives. In other words, the advertisement strongly implies that Coke can localize them all into wantoks.

The advertisement also implies that Coke can nationalize them into citizens. The Papua New Guinean impulse to share, which the young man's offer catalyzes, is responsible for transforming the strangers into an instant community based on empathy, based on the recognition that everyone likes Coke and, perhaps therefore, that everyone is likable. In this manner, Coke can commit, or at least dispose, such strangers to a relationship of positive reciprocity. Moreover, the social and spatial indeterminacy of those on the truck—that they represent "everyman" from "any place"—suggests an imagined, pan–Papua New Guinea community of Coke gatherings and sharings. Thus, as wantoks and as citizens, Coke makes Papua New Guineans more sociable, more socially linked, in a Papua New Guinean sort of way.

Indeed, as virtually anyone traveling in contemporary Papua New Guinea can attest, Coke is by far the most available source of liquid refreshment. This is so whether or not it would offset the tensions and hazards of road travel, or whether or not it might bring about an instant and easy sociability of kin and community. In fact, Robert Foster, who studies Coke extensively in both Papua New Guinea and elsewhere, writes that it is the company's goal to make its product preferable to water. Foster quotes a 1996 address to shareholders given by Roberto C. Goizueta, between 1981 and 1997 the chairman and CEO of the Coca-Cola Company: "[W]e have become increasingly mindful of one undeniable fact—the average human body requires at least 64 ounces of liquid every day just to survive, and our beverages account for not even 2 of those ounces. For every person on this planet consuming at least 64 ounces is not an option; but choosing where those ounces come from is" (2002: 11). Goizueta concludes by assuring the shareholders that he is "resolutely focused on going after the other 62." Thus, Foster wryly comments "the global expansion of soft drink consumption is a war against tap water or, more accurately, the transformation of tap water from an end product to an ingredient" (12).

In traveling, as the two of us have, from Lae to Gusap—from the metropolis where Coke is produced and bottled to the hinterland where the sugar, an ingredient of Coke, is grown and processed—we can see the extent of Coke's reach at every roadside stop. (In fact, with Pepsi Cola's withdrawal from the Papua New Guinea soft drink market in 1998, CCA became the sole purveyor of soft drinks in the country.)[1] Along this stretch of highway there are three large and many small markets selling products ranging from betel nut to used clothing. The large markets all have prominent, Coke-emblazoned signs announcing the name of the market and indicating the availability of Coca-Cola. In addition, both at the large and small markets, there are numerous CCA-issued pushcarts from which Coke and the Coke-line of soft drinks are available. Significantly, each of these carts is conspicuously labeled as a "Coke Ples." Thus, at least according to CCA's definition of geography, wherever one travels in Papua New Guinea, one either is, or soon will be, at a location that, whatever its local meaning, is a place of Coke (cf. Miller 1997).

We recognize, of course, that there is a difference between Coke's advertising claims and Coke's actually claiming a ples. However, to judge from the lives of those at RSL, Coke's penetration is, in fact, remarkably thorough. Coke not only features in everyday RSL life, but also is part of the grammar of that life, signifying work, leisure, hospitality, and, as we shall see, intimacy. Coke is drunk frequently by workers and managers, both as a way to provide the body with fluid and to provide a pause that refreshes. It is readily available for sale from coolers supplied free of charge by CCA—so long as the only products refrigerated therein are theirs. (A CCA official told us that he was always sorry when he had to remove a cooler from a remote area because it was being used for stocking non-Coke products, like Milo, which might, in fact, be better for children.) One of our friends, a mechanic for RSL, is in charge of the transport section's cooler. He posted a sign saying that no one will be allowed to acquire a Coke on credit. But then he also posted a list of those who did so. Moreover, in our interviews with senior managers, both RSL and BTL, we are often asked whether we wanted tea, coffee, or a soft drink—from a CCA cooler. One Papua New Guinean agronomist often takes several bottles of Coke with him into the fields. When we wanted to photograph him alongside a cane field, he put aside his Coke, joking that while he really likes Coke, he doesn't "want to be an advertisement for globalism."

Coke, it seems, is always welcome. Once, as we dropped Paul, our research assistant, at his village of Bumbu, we saw a young and unfamiliar boy near his house. No one knew who this boy was, and he did not seem to speak Pidgin English. Perhaps he had strayed from his parents while traveling between the Highlands and Madang. The police were notified, and, meanwhile, Bumbu people looked after him. Drinking a Coke we had just purchased for him, Paul handed it to the boy. Although the boy was lost, confused, and perhaps not even a Pidgin-speaker, he was assumed to be—and evidently was—a Coke drinker. Coke, it will be recalled, was distributed widely at the birthday party Kamdan held for his son, both as sufficient in itself and as mixer for stronger drinks. And, of course, Coke is often consumed at the Management Club, either by those trying to lay off the booze for a while or as a mixer by the confirmed rum drinkers (as many BTL sugar men are proud to be).

We became most fully aware of the way in which Coke operates within the grammar of everyday life during one session of the village court. As a pause that refreshes, it also proved in one case to be a pause that implicates. Sarah Bama (we use pseudonyms here) accused her husband, Simon Kulapi, of abandoning her for a second wife, Philomina. Simon admitted marrying Philomina, but said he did so only after considering himself no longer married to Sarah. Why did he conclude that he was no longer married to Sarah, the magistrates asked? Because she had left him for another man. He knew this because he saw Sarah and this man drinking Coke and eating scones together on five occasions under a tree near one of the minimarkets.

The significance of this evidence seemed to rest on an implied contrast apparent to all, certainly to all at the village court. One referent was the locally grown subsistence meal: a traditionalist coconut-milk and yam shared at one's home-ples among kinsmen and in-laws was thoroughly grounded—not only socially but also agriculturally—and therefore sober and domestic. The other referent was the money-dependent, pleasure-driven snack: a modernist Coke-drinking, scone-eating interlude occurring among the quasi-urban crowds at Gusap was evidently unentailed and therefore licentious and extramarital. Indeed, both Simon and the magistrates viewed the pleasure-driven snack as incontrovertible evidence of what else Sarah and the man were doing. In fact, so transparently egregious would even one such incident have been—to say nothing of five—that the court simply did not believe that Simon witnessed these events and did nothing about them at the time. Why, the magistrates demanded, had he not confronted Sarah and the man or taken them to court? Surely, they reasoned, these events had not, in fact, occurred; and they ruled in favor of Sarah.

RSL's most fundamental connection with Coke, however, has more to do with production than consumption. Michael Quenby, RSL's general manager, told us that the company would be hard-pressed to survive if CCA stopped buying sugar from RSL: the 9,000 tons CCA had purchased in recent years accounted for between 20 and 25 percent of RSL's production. Quenby also told us, as others had, of the difficult history between RSL and CCA. The mill-white grade of sugar produced by RSL, though far superior to the brown sugar rejected by the nationalists, was not as white or fine-grained as refined sugar. Although RSL's initial decision to produce mill-white sugar was made in consultation not only with politicians, but also with industrial users, including CCA and other producers of soft drinks, CCA soon began to insist that RSL's quality was inadequate. For instance, RSL's mill-white sugar made Coke products look cloudy—a problem especially for "clear" beverages such as Sprite. Claiming that it had its own obligations to meet the exacting standards of Coca-Cola International, CCA began to challenge RSL under the terms of the monopoly agreement. This did permit importation of the sorts of sugar (for instance, icing sugar) not produced by RSL. In effect, CCA, the company's largest customer, demanded that RSL either produce refined sugar or that CCA be allowed to import it, presumably from Australia.

This virtually forced RSL to spend K2.5 million in 1995 (then about $U.S.1.9 million) to construct a refinery. However, in the end, CCA decided to alter the appearance of its soft drinks through filters and its own processors rather than use the more refined and expensive ingredient. Thus RSL was left with a refinery but no real market for refined sugar. Subsequently, through lack of use, the refinery deteriorated to such a degree that it could not easily be brought back on line. From RSL's point of view, the investment was virtually a total loss. From CCA's point of view, RSL's sugar, even with CCA's tweaking, remained below Coke's own international standards for sugar purity, the most demanding in the world.

RSL's position relative to CCA's continued to weaken. In the beginning of 1997, RSL's monopoly expired (the initial ten-year period had been extended owing to the exigencies of the outbreak of Ramu stunt) and was replaced by tariff protection. Moreover, this tariff protection was scheduled to decline. Indeed, by 2000, with tariff protection at 82 percent (down from the initial level of 85 percent), RSL was feeling quite vulnerable. Australian sugar was of a quality that CCA desired and of a price, especially for a big buyer like CCA, sufficiently low to offset substantially Papua New Guinea's import tariff. RSL was certain that, if the tariff were to fall to 40 percent as it was scheduled to do by 2006, the company would succumb to foreign competition. In Australia, for instance, not only were there substantial economies of scale in sugar production, but Australia did not rely on a sugar industry to provide local infrastructure, to say nothing of social services. RSL thought that it could just manage to stay in business at a tariff rate of 70 percent, provided it worked very hard to increase efficiency and curtail expenses. Thus, RSL's new policies toward the Mari can be seen as efforts to relieve the company of peripheral expenses. Through the Outgrowers Association and the Rabaul Study Tour, it was hoped, the Mari would be better able to help themselves.

Exacerbating the squeeze RSL was experiencing, Coca-Cola International, in response to quality-control problems in France, decided in 2000 to further tighten up its standards and sent inspectors from Australia to look at RSL's operation. These inspectors decided that, at the very least, RSL had to make changes in the factory and packinghouse. In particular, RSL had to (1) replace the glass test tubes and slides used to monitor the production process with plastic ones to ensure that no broken glass could contaminate the sugar; (2) add a specified number of laboratory tests to increase the sugar's uniformity; (3) build covers over the belts that conveyed sugar from the factory to the packinghouse to prevent dirt and debris from falling onto the sugar; (4) limit access of workers to the packinghouse so as to keep it generally cleaner.

At this point, RSL and CCA reached an interim agreement for the next contract period: RSL agreed that these changes were reasonable and would be implemented; CCA agreed to fill its Papua New Guinean sugar needs with RSL's mill white. But both knew that matters were not fully resolved. So, not to our surprise, when we visited the CCA plant in Lae on April 25, 2000, with the Coke expert Robert Foster, the Australian technical operations manager, David Lane, told us that Coke still had "a lot of issues with Ramu Sugar." Ramu sugar remained "inconsistent," had a high mud content, and caused problems "with both taste and color." Not only in clear drinks like Sprite but also in Coke, the CSR sugar imported from Australia was far superior for ensuring "a uniform product." Foster asked if Papua New Guinean drinkers had such cultivated tastes that they would notice or care about these things. No, Lane thought, but it was nonetheless important for CCA to make an internationally uniform product. "We have our standards," he insisted, and therefore CCA was seriously considering switching and paying the duty on imported sugar.

Then Lane offered to show us his "state-of-the-art" operation, in which attention to quality control was indeed remarkable. The technologies and techniques of management and production were precisely focused so as to conjoin cleanliness with efficiency. Workers wore hairnets and white coveralls and were not allowed to wander from their stations. Lines were painted on the floor where those overseeing the filling of Coke cans and bottles were to stand. Everyone had a clearly designated job to do and a place to do it. Everyone, as well, wore ID tags to prevent unauthorized and potentially contaminating people from entering the plant. We ourselves were given ID tags and, as we entered the work area, hairnets.

Everything that went into the product, whether container or content, was closely monitored. Thus Lane showed us the large plastic-sheathed pallets of empty Coke cans, which the company imported from New Zealand. One had obviously been tampered with. Its protective wrapper had been cut and several cans removed. Such tampering, Lane assured us, was rare; when it did happen, the entire contents of the pallet were destroyed even though the remaining neatly stacked cans appeared undisturbed. He simply could not take a chance that contamination had been introduced.

In fact, he was rapidly phasing out the use of glass bottles because he could not control their quality once they were recycled. All sorts of things happened to these bottles in villages. People threw them into fires, put betel-nut lime—or who knew what else—in them. It was difficult and expensive to ensure their structural integrity and cleanliness. Cans were better, but it was the plastic bottles (PET) that were most efficient to use. Then, with noticeable pride, he showed us how these plastic bottles were formed, right in his factory.

The "blanks" arrived from Australia, looking like little plastic test tubes, with a threaded neck for the cap. Lightweight and sealed in large heavy plastic bags, they were cheap and easy to ship and handle. We watched as the blanks were "blown" into full-sized bottles in an immaculate, French-made, fully automated machine—the latest model, Lane said, and kept in "showroom condition." The blanks, passing through the computerized machine at the rate of several a second, were first softened by a set of heat lights such that different parts of each blank were heated differentially. Next, held by a mold, they were inflated by blasts of filtered air. Then they were zipped out on a track into a different part of the factory for filling. Finally, a laserlike printer applied a code on each filled bottle. No bottle or can left the factory without this code, which also was crucial for quality control. If a bottle or can was found to be substandard in any way, the code would allow Lane to track the problem down. Then, after determining whether the problem involved ingredients, mechanics, or personnel, he could seek appropriate remedial action. That might include assigning responsibility and, if necessary, recalling the relevant batch.

Lane described the care they at the Lae plant took to ensure the purity of Coke's ingredients. The syrup was imported and the water, from on-site wells, was extensively filtered and stored in large stainless steel tanks. They also made their own carbon dioxide. The principal ingredient over which they had insufficient control—and, in fact, the only significant ingredient purchased in Papua New Guinea—was their sugar, which we saw in fifty-kilo bags stamped "Ramu Sugar" and stacked on RSL pallets.

Coke's market was expanding in Papua New Guinea, Lane was happy to report. Its marketing was aggressive and had been successful in reaching into the very local level. Coke signs and pushcarts were everywhere. One very good way to involve local Papua New Guineans was with promotions. Once in a while, they would give away a big item, such as a generator. But mostly they relied on smaller items, such as Coke-trademarked backpacks, which could be acquired with winning bottle tops. In fact, of more than a hundred thousand backpacks made available, there was a nearly 100 percent redemption rate. And Coke wristwatches and umbrellas were popular too.

Currently, the factory was running two twelve-hour shifts. CCA employed 160 Papua New Guineans at its plants in Lae and in Port Moresby, and another 500 in marketing and sales. Those in marketing and sales also delivered soft drinks to the various "Coke pleses" and coolers. In addition, they employed a number of casual workers at their depots and secondary warehouses. Altogether, it was a remarkably efficient operation, making optimal use of state-of-the-art machinery and inexpensive urban labor willing to work for minimal wages and without benefits such as housing.

Indeed, during the next year, Coke's market continued to grow, one of the few businesses in Papua New Guinea that was thriving despite general economic conditions of stagnation if not decline.[2] And RSL continued to supply it with sugar. CCA apparently had negotiated something of a truce with RSL.[3] Perhaps this was either to save a bit of money by continuing to buy from RSL under the existing tariffs or to avoid the bad publicity that would likely follow from dumping Ramu Sugar in favor of an Australian-produced substitute. In fact, RSL's general manager told us that Coke had expressed interest in increasing its purchases, up to perhaps 20,000 tons annually. It might be planning to export from Papua New Guinea to other countries in the region. For its part, RSL not only implemented the changes Coke demanded in order to protect the sugar from contamination, but also was working to improve the color of its mill white.[4]

On Tariffs and Taxes

The present arrangements between CCA and RSL are clearly provisional. RSL knows that as soon as it becomes politically feasible and economically advantageous, CCA will import refined sugar from elsewhere. Certainly, RSL's well-being is not central to CCA's perception of its own long-term interests. Indeed, it may serve CCA's interests better if RSL simply goes under. Then, with no domestic industry to protect, Papua New Guinea will presumably lower its duties, thus allowing CCA to import cheaper and more highly refined sugar. In fact, CCA's coercion of RSL to build a refinery could be viewed as part of a strategy to weaken it. RSL, for its part, is convinced that its very existence requires that its domestic market be protected from the full force of external competition. It also knows that protecting its domestic market is becoming increasingly difficult. Clearly, the world into which RSL was introduced is no longer the world in which it now must operate: the vision of nationalist self-sufficiency is being incrementally displaced by a vision of worldwide market penetration.

As we have seen, in the early days of Papua New Guinea's independence and as part of a policy of import substitution, RSL was created to establish Papua New Guinea's self-sufficiency in a product deemed both quintessentially indigenous and modern. And to ensure RSL's initial survival, as well as to assert appropriately the newly won sovereignty through the control of national borders, RSL was given an important measure of protection from outside competition.

But RSL as a big project generated considerable controversy. Far from diminishing, this controversy has grown in succeeding years, forcing the government to reevaluate the desirability of maintaining a domestic sugar industry at all, especially if that industry requires protection. Unlike the initial debate, when the issue was whether such a big project made economic sense or fit with the Eight Aims, this later reevaluation has, of course, to take into account the fact that RSL already exists. Mistake or not, the loans were taken, the capital expended, the factory built, the manning exercise completed, the outgrowers engaged, the valley transformed.

Precipitating the reevaluation has been the sharp change in world sugar prices in the years following RSL's creation. When world sugar prices were high, as they initially were, giving RSL a domestic monopoly was merely prudent protection of a new industry. Rather than propping up sugar prices at the expense of consumers, it was seen as a long-term protection of these consumers and their national sugar industry from the potential gouging of international producers. However, when world sugar prices fell precipitously and RSL could less easily be defended as an infant industry, the degree of protection RSL would need and deserve became increasingly debatable. While it could be argued that RSL must receive substantial protection from the world market lest it go out of business, it could also be argued that Papua New Guinean consumers have been—and for some time—paying quite a lot more for their domestically protected sugar than they otherwise might pay.

During this period of reevaluation, there were Papua New Guineans and others who found RSL seriously wanting and certainly not deserving of continued protection, at least when evaluated in a narrow economic sense. Thus, Rufina Peter, a Papua New Guinean student of economics in Australia, argues in her M.A. thesis, "Evaluation of Comparative Advantage in Producing Sugar under the Current Industry Structure in Papua New Guinea," that because Papua New Guinea does not have a comparative advantage in the production of sugar, "production should cease." Although she does admit that "other social benefits of the industry" not quantified in her study might be reasonably "felt by the government to outweigh the economic costs," she thinks this unlikely (1993: 92).

RSL's continuing importance in Papua New Guinea's future was also the subject of explicit reevaluation in the seminar "Employment, Agriculture, and Industrialisation" sponsored by the Papua New Guinean government itself. John Gibson, working for Papua New Guinea's Department of Agriculture and Livestock, stressed in his presentation that RSL sugar was unduly expensive and that "[h]ouseholds face the most important costs, with higher sugar prices acting as an implicit tax. This tax appears highly regressive" (1993a: 129). In addition, he worried that the tariff might stifle enterprise, might, for instance, prevent the establishment of "food processing industries . . . because of high sugar prices (jam?) and higher wage demands as a result of more expensive sugar" (129).[5]

Yet those present at the seminar could not deny that RSL was already a fact—indeed, a "big project." Therefore, Gibson also reminded participants that "[s]ugar plantations are long-lived projects; I think we can assume that Ramu Sugar is going to be a long-standing feature of the Papua New Guinean economy in some way, shape or form" (1993b: 153). Significantly, Peter Colton, RSL's long-standing chairman, did not let the matter rest with Gibson's acknowledgment that RSL would likely continue for some time. His response challenged Gibson's economic perspective as excessively narrow. Colton's position was that the indirect tax on sugar consumers was justified by the social and economic benefits that RSL provided for its workers, for those in the Ramu Valley, and for the nation at large. This position is one we often heard, articulated by Colton and others connected with RSL. Colton finished his argument with a final dig at Port Moresby elites:

> I would suggest that Ramu wasn't a blunder. We have replaced imported sugar, we have created 2,500 jobs in an area which was totally undeveloped. I suspect if Ramu Sugar wasn't there there would be nothing there still; nothing else would have come along to take on what Ramu has taken on. We have today a community of between 15,000 and 20,000 people, not just our employees but surrounding villages who, to one degree or another, rely on Ramu Sugar for their economic welfare. . . . People come down from as far as Kainantu to sell their produce at Ramu Sugar. These are all benefits which need to be

looked at when one looks at Ramu Sugar. . . . Despite the problems of the last 3 to 4 years we believe that there will be a steady growth in sugar consumption. This will allow Ramu Sugar to involve more out-growers so that the community at Ramu will survive and become larger and larger over the years. If those 15,000-odd people were not involved at Ramu a reasonable proportion of them may be climbing over your fences in Port Moresby and Lae and trying to get money that they couldn't get from Ramu.[6] One has to recognize that these benefits are real.

Gibson, in his reply—and in statements elsewhere, including in sub-sequent conversations with us—was quite willing to accept the impor-tance of social factors and, indeed, that social and economic factors were likely conjoined (see, for example, Gibson 1994 and 1995). Nonetheless, he still questioned Colton's assessment:

I have been fairly careful to say that I am not necessarily saying that Ramu Sugar was a blunder. It is commonly perceived as that and one of the aspects of that was the exposure to risk [the lower price of sugar on the world market] which neither the government, nor Booker Tate, nor anyone expected to occur. As to the regional development effects, yes, these are important given the poor results that we have got from [other] places. . . . Let's call it Ramu Integrated Rural Development, rather than Ramu Sugar. . . .[7] [Yet] I would say that in regional devel-opment, we could have got a "bigger bang for our buck" from other areas in Papua New Guinea. . . . And, we do not know what the regional impacts have been for people who have had to pay higher sugar prices in isolated areas, and what developments they may have come up with if sugar prices were lower.

Thus Colton viewed projects like RSL as more important in creating development than did Gibson. And Gibson viewed market mechanisms as more important in creating development than did Colton. But this dis-agreement was one of relative weighting, a disagreement between those who shared certain key assumptions. Both thought that Papua New Guinea should tailor its economic policies to further its own nationalist objectives: to create policies that brought development to its myriad pleses so as to establish an independent and viable nation. Both thought that Papua New Guinea should do this in a cost-effective, that is, rational and efficient, manner. Indeed, both considered it appropriate that the

government might wish to establish integrated rural development projects. Correspondingly, in appraising such projects, both seemed willing
to accept that economic costs might be calculated so as to take into
account such variables as the relationship between unemployment and
crime.

However, the discussion between RSL and its critics has become far
more acrimonious. While still focusing on whether development might
best proceed through reliance on government support or though reliance
on market mechanisms, the positions are increasingly polarized: efforts
to find common ground are undermined by what we see as the absolutist
narrative of global capitalism.

On the Equality of Comparative Advantage

We made our first visit to BTL headquarters in Thame, England, in 1998.
Our first conversation with a BTL representative was with Dr. Martin
Evans, an economist and BTL's project director for the RSL operation as
well as BTL's new business director. Evans told us that RSL was under
attack by those advocating economic liberalization, by the "free marketeers" in the World Bank, World Trade Organization (WTO), International
Monetary Fund (IMF), and Asia-Pacific Economic Cooperation (APEC):
these institutions all believed in letting "market forces rip" and allowing
"anarchy or chaos to reign." Evans was particularly concerned about the
effects of these free marketeers on Papua New Guinea. Taking what was,
in essence, a moral and an economic-development perspective, Evans
argued that if free marketeers had their way, Papua New Guineans would
forever remain stuck in primary-sector activities—farming, forestry, and
mining—as "hewers of wood and drawers of water" while others in the
world got on with deepening and broadening their economies by developing secondary and tertiary sectors with attendant employment diversification and demand for higher skills. And to this, we would add that
Papua New Guineans would remain "hewers of wood and drawers of
water" until their natural resources—their gold, copper, oil, and forests—
were gone and they would become worse off than they were before
development began.

It had become widely understood in Papua New Guinea that the World
Bank (from which the country was borrowing substantially) and the WTO
(of which the country was a member) were strongly suggesting that the
Papua New Guinean government reduce the state's presence in the economy through "structural adjustments" and market "liberalization." These

adjustments included privatization through the sale of state interests in companies both wholly or partially owned by the state: telegraphs and communications, the postal service, the national airline, and RSL. In addition, this liberalization included the rapid phasing out of tariff protection for all industries.

Certainly, when we were at RSL during 2000 and 2001, privatization was a highly politicized issue throughout the country. Led by outraged university students, large demonstrations were held in the capital and elsewhere, with protesters claiming that outsiders were interfering with the autonomy of their nation; that the World Bank, WTO, IMF, and APEC were neocolonial oppressors; that those politicians who capitulated to the demands for structural adjustments were weak, if not traitorous.[8]

Partly in response to these protests, the Institute for National Affairs (INA) asked Professors Kym Anderson of Adelaide University and Malcolm Bosworth of the Australian National University to produce a "reasoned argument about the effects of WTO and APEC, primarily [on] how they affect PNG but also . . . [on] how they affect other small Pacific nations" (Manning 2001: vii). Clearly, Anderson and Bosworth were selected because they were already committed to a free-market policy. INA's director, Michael Manning, describes them as such in his foreword to their *Reforming Trade Policy in Papua New Guinea and the Pacific Islands* (Bosworth and Anderson 2000). He characterizes them as "strong supporters of the multilateral trading system, having each spent several years working at the GATT [General Agreement on Tariffs and Trade]/WTO Secretariat. They see the gains from trade as far outweighing the short term costs that will be felt as adjustments are made to allow greater gains from trade to flow" (Manning 2001: ix).[9]

As it turned out, Bosworth and Anderson were to pay "particular attention to PNG's sugar industry because [the foreword claims] it is a classic example of the problems that a small economy faces when it encourages, through protection from import protection and other measures, a large investment in a remote area." (Manning 2001: viii). In fact, Bosworth did spend one of his six days in the country at RSL (at RSL's expense) so that he could decide whether RSL might warrant an exemption from Papua New Guinea's general commitment to tariff reduction. We were invited to a meeting Bosworth held with Papua New Guineans (eight RSL supervisors and managers, six outgrowers, including Wilson Gagas, and a local government councilor). In addition, we were invited to a lunch that senior BTL and RSL managers held for him at the Management Club.

The meeting (at which Cokes were offered) lasted about two hours. Bosworth spoke entirely in English—and often rather academic English, at that. He began by explaining that he had been asked by the INA to write a report about "the possible effects of WTO/APEC strictures on Papua New Guinea." Papua New Guinea is a founding member of the WTO, he continued, as are Fiji and the Solomon Islands. Three other countries in this area—Vanuatu, Tonga, and Samoa—are also keen to join. Indeed, it is "an international trend," with lots of developing countries wishing to belong to the WTO. The philosophy of the WTO involves "an opening up of trade, a neutralization of protection." The WTO believes that "all countries will gain from free trade"; that countries are "better off specializing in what they can do best and importing what they can produce less efficiently." This philosophy has already been adopted by Papua New Guinea, which has "decided over the next six to eight years to reduce the protection it is providing to various industries, including cement, tinned mackerel, and sugar." It also has adopted a "value-added tax to fund this reform of the tariff program. The tariff on Ramu Sugar, which was set last year on July 1, at 82 percent is to be reduced to 40 percent by 2006." After thus presenting this fait accompli, Bosworth concluded his introductory remarks by inviting the audience to explore the implications of this adjustment process at RSL.

Various people had various things to say. Robin Wilson, as the outgrowers' manager, said that he thought there would be a loss of livelihood. If there was a reduction in tariff, especially in bringing it down to 40 percent, RSL would have a real problem and RSL was "the only lane for the outgrowers." Bosworth asked, in reply, what would people do. Would people continue to live here? Perhaps farmers could be retrained to grow something other than sugar. Were there any alternative crops?

Philip Kepas, the manager of the nucleus estate, said that peanuts had been tried once, but peanuts were not very successful as a money-generating crop because too many people grew them closer to Lae, where they were more easily processed. He also said that RSL workers would all lose their jobs. Bosworth appreciated this as a concern but again suggested that perhaps there could be retraining possibilities. Or perhaps some people currently dependent on RSL could move to another area where jobs would be expanded, and, thus, such a person might well do better.

Dr. Lastus Kuniata, the head of the agronomy section, pointed out that Papua New Guinea remained dependent on imported foodstuffs, except for chickens and sugar. Rice was eaten by everyone, but the country certainly was not self-sufficient in rice. The government policy was to encourage self-sufficiency, but even the cash crops Papua New Guineans did grow were mostly sold back to them after being processed by firms like Nestles. If the tariff on sugar were to be reduced, it would kill the development of this local industry: then we would buy almost everything from Australia. We have been able to grow sugar because it is indigenous here; we have always grown it in our backyards. It has fit into our culture. There have been experiments in growing rice, but the project survived only as long as there were Taiwanese around to encourage it. We haven't grown up growing rice. Tariffs should be kept on selected items, such as basic foods, to encourage people to grow them rather than import them. In the United States, there was a 200 percent tariff protection on sugar, yet Papua New Guinea, with an eighteen-year-old industry, has been forced to reduce its tariffs. Many countries have been able to compete in a commercial market better than Papua New Guinea because their sugar industries are much older. Forcing us to reduce tariffs would be unfair and unjust.

Bosworth expressed sympathy for this perspective, but said he had a different one. Of course, he would not defend the farm subsidization policies of the European Union and the United States. In fact, through the WTO, little countries can be critical of European and American policies. It is true, however, that big countries were slow to hear criticisms. But as an economist, he believed that there could be no free lunch. Tariffs on food items meant that the consumers were taxed by paying higher prices for food. Now, concerning sugar, one had to consider the downstream processing. For example, people who might wish to establish a confectionery industry in Papua New Guinea were deterred because they would have to pay such a high price for sugar. You had to allow them to have access to sugar at world prices. Some protection might be good for the sugar industry and certainly the sugar industry created employment, but you had to consider that you might be reducing employment in other industries. Generally speaking, economists thought that tariffs protect inefficiency. This has become a fundamental principle in economics: if you can import more cheaply than you can produce, you should import. Industries then would develop at home that would provide efficiency and gains to the economy. Empirical evidence has supported these principles. The Australian car industry was a case in point. It did not collapse as some feared when its heavy tariff protection was removed. Instead, it became far more streamlined and efficient, producing a better product for a better price. Those economies that have opened up have enjoyed greater trade.

In the course of continued discussion, it was pointed out that the kina had been devalued, making it hard for people to get by. Indeed, the items imported into the country were prohibitively expensive for many. Bosworth asked for clarification about the rate of exchange. Although surprised at the degree to which the kina had fluctuated within the past year (from U.S.$0.41 to U.S.$0.29), he nonetheless insisted that for things to get better—to ensure "macroeconomic stability, policy security, sustained commitment to growth, and general security"—foreign investors must be attracted to the country and the best way to do this was to remove trade barriers. Moreover, the policy to reduce tariffs had already been decided upon: it was now the only program in town. Indeed, to change the program would be to indicate instability.

Kuniata argued that, unlike RSL, the government was incapable of providing necessary services: it could not even supply basic health and education, leaving these things to various industries. Bosworth agreed that the Papua New Guinean government seemed to have prioritized badly by not spending its limited resources on infrastructure. Perhaps overseas donors might help with roads, bridges, even with health. Kuniata countered that roads and bridges would get built by foreign donors only if the government did not get its hands on the money. The government was a bottomless pit when it came to money. Then, Bosworth rejoined, the government should be held responsible. Kelly Thom, the housing manager, then pointed out that RSL was not like a factory in Lae. Companies in rural areas that provided health services, roads, schools, the courts—everything—should be protected. If RSL were to go, everything here would disappear. Bosworth thought this a valuable point, but also thought that community assistance should nonetheless not be provided through tariff protection.

The discussion continued in this vein. No outgrowers participated. Few, if any, could understand Bosworth's level of English. Finally, lunchtime approaching, Robin Wilson thanked Bosworth for his very informative views. Bosworth, in turn, thanked the group for listening to him and wished us the best in the future. He hoped that things would not be as "gloomy and doomy" as they seemed.

At lunch, only the BTL managers expressed opinions. Steve Vaux, head of agriculture, spoke rather movingly about the social benefits of RSL: its creation of a trained workforce and a petit bourgeoisie, both necessary for social stability. If the tariffs were to be reduced worldwide, he thought, rich countries should do so first. Otherwise, the poor countries would simply get poorer, and the rich countries would become razor-wire enclosures, with the poor hankering to get in. Bosworth asked the general manager whether RSL would go under if the tariff fell to 40 percent. Yes, without a doubt, was the reply.

We said that if that were the case, many of those now currently supported by RSL would be forced into cities like Lae, already notorious for their squatter settlements, crime, and high unemployment.[10] Bosworth's response, that "at least these people will be taking a chance on a better life," seemed more a recitation of a preestablished position than a realistic appraisal of Papua New Guinean circumstances.

Indeed, it is difficult to imagine any evidence or argument that would have dissuaded Bosworth from his prior commitment to free trade. And, not surprisingly, Bosworth and Anderson's final report is fully consistent with the position Bosworth expressed at both the meeting and lunch:

> The sugar industry's competitive position is weak because of unsuitable climate, which lowers sugar content of cane and encourages pests, and from lack of economies of scale because of small throughput of the milling factory of some 40,000 to 50,000 tonnes annually. Current indications are that the survival of Ramu sugar will need a tariff of substantially above the long term rate of 40% if it is to remain viable. Thus, there is the possibility of closure of Ramu sugar (as would be in the national interest if it cannot be competitive without a tariff of any size, let alone one as high as 40%). That would have major structural adjustment implications for the Ramu workers and the community, of course.
>
> These one-off adjustment costs, however, need to be considered in relation to the benefits that will forever flow afterwards to the economy. One source of benefits would come from downstream food processors and consumers having access to better-quality sugar at much lower— about half—existing prices. (2000: 54)

RSL had been invited to respond to a draft of Anderson and Bosworth's report, and the company understood that its response would be included in the final version. After all, its continued existence was the subject under discussion. Evans, as both an economist and RSL project director, wrote the response, which he kindly shared with us. In it, he counters many of the "conventional economic argument[s] in favour of trade liberalisation and the reduction or elimination of industry protection." Evans argues:

> Unpalatable though it may be to economists who are convinced of the benefits of trade liberalisation, the fact is that all developing country

sugar producers protect their domestic industries with import tariffs. Furthermore, . . . developing countries are most reluctant to agree to further sugar tariff reductions without substantial and simultaneous reductions by the EU and US. Even China, which is yet to join the WTO, will come in with non-quota sugar tariffs of 75% reducing to 67% by 2004.

The [Anderson-Bosworth] report says that "[s]imply because other governments select bad policies is no reason for PNG to follow suit." But can we be so sure—in the present circumstances of the world sugar market—that a sugar tariff is bad policy and that all other sugar producing developing countries have therefore got it wrong? And can we be so sure that PNG will not suffer by being made a guinea pig for a trade liberalisation experiment which other developing countries have rejected as too risky at the present time?

. . . RSL believes that there is too much at stake, in terms of the actual development created in the Ramu Valley as a result of RSL, to justify a substantial reduction of the present sugar tariffs on the grounds that it will otherwise remain an untidy exception to the overall pattern of PNG tariffs. A vaguely argued conviction that cheaper sugar will be a benefit to everyone is no substitute for the actuality of jobs, businesses, livelihoods and communities supported on the ground in Morobe and Madang Provinces.

However, this does not mean that RSL should not be put under pressure to strive for improved efficiency and lower production costs. (Evans 2000: 2–3)

As it turned out, Evans's response was not included as a rejoinder in the published report. Nor, as far as both Evans and we could tell, did it have any discernible effect on that report.

It has long been apparent to everyone that RSL cannot directly compete against overseas sugar producers, whose operations benefit from tariff protections and a range of subsidies, as well as from economies of scale. But if Papua New Guinea lacks a comparative advantage in sugar production, is the appropriate response for the government simply to allow RSL to go under? This prospect is rather blithely glossed by Bosworth and Anderson as "one-off adjustment costs" from which "benefits . . . will forever flow afterwards to the economy" (2000: 54). But from Evans's perspective, as well as our own, there are actual "jobs, businesses, livelihoods and communities . . . [at stake] in Morobe and Madang Provinces" (Evans 2000: 2).

Moreover, given the realities of contemporary Papua New Guinea, with its weak state, inadequate infrastructure, devalued currency, and rampant corruption, the likelihood of a fluorescence of entrepreneurial activity stimulated by lower sugar prices would strike anyone who was in the country for more than six days as dubious. Indeed, even a company already as well financed and established as the Lae-based Coca-Cola operation would likely hire only a few more employees (and probably none from the Upper Ramu Valley) if its operations were enhanced by the availability of higher-quality sugar at a lower price.

But more fundamentally, what would contemporary Papua New Guineans have a comparative advantage in producing? How would commitment to this logic play out for them? Their tropical tree crops would bring an uncertain price on a frequently glutted world market. Their mineral and timber resources are finite, extracted with considerable environmental damage and, at least for minerals, not even potentially renewable. This logic, it seems to us, would likely foster a future in which Papua New Guineans will remain impoverished, poorly trained, and angry: hewers of wood, drawers of water, and—for the more agile and agitated—climbers of fences in Port Moresby.

Dueling Narratives

RSL's position is actively promoted in a range of venues. On several occasions, for example, Colton and Evans organized "sugar seminars" followed by site visits to convince ministers, government officials, and other policymakers that RSL should not be sacrificed on the altar of free trade. The seminars are intended to provide counterarguments to the arguments of, for example, Bosworth and Anderson. The site visits are meant to bring the counterarguments home by demonstrating what RSL has, in fact, become. Together the sugar seminars and site visits are intended to displace the WTO narrative with the RSL narrative. RSL wants to make it very clear that the projected benefits of comparative advantage in a brave new global world of free trade will certainly not offset the immediate and tragic effects of eliminating the hard-won and nationally significant development of the Upper Ramu Valley.

The seminar we attended, after the Rabaul Study Tour, took place on April 11, 2000, in Port Moresby at the Park Royal, the most luxurious hotel in town. Mao Zeming, the minister of agriculture, and many other dignitaries were invited to hear papers, eat lunch, and on the following day fly by private plane to RSL to see for themselves the development the company was fostering. Moderated by Manning, as director of the INA, the seminar included speeches by the minister of agriculture (delivered by his representative), Colton, Evans, and A. C. Hannah, head of the economics and statistics division of the London-based International Sugar Organization. After Manning welcomed the forty or so in attendance, the minister's representative stated that the subjects of tariffs and of RSL's contribution to the development of the Upper Ramu Valley were currently under consideration by the government.

Colton's speech, "History and Role of Ramu" (2000), was consistent with his perspective concerning RSL's contribution to social and economic development, as we have described it earlier. In addition, he stressed that the operation at RSL was "unlike mines and oil exploration business in that we are not exhausting the nation's natural resources" (2000: 8).

Evans's presentation, "RSL from an International Perspective" (2000]), was conveyed principally through slides comparing relative costs of production, amount of sugar subsidy/protection, and cost of product worldwide. He concluded that the degree of protection that RSL received was not out of line with that received in most other comparable countries; moreover, he said RSL's sugar price was "not high in relation to other countries' sugar prices" (slide 32).

RSL had invited Hannah to participate because he was an outsider and an authority—indeed, a notable expert at predicting the price of sugar on the world market. Although Colton and Evans were not completely sure of what he would say, they thought he would likely confirm Evans's comparative analysis of the world sugar market and RSL's position within it. Hannah ended up doing this and more. Indeed, the RSL contingent was gratified by his variant of the narrative concerning hewers of wood and drawers of water. We quote from the conclusions of his prepared paper:

> In my view any reform should have a moral underpinning, and in the case of trade reform this should be a redistribution from richer to poorer. Using this criteria, I have no problem with getting rid of the tariff quota and the support it underpins (in the US) or subsidized exports (the EU). These are trade distorting regimes. . . . But where I take exception with the mad reformers, the obsessive free traders, is their disregard for the sovereign rights and legitimate interests of developing countries with their own sugar industries. I discussed earlier the real, legitimate and important role that sugar plays in development,

particularly by generating employment and social services. . . . I can only encourage Papua New Guinea to continue to support and defend its sugar industry, which has achieved much in terms of industrial and social development in a relatively short time.

Protection *is* a problem. The US and EU distort the world sugar market—the US by restricting trade and the EU by selling large quantities of subsidized exports onto the market. My recipe for continuing reform . . . is, attack the big, rich boys, but leave developing countries alone. (2000: 8)

Manning, however, apparently unswayed by these arguments, summed up in a way consistent with his foreword to Bosworth and Anderson's book. In particular, he spoke about the enterprise-discouraging effects of tariffs as indirect taxes and about the need to encourage businesses to become more efficient. Moreover, he said, Papua New Guinea has few options: "Eventually, whether we like it or not, we are going to have to become part of the world economic community. WTO and APEC are going to go ahead whether or not PNG wants to become a part of it. There's doubt that we can influence anybody. We're a tiny country in terms of those sorts of things. So, we are going to have to come to terms with it."

Colton and Evans were, of course, somewhat disappointed with Manning's assessment. But they were even more let down by the fact that, because Parliament was unexpectedly called back into session, few of their desired audience were available for either the seminar or the site visit. RSL advocates have been well aware that the best argument they can make is to show politicians and policymakers the actual RSL operation. Once they see this immense physical as well as social presence, they will be reluctant to sacrifice it for a "vaguely argued conviction" that cheaper sugar would be a benefit. It is hoped, as one BTL executive told us, that the visitors will recognize RSL as "a real platform for development which actually delivers economic diversification, infrastructure, employment, vocational training, entrepreneurial opportunities, township amenities and community services into an underdeveloped area, objectives which successive Papua New Guinean governments often struggle to achieve elsewhere and by other means."

· · ·

During such site visits, including one made by Prime Minister Bill Skate in May 1999, shortly before we first arrived at RSL, the company's intent has been to convey the idea that all things considered, RSL delivers very good value. Not only is the size and complexity of the sugar operation impressive, but also the extent of its support to the community makes it indispensable to the Papua New Guineans in the Ramu Valley. Ross Masterman, RSL's financial comptroller, told us what he said to Skate: There is no way that Ramu can compete with Brazil, for example, if the tariff is reduced to 40 percent. Brazil produces 17,000,000 tons of sugar, compared to RSL's 45,000 tons, and Brazil dumps its sugar surpluses on the world. Therefore, the world price of sugar, which has been holding rather steady at ten cents per pound, has fallen during 1998 to four cents per pound. The world price of sugar is not what it takes to produce sugar, but what it takes to buy dumped sugar. In addition, RSL supports the community, unlike Brazilian producers. Hence, what looks to some like RSL's inefficiency is actually its social responsibility.

Even the World Bank's resident coordinator in Papua New Guinea was impressed during his visit to RSL in 2000. Dan Weise told us when we interviewed him at his Port Moresby office he thought RSL was doing a good job under the circumstances. "RSL runs a tight operation," he said. "The general manager lives in a modest little house; the management drives reasonably priced four-by-fours. Nobody is exploiting anybody else. The board members have prevented interference from the government and they also haven't raked things off from the company."

Nonetheless, Weise remained strongly committed to an antitariff position, partly because he feared that bilateral tariffs in places like Papua New Guinea would encourage corruption, with tariff protections negotiated in private over suitcases of money.[11] In addition, he favored free trade for precisely those reasons Bosworth had, believing that if RSL could not compete on an international market, it should not exist. After all, he told us, the indirect tax on sugar might prevent the flourishing of, for instance, a small tee-shirt factory someplace in the country. Of course, the Papua New Guinean government did not have to agree with World Bank recommendations concerning tariff reduction. But if it did not, then it would not get World Bank loans. The country could get other loans and at almost the same interest rate, but other banks would demand as security the country's future revenues—for example, first shot at mining royalties. This would be "a real mortgaging of the future."

Because Papua New Guinea accepted World Bank loans, Weise continued, the government was obliged to listen to World Bank advice. The fact that RSL provided employment, services, safety, good schools, and the like was not sufficient grounds for the World Bank to support a sugar tariff.[12] Rather, the government should be pressured into working properly. To effect this pressure, the K220 million in loans the World Bank approved—together with an additional K100 million from the IMF, K110 million from Australia, K50 million from Japan, and K10 million from the European Union—were all tied to structural adjustments involving, among other things, privatization. RSL was on the privatization list, and if a buyer of the government shares could be found, all the better.

Weise agreed that RSL had symbolic importance to Papua New Guineans. But he tried not to think about such value. If he did, he would "go mad." Every company, after all, was trying to justify itself to the government by arguing that it had added value. But the fact of the matter was that everyone in Papua New Guinea paid for RSL by buying expensive sugar. And, if RSL closed, it might give people a different kind of opportunity since "the essence of development is migration to cities." Such migration gave people "a dynamic." It provided them with "a chance to change."[13] The hardest thing was to figure out when to sell—when to cut your losses. And there may come a time to do this with RSL.[14]

· · ·

RSL is trying to forestall that time—although it knows that its narrative of import substitution leading to national development is no longer persuasive in a Papua New Guinea increasingly dependent on massive loans and increasingly subject to the structural adjustments those loans entail.[15]

In the meantime, RSL is trying to become more competitive—more productive, more efficient. It is trying to increase crop yields so as to get more sugar through its existing factory; it is trying, for instance, to keep costs down by giving only minimal raises (of 3 percent), by cutting back on expenditures in housing maintenance, and it is thinking of charging workers for excess water and electricity. It is also exploring additional sources of income, including diversifying into oil palm production, perhaps on its own estate as well as on land farther down the Ramu Valley near the subdistrict headquarters of Walium.

Most strikingly, RSL has already been restructuring its relationship to BTL: RSL's board of directors has decided to "wean" the company from BTL. As a first step in a major reformulation of existing arrangements, the general manager, provided to RSL by BTL, has been replaced with a CEO of the board's own choosing. The new appointee, who works directly for RSL, is an Australian of Fijian-Indian origin. In addition, RSL is claiming the right to hire in due course other top management "locally" (in an extended sense, as encompassing the Pacific, Southeast Asia, and Australia). These personnel changes will appreciably reduce costs, since RSL pays the salaries of the BTL employees seconded to it in British Pounds—salaries made additionally expensive given the depreciation of the kina. Furthermore, the board feels that this change enhances efficiency by giving it more immediate control of the company. Management will become more direct when decisions can be made on site without having to be approved in England. In addition, potential conflicts of interest might be reduced. Such conflicts might arise, for instance, if BTL becomes committed to a particular decision that will preserve its corporate reputation more than benefit RSL.

BTL, for its part, recognizes that RSL's connection to BTL is expensive. It also expects eventually to be entirely replaced. However, that its general manager has been superseded by another expatriate, rather than by an indigenous manager trained by BTL, is not what the parent company has in mind with its oft-repeated axiom that its job is to work itself out of a job. For this reason, and because the fate of RSL is uncertain, many BTL managers are taking stock of the enterprise and BTL's role in it. To be sure, Papua New Guinea, with its complex social and physical environment, has not been an easy place in which to run a complicated sugar operation. Nonetheless, some BTL managers believe that errors have been made at RSL over the years. They think that BTL's leadership, whether of general managers or heads of departments, has been sufficiently uneven to weaken morale and efficiency: at times, leadership was so weak and enforcement of rules and procedures was so ineffectual as to be debilitating; at times leadership was so authoritarian and enforcement of rules and procedures so stringent as to be alienating.

BTL managers, in hindsight, also think that a serious error was made in relying initially on a single variety of cane. Despite the compelling reasons for having planted so much Ragnor, the risk of encountering unknown indigenous pathogens proved too great, and the company almost went under. Other errors were made. Some alterations to the factory have not proven cost-effective. Certain agricultural schemes, such as a rather expensive trial of an irrigation system, have not worked out and in fact increased the depredation of certain pests. Finally, miscalculations have exacerbated RSL's often cash-short circumstances. Once, for instance, based on an overoptimistic prediction of cane yield, BTL filled its U.S. quota early in the season so as to obtain ready cash. However, the subsequent production shortfall forced it to import sugar, at high tariff, so as to meet domestic commitments. Nonetheless, most BTL managers feel that they have done the best they could under very difficult circumstances.

BTL's managers have asked us to evaluate their performance at RSL relative to that of the managers of other large businesses in Papua New Guinea. Compared with others, we think RSL under BTL's guidance has done quite well. In providing a livelihood and many vital social services for thousands of Papua New Guineans, RSL compares favorably to the Papua New Guinean operations of a company like Coca-Cola Amatil (and, we might add, the mining giant BHP Billiton, which until recently ran the environmentally devastating Ok Tedi mining complex). Significantly, though, it is global companies that seem to be the business most favored—best served—by the World Bank and WTO. Despite the rhetoric suggesting that the World Bank and WTO are small-project friendly (as in Weise's small tee-shirt factory), it is large companies like Coca-Cola (and its subsidiaries) that will benefit most from the tariff reduction and the ease of capital flows that will follow trade liberalization. Indeed, because of its global efficiency and profitability, Coca-Cola embodies the touted advantages of free trade.

Yet, of course, Coca-Cola's entire Papua New Guinea operation, including the undeniable efficiencies of its Lae factory, are premised on creating profits for largely overseas stockholders. Correspondingly, the permeability of national borders that serves CCA's interests for a cheaper and whiter sugar—and a Sprite meeting Coke's international quality-control standards—will inevitably undermine its long-term commitment to any place, much less, to any ples.

The Weight versus the Trajectory of History

Although we are not professional economists, we agree with those connected to RSL, both expatriates and nationals, who believe that closing the factory would be devastating. Few think that anything, certainly anything that will provide comparable employment, training, and services, can replace it in a Papua New Guinea of increasing inequality, corruption, and turmoil. Moreover, our years in Papua New Guinea (not days, as in Bosworth's case) lead us to concur with Evans's argument that the few kina a year Papua New Guineans might save from cheaper sugar would be unlikely to result in any significant upsurge in entrepreneurial activity. In addition, we strongly doubt that Weise's tee-shirt factory (inspired, somehow, by the spirit of capitalism) would prove competitive with, for example, cheap textiles from bordering Indonesia. It too would fall victim to the very trade liberalization that supposedly created it. Likewise, it seems to us that Boswell's analogy between the Australian car industry and RSL concerning the overall benefits of tariff reduction has not been sufficiently thought through. Australia, with a well-trained workforce, substantial social services, capital for investment, and a wide industrial base, was in very different social and economic circumstances when it liberalized the car industry than Papua New Guinea would be in if it liberalizes the sugar industry.

In these regards, we find the work of the economists at the Economic Policy Institute informative. In a recent position paper entitled "The Unremarkable Record of Liberalized Trade," Weller, Scott, and Hersh conclude that, contrary to belief that global deregulation will reduce poverty and promote equality between countries,

> [i]ncome distribution between countries worsened in the 1980s, and its apparent improvement (or leveling off) in the 1990s is the result solely of rising per capita income in China, where the enormous population tends to distort world averages. Within-country income inequality is also growing and is a widespread trend in countries with both advanced and developing economies. Success in reducing poverty has been limited. . . . The promises of more equal income distribution and reduced poverty around the globe have failed to materialize under the current form of unregulated globalism. Thus, it is time for multi-national institutions and other international policy makers to develop a different set of strategies and programs to provide real benefits to the poor. (2001: 8)

Likewise, the Harvard University economist Dani Rodrik argues that "[g]lobal integration has become, for all practical purposes, a substitute for a development strategy." In fact, he maintains, this "trend is bad news for the world's poor." Not only does Rodrik find that the "new agenda of global integration rests on shaky empirical ground and seriously distorts policymakers' priorities," but also that the costs of implementing WTO agreements are unduly expensive. As evidence, he cites an estimate from a World Bank economist indicating that to implement only three of the WTO requirements—pertaining to customs valuation, sanitary and phytosanitary measures, and trade-related intellectual property rights—would cost a typical developing country $U.S. 150 million. Therefore by "focusing on international integration, governments in poor nations divert human resources, administrative capabilities, and political capital away from more urgent development priorities such as education, public health, industrial capacity, and social cohesion. This emphasis also undermines nascent democratic institutions by removing the choice of development strategy from public debate" (Rodrik 2001: 55).

This is to say, the trajectory of history envisioned by the free traders seems to be exacerbating, rather than alleviating, the weight of history that bears down on poor people in developing (as well as developed) countries.

· · ·

At the beginning of this chapter we suggested that the narrative used by the free traders grows out of and undermines, continues yet contradicts, three earlier narratives: that of Wilson Gagas concerning a primordial connection to ples; that of Stuart Hayes concerning the rational evaluation of the technologies and techniques most appropriate to solving the problems set by a particular place; and that of the Papua New Guinean nationalists concerning the equality and distinctiveness of Papua New Guinea's place among the nations of the world. This free-trade narrative is transforming Gagas's ples into a Coke-ples, wherein Bumbu is less to be understood as a home for ancestral presences (indeed, also less to be understood as BUMBU, a focus of colonial control) than as a retail outlet on the Lae-Madang Highway, an outpost of Coke's worldwide war against water. This new narrative is transforming Hayes's place into a locus of sugar production in and for the global marketplace, wherein RSL is less to be appraised as rational and efficient within Papua New Guinea than as one sugar operation among the many in the world. It is transforming the nationalists' Papua New Guinea into a node in global flows, wherein the nation's development and valued individuality are to be pursued less through import substitution as a strategy of autonomy than through free trade as a strategy for global integration.

But there is one narrative that the free traders do not significantly transform, undermine, or contradict, but simply (post)modernize. This is the narrative we described as Diamond's—a broad historical narrative in which history is the evident and the apparently inevitable playing out of the technologies and techniques that maximize control. To be sure, the global agents of economic and political penetration are mostly transnational interests backed by bank loans and trade agreements rather than conquistadors backed by the germs and steel of efficient destruction: Coke-ples carts and coolers, rather than disease and subjugation, have become, it seems, the immediate manifestations of ultimate causes.

Diamond's history and Bosworth's economics use the same language and sustain the same politics. Diamond's history is of an all-encompassing inevitability that silences those who consider motives and morality important in dealing with the causes and consequences of inequality. Efforts to foster responsibility, seek rectification, and perhaps effect reconciliation languish in this world of ultimate and inevitable causes: they languish in this world where what happened had to happen, where that was that.

Bosworth's economics, though less ambitious than Diamond's history, also claims to have discerned the inevitable course of events. Indeed, Bosworth's economics focuses on the capitalist subset of Diamond's history. And Bosworth, like Diamond, uses his theory as a juggernaut: economic inevitability renders objections misguided and irrelevant. In addition, while arguing that lives of rural farmers in the Ramu Valley should matter, Bosworth, in actuality, undermines efforts to sustain these lives—except in recommending that a better future might be found in a squalid squatter settlement with the money saved from cheaper sugar.

Diamond and Bosworth thus seamlessly merge explanation of existing inequalities with justification and perpetuation of these inequalities. Papua New Guineans, according to both, will likely be condemned to economic marginality—whether by the inevitable playing out of the forces of history, in general, or by the inevitable playing out of the invisible hand of capitalism, in particular. Moreover, in so buttressing their authority with the trajectory of history, in so rendering whole categories of objections moot, their arguments themselves serve as technologies and techniques of control: the only morality or responsibility either position allows is that outcomes are no one's fault; it is just how the game must be played.

This, of course, is Diamond's answer to Yali. It is also Bosworth's answer to Wilson Gagas and the others present at the meeting he held at RSL—and by extension, his answer to Kamdan and the many sustained by RSL. And what might they say in response? Perhaps the conversation, echoing Colton's with "a young cargo cult leader," might go like this:

Yali, Gagas, and the RSL Others: Why have so many of us remained
hewers of wood and drawers of water?
Diamond and Bosworth: Drawers are the luck of the draw.
Yali, Gagas, and the RSL Others: You're not treating us with
respect—and we've been had.
Diamond and Bosworth: Sorry about that—nothing personal. But,
have a Coke, or maybe a Sprite of international standard, on us.

Conclusion: *On Listening*

IN COMING TO TERMS with big, startling, and transforming RSL, we have considered the various visions of the desirable and feasible that brought it into existence. And, of these, there is no doubt that the broad narratives we glossed as Gagas's, Hayes's, and the nationalists'—as well as the free traders'—still remain in play. However, it is also the case that RSL's fields and factory have been organized more according to Hayes's development-focused vision of efficiency than to Gagas's ples-centered vision of entailment. Correspondingly, it is doubtless the case that RSL's decision to spend K18,000 for the Mari to attend Robin Wilson's burial stemmed more from a BTL commitment to a "sensible, pleasant, civilized society" than from some recognition of an inalienable, Nahiyel-based, landowners' due. Moreover, not only has Gagas's primordial ples been considerably subsumed by Hayes's modernist place, but also RSL as a nationalist place is itself being significantly subsumed. No longer a distinctive manifestation of the national will and autonomy of a newly independent Papua New Guinea, RSL and the nation itself are being transformed into the faltering and the peripheral. Primordial ples, modernist place, and nationalist place are becoming just another, rather minor node in the global marketplace.

In other words, some of the narratives we have described have more apparent effect, more clout, than others. What do we make of this? What does it mean for our claims about how history—about how places like RSL—must be understood? If the strong always win, what is the point of telling the story of RSL as we have told it? If the Gagases will usually lose out to the Hayeses, and the Papua New Guinean nationalists will likely lose out to the free traders, and RSL will probably lose out to CCA, does this mean that the Gagases, the Papua New Guinean nationalists, and RSL are just some "noise" in history's inevitable and inexorable course? And if this is the case, does anthropology have anything important to contribute? Is its value just to document the voices of the Yalis and other losers, the have-nots? Or perhaps to provide some tips on cultural sensitivity so that U.S. business travelers, the haves, can avoid cultural gaffes and unnecessary friction? If this is all there is to it, why bother?

We should bother because, if we do not, we will never know ourselves and others for what we all are: humans who are influenced strongly by context and hence are motivated by a range of historical and cultural ideas about life's nature and possibilities. Thus, those in our RSL story have often varied substantially in what they believed desirable and feasible. They often varied in their ideas and practices about whether families should be extended or nuclear, whether communities should be dispersed or concentrated, and whether nations should be composed of clansmen or citizen-workers. They often varied in their ideas and practices about whether connections to ples/place should be understood as inalienable or alienable; whether objects should be used to create social relationships or to pursue private objectives. They often varied in their ideas and practices about whether a well-lived life would be one of thickened obligations or of career opportunities; whether conflicts should best be resolved through mediation or litigation.

Indeed, the recognition that there is an enormous range of ideas and practices in the world is basic to anthropology. This range becomes evidence that such ideas and practices are not innate, but are culturally and historically shaped. There are, in other words, all sorts of different ways to lead reasonable lives, and in the same way that our lives seem plausible to us by virtue of our cultural and historical circumstances, other peoples' lives seem plausible to them. And, just as we can, if we work hard, understand how other peoples' visions of the desirable and the feasible reflect their histories and cultures, so too we can, if we work hard, understand our own taken-for-granted visions as reflecting our histories and cultures. In fact, implicit in such a comparative undertaking is the means by which we can strive to understand both others and ourselves. What the Gagases of the world want and seek and why they seek it become clarified as we think about what (and why) the Hayeses want and seek—and vice versa. This is to say, anthropology and its intellectual toolkit prompt and enable us to stretch our imagination so as to understand not only an unfamiliar other but an all too familiar self.

Hence, we should not simply conclude from our RSL story that our familiar perspectives about the world and how it works have won—and that is the end of it. That we, as the haves, are able (virtually by definition) to call many of the shots should not prevent us from probing objectives and motives. Indeed, it is especially those who have won who might well think through what constitutes winning itself—what is won, for whom, at what cost, at whose expense, and with what consequences? If, to reiterate, guns, germs, and steel might be used to pursue particular objectives, to secure particular outcomes, and to win particular prizes, this does not mean that they had to be employed in these ways. Comparably, that the Australians had the necessary power to deny Yali his worth is not a sufficient explanation—or justification—for their having done so.

We think that such an anthropological perspective is especially important at the present moment. We write during a time of serious American concern about the extent of corporate fraud, greed, and political influence at home as well as about the extent of military and other forms of coercion abroad. It is at just such a time that we need to be prompted to think especially carefully, self-reflexively, about the outcomes being pursued. With what objectives and with what ramifications—economical, environmental, political, national, international—are the techniques and technologies of power being employed? Even if we fail to take responsibility for the outcomes of our actions, others elsewhere will insist that we do so.

·   ·   ·

The anthropological view of history we are presenting is crucially unlike Diamond's in its emphasis on what needs to be taken into account. Diamond, less by default than by design, denies significance to cultural differences—to particular, historically located visions of the desirable and the feasible. The dissimilarity in our approaches is clarified by what we make of Diamond's book cover. This cover reproduces a large oil painting by John Everett Millais entitled *Pizarro Seizing the Inca of Peru* (fig. 20).

Figure 20. John Everett Millais, *Pizarro Seizing the Inca of Peru*, oil on canvas, 50½ × 67⅞ inches. Victoria and Albert Museum

Completed in 1845, the painting, which hangs in London's Victoria and Albert Museum, is part of a collection begun in 1852 representing the various, often diverse, aesthetic currents of the Victorian age. In the center, Pizarro, sword in hand, is seizing a darkly handsome, grandly exotic Inca leader from his partially overturned palanquin. On the left are massed Spanish soldiers, with a priest holding up a cross for their inspiration. In the right foreground, two Peruvian women and a child are clutching each other in fear. In the right somewhat blurred and darker background, Spanish soldiers are putting Peruvians to the sword. The painting, perhaps anticipating Millais's later anti-Catholic work, seems directly critical of Spanish conquest. Certainly, this is the perspective of Joseph Kestner, who describes the picture as an "anti-Imperialist canvas during a decade of British expansionism and colonial defense" (1995: 55).

When we look at this painting and think about the big, startling, and transforming place in which it hangs, we reflect on a particular and complex history—on the range of sensibilities and political perspectives that existed within this age dominated by capitalism and empire. However, when we look at this painting as it appears on the cover of Diamond's book, we find it interesting because of the extent to which it is

decontextualized and, we think, misunderstood. Rather than a historically located castigation of Spanish imperialism, it is offered as a synop-
sis of human history in general—a history of morally neutral conquest
through the use of techniques and technologies of physical domination.
In other words, from our anthropological perspective, we see Millais's
vision, itself critical of the dominant expansionist perspective of his age,
transformed into a model that justifies as well as universalizes expansionism: it is used to explain what happened to "everybody for the last
13,000 years" (1997: 9).[1] His transformation of Millais's critique of imperialism strikes us as consistent with Diamond's position about the irrele-
vance of cultural and historical contexts in understanding what people
do. Indeed, given Diamond's view of history, the conquest that he rather
mechanistically entitles "Collision at Cajamarca" was inevitable (67).
From his perspective, if it hadn't been Pizarro who had seized the Inca of
Peru, it would have been some other European at some time.

Interestingly, in Kestner's discussion of Millais's painting, he quotes
Bartolome de Las Casas, whose *Short Account of the Destruction of the Indies*
(1552) was a primary source of information concerning the incident
depicted in it. Las Casas, citing eyewitnesses and writing only two decades
after the event, conveys the massacre as remarkably cruel and entirely
unjustified. From his contemporary Spanish perspective, Pizarro was,
even by the standards of the time, a "great villain" whose "cruelty came to
outstrip even that of his predecessors. . . . His wickedness was on such a
scale that nobody will ever really learn the full extent of it until all is
revealed on the Day of Judgment" (in Kestner 1995: 54).

We do not think that Diamond, given his history of grand inevitability,
would be much interested in such alternative voices as Las Casas's. From
his perspective, there is little value in extended conversation to probe the
perspectives of anyone.[2] Certainly, the voices of those like Yali would
scarcely register: their concerns and sense of injustice would not be heard,
their claims to moral worth would not be recognized. Moreover, in the
absence of such conversations, voices would be eliminated that might challenge and contextualize our own more familiar ones. And this elimination
would come about, in our view, not just as a function of the scale on which
history was written, not just as a function of an interest in broad patterns.

•   •   •

How, then, might we respond to Yali's question. Why did white people
deny equality and full humanity to black people? Our full response would

be more proximate, more complex, and more messy than Diamond's. It would consider, as essential background, the rhetorics, practices, contingencies, and exigencies of nineteenth-and twentieth-century global expansionism. Such a consideration would involve, among other matters, the often contesting perspectives concerning how human beings might legitimately derive profit through the use of others, at home and abroad: whether used as slaves, indentured laborers, pieceworkers, or wage earners. It would also consider, as we have done in this book, the often contesting perspectives concerning what might be done for Yali and others to achieve worth in an independent Papua New Guinea. Although our book is only a partial answer to Yali's question, and one addressed more to the several generations that have followed Yali than to Yali himself, it is, we think, an example of the form any answer should take. It is the kind of answer that anthropologists (and many historians) do provide in their willingness to listen seriously to others and scrutinize their own taken-for-granted understandings.

It is the kind of answer that reveals the differences between the necessary and sufficient causes of historical phenomena, that insists that people who have the power to dominate others in faraway places do not automatically find it desirable to do so. It is the kind of answer that shows colonial expansionism and domination to be the product of the historical and cultural circumstances of capitalism, rather than the product of the inevitable workings of human nature. Moreover, it is the kind of answer that shows capitalism, as well as expansionism and domination, as often justified through seemingly inexorable narratives about human nature.

This kind of answer would also be appropriate to the question of what Yali and the other Papua New Guineans might do if they had long been the ones with significant power—if various historical shoes had been, as it were, on other feet. In fact, we are often asked by students whether Yali, with guns, germs, and steel on his side, would have acted as Pizarro did. Our response must be that it all depends on what conditions, on what contexts, are assumed. If Yali were the product of the sort of history that produced the concentrations of power that made Pizarro's conquest feasible, Yali would not be Yali. Under such conditions, he might be Pizarro, or he might be Las Casas. On the other hand, if Yali and the other Papua New Guineans who feature in our story were the products of the history they actually had, we venture that (at the very least) they would be reluctant to leave kin and ples for lives of reckless and ruthless conquest on behalf of god, king, or gold. Their preferred world, while doubtless still assertive and contentious, would, we think, be one of maximized entailments rather than maximized annihilations.[3]

It is true, as we have said, that people not only make war, but also peace; they not only employ techniques and technologies, but also think about how these resources should, or should not, be used; and they not only pursue outcomes, but also evaluate outcomes. To understand all of this—to understand how history happens—requires attentive listening. It requires conversations that probe and interrogate the range of perspectives held by culturally and historically located actors, ourselves included.

Notes

Introduction

1. The literature on the importance of narrative has burgeoned in recent years. Finnegan, in contextualizing the stories she examines about England's newly created community of Milton Keynes, characterizes this work well. (Finnegan's stories include those of critics, residents, and planners. We were brought to her book because one of the key planners was Lord Campbell of Eskan, a figure of significance to RSL.) She explains that her book builds on a range of works about narrative:

> It draws on the view of story as art-ful communication—a view consonant with traditional literary analysis but no longer confined just to that; on the role of myth as elucidated in anthropology and folklore; on the idea of self-as-narrative that now appears across so many disciplines, most notably in psychology; on the relevance of contexting, performance and process from folklore, sociology and, above all, from anthropology; on structured conventions of plot, style and protagonists from literary, anthropological and narratological studies; and on issues about relativism, the multiplicity of our storied views of "reality" and the construction of narratives now being debated among postmodern writers and their critics (1998: 8).

In our book we are especially interested in how contesting narratives compel historical process. We find this perspective useful concerning RSL because RSL did not have to happen (and almost did not), but was brought into being to fulfill certain, often explicitly discussed, objectives. In this regard, in addition to Finnegan, we find Donham 1999 particularly helpful.

2. As aspects of culture, such narrative forms, contexts, and scales show some measure of consistency, are linked. That, for example, contemporary American students are enjoined by their parents to do well on high school exams is linked to ideas of successful careers in a market economy, of coveted lifestyles, of affluent and satisfying retirements—of lives well lived (and well lauded), or not. Or, to anticipate, that young, male, Australian colonial officers are enjoined by their superiors to conduct patrols, with efficiency and dispatch, into remote areas so as to develop Papua New Guineans (through counting, taxing, inspecting, and otherwise regimenting) is linked to ideas of successful careers in a hierarchical state, of masculine efficacy, of modernity's transformative benefits—of challenges met and patriotism proven. Moreover, our concern with tracing out these links, ones conjoining, for instance, ideas about the state with ideas about the career, will be situational. We will not be creating an exhaustive genealogy specifying type and subtype, specifying what narratives logically (or historically) encompass others. Rather, we will be focusing on those narratives, whether broad or particular in scale, that people actually bring to bear in appraising their pasts, coping with their presents, and pursuing their futures. The narratives people use and on what scale vary, of course, according to context. Those relevant to dealing with a threat to national security are different from those relevant to dealing with a reprimand from a boss. Moreover, and as our examples of contemporary American students and Australian colonial officers imply, narratives may also be inflected by class, gender, race, ethnicity, and similar identifiers. The desirability and feasibility of academic success or of a colonial career depend on who one is. We also wish to make it clear that the workings of narratives and the ways in which they construct futures—indeed, the ways in which futures (and pasts and presents) are understood—can be culturally quite variable. This is so because the workings of narratives are contingent on concepts of time and process that give rise to different experiences of transformation and continuity. See Leenhardt [1947] 1979 and Van Heekeren n.d. for Melanesian examples of such variability.

3. For Diamond's studies of Pacific birds, see, especially, Diamond 1972 and Diamond and Mayr 2001. Diamond also writes extensively about conservation issues (see, for instance, Diamond 1984). Finally, he writes popular essays and, in addition to *Guns, Germs, and Steel* (1997), has written one popular book, *The Rise and Fall of the Third Chimpanzee* (1992), which is about the continuities between humans and other primates.

4. As a "big" thinker, Diamond is necessarily concerned more with broad patterns than with messy details. Yet, as other big thinkers like Weber ([1944] 1976), Polanyi (1944), and Foucault (1977, 1978) show, it is possible to depict broad historical patterns, patterns covering whole civilizations and epochs, quite differently. These big thinkers construct their histories in terms of the complex relationships between ethical concerns and material forces, between ideas and interests. They consider the role of accidents and of contingencies, the role played by events coming together in unpredictable ways. They consider the centrality of individuals struggling to make meaning under circumstances of anxiety and confusion. In so doing, their histories take into account many more dimensions of human life and do so in a far less deterministic fashion than does Diamond's history. As Foucault urges historians:

[We must] adopt the methical precaution and the radical but unaggressive skepticism which makes it a principle not to regard the point in time where we are now standing as the outcome of a teleological progression which it would be one's business to reconstruct historically: that skepticism regarding ourselves and what we are, our here and now, which prevents one from assuming that what we have is better than—or more than—in the past. This doesn't mean not attempting to reconstruct generative processes, but that we must do this without imposing on them a positivity or a valorization. (1980: 49)

5. Correspondingly, for those who incline toward race-centered explanations, Diamond's book is an important corrective.

6. Ultimate causes inhere in the nature of things, like gravity, for instance, which causes objects to fall. Proximate causes lead to a particular event, as when an apple falls on one's head. From an ultimate perspective, the said apple falls because of gravity; from a proximate one, it falls because, let us say, a current of air has shaken it loose. The implication, of course, is that once Diamond properly explained things to Yali, Yali would recognize that the apple (or, since the context is Papua New Guinea, the coconut) was both entirely blameless for falling on his head and would continue to behave precisely this way in the future anytime a sufficient breeze occurred. After all, it was in the nature of things. Yali's best strategy would be simply to get out of the way.

7. Anthropologists, especially in introducing students to their discipline, frequently confront views—either explicit or implicit—about purported human nature. In response to such claims as "people just find the grass greener on the other side," anthropologists often try, through the use of comparative material, to convince students that these universalizing statements are ethnocentric. They try to convince them that, while a view of wants as infinite (a view of commodity desires as insatiable) might appear to Americans as mere common sense, as natural, such a view would not necessarily appear as reasonable and natural to those elsewhere.

8. Many of our comments about Diamond might also be applied to the kinds of explanations sociobiologists offer (and E. O. Wilson, perhaps the most distinguished of the sociobiologists, writes a most laudatory blurb for Diamond's book): these are explanations which account for the present and (although sociobiologists often deny this) the future in terms of fixed and still active—ultimate—causes. In effect, sociobiologists argue that it is in the genetic nature of things for human beings (like all other life forms) to maximize their genetic fitness, to prevail by passing on as many of their genes as possible to as many people as possible. To use a particularly egregious example—one that we do not claim Diamond accepts—some sociobiologists account for rape as one of three possible "tactics" available for the passing on of genes, the other two being the cooperative bonding of marriage and the manipulative courtship of seduction. As the biologist Fausto-Sterling elaborates in her criticism of this argument, "Plainly put, all men have the potential to rape, and may be expected to do so if they can get away with it." She continues with a discussion of the problem of distinguishing between ultimate and proximate causes:

These authors do not argue that men consciously think through the possible genetic advantages of rape. Rather, they view this non-conscious calculation as an "ultimate cause," one that originated in our evolutionary history. Rape, they acknowledge quite freely, may have "proximate causes" such as aggression, the desire to humiliate, or sexual gratification—just as many feminists have argued. But those proximate causes, say [certain sociobiologists] represent evolution's way of carrying out its ultimate desire of maximizing genetic fitness. . . . The use of the ultimate-proximate distinction is clever, because it is totally unassailable. Any motivation for rape, regardless of how little it has to do with reproduction, can still be explained on an evolutionary basis by arguing that it is the proximate effecter of the ultimate genetic cause! (1985: 193–94)

Such virtual unassailability makes poor science, as many biologists show (Gould 1980; Bleier 1985; and Fausto-Sterling 1985). However, such science also makes effective ideology by providing readily convincing justifications of the status quo. Sahlins (1976) has articulated this last point particularly well.

9. Because writing this homophonic language "required" an ideographic transcription that was hard to learn, Diamond concludes that a causative sequence arose: a pervasive hierarchy came into being that concentrated power in the hands of a literate elite; this hierarchy ultimately resulted in a single very powerful ruler; this ruler was effectively able to insulate China from outside influences and innovations; an insular China inevitably was overcome by forces from Western Europe rather than vice versa. However, for Diamond to argue that homophones, as arbitrarily given but causatively decisive—just the luck of the environmental-ish draw, as it were—caused hierarchy (or Confucianism, or cultural conservatism) reflects, we think, a misplaced and reductionist causality. Ideographs, we venture, as with other politically consequential esoterica, could be caught up in a whole range of social forms and processes, their uses shaped by pervasive narrative conventions of the feasible, the appropriate, the desirable. Thus, comprehension of the role that Chinese ideographs played in a system of hierarchy requires less an understanding of the possible problems there might, or might not, be in transcribing a homophonic language. Rather, it requires an understanding of the broader social and political contexts (never, of course, completely independent of the environment) in which ideographs were taught and used. This context would have included, for instance, the Chinese system of education and the Chinese system of public administration, which placed the mastery of ideographs within a convincing narrative of career and country.

10. See Cronon 1983 for an instructive discussion of the different objectives—narratives—of English settlers and Native Americans concerning land use in New England. The settlers, seeking to produce surplus for an international market, were committed to expansionist policies in ways that the Native Americans were not.

11. Although our concern here with Diamond is limited to his *Guns, Germs, and Steel* (1997), he expounds his view of human nature more explicitly in *The Rise and Fall of the Third Chimpanzee* (1992).

12. By dissolving actors from historical process and by absolving them from historical responsibility, Diamond's history is far from morally neutral. In this regard, we find unsatisfactory his position that one can distinguish between the "explanation of causes . . . [and] the justification or acceptance of results" (1999: 17). Correspondingly, we find unconvincing, at least with respect to the history he presents, his statement that "[w]hat use one makes of a historical explanation is a

question separate from the explanation itself" (17). In our view, to explain a process by describing it as fundamentally inevitable is, in effect, to curtail the possible uses one can make of that explanation—other than to accept it as fate, as in the nature of things, as morally irrelevant.

13. Even if it is the case that no significant military technology ever went unused, this would not explain adequately the reasons that people used it, much less explain why they used it for maximum effect—without restraint. Nor would it absolve them from having done so.

14. This is to say, hegemony is never fully complete; *doxa* generally remains heterodox; truth regimes are often in competition; consciousness is never totally colonized.

15. It is difficult to know how to appraise historically remote activities—those of Genghis Khan and his Mongol hordes, for instance—in terms of choice and, hence, responsibility. However, during the more recent periods of mercantilism and capitalism (again, the periods in which guns, germs, and steel were used with particular effect), choices can be shown to have existed. Thus, to take an example from closer to our home: Lord Jeffrey Amherst furthered his career and cause by strongly advocating the introduction of smallpox-infected blankets to a completely disease-susceptible Native American population (see Fenn 2000). That he did so was not the morally neutral, because inevitable, consequence of human nature; it was, likewise, not the morally neutral, because inevitable, consequence of cultural determinants. Even at the time, such biological warfare, including British biological warfare against American colonists during the Revolutionary War, was seen by some as morally suspect, if not outright reprehensible. For instance, Quaker evangelists such as John Woolman never doubted that because the English and the Native Americans all shared a common humanity, the latter should be treated according to "pure universal righteousness as to give no just cause of offense" (quoted in Moulton 1971: 128–29). Moreover, even some among Amherst's advisors argued that such tactics were so immoral as to be shortsighted, sure to alienate and infuriate potential Native American allies. Sir William Johnson's view was that Amherst "is not at all a friend of Indians which I am afraid will have bad consequences" (quoted in Nester 2000: 10–11). In addition, it should be recognized that, more than a hundred years earlier, the American colonist Roger Williams argued that the settlement of the New World should rest on the purchase rather than on the conquest of Native American lands. See, in this regard, Williams 1643, chap.16, as cited in Waldrop 1994: xvii.

16. For an excellent and somewhat comparable ethnography of a multinational corporation, see Trouillot 1988.

17. In chapter 6, we will learn about Lord Campbell of Eskan and his role in shaping BTL. He also initiated the company's interest in literature. His obituary in the London *Times*, December 28, 1994, describes how this came about:

> In a highly original business move Bookers also expanded into literature when, in 1964, it took over a 51 percent interest in Glidros Productions which held the copyright on Ian Fleming's novels. Campbell was a great friend of Fleming and had clinched the deal over a round of golf. It proved an extremely lucrative move for Bookers, who were then set to exploit James Bond's vast merchandising possibilities only two years after "Cubby" Broccoli's first Bond

film, *Dr. No.* It was only fitting, therefore, that Bookers set up the Booker Prize for literature in 1969.

For a fascinating analysis of the Booker Prize winners through 1999, as concerned with the legacy of the British Empire, see Strongman 2002.

18. In 1886, the northern half of what became Papua New Guinea was a colony of Germany and the southern half was a colony of Britain. In 1921, after World War One, the northern half—New Guinea—came under Australian administration, first as a League of Nations Mandated Territory, and later as a United Nations Trust Territory. In 1906, the southern half—Papua—though still formally controlled by Britain, also came under Australian administration. The two territories—New Guinea and Papua—were separately administered by Australia until 1942. Subsequently, Australia brought both under a single administration, although the United Nations retained some responsibility for the New Guinea portion. This condition prevailed until Papua New Guinea's independence as a single nation in 1975.

19. For an excellent analysis of the local impact of sugar operations under postcolonial, albeit equally grim, circumstances, see Scheper-Hughes 1992.

20. As we shall see in chapter 2, the land that eventually became RSL was purchased from indigenous people in 1956 by the Australian administration to be offered to Europeans in pastoral leases. When RSL was established, it had to buy the leases from these Europeans. The leases came as a package involving several small cattle ranches scattered down the Markham Valley and one large ranch in the Upper Ramu Valley. The Ramu Valley parcel was divided: a portion became the sugar operation and a portion remained as a ranching operation. Although there is some synergy between the ranching and the sugar operations (cattle, for example, are sometimes fed molasses and cane tops), the two are quite different kinds of operations. This book focuses exclusively on RSL's sugar operation, by far the more economically and organizationally important of the two.

21. These terms are commonly used by both nationals and expatriates to refer to themselves and to the other.

22. For informative discussions of the development of sugarcane processing technology, including its great improvement in the nineteenth century, see Deerr 1950 and Mintz 1985. See Bakker 1999 for a state-of-art specification of sugarcane growing techniques.

23. Arce and Long continue in ways that resonate with our focus with questions concerning studies of development projects: "How can anthropology capture the dynamics of these situations and processes? How can one deal theoretically and pragmatically with the partial connections, ambiguities and incompatibilities in the meanings and social practices? How can the researcher construct a convincing narrative of events and outcomes that does full, or at least adequate, justice to these complexities?" (2000: 3).

24. In his challenge to anthropologists who are inclined to view themselves as the ones who travel and the people they study as the homebodies, Clifford (1997) describes the visa-filled passports of Middle Eastern villagers who spend much of their lives working away from home. Such lives, he argues, are now common. It seems to us that RSL, as a Papua New Guinean metropole, is an important context for understanding how such multisited lives are constituted and experienced. In effect,

such lives—both at RSL and at "home"—are examples of what Knauft (2002) calls the "locally modern."

25. In his prologue, Diamond says that cultural anthropologists, along with a range of other scholars, "have called attention to parts of the puzzle, but they provide only pieces of the needed broad synthesis that has been missing" (1997: 24). If he finds anthropologists useful though excessively particularistic, we find him useful but excessively homogenizing. As shall be made clear in this book, we think that he homogenizes humanity by making differences in cultural perspectives dissolve unproblematically into a single, uniform and ultimately Western perspective. To be sure, not all contemporary anthropologists would agree with our critique of Diamond. In particular, biological determinists and economic determinists would likely be sympathetic to Diamond's endeavor. We also might add that nineteenth-century cultural anthropologists like Lewis Henry Morgan ([1877] 1969) who propounded unilinear evolutionism might agree with him as well.

Chapter One

1. On desire and its social and linguistic transformations, see Lacan 1981 and Turkle 1992. Concerning the social construction of desire in a Pacific society, see Lindstrom 1990.

2. We thank Bryant Allen for drawing our attention to this photograph. For a brief biography of Yali, see Hermann 2002. On Yali and his people, see Hermann 1992a, 1992b, 1995.

3. See Errington and Gewertz 1995b and 1995c. See also *Mambu* (1960), Burridge's pioneering study of the cargo-focused efforts by Papua New Guinea's Tangu villagers to achieve moral equality.

4. That Papua New Guineans, like Yali, wanted Australians to recognize them as equals does not mean that they themselves were always willing to grant full equality, much less, full humanity, to all other Papua New Guineans. Nonetheless, in our experience, virtually regardless of the relationships at any particular moment between Papua New Guinean groups, these groups remain alert to the possibilities of establishing positive, mutually validating ties.

5. Collective, language-focused identities, rather than more particularistic, hamlet or clan-focused identities, are increasingly significant in contemporary politics, particularly in efforts to make effective land claims. We undertake a more extensive discussion of those defining themselves as Mari, Raikos, and Kafe, including reference to the ethnographies about them, in chapter 7.

6. As a modernist perspective applied to the recounting of the process of modernization itself, such accounts are particularly clear and instructive renditions of the broad narrative of modernism.

7. On the relationship between time, space, and human action in modernity, see especially Giddens 1998, 2000.

8. There are many discussions, if not debates, concerning the philosophical bases and the political and economic effects of development visions and rhetorics. Among others, see Cowen and Shenton 1996, for a probing of development's philosophical bases; Marglin and Marglin 1990, for a discussion of the relationship between development and Western forms of knowledge; Frank 1967, for a consideration of the relationship between development and underdevelopment; Cowen and

MacWilliam 1996, for an examination of the relationship between development and class formation; and Kelly and Kaplan 2001, for an elucidation of the relationship between development, decolonization, and the construction of the nation state.

9. Many patrol officers likely accepted some variant of a view known as unilinear evolutionism. This view, first prevalent during the late nineteenth century among members of the Euro-American public (including anthropologists of the time), holds that there is a single trajectory of human development from simple to complex, from savage to civilized. All existing societies can be placed along this trajectory with, of course, Euro-American societies being most evolved. According to this framework, Papua New Guinean natives had to recapitulate, ideally in accelerated fashion, the historical trajectory that moved Europeans from savagery to civilization.

10. Thus "models of" were linked with "models for" (Geertz 1973).

11. Healy writes concerning cargo-cult sentiments that he encountered in the Ramu region: "The general languid feeling noticed throughout will be cast aside gradually as the greater majority of natives become convinced that the old doctrines cannot bear fruit. At present, I gathered only the minority were convinced of the use-lessness of waiting [for cargo to come through magical means] and time alone and their own better appreciation of the European's way of life will bring about the desired change in the natives mind" (1953: 8).

12. McPherson provides subsidiary evidence: "Patrol officers, by the very nature of their job requirements, were essentially unsupervised in the performance of their duties. Since their hours of work 'could not be accurately determined,' kiaps [patrol officers] on patrol were required to maintain a journal that included shorthand accounts of time and distance traveled, duties performed on an hourly and daily basis, and events encountered during the patrol" (2001: 90). Thus, patrol officers not only monitored what was done, but also what could be done. They imposed a time/space grid of not only what a hard-working and efficient patrol officer did accomplish, but also what he should/must accomplish.

13. Nash describes such comparisons as they differentiated between villages in Bougainville: "From the beginning, patrol reports freely used language implying stages of development: the Nagovisi were 'backward,' real 'bush kanakas' . . . , and, sometimes, 'the most backward' in the district" (2001: 116).

14. Although patrol officers were the agents of this transformation, their agency was provisional, and they were also frequently put into their place. In fact, each patrol report, following the principle that files should be added to the front, accrued letters of evaluation attached by superiors as the report moved up a chain of command, from patrol officer, to assistant district officer, to district officer and then to the director of district services and native affairs (for example, from Bundi, to the district capital of Madang and, finally, to the Territory capital of Port Moresby).

15. In "Bundi Patrol Report No. 3 for 1956–57," patrol officer Neil McNamara records that the census total for Bopirumpun was 103; for Bumpu, 123; for Kaigulan, 153; and for Sankian, 148. Based upon the International Monetary Fund's *International Financial Statistics*, A£8,412.12.0 was worth approximately U.S.$18,843.15 in 1956 (International Monetary Fund 1956: 14). According to the Economic History Services Web site (www.eh.net/hmit), this amount converted, using the Consumer Price Index, into about U.S.$122,000 in 2001.

16. Geertz (1973: 3–30) explains the difference between a thin description and thick description with reference to the differences between winks, twitches, and parodies of winks and twitches. A thin description equates them all as simply rapid contractions of the eyelid. A thick description contextualizes each as having a very different significance in social life.

Chapter Two

1. Dyer's own responsibility was to prepare the agricultural land. This involved plowing the grasslands under, arranging the fields and rows to cut across the slopes rather than down the slopes (so as to avoid erosion and conserve water), and constructing channels for water runoff. The channels, lined with well-rooting grass, prevented torrents and gullies.

2. Thus McCarthy reports that Yali said, upon returning from Australia: "I have seen how the white man lives in his own country. He has good houses, much food, and he obeys the law. Every day, except on Sunday, he goes to work and earns money to buy the things and the food he wants. Even the white women and the children also work hard at school" (1963: 225).

3. Significantly, Karavarans often asked Fred questions about "factories" and, in fact, offered him money so that he would build them one. However, once again, their concern was not primarily to have factories per se but to win European respect by having something that Europeans so obviously valued.

4. There were those at the time who objected to what they considered the bias of Australian planners toward large-scale development projects. See, in particular, Crocombe 1967, 1968, and 1969.

5. Kelly and Kaplan (2001) argue that the formation of nation-states after World War Two was not the product of some inherent trajectory of modernity, as they claim Anderson (1983) holds. Rather, they see such a formation as orchestrated by the United States and the United Nations. This vision, which "eventually routinized the idea of a globeful of egalitarian, community nation-states" (Kelly and Kaplan 2001: 9), seems especially pertinent to processes of decolonization in what became Papua New Guinea.

6. It was, after all, as early as 1951 that, as a step toward a democratically elected parliamentary government, Papua New Guineans were placed upon the first Legislative Council. John Guise was among those serving on this council. He later served as the first governor-general of an independent Papua New Guinea between 1975 and 1977 and thus figures importantly in our story about RSL.

7. Concerning Australia's desire to disentangle itself from Papua New Guinea, Zimmer-Tamakoshi writes: "In December 1973, Papua New Guinea became self-governing. Although little had been done to implement the goals of the Eight Point Plan and Papua New Guinea was far from economically self-sufficient, Australia was facing economic problems of its own and was committed to getting out of Papua New Guinea as quickly as it could decently do so" (1998a: 8).

8. We owe a special debt to Robin Hide, who not only generously shared with us his extensive personal and bibliographic knowledge of Papua New Guinea, but also searched the Australian Government Archives for information about early attempts at producing commercial sugar in Papua New Guinea.

9. As Marks and Maskus concisely explain in the introduction to The Economics and Politics of World Sugar Prices: "That sugar production is heavily supported around the

world is partly a response to the periodic boom-and-bust cycles that sugar markets have experienced historically. Such price cycles are typical of many agricultural commodities for which demand and supply are price-inelastic. Sugar prices have been highly volatile, even in comparison with other farm commodities, however. Typically, the cycle begins with an upward spike in the world price caused by production shortfalls associated with bad weather in some important producing region. After stocks are depleted, producers worldwide react by planting significantly more acreage in sugar cane and sugar beets. Expanding cane acreage tends to generate structural output surpluses over time because cane, once planted, continues to produce sugar for several years. This feature is exacerbated by the tendency of sugar farmers in most countries to lobby for additional protection to support their additional output. The result is a period of depressed world prices for sugar, generating additional impetus for protection. As a consequence of economic and political dynamics of this sort, monthly [world] sugar prices ranged from a low of 2.7 U.S. cents per pound to a high of 41.1 U.S. cents per pound during the 1980's" (1993: 4). Thus, as BTL experts frequently stressed to us, rather than reflecting actual costs of production, such very low prices resulted from "dumping"—fostered, in part, by domestic subsidies and protections.

10. Schmitz and Christian note: "In 1974, shortages in the world market resulted in an approximate tripling in sugar prices" (1993: 51).

11. In telling this part of RSL's story, we learned from Thomas's analysis (1984) of the development of Guyana's sugar economy. In particular, we benefited from his examination of the state's role in "consolidating the dominant position of the plantation and, later, after nationalization, in holding the key to rural development and transformation" (xvii).

12. Both "open pan" and "vacuum pan" refer to methods by which the juice from crushed sugarcane is heated to the extent that the excess moisture evaporates and sugar crystals form in the resulting concentrate. In the open-pan Khandsari system, the sugar juice is heated in open vessels (pans) with the excess water simply boiling off as steam. The resulting concentrate includes both sugar crystals and molasses. It is considered ready for sale with no further significant processing. In the vacuum-pan method, the sugar juice is heated in a series of closed vessels. That these vessels are closed allows for the creation of a partial vacuum. With a partial vacuum, the boiling point of the liquid is reached at a lower temperature than if the vessels are at normal atmospheric pressure. In addition, the steam boiled off from the first pan is captured and used to heat the juice in the next pan. That this next pan is at a yet higher vacuum means that the liquid boils even more easily—at essentially the temperature of the incoming steam from the first vessel. This process continues, pan to pan. Such a method not only saves fuel; it also produces higher-quality sugar through the use of lower boiling points. In addition, vacuum pans are integrated into a comprehensive system of processing, including the use of centrifuges to spin off much of the molasses. The investigation of the feasibility of a small vacuum-pan system in Papua New Guinea was, in effect, the investigation of the feasibility of a small-scale modern sugar factory, designed to provide superior sugar quality, enhanced process control, and better fuel economy.

13. If it were not for David Freyne and John Mosusu, we would never have found the Christensen files. We thank them both for their engagement with our project and efforts on our behalf.

14. A BAI staff member, who worked extensively with Christensen, found him knowledgeable, thorough, hardworking, invariably courteous and "totally committed to PNG's development to which he gave many years of unstinting service." After Christensen's employment in Papua New Guinea was terminated, he returned to Australia. This staff member speculated to us that Christensen's later tragic suicide in Australia was prompted by the loss of the work to which he had been completely dedicated.

15. Shaw defines the difference between small and grand development as one between "adaptive" and "radical" food production strategies. Adaptive strategies require "only minor shifts in the pattern of land and resource use. They recognize and utilise existing social systems and human resources and build upon these and graft new techniques or crops onto existing production systems" (1982a: 12). In contrast, radical strategies, such as those employed by RSL and oil palm projects, emphasize "'universal' rather than 'unique' solutions and require considerable shifts in resources such as land, labour, technology, money and other inputs.... Radical solutions also have important political implications. National and regional politicians like them since they are highly visible and give an impression of action and impact. Because of their financial and capital requirements, they are attractive to multilateral and bilateral lending agencies and aid donors. They can also be implemented by foreign investors. While they may create employment, they also have important indirect effects which may be undesirable, such as increasing [the need for] energy, raw materials, capital goods and skill imports, and foreign remittances" (1982a: 14). See also, Shaw 1980, 1982b, and 1985.

16. Correspondingly, as suggested to us by another observer, Chan seemed more interested in creating an elite class of Papua New Guinean capitalists than in enhancing indigenous rural communities. Overall, his vision of development could certainly be seen as reflecting his social status and economic interests.

17. According to a senior BAI/BTL source, because the company is both an agricultural consultancy and a management company it differs from its competitors in three major ways: it carries out feasibility studies and implements the results of these studies; it is willing to take a minority investment in any major project it manages; and it employs a cadre of professional management staff, who are full-time pensionable employees. In this latter regard, since the company does not hire and fire as and when needed for particular jobs, its staff has a high degree of company loyalty and professional commitment.

18. Lévi-Strauss (1962) states that because food features in systems of human classification, it is not only good to eat, but good to think—with and about. Thus the difference between brown and white sugar was more than a matter of physical taste.

19. Fiji produced raw sugar that was refined elsewhere, for example, in Australia and New Zealand. For a history of the Colonial Sugar Refining Company (CSR), the major player in the production and refining of Fijian sugar, see Lowndes 1956.

Chapter Three

1. As Rodman argues, "places, not only feature in inhabitants' ... narratives, they are narratives in their own right; 'a place comes explicitly into being in the discourse of its inhabitants and particularly in the rhetoric it promotes'" (Rodman 1992:

642, quoting Berdoulay). Among the other provocative writings on place, see Casey 1993, Hirsch and O'Hanlon 1995, and Feld and Basso 1996.

2. Thus, when we traveled in central Australia, we discovered that the geological formation known as Ayers Rock to white Australians and as Uluru to Australian Aborigines is a different place to each: to the former, it is a tourist attraction to be climbed and mastered as an expression of national vigor and pride; to the latter, it is a sacred site to be respected and protected as an expression of indigenous rights and responsibilities.

3. Without implying that Gagas is a cargo cultist, his description of the earphones and television screen used by RSL's Japanese engineers reminds us of the ways in which Kaliai cargo cultists incorporate reconfigured items of Western technology, especially telephones and cameras, in a renarration of race relations under contemporary Papua New Guinean circumstances. See Lattas 2000.

4. Hayes told us that the RSL factory is less than half the size of the smallest factory operating in Australia. Australia's smallest factory crushes 8,000 tons of sugarcane a day, while RSL's factory crushes only 3,000 tons a day in processing its annual crop. With a guaranteed market in Papua New Guinea of only 30,000 tons per year, it was hard for him to justify building RSL's factory, at least on narrow economic grounds: it would always produce expensive sugar; and there would always be commercial pressure to import cheap sugar. After all, in a few countries such as Brazil and Thailand, companies can make a profit by charging $U.S.0.08 a pound for raw sugar. But in Papua New Guinea, RSL cannot make a profit unless it charges $U.S.0.25 a pound for the mill-white sugar leaving its factory. (Granted, the comparison of products here is not precisely equivalent—raw sugar versus mill-white sugar. However, the cost of converting the former to the latter is relatively slight.)

5. As an example of the rationalized, impersonal arguments that Hayes and BTL employees at RSL find compelling, consider the language used in the BAI Feasibility Study concerning RSL's prospective factory (Booker Agriculture International 1978b: 4–5):

1.9. *Mill Capacity and Size.* Mill capacity is largely related to the fibre in cane. This quantity is dependent upon cane varieties, climate, harvesting methods, supervision and control of harvesting, and other agricultural practices and procedures.

1.9.1. The initial cane varieties are expected to be taken from those currently favoured in Australia with about 12.5% fibre on clean ("net") cane. . . . The regime at Gusap might result in 13% fibre in actual ("gross") cane milled. The initial mill capacity therefore should secure:

$$(2800/24 \times 0.13) + 10\% \text{ peaks, i.e., 16.7t fibre/h}$$

6. The literature on essentialism and its discontents is large. For a particularly comprehensive discussion, see the articles in Carrier 1995.

7. The BAI pamphlet, written to provide expatriates with the information they would need to decide whether to accept employment at Papua New Guinea's RSL, includes details about the country, climate, history, government, economy, development prospects, population, peoples, and cultures. It also concludes with a brief

outline of the RSL project and with "general information" about visas, medical requirements, facilities for babies, baggage, freight and insurance, the journey to Papua New Guinea, the currency, banking, communications, personal security and insurance, housing, services, servants, shopping, health, clothing, recreation, schooling, transport, employment of wives, pets, and hours of work.

8. Thus, as Mintz writes about plantations in Puerto Rico, and everywhere else that he knew of, "the roles of the laboring and employing classes were set sharply apart" (1953: 225).

9. With an increasing number of managers' children wishing to attend the international school, a separate building was constructed during 2000 (still within the Management Compound) and an additional teacher was hired.

10. This arrangement is, in effect, what Wolf would predict from his studies of plantations of the "New World." He writes that "[e]verywhere these new communities also follow a basic plan which translates into spatial terms the chain of command of owners, managers, overseers, permanent workers and seasonal workers" (1959: 137).

11. The 1990 official census figures for "Ramu Urban," which included those living at RSL and those living at Gusap—but not those living in surrounding indigenous villages—was 7,946, including 41 noncitizens. Given that many people actually resident at RSL were not, according to company policy, supposed to be there, we imagine this figure was an undercount.

12. This was, we might mention, a general practice by such national organizations as the police and army during the 1960s and 1970s. For another discussion of comparable hiring procedures in Papua New Guinea, see Imbun 2000.

13. During 2000, twenty-one of the permanent workers came from Central; thirty from East New Britain; sixty-one from East Sepik; forty-three from Enga; ten from Gulf; twenty-three from Manus; eleven from Milne Bay; four from New Ireland; nine from North Solomons; eleven from Oro; seventeen from Sandaun; seventy-five from Simbu; twenty-nine from Southern Highlands; thirty-six from Western Highlands; nine from West New Britain; and one whose province of origin we do not know.

14. For comparative examples see Thompson 1967 and Cooper 1992.

15. As LiPuma well puts it: "For the imagined community to become possible . . . there must come into being a horizon that transcends and seeks to pre-empt local culture and community. For kinspeople to become 'citizens,' they must be enveloped in a new social space" (1995: 61).

16. On the importance of narrative in nation making, see, in particular, Bhabba 1990, Layoun 1992, and Foster 1995.

17. Hence, America as a distinct nation is composed of Americans who are taught that their unity as brave, resourceful, freedom-loving citizens is derived from a common history; according to this often repeated narrative, their shared, and ongoing, heritage defines them as vigilant defenders of liberties and as daring conquerors of frontiers.

Chapter Four

1. During 2000, of the 668 permanent employees, 39 were women; of the 789 seasonal employees, 15 were women.

2. RSL is systematically mechanizing its agricultural procedures (primarily through the use of mechanical cane-harvesters). This is not only to alleviate the

social problems created by the very large numbers of "seasonals" but to save money. The costs of wages as well as of housing (including utilities) make it more expensive to use seasonal workers than to run machines.

3. On shifting priorities among Papua New Guinea wage earners, see, among others, King 1998, Zimmer-Tamakoshi 1998b, and Gewertz and Errington 1991, 1999.

4. The RSL *Employees Handbook* specifies that "unauthorized absence for a full working week or more is a serious offense and in such cases an employee will be treated as having deserted and left employment permanently" (Ramu Sugar Limited 1993: app. 3, 1).

5. Tribal fighting, focusing largely on land disputes, is both common and, with the use of guns, very dangerous throughout the Highlands. In fact, one RSL seasonal we know well spent much of his wage on ammunition to supply kinsmen at home. Moreover, the country is plagued by criminals (Pidgin English, "raskols") who, generally in groups, engage in a variety of felonious activities, from rape to robbery to murder. For recent analyses of "raskolism" in Papua New Guinea, see Goddard 1992, 1995; Hart Nibbrig 1992; Kulick 1991, 1993; Roscoe 1999; and Sykes 1999.

6. We describe such a settlement in the town of Wewak in Gewertz and Errington 1991, 1999.

7. RSL's employees and RSL on behalf of its employees pay regularly, as obligated by law, into the National Provident Fund (NPF). However, the prospects that this fund will significantly supplement the income of retirees were recently dealt two blows. One involves the steady depreciation in the value of the kina (about which we shall say more in chapter 9). The other involves the drastic decrease in the value of NPF holdings through mismanagement, which likely included outright theft. When this decrease was revealed, workers at RSL reacted with general and angry consternation at the likely loss of much of their savings.

8. For an overview concerning the importance of custom, or "kastom," in the Pacific, see Keesing and Tonkinson 1982. In addition, see Keesing 1992 for the ways in which ideas about custom became significant in contemporary political struggles in the Solomon Islands. Also, for interesting discussions about the relationship between custom and European business practices, see Foster 1990 (concerning Papua New Guinea) and Thomas 1992 (concerning Fiji). Finally, for the manner in which customs are being rendered generic in Papua New Guinea, see Errington and Gewertz 2001.

9. Attachments to ples, particularly among elite Papua New Guineans, are increasingly described as protecting "assets," protecting what can generate income from, for example, cash crops or mineral and timber resources. See, in this regard, Gewertz and Errington 1999. Correspondingly, for an analysis of the ways in which commodifiable resources are precipitating a redefinition of social groups and their boundaries, see Ernst 1999.

10. Strathern (1988) contrasts Papua New Guinean "sociality" with Western "society." The former she considers more fluid and situational; the latter, more bounded and structured. RSL, not to mention the BUMBU of the patrol officers, is formally organized as a society.

11. On village courts in Papua New Guinea, see, among others, Gordon and Meggitt 1985; Scaglion 1979, 1985; Westermark 1986, 1997; and Zorn 1992.

12. Of course, it must also be true that what being a Minj has shifted for him, given these other things he has become. And, presumably, being a Minj has changed for other Minj, given what Kamdan has become.

Chapter Five

1. Sontag's statement appears in her evaluation of the "Family of Man" photographic exhibition. She thinks this exhibition, in its emphasis on common worldwide humanity, glosses over crucial and persisting differences. It is worth noting that the book reproducing the photographs from this exhibition is still in press. See Steichen 1955.

2. This description of BTL's offerings appeared on its Web site in 2000 (www.booker-tate.co.uk/Comp_main.htm).

3. Because BTL is a British-based company, most of its employees at RSL are from the United Kingdom. However, some come from elsewhere, generally from Australia, where BTL has, until relatively recently, operated an office to oversee its Pacific operations.

4. In a personal communication, Robert Foster suggests that, with global capital, the era of transporting England, for instance, to the former colonies has largely ended. Contemporary technicians, regardless of their specific place of origin, are trained to view cultural preoccupations and allegiances as impediments to efficiency.

5. For an informative, cross-cultural example, focusing on the Apache, of the benefits and risks of establishing and breaking through the ethos of banter, see Basso 1979.

6. For informative ethnographies about the importance of discourse in the Pacific see Lindstrom 1990, Brenneis and Myers 1991, and Brison 1992.

7. There are notable exceptions to this characterization of the literature on expatriates as thin. (See chapter 1, note16, for a more complete discussion of "thin" versus "thick" descriptions.) On Papua New Guinea, see Nelson 1982, Huber 1988, Bourke et al. 1993, and Upton 1998. In addition, see West's biography of Murray (1968), Hasluck's autobiography 1977, and Sack and Clark's biography of Hahl 1980. For a general discussion of expatriate life, see Cohen 1977.

8. On colonialism and its culture in the Pacific, see especially Thomas 1994 and Douglas 1999.

9. We include our own work on tourists here (Errington and Gewertz 1989); Gewertz and Errington 1991: 25–57), as well as that of Silverman (1999, 2000). We particularly commend Huber for her exceptional study of missionaries (1988).

10. See, especially, Street 1992, O'Hanlon 1993: 7–13, and Lutz and Collins 1993: 188–216.

11. Some of this moral uneasiness might well be felt concerning anthropological representation in more "conventional" field studies. While anthropologists often make it clear to "natives" (as opposed to expatriates) that anthropology is being done among them, the "natives" may not be entirely clear what anthropology is. While anthropologists often help local people, for example, by providing medical care, transportation, or school fees, such help is likely to be most focused on those who provide research assistance. And while anthropologists may, through their representations of local people, help provide a voice heard by the more powerful (see Myers 1988), any particular representation likely serves some local political ends

better than others. This circumstance is wonderfully depicted in Shearston's short story set in Papua New Guinea about an archaeological discovery that, by favoring one group as the area's original occupant, undermined regional harmony (1979: 11–26; see also Errington and Gewertz 1987).

12. Based upon our own research among expatriates in Wewak, we find *Rascal Rain* (Baranay 1995), an account by a volunteer of her time in Papua New Guinea, a particularly egregious instance of invasive misrepresentation.

13. Most expatriates employed by mining operations in Papua New Guinea work intensively for a several-week stint and then fly home (generally to Australia) for a leave. This pattern is repeated for the duration of their contract.

14. Bettison found, before Papua New Guinea's independence, that interracial socializing was "most pronounced between expatriates and better paid [nationals]" (1966: 230). This has continued to be the case since independence. However, in our experience, the degree of actual mixing between expatriates and affluent nationals may still be limited—as much by ethos as economics.

15. Upton describes a number of club-centered, expatriate cliques that formed in Lae during the late 1980s. She cautions, however, that expatriates living there then were, in fact, a rather various bunch who could not easily be characterized as falling within the stereotypes "mercenary," "missionary," or "misfit" (1998: 18–20).

16. Such diseases were always recognized as a significant threat to commercial cane production in Papua New Guinea. Because sugarcane had originated in Papua New Guinea, a large number of (possibly unknown) local pathogens that could have developed along with the cane might still be there. Moreover, by the time RSL was established, sugarcane had been greatly transformed away from its place of origin by centuries of commercial breeding. This meant that when these commercial varieties were brought to Papua New Guinea they would be especially vulnerable to disease: they would be (re)exposed not only to a great many indigenous pathogens but to pathogens for which they might well have lost earlier resistance. (On the history of Ramu stunt and its consequences at RSL, see Eastwood 1990.) Under these circumstances, it would have been especially prudent at RSL to plant a substantial range of cane varieties, with a presumed range of resistances. However, as Bryan Dyer, RSL's first agriculture manager, explained to us, only about eighteen cane varieties were available to him. These varieties, in semiabandoned plots, had been imported previously from Queensland by the Department of Primary Industry. Although Dyer would have liked at least one hundred varieties to set things up properly, he concluded that he had to make do, at least initially, with a very limited genetic base. And, of what he had, only one variety—Ragnor—gave high yields. Thus, rather than delay the whole project until it was possible to establish the agreements necessary to import additional varieties, it was decided to risk planting most of the estate in Ragnor. Ragnor's yields, it was hoped, would get RSL off the ground: of particular importance, it would enable RSL to deal with its heavy burden of offshore debts. Dyer stressed to us that it was a matter of "risk management" and that he hoped "with good crop husbandry and a prayer" RSL could make it until he could establish the requisite trade agreements with Caribbean and Australian sugar-breeding stations.

17. On expatriate domestic coping, focusing on missionaries living in West Papua between 1953 and 1998, see Lake 2001. In a personal communication, Lake

describes his missionary father often coming home after a hard day and asking in jest, "What's for dinner, Baked Alaska?" Indeed, in what was generally regarded as a triumph of coping, one missionary wife actually made Baked Alaska without refrigeration. Coping, in this sense, sought to maintain the amenities of a Western way of life in a difficult and exotic context.

18. This was not just a private polling, but a public substantiation: a model *of* conviviality and a model *for* conviviality (Geertz 1973: 93–94).

19. On nostalgia, see also, Rosaldo 1993, Battaglia 1995, and Ferguson 2002.

20. In other words, the *Sugar Valley News* promulgates a selective vision of moral regulation that renders "natural and taken-for-granted a set of particular and historical premises about social life." It produces and disseminates, "in relatively self-conscious fashion, collective representations—images and ideals of the collectivity and of the persons who compose the collectivity" (Foster 1992: 33).

21. On the aesthetics of work in another Papua New Guinean context, see Demian 2000.

22. For a comparable example of the importance of homes and gardens in the colonial enterprise, see Macintyre 1989.

Chapter Six

1. Robinson had been with BTL from its beginning. Indeed, he was a personnel director of BTL's predecessor organization, Booker Agriculture International. BAI, it will be recalled, was the company that carried out RSL's initial feasibility study. Subsequently, in 1988, it joined with the agricultural and project management division of sugar giant Tate and Lyle to became Booker Tate Limited.

2. The Guyanese sugar industry, much of which was consolidated under Bookers control, was nationalized in 1975–76 at a time in which world sugar prices were high. After a period of state farming, the company (in the form of Booker Tate) was called back in 1991 to manage the failing plantations. An article about this event in the *Economist* is ironically titled, "Come Back, Slavemasters" (1992). On the history of this sugar industry, see Adamson 1972 and Thomas 1984.

3. On the different social and economic mechanisms used to control labor on sugar plantations throughout the Caribbean, see Adamson 1972; Crayton and Walvin 1970; Hagelberg 1974; Mandle 1973; Mangru 1996; Mintz 1953, 1958, 1959, 1960, 1985; and Smith 1962, 1967.

Concerning "Bookers' Guiana," Smith elaborates:

When Guianese refer to their country as "Bookers' Guiana" they refer not only to the fact that the firm has a hand in practically every economic activity in the country but also to the fact that the real control centre of Bookers' is London, that it is an English company run almost wholly by Englishmen answerable to English shareholders, and that in the past Guianese were rarely able to aspire to any but the lower status positions within its hierarchy. Some of these factors may not have been so objectionable had the British not behaved very much as a dominant caste group. (1962: 84)

Curtis extends Smith's argument concerning Bookers' role in Guiana: In 1953 after Cheddi Jagan's democratically elected People's Progressive Party (PPP) called for a strike by sugar workers seeking union recognition from the Sugar Producers Association, Bookers "stated that the strike meant 'a loss of profits' and that 'the present situation can only be dealt with effectively by the Colonial Office.' Indeed, 'unless something drastic is done, Bookers will cease to exist as a large firm in five years.'" A month later "the British Governor announced that the constitution was being suspended and the elected members were being removed from office. A few hundred British troops landed and three warships remained stationed off the Guianan coast" (Curtis 2003: 350). It was only because the PPP had been removed from office after the 1964 elections that Britain granted British Guiana independence in 1966. Curtis concludes that this left Bookers with a "remarkable degree of control over the economy, both through its dominant interest in the sugar industry and through its interests in fisheries, cattle, timber, insurance, advertising and retail commerce" (354).

4. In fact, many of the expatriates replaced in supervisory positions were the Filipinos seconded from Victorias Milling (see chapter 3). Below are the data compiled during 2001 concerning localization:

EXPATRIATE MANNING SCHEDULE

Year	Management	Supervisory	Total
1983	55	27	82
1984	56	19	74
1985	50	10	60
1986	50	3	53
1987	49	3	52
1988	49	1	50
1989	37	2	39
1990	36	2	38
1991	28	2	30
1992	24	2	26
1993	26		26
1994	26		26
1995	27		27
1996	23		23
1997	22		22
1998	21		21
1999	20		20
2000	16		16
2001 Jan.	12		12
2001 Apr.	11		11

For comparison, we provide our calculations of the number of national managers, management trainees, and supervisors who were permanently employed during 1999 and 2000 (which are the only years for which we have data):

NATIONAL EMPLOYEES

Year	Managers	Management Trainees	Supervisors
1999	37	4	66
2000	40	3	65

5. It is perhaps worth noting, again, that the mastery of technologies and techniques like those crucial to the operation of a sugar industry take their significance from their complex contexts. In the Papua New Guinean instance, such mastery has been set in a narrative of nationalist aspiration; in contrast, in prewar British Guiana ("Bookers' Guiana"), such mastery was set in another sort of narrative, with a different sort of significance. Hence, these technologies and techniques were not, in and of themselves, historically causative—they did not, in and of themselves, drive history.

6. The Ramu Sugar National Employees Union represents nonmanagers and nonsupervisors. During its one major strike in 1983, eight hundred factory workers joined five hundred field workers in a wildcat action that some describe as a riot, which resulted in the burning of two acres of sugarcane and a two-day loss in production. Two riot squads, totaling some sixty men, were summoned from Lae and Goroka by RSL's expatriate personnel manager to suppress the strikers. The cause of the strike, according to the workers, was that the management had ignored union submissions requesting an increase in allowances, including pay. Management countered that the strike was triggered by the suspension of two employees involved in an alcohol-related offense. During early 2000, the union's agenda, as it prepared for contract negotiations, focused on increases in severance pay, wages and tool allowances, as well as the provision of grade D houses for *all* workers. The company, however, responded with only modest concessions, expressing apprehension for its very existence during the current economic circumstances. Later in 2000, the company again faced demands for higher wages. At that time, there was a proposal by the government's Minimum Wages Board to increase the minimum wage to K60 per week. Since there were only a few employees at RSL—some seasonals—not already getting K60 a week, raising their pay would not be a great problem. More worrying for RSL's management was an anticipated "knock-on" effect: as those at the bottom got more pay, the workers above them would demand that the pay differentials be maintained. Eventually, as relatively unskilled workers were moved closer to, or into, the wage scale of the skilled artisans, there were fears that these artisans would simply stop work unless something was done.

7. We are extremely grateful to Joe Herman for his permission to use his autobiography in this way.

8. Our metaphor here, though irresistible to us, may not be fully appropriate. Money can be used in a range of ways. Thus, in Papua New Guinea, it can be used along with, or in substitution for, shell valuables in "traditional" exchanges—even "te" exchanges. Yet, because money is a universal currency, it tends to change the dynamics of gift exchanges once it infiltrates them. That money can be used, not only in marriage exchanges but also in buying a pick-up truck or a case of beer, suggests

an equivalence between a bride and these commodities that did not exist before. On money and its various uses in Melanesia, see Errington and Gewertz 1987, Robbins and Akin 1999, and LiPuma 2000.

9. Placed by RSL in Air Niugini's airline magazine and elsewhere, the advertisement pictures well-cared-for, middle-class Papua New Guinea children, engaged in a jubilant sack race. They use as sacks some packing bags clearly marked Ramu Sugar. The strategy of this advertisement is to associate the sugar produced by RSL with a middle-class lifestyle. Like many advertisements in Papua New Guinea, it seems intended to create capitalist consumers; to create units of consumption, in this case middle-class, nuclear families; and to create consumers interested in a particular product, in this instance, sugar produced by RSL. The caption "Natural as Life"—provides the thread that links all of these and allows each to reinforce the others: the product is as natural as life; the lifestyle is as natural as the product; consuming the product is as natural as living the (natural) lifestyle. During the course of its history, RSL has used three different slogans to advertise its product, according to John Piawu, manager of sales and marketing at RSL's Lae office: "Ramu is sweet energy"; "Put some Ramu in it"; and "Ramu is natural as life." In the future, RSL will likely introduce a fourth, "Ramu, it's traditional in PNG," which Piawu explained, means that "it's like a 'Barbie' doll in America, or a bottle of beer in Australia." On Papua New Guinean advertising, see especially Foster 1995, 1996–97.

10. Concerning exclusivity: When it became clear that the international school within the Management Compound was too small to accommodate the children of all managers, RSL debated whether to build a new, larger building within the compound or to use the money that building, staffing, and maintaining a new school would cost to subsidize the community school located in Gusap and available to everyone in the area. The national managers overwhelmingly favored the former and the new school was built in 2000. All managers, national and expatriate, can send their children to this international school for free.

11. Expatriates also juggle their sometimes conflicting obligations to company, clients, family, and colleagues. However, the narrative of career, which prioritizes obligations, is generally far more compelling to them than to nationals. This narrative provides a storyline such that, by furthering one's career, one serves one's family, one's company, one's client, and one's colleagues. Although, for instance, one might sometimes out of friendship turn a blind eye to a colleague's impropriety, it is understood that it would be foolish to do so at the expense of one's career.

12. Expatriates are accused by nationals of receiving special privileges, for example, when their medical problems are dealt with in Australia rather than Papua New Guinea, or when their office affairs are ignored, or when their end-of-contract shipping allowances are larger than those guaranteed by company policy. Nationals are accused by other nationals of currying favor, for example, when only some are selected to go on study tours, or when only some get permission to overstay the requisite leave to attend a kinsmen's funeral. This also means that managers responsible for personnel matters—whether expatriate or national—may be accused by some as being dictatorial, weak, disorganized, or erratic and praised by others as being decisive, democratic, flexible, or responsive.

13. The company, for instance, cannot afford to give workers more time off to attend rituals back home; it cannot afford the water and electricity uses of workers'

wantoks; it cannot afford overseas training trips for everyone. However, from the point of view of many nationals at RSL, including many managers, a major aspect of the business of business is to facilitate a whole range of what BTL people might regard as) nonbusiness objectives. BTL people can counter that these objectives are up to individual workers to fulfill through the prudent allocation of their resources. And this can lead Papua New Guinean employees to claim that BTL people can reduce their own expenses if they do not fly business class, or call in consultants whose visits are not really necessary given that nationals on site can probably solve the problems better.

14. We might point out that Diamond's history rests on a view of the bottom line that we see, not as transcultural and transhistorical, but as closely linked with capitalism. He assumes that what inexorably drives history is an inherent rationality, one that defines the unencumbered and unimpeded individual as being the essential manifestation of human nature. This inherent (and thus morally neutral) rationality, he suggests, drives everyone to maximize his control over and extraction from others: those who have guns, germs, and steel will inevitably and unproblematically use them for conquest and profit. Such a view, to repeat, does not examine our own taken-for-granted assumptions about why people—at different times and places—do what they do.

Chapter Seven

1. Entitled "Mumias Sugar Company Limited: A Success Story," Janet Shaner's forty-page Harvard Business School Study includes statistics, ranging from "Booker, PLC Consolidated Profit and Loss Account" (Shaner 1989: 16) to "Mumias Sugar Company Limited . . . Summary of Long-Term Plan Cash Flows" (40). It also includes descriptions of the history, goals, and structure of the Mumias project.

2. Many of the points we make below reiterate those in the report we did, in fact, submit to RSL in 2001.

3. Ethnographic descriptions of those calling themselves the Kafe can be found in Faithorn 1974; the Raikos, in Dalton 1996, Claassen 1970 and 1971, and Toland and Toland 1983; and the Mari, in H. Holzknecht 1974, S. Holzknecht 1989, and May and Tuckson 2000.

4. The written records that might give evidence about who was living where and when are very limited and ambiguous. The earliest specific mention we could find of a Mari village appears in the unpublished station reports kept by Lutheran missionaries at Kaiapit in the neighboring Markham Valley (excerpted and translated from German by various missionary assistants and kindly shared with us by Hartmut Holzknecht). In the introductory pages outlining the major events at this station, there is reference to mission helpers stationed at "Bapirompon" during 1927. We do not know, however, where exactly the village was at this time—whether it was actually in the Ramu Valley. Even present-day Bopirumpun is built very close to the foothills. In another station report, written in 1930, missionary Streicher "visited the helpers station Bopirompon, besides the stations of the Mari territory where, at the same time, I inspected the schools." Again, what the Mari territory consisted of is unclear.

5. Papua New Guineans are being taught that admissible evidence must follow a certain form. This form accords with what is, in effect, a modern, natural-history

model in which credible evidence is based on visual perception as corroborated by the process of consensus. As this model is playing out in Papua New Guinea, compelling visual evidence includes written texts, such as the book the Mari knew we would be writing. On this natural history model, see Foucault 1970. See, too, O'Hanlon 1995 and Errington and Gewertz 2001 for a more extensive discussion of the effects of this new model elsewhere in Papua New Guinea.

6. In an interesting description of land courts among the Agarabi of the Eastern Highlands, Westermark writes: "[M]any of the mediators typically searched for the marks of occupation on the land to determine if it had been used before. Old garden ditches or cordyline plants might demonstrate that the parcel of land was indeed a former garden; the presence of other trees might show that it was a habitation site." He suggests also that the use of these principles reflects traditional "ideas regarding the land . . . where work and interaction with the land were significant for the formation of group identity" (1997: 223). We think, however, that the use of such principles also reflects a more general preoccupation with objective evidence.

7. One such logo, belonging to the Yabobumusa Land Owners Association, Inc., is in effect a visual summary of some of the stories we were told by the Mari as well as a record of some of their handmarks. The logo depicts a wooden pillow (which features in a longer version of the story we told above about the female spirit Sararingu), the tusks of Kwasing and of another horse-sized pig, the ancestral salt (some of which the Mari still possess), and some ancestral shells (also significant in the longer version of the story). We first saw this logo on a letter in the general manager's file on traditional land ownership. He had circulated it to his staff with the hand-written inquiry, "does anyone know who these people are?"

8. Through Tom Muliap's efforts, in 1990 the national government gave the Mari some K86,000 (then about U.S.$90,300) in final compensation for the low price originally paid for their land.

9. In a personal communication, Hartmut Holzknecht, who was asked by the Madang Provincial Government to report on the social impact of RSL during the early days (a report he unfortunately misplaced and which we could not find in the offices we checked), told us that he found the Mari short of gardening land. Indeed, he recalls feeling sorry that they had to squeeze crops into the areas between their houses because their fields were taken up with sugarcane. Although we did no systematic study of garden-land availability, we did ask many Mari whether they have enough to grow what they need. All—both men and women—feel they do. Also, as we noted, subsequent to Holzknecht's study, most Mari divided their land into family-owned rather than clan-owned holdings. And each family can decide how much of its land it wishes to use for cane and how much it wishes to hold back for gardens. Nonetheless, it should also be noted that, while the women do not want more land for gardens, they do want more of a share of the money their husbands and fathers gain from the sale of cane.

10. In 2000, a kina was worth U.S.$0.3623.

11. Moreover, that the company is profiting at their expense is also implicit in the Mari's periodic concerns that agricultural chemicals are poisoning their food and water supply. In this regard, we note a news item in which "Ramu villagers claim chemical spraying by Ramu Sugar Limited at the Gusap sugarcane estate has resulted in the deaths of two people early this month . . . after eating vegetables they

had harvested in their gardens, located close to one of the sugarcane fields" (*Post-Courier* [Port Moresby], February 21–22, 2003). According to the article, RSL ordered a toxicology test on the deceased to support its position that the chemicals employed had no adverse effect on animals and humans. Although a subsequent article reported that "the young woman had died from cerebral malaria and the man from a ruptured appendix, causing sepsis" (*Post-Courier*, February 26, 2003), we expect that the Mari will continue to worry about living so close to areas intensively treated with agricultural chemicals.

12. It will be recalled from chapter 1 that Parrish and McNamara, the patrol officers who had purchased the Upper Ramu Valley on behalf of the Territory of Papua and New Guinea for pastoral leases in 1956, make it clear in the document "Transfer of Title from the Native/s to the Administration," that they sought to establish a quitclaim. Thus, they write: "Occupation by the Natives is to cease when the new villages outside the boundaries of this land are completed and when the present crop has been harvested but in any case no later than the thirty-first day of December in the year one thousand nine hundred and fifty-six" (Territory of Papua and New Guinea 1956: 4). Those who came to be known as Mushuans, but were then referred to as Kaigulans, were to move across the Ramu River. This they eventually did, but not because they recognized the sale of their land as a quitclaim. Rather, they told us, that when they refused to abandon their land on (or about) the thirty-first day of December in the year one thousand nine hundred and fifty-six, they were forced to do so at gunpoint.

13. Barker's description of Rivers's study continues with a fascinating description of the dismay a local woman felt when she realized that Rivers was not obligated to share with his kin:

> [O]ne of the women caught his arm and pulled him down again. Poking him playfully in the chest, she retrieved two words of English from her small store: "Your turn."
>
> The questions were posed again and in the same order. When he told them that, since he was unmarried and had no children, he would not necessarily feel obliged to share his guinea with anybody, they at first refused to believe him. Had he no parents living? Yes, a father. Brothers and sisters? One brother, two sisters. Same mother, same father? Yes. But he would not *automatically* share the guinea with them, though he might *choose* to do so.
>
> The woman who'd pulled his arm looked amused at first, then, when she was sure she'd understood, horrified. (1995: 119)

14. Finney (1971), Moulik (1973), and Christie (1980) are concerned to compare regions in Papua New Guinea with respect to interest in engaging in cash cropping or in other business enterprises. To this end, they provide economic and sociopsychological data that include accounts by respondents of what they would do with substantial sums of money (£500 for Finney; A$50 and A$500, for Moulik; and K10, K100, and K5,000 for Christie). The accounts are scored concerning the degree to which different peoples are oriented toward immediate or deferred gratification. Our desire is not to differentiate between cultures or regions according to propensity to engage in business enterprise. Rather, we hope to probe how members of the same

cultural group, differently positioned according to access to money, feel their lives to be constrained.

15. We do recognize that this comparison is imprecise: that there are different sums involved within and between the two sets of cases; that those at Bumbu are fantasizing while those at Mushuan are supposedly recollecting. This is to say, Bumbu villagers may actually spend K100 differently than they anticipate and Mushuan villagers may actually have spent their money differently than they report.

16. The RSL Outgrowers Association is based on a Ugandan prototype modified to Papua New Guinean conditions. Indeed, many of the policies implemented at RSL were developed in other social and cultural contexts. A long-term BTL employee explained this variation on industrial modularity: "The company policy used to be that you would spend two to three years in a place and then move on. The systems we used were all the same, no matter where we went. Booker could send people anywhere, but this is breaking down because there are few people left who know the system, and these people are expensive to keep on, and what they know has not been written down. Solutions are in people's heads." This man himself said that he had archives on his computer of situations he faced and of solutions he implemented. He could simply adapt and apply these solutions wherever and whenever necessary. By way of verification, he showed us an early employment manual used at RSL and said he could locate the particular countries in which various rules and regulations came into existence. Thus, the bicycle-loan allowance, to purchase a bicycle in installments from wages, came from the Nigerian manual and was simply transported to Papua New Guinea.

17. We were asked by a colleague why the Mari outgrowers had not formed an association earlier. After all, there existed a number of cooperative associations elsewhere in Papua New Guinea among, for example, coffee and cocoa growers. Our answer must be speculative. There is, we think, an important difference in the production and processing of coffee and cocoa and of sugar. For coffee as well as cocoa growers, a local association is able to build the facilities to process their raw products. For the Mari, an association could serve no such interest—a sugar factory is already in place (and, unlike a cocoa fermentery, would in any case greatly exceed any local capacity to construct). Whether an association would serve the interests of Mari outgrowers in, for instance, negotiating prices with RSL is not clear. The price that RSL pays for sugar is determined by a quite technical formula set out in the MA between RSL and the Papua New Guinean government (see table 1 for the formula). Consequently, any (re)negotiation by outgrowers would likely be difficult. In addition, Mari powers to negotiate are limited by the fact that RSL has additional land of its own to put into sugar production if relations with outgrowers become too difficult. On the other hand, RSL is interested in maintaining amicable relations with outgrowers, for a number of reasons: these include avoiding bad publicity as well as damage to its sugar fields by arson. Moreover, Mari regard themselves, not primarily as agricultural producers, but as landowners. Consequently, their models for effective action are not those of agriculturalists concerned with producing and processing, but of militant landowners concerned with applying pressure to large companies, as well as to the government. For its part, RSL definitely has not encouraged them to become more united and effective landowners. Indeed, as we elaborate later in this chapter and in chapter 8, RSL is careful not to recognize them as

landowners at all, but only as outgrowers, saying, for instance, that whatever concerns Mari have about whether they were fairly compensated for their land should be directed not to RSL but to the Papua New Guinean government. In the one instance that the Mari grievances about land did receive official recognition, it was not through collective action. Instead, it was through the intervention of Tom Muliap, a politically important Mari (a former member of parliament for the district that included the Mari) who, in 1990, got additional payment from the government. Significantly, Mari accounts, as well as newspaper accounts, speak of Muliap as a "landowners' spokesman" but do not refer to any formal organization of Mari landowners. Finally and consistently, Mari are dubious about their own capacity to muster the skills and discipline to organize themselves to pursue collective projects. Correspondingly, as we shall see in chapter 8, they were greatly impressed by the Tolai capacity to pursue such projects when they visited East New Britain on a RSL-organized study tour in 2000.

18. RSL's factory manager, Annamale Naicker, explained this quota to us: The United States quota for Papua New Guinea stands at 7,000 tons of raw sugar per year. (This sugar is far less processed than the mill white RSL sells in Papua New Guinea.) The quota was once 12,000 tons, but was reduced to this "minimum" quota because, during the Ramu stunt years, RSL was unable to produce for export. The United States purchases a certain percentage of its own consumption needs from its allies. Then the United States Department of Agriculture says to various U.S. purchasers that a certain amount of sugar will be available from an ally—Papua New Guinea, for instance—and asks which of them wants it. Generally RSL sugar is purchased for further processing by C. & H. (California and Hawaii), a milling firm conveniently located from the perspective of freighting on the West Coast. Such a sale is possible for RSL because the U.S. government subsidizes its farmers, in part by controlling imports. The government likes, and generally ensures through its level of price supports and import duties, that American farmers get $0.18 per pound when they sell their sugar to U.S. sugar mills for processing. Thus, because RSL prices its sugar a bit below that—and comes in without duties—its sugar will be acceptable to these U.S. sugar mills. Since RSL's cost of production of raw sugar is about $0.15 a pound, the U.S. quota provides important revenues. All of this can change, however, because there is considerable pressure from the World Bank and World Trade Organization for subsidies to be lifted in the United States and Europe.

19. Rabaul, though no longer East New Britain's capital and business center after its inundation by volcanic ash in 1994, is still regarded as representing the region.

20. Shell money, or "tambu," consists of small cowrie shells strung onto strips of rattan and counted either individually or measured on the body in standard lengths.

Chapter Eight

1. For elaboration, see Errington and Gewertz 1995a. Of course, responses to colonial oppression varied and not all Papua New Guineans proved bloody-minded. Thus, Lattas finds among the Kaliai that

[c]olonial and neo-colonial inequalities come to be personalized, in that they become expressions of moral identities and moral differences. . . . Here social

inequalities become part of a moral economy where the whiteman's power and wealth are seen as extensions of his moral laws and moral person-hood. . . . Such moral beliefs are part of the process of internalizing the conditions of colonial domination; that is, they are part of the process of making one's race morally responsible for the conditions of its own subjugation. (1992: 32)

There should be no doubt that colonial definitions of unequal worth were propagated and, in some cases, accepted as true. Yet, in our view, although many Papua New Guineans might have come to regard themselves as in some ways deficient, they never regarded their deficiency as the product of inherent nature, but rather of immediate and rectifiable circumstances (cf. Lattas 1998).

2. Michael Leahy himself provided such first-contact refresher courses. Thus, in *The Land that Time Forgot*, he describes a 1932 trip to the coastal city of Lae he arranged for Narmu, a young Highlander he "first contacted" some two years earlier:

Gurney [the pilot who flew the boy to Lae] took him on a shopping expedition and bought him a great collection of coloured gimcracks and baubles, as well as a red lap lap [a piece of cloth to be worn as a wrap-around skirt], a mouth organ, a couple of small mirrors, a leather belt, a white cotton singlet, a pound or so of glass beads, and a few knives. He was taken inside a refrigeration chamber in one of the stores, and given a small piece of ice. He had a look at the sea, and saw a fortune in shells lying unclaimed on the beach. He listened to a phonograph, and saw an electric light, and wore out the switch turning the light on and off again. Gurney said that next to the light the thing that seemed to interest Narmu most was the heap of tin cans and empty bottles. (Quoted in Connolly and Anderson 1987: 164)

Connolly and Anderson conclude that "Leahy could see the public relations value in this exercise and was to repeat it many times" (165).

3. Papua New Guinean managers, considered to be on a career trajectory, are usually sent as individuals to various mini-courses held, for instance, at BTL-managed sugar estates in Guyana, Swaziland, or Indonesia. Supervisors, not yet assured of such a career trajectory, tend to be conveyed in groups. Thus, one expatriate manager annually takes a group of ten or so Papua New Guinean supervisors to tour sugar operations in Queensland, Australia.

4. Brown's arrival was in August 1875 in the neighboring Duke of York Islands. Mission influence soon after spread to the Tolai.

5. On the Tolai, see T. S. Epstein 1968; A. L. Epstein 1969, 1992; Salisbury 1970; Neumann 1992. Also see Errington 1974 and Errington and Gewertz 1995a.

6. Tolai shell money, comprising lengths of cane strung with small cowrie shells, has many of the attributes of Western currency. It is readily divisible, enduring, not greatly subject to inflation, and can be used to acquire a range of items as well as to compensate for a range of services.

7. Wilson's vision of the Tolai's success was perhaps selective and somewhat partisan, underplaying the fact that it was often at the expense of other Papua New

Guineans, including such neighbors as the Baining, on whose land the Tolai have long encroached. See in this regard, Fajans 1997.

8. Much Tolai sociability focuses on the distribution and consumption of betel nuts, accompanied by lime powder and a leaf or catkin of the betel pepper vine.

9. The fathom is a European term referring to a standardized length of shell money, about six feet long as measured on the body: it is a loop running from the fingertips of an extended arm and hand, to the center of the chest and back to the fingertips.

10. It is becoming increasingly frequent for affluent Tolai and other Papua New Guineans to convert collectively held traditional land into privately owned and formally registered land. This is so especially if the land is to be used for permanent buildings or cash crops. In Wilson's case, the traditional land did not come from Wilson's own primary kin group—his matrilineage—but from the matrilineage of his father. With an increase in the importance of nuclear families in postcolonial Papua New Guinea, fathers tend to favor their own sons over other kinsmen. In the Tolai instance, this means that Wilson's father is likely to favor him at the expense of his sister's sons, his junior matrilineal kin.

11. When we mentioned to Nerrie Wilson that the Mari remain perplexed about how to deal with the jealousy of others— jealously that, they fear, would lead to their ensorcellment—she expressed surprise. She said that among the Tolai there is no such jealousy: "If someone does something like build a good house then everyone else wants to better him. It's a competition. Also, people help one another. Thus when a man spends money on a house or a water tank, he will give a party and people will come with presents which they know he needs, having spent so much." We might add, however, that a serious competitor—certainly a major competitor like Torot—does not likely worry unduly about sorcery because he himself controls powerful magic: otherwise, his affairs would not have gone so well and he would not be so important. In contrast, among the Mari, control of powerful magic does not seem to be a standard part of the male toolkit and sorcery fears do seem greatly to limit competition. For discussion of the ways these differences might reflect "stable" and "fluid" social organizations, see Lawrence and Meggitt 1965: 16–18.

12. According to a recent World Bank publication, "100 of the 121 savings and loan societies" established in the ten years prior to 1999 in Papua New Guinea failed (World Bank 1999: 234). On statistical grounds alone, we would not bank on the Mari's success in this project.

13. As Evans elaborated to us in a personal communication in 2001: "[T]he Outgrowers attitude towards cane farming was an entirely rational response and indeed fully consistent with the economic theory of factor proportions. This says that owners of resources will select activities which enable the owners to use their most abundant resources to maximise the returns they receive from their scarcest resource. Thus in the Mekong Delta a Vietnamese peasant will put in long hours of his own and his family's labour on their tiny parcel of land in order to get the highest returns per hectare. A similar response might even be observed in some of the densely populated areas of West New Britain where oil palm smallholders work their land alongside the nucleus estates. In the Ramu Valley, however, the resource which the Outgrowers have in abundance is land and the resource in shortest supply is labour. It is therefore . . . sensible of the Ramu Outgrowers to 'lend' their land to RSL

to farm since this gives them quite a good return per person-day of their own labour at very little risk. While it might be true that they could in principle earn more by farming these relatively large tracts themselves, this would involve a high level of borrowing to finance the necessary capital investment in farm machinery and equipment."

Chapter Nine

1. David Lane, the Australian technical operations manager of Coke's Lae-based operation, told us that Pepsi lost its share of the Papua New Guinea market owing to a corporate buyout. (He expected its absence, given the ongoing "cola wars," to be only temporary.) More specifically, Pepsi was produced in Papua New Guinea by South Pacific Breweries, which also produced the Schweppes line of soft drinks. But when Schweppes sold out to Coke in both Australia and Papua New Guinea, it was no longer cost-effective for South Pacific Breweries to make Pepsi as its sole soft drink.

2. Thus, on November 8, 2001, Gomez reported in the *National* (Port Moresby), one of Papua New Guinea's two English-language dailies:

Recently released data from the International Monetary Fund shows that Papua New Guinea's gross domestic product contracted by 1.8 per cent last year compared with official government figures showing a growth of 0.8 percent. . . .

The data shows that Papua New Guineans have been undergoing one of the most difficult economic periods in [the country's] recent history. . . .

Earlier government forecasts of 3.1 per cent growth this year have been downgraded to a projection for a minus 2 per cent change this year.

The economic contraction projected for this year and the next year comes on top of a minus 3.8. per cent showing in 1998 and a minus 3.7. percent in 1997. . . .

These figures suggest that, since the population is growing by 3.1 per cent annually, per capita incomes would have fallen by about 16 per cent in the past four years with worse to come in 2002.

3. One BTL manager described Coca-Cola International as absolutely ruthless. In fact, he fully expected that it might well go to BTL and threaten to stop buying from *any* of its worldwide operations if such a threat suited its purposes. He also said that if Coke were to stop buying from RSL, he would authorize newspaper ads to publicize the betrayal of this national industry.

4. Coca-Cola International wanted its ICUMSA (International Commission for Uniform Methods of Sugar Analysis) Color to be below 35, while RSL's was often between 500 and 600. The compromise that was reached between CCA and RSL, at least for the time being, was that CCA would bring in some equipment from the Philippines that could improve the color if RSL could provide sugar with an ICU below 300. BTL consultants thought RSL could augment some old equipment from the refinery with some new equipment to do just that. During 2000, RSL ran a trial of 900 tons, which was successful.

5. Indeed, Gibson did describe RSL as a "major policy blunder" (Gibson 1993a: 119). In so doing, he cites Shaw 1985, Jarrett and Anderson 1989, and the World Bank 1991.

6. We are reminded of the wonderful protest song performed by "Country Joe and the Fish": "Come to beautiful Harlem, in New York City; because if you don't come to Harlem, someday Harlem's gonna come to you."

7. Connell explains the role of such projects in Papua New Guinea's development history: "Formal integrated rural development projects (IRDP) were a major element of rural development between 1976 and 1986 in five provinces—East and West Sepik, Southern Highlands, Enga and Simbu—some of the least developed provinces in the country. Though largely funded by the World Bank and the Asian Development Bank, they cost the PNG government more than K80 million. The IRDPs emerged from the Less Developed Areas strategy, formulated under the Eight Aims in 1975, and combined a mix of infrastructure (roads, bridges and buildings), income-generation (plantations, rural industries and smallholder cash-cropping schemes) and social welfare (schools, aid posts, health centres and nutritional centres)" (Connell 1997: 116).

8. There were widespread rumors that these students were supported by various politicians who, under the guise of populist rhetoric, sought to destabilize the current government and to maintain their own access to the resources of state-owned enterprises.

9. The WTO Web site conveys the following history:

The World Trade Organization came into being in 1995. One of the youngest of the international organizations, the WTO is the successor to the General Agreement on Tariffs and Trade (GATT) established in the wake of the Second Word War.

So while the WTO is still young, the multilateral trading system that was originally set up under GATT is well over 50 years old.

The past 50 years have seen exceptional growth in world trade. Merchandise exports grew on average by 6% annually. Total trade in 2000 was 22-times the level of 1950. GATT and the WTO have helped to create a strong and prosperous trading system contributing to unprecedented growth.

The system was developed through a series of trade negotiations, or rounds, held under GATT. The first rounds dealt mainly with tariff reductions but later negotiations included other areas such as anti-dumping and non-tariff measures. The last round—1986–94 Uruguay Round—led to the WTO's creation. (www.wto.org/english/thewto_e/whatis_e/inbrief_e/inbr01_e.htm)

10. "No Justification for Illegal Settlements," a recent editorial in the *National*, describes squatter settlements in Lae as "a breeding ground for disease, crime, and for the kind of grinding poverty that simply should not exist in Papua New Guinea" (*National*, February 21, 2002).

11. On the World Bank's position concerning corruption in Papua New Guinea and on its explicit support for WTO objectives, see World Bank 1999.

12. For another World Bank view concerning free trade as it affects sugar industries worldwide, one somewhat less committed to rapid privatization, see Larson and Borrell 2001.

13. Weise's position seems consistent with Stirrat's discussion of the World Bank's approach to development in Africa. He quotes the bank as regarding rapidly

expanding urban centers to be the "crucibles of acculturation to modernity and the market economy" (Stirrat 1992: 206).

14. While on leave in Australia in February 2001, Weise was abruptly informed of the expiration of his entry visa to Papua New Guinea. The reasons for this virtual expulsion remain somewhat unclear. He and his supporters claim that his anticorruption stance made him unwelcome. His detractors claim that he was meddling in issues pertaining to Papua New Guinean sovereignty. He subsequently resigned from the World Bank. Australian Broadcasting Corporation devoted a *Four Corners* television program on June 24, 2002, to this subject. A transcript can be found at www.abc.net.au/4corners/stories/s590512.htm.

15. The rhetoric of self-sufficiency still remains salient. Thus, Sir Michael Somare—once again in 2002 prime minister of Papua New Guinea and often regarded as father of the nation—was recently quoted: "PNG is a very fortunate country. God has given us everything we want. We've got land, a market. But if we want to prosper and be like China we must change. It is a challenge to everyone of us. . . . We've proven that we can grow sugar on a commercial basis so why can't we do it too with rice and other food crops. We've to learn to be self reliant through sweat and hard work" (*National*, November 10, 1997). Shortly after this news item appeared, a Papua New Guinean student studying agriculture in Melbourne submitted a letter to the editor in support of Somare's perspective. Signing himself "Markham Student," he writes: "Thus PNG imports all its rice from Australia—and the Australian farmers are happy they have a market in PNG. We have done this to sugar—Ramu has replaced imported sugar and we can do so with rice" (*National*, November 25, 1997).

Conclusion

1. In contrast, consider Obeyesekere's examination of the Philip Wouvermann engraving depicting Captain Cook's direct ascension into heaven, which Obeyesekere used as the cover to *The Apotheosis of Captain Cook* (1992). He thoroughly discusses it in terms of the eighteenth-century sensibility that produced it.

2. As Geertz suggests, anthropologists seek: "in the widened sense of the term in which it encompasses very much more than talk, to converse with [others], a matter a great deal more difficult . . . than is commonly recognized" (1973: 13).

3. Although there were regional differences and routing did take place, warfare in precontact Papua New Guinea was usually conducted with the moderating recognition that deaths inflicted would require either revenge or compensation. Even where warfare was endemic, there were, as with the Mari, frequent truces cemented with marriages and adoptions. On warfare in Papua New Guinea, see, among others, Meggitt 1977, Harrison 1993, and Roscoe 1996.

References

Adamson, Alan. 1972. *Sugar without slaves*. New Haven: Yale University Press.

Allen, Bryant. 1983. Paradise lost? Rural development in an export-led economy: The case of Papua New Guinea. In *Rural development and the state*, ed. David Lea and D. P. Chaudhri, 215–40. London: Methuen.

Anderson, Benedict. 1983. *Imagined communities*. London: Verso.

Appadurai, Arjun, ed. 1986. *The social life of things*. Cambridge: Cambridge University Press.

Arce, Alberto, and Norman Long. 2000. *Anthropology, development, and modernities*. London: Routledge.

Bakker, Henk. 1999. *Sugar cane cultivation and management*. New York: Kluwer Academic/Plenum.

Baranay, Inez. 1995. *Rascal rain*. Sydney: Angus and Robertson.

Barker, Pat. 1995. *The ghost road*. New York: Dutton.

Barth, Fredrik. 1966. *Models of social organization*. Royal Anthropological Institute Occasional Papers, no. 23. London.

Bashkow, Ira. 1999. "Whitemen" in the moral world of Orokaiva of Papua New Guinea. Ph.D. diss., University of Chicago.

Basso, Keith. 1979. *Portraits of the "whiteman."* Cambridge: Cambridge University Press.

Bateson, Gregory. 1958. *Naven*. Stanford: Stanford University Press.

Battaglia, Debbora. 1995. On practical nostalgia. In *Rhetorics of self-making*, ed. Debbora Battaglia, 77–96. Berkeley and Los Angeles: University of California Press.

Bego, Henry. 1985. Profile on Kevin Hecko. *Sugar Valley News* 11:9.

———. 1990. Ramu should be a "model" community. *Sugar Valley News* 21:16–17.

Bettison, D. G. 1966. The expatriate community. In *New Guinea on the threshold*, ed. E. K. Fisk, 222–42. Canberra: Australian National University Press.

Bhabba, Homi, ed. 1990. *Nation and narration*. London: Routledge.

Bleier, Ruth. 1984. *Science and gender*. New York: Pergamon Press.

Booker Agriculture International. 1978a. *Papua New Guinea sugar study*. Vol. 1, Main report. London.

———. 1978b. *Papua New Guinea sugar study*. Vol. 4, *Appendix 4*. London.

———. 1978c. *Papua New Guinea sugar study*. Vol. 5, *Appendices 5–8*. London.

———. 1981. *Notes on Papua New Guinea and Ramu Sugar Limited*. Booklet, London.

Booker Tate Limited. N.d. *Booker Tate*. Promotional pamphlet, Thame, England.

Bosworth, Malcolm, and Kym Anderson. 2000. *Reforming trade policy in Papua New Guinea and the Pacific islands*. Adelaide: Centre for International and Economic Studies; Port Moresby: Institute for National Affairs.

Bourdieu, Pierre. 1977. *Outline of a theory of practice*. Cambridge: Cambridge University Press.

Bourke, M. J., et al., eds. 1993. *Our time but not our place: Voices of expatriate women in Papua New Guinea*. Melbourne: Melbourne University Press.

Brenneis, Donald, and Fred Myers, eds. 1991. *Dangerous words*. Prospect Heights, Ill.: Waveland Press.

Brison, Karen. 1992. *Just talk*. Berkeley and Los Angeles: University of California Press.

Burridge, Kenelm. 1960. *Mambu*. New York: Harper and Row.

Cameron, Bruce. 1985. History of malaria. *Sugar Valley News* 10:24–25.

Campbell, Jock. 1966. Private enterprise and public morality. *New Statesman*, May 27, 765–66.

Carr, David. 1986. *Time, narrative, and history*. Bloomington: Indiana University Press.

Carrier, James, ed. 1995. *Occidentalism*. Oxford: Clarendon Press.

Casey, Edward, 1993. *Getting back into place*. Bloomington: Indiana University Press.

Chan, Julius. 1977. Sugar industry—policy. Letter, Ministry for Primary Industry, Papua New Guinea.

Christensen, John, and D. R. J. Densley. 1977. Oil palm. *Agriculture in the Economy of Papua New Guinea* 2:1–17.

Christie, Marion. 1980. *Changing consumer behaviour in Papua New Guinea*. Canberra: Centre for Resource and Environmental Studies, Australian National University.

Claassen, Oren. 1970. Folklore and religion in a New Guinea tribe. Manuscript submitted to Professor David Bidney in partial fulfillment of the requirements for a reading course in anthropology, Columbia University.

———. 1971. Rawa: Ethnography and acculturation of a New Guinea society. Portion of an M.A. thesis, Summer Institute of Linguistics, Ukarumpa, Papua New Guinea.

Clifford, James. 1997. *Routes*. Cambridge: Harvard University Press.

Cohen, Abner. 1974. *Urban ethnicity*. London: Tavistock.

Cohen, Erik. 1977. Expatriate communities. *Current Sociology* 24:5–90.

Colton, Peter. 1971. Madang patrol report no. 17, 1969–70. Mandeville Special Collections Library, University of California, San Diego.

———. 1993. Comment during the second discussion period of the paper "Import Substitution, Risk, and Consumer Costs," by John Gibson. In *Seminar on employment, agriculture, and industrialisation*, ed. John Millett, 154–55. Port Moresby: Institute for National Affairs and National Research Institute.

———. 1995. Press release. Ramu Sugar Limited, Gusap, Papua New Guinea.

———. 2000. History and role of Ramu. Paper presented at Ramu Sugar Limited's Sugar Seminar, Port Moresby, April 11.

Come back, slavemasters. 1992. *Economist*. February 29, 46.

Connell, John. 1997. *Papua New Guinea: The struggle for development*. London: Routledge.

Connolly, Bob, and Robin Anderson. 1984. *First contact*. Videocassette. New York: Arundel Productions.

———. 1987. *First contact*. New York: Penguin Books.

Cooper, Frederick. 1992. Colonizing time. In *Colonialism and culture*, ed. Nicholas Dirks, 209–45. Ann Arbor: University of Michigan Press.

Cowen, Michael, and Scott MacWilliam. 1996. *Indigenous capital in Kenya*. Helsinki: Interkont Books.

Cowen, M. P., and E. W. Shenton. 1996. *Doctrines of development*. London: Routledge.

Crayton, Michael, and James Walvin. 1970. *A Jamaican plantation*. London: W. H. Allen.

Crocombe, Ronald. 1967. A Canberra view of economic development in New Guinea. *Australian Journal of Agricultural Economics* 11:208–10.

———. 1968. That five-year plan: For New Guineans—token development. *New Guinea (and Australia, the Pacific, and South-East Asia)* 3:57–70.

———. 1969. Crocombe to his critics—the debate goes on. *New Guinea (and Australia, the Pacific, and South-East Asia)* 4:49–58.

Cronon, William. 1983. *Changes in the land*. New York: Hill and Wang.

Curtis, Mark. 2003. *Web of deceit*. London: Vintage.

Dalton, Douglas. 1996. Cargo, cards, and excess. *Research in Economic Anthropology* 17:83–147.

Deerr, Noël. 1950. *The history of sugar*. London: Chapman and Hall.

Demian, Melissa. 2000. Longing for completion: Toward an aesthetics of work in Suau. *Oceania* 71:94–109.

Densley, D. R. J. 1977. Sugar. *Agriculture in the Economy of Papua New Guinea* 3:1–17.

Diamond, Jared. 1972. *Aviafauna of the Eastern Highlands of New Guinea*. Cambridge, Mass.: Nuttall Ornithological Club.

———. 1984. Biological principles relevant to protected areas design in the New Guinea region. In *National Parks, Conservation, and Development*, ed. Jeffrey NcNeely and Kenton Miller, 330–32. Washington: Smithsonian Institution Press.

———. 1992. *The rise and fall of the third chimpanzee*. New York: Harper Collins.

———. 1997. *Guns, germs, and steel*. New York: Norton.

Diamond, Jared, and Ernst Mayr. 2001. *The birds of northern Melanesia*. New York: Oxford University Press.

Doery, Richard. 1976. Summary of discussion between Dr. G. Fox of World Bank and secretary for primary industry. Document, Policy Review and Co-Ordination, Department of Primary Industry, Port Moresby.

———. 1977. Notes on sugar in P.N.G. Document, Policy Review and Co-Ordination, Department of Primary Industry, Port Moresby.

Donham, Donald. 1999. *Marxist modern*. Berkeley and Los Angeles: University of California Press.

Douglas, Bronwen. 1999. Science and the art of representing "savages." In *The politics of knowledge: Science and evolution in Asia and the Pacific*, ed. Morris Low and Christine Dureau, 157–201. Special issue, *History and Anthropology* 11.

Dumpu and the Jephcott family. 1985. *Sugar Valley News* 11:35–38.

Durkheim, Emile. [1933] 1984. *The division of labor in society*. New York: Free Press.

———. 1965. *Elementary forms of the religious life*. New York: Free Press.

Eastwood, David. 1990. Ramu stunt disease. *Sugar Cane* 2:15–19.

Epstein, A. L. 1969. *Matupit*. Berkeley and Los Angeles: University of California Press.

———. 1992. *In the midst of life*. Berkeley and Los Angeles: University of California Press.

Epstein, T. S. 1968. *Capitalism, primitive and modern*. Canberra: Australian National University Press.

Ernst, Thomas. 1999. Land stories and resources: Discourse and entification in Onabasulu modernity. *American Anthropologist* 101:88–97.

Errington, Frederick. 1974. *Karavar*. Ithaca: Cornell University Press.

Errington, Frederick, and Deborah Gewertz. 1987. On unfinished dialogues and paper pigs. *American Ethnologist* 14:367–76.

———. 1989. Tourism and anthropology in a post-modern world. *Oceania* 60:37–54.

———. 1995a. *Articulating change in the "last unknown."* Boulder: Westview.

———. 1995b. First contact with God. In *Articulating change in the "last unknown,"* ed. Frederick Errington and Deborah Gewertz, 107–34. Boulder: Westview.

———. 1995c. Resistance through emulation: On patrols, reports, and "cults" in colonial New Britain. In *Articulating change in the "last unknown,"* ed. Frederick Errington and Deborah Gewertz, 19–47. Boulder: Westview.

———. 2001. On the generification of culture: From blow fish to Melanesian. *Journal of the Royal Anthropological Institute* 7:509–25.

Escobar, Arturo. 1995. *Encountering development*. Princeton: Princeton University Press.

Esteva, Gustavo. 1992. Development. In *The development dictionary*, ed. Wolfgang Sachs, 6–25. London: Zed Books.

Evans, Martin. 2000. RSL from an international perspective. Paper presented at Ramu Sugar Limited's Sugar Seminar, Port Moresby, April 11.

Evara, Roy. 1979. *Papua New Guinea sugar industry*. Information Paper No. 79, for Members of the National Executive Council, Ministry for Primary Industry, Papua New Guinea.

Faber, M., et al. 1973. *A report on development strategies for Papua New Guinea*. Washington, D.C.: International Bank for Reconstruction and Development, United Nations Development Programme.

Faithorn, Elizabeth. 1976. Women as persons. In *Man and woman in the New Guinea Highlands*, ed. Paula Brown and Georgeda Buchbinder, 86–95. Washington, D.C.: American Anthropological Association.

Fajans, Jane. 1997. *They make themselves: Work and play among the Baining of Papua New Guinea*. Chicago: University of Chicago Press.

Fausto-Sterling, Anne. 1985. *Myths of gender*. New York: Basic Books.

Feather, N. T. 1981. Culture contact and national sentiment. *Australian Journal of Psychology* 33:149–56.

Feil, D. K. 1984. *Ways of Exchange*. St. Lucia: University of Queensland Press.

Feld, Steven, and Keith Basso, eds. 1996. *Senses of place*. Santa Fe: School of American Research.

Fenn, Elizabeth. 2000. Biological warfare in eighteenth-century America: Beyond Jeffery Amherst. *Journal of American History* 86:1552–80.

Ferguson, James. 1990. *The anti-politics machine: Development, depoliticization, and power in Lesotho*. Cambridge: Cambridge University Press.

———. 2002. Of mimicry and membership. *Cultural Anthropology* 17: 551–69.

Finnegan, Ruth. 1998. *Tales of the city: A study of narrative and urban life*. Cambridge: Cambridge University Press.

Finney, Ruth. 1971. *Would-be entrepreneurs?* Boroko, Papua New Guinea: New Guinea Research Unit.

Fitzpatrick, Peter. 1985. The making and unmaking of the Eight Aims. In *From rhetoric to reality?* ed. Peter King, Wendy Lee, and Vincent Warakai, 22–31. Port Moresby: University of Papua New Guinea Press.

Foster, Robert. 1992. Take care of public telephones. *Public Culture* 4:31–45.

———. 1995. Nation making and print advertisements in Papua New Guinea. In *Nation-Making*, ed. Robert Foster, 151–81. Ann Arbor: University of Michigan Press.

———. 1996–97. Commercial mass media in Papua New Guinea. *Visual Anthropology Review* 12:1–17.

———. 2002. *Materializing a nation*. Urbana-Champaign: University of Illinois Press.

———. N.d. Commoditization and the emergence of kastam as a cultural category. Manuscript.

Foucault, Michel. 1970. *The order of things*. New York: Random House.

———. 1977. *Discipline and punish*. New York: Pantheon.

———. 1978. *The history of sexuality*. New York: Pantheon.

———. 1980. *Power/Knowledge*. New York: Pantheon.

Frank, Andre Gunder. 1967. *Capitalism and underdevelopment in Latin America*. New York: Monthly Review Press.

Fred, Henkel. 1990. Safety warning. *Sugar Valley News* 21:14–15.

Gagau, Roy. 1985. My three month course in England. *Sugar Valley News* 12:6–10.

Garnsworthy, Philip. 1985. Pet's corner. *Sugar Valley News* 10:27–29.

Geertz, Clifford. 1973. *The interpretation of cultures*. New York: Basic Books.

Gewertz, Deborah, and Frederick Errington. 1991. *Twisted histories, altered contexts*. Cambridge: Cambridge University Press.

———. 1999. *Emerging class in Papua New Guinea*. Cambridge: Cambridge University Press.

Gibson, John. 1993a. Import substitution, risk, and consumer costs: The Papua New Guinea sugar industry. In *Seminar on employment, agriculture, and industrialisation*, ed. John Millett, 119–36. Port Moresby: Institute for National Affairs and National Research Institute.

———. 1993b Comment during the second discussion period of the paper "Import Substitution, Risk, and Consumer Costs," by John Gibson. In *Seminar on employment, agriculture, and industrialisation*, ed. John Millett, 153–56. Port Moresby: Institute for National Affairs and National Research Institute.

———. 1994. Rice import substitution and employment in Papua New Guinea. *Pacific Economic Bulletin* 9:46–52.

————. 1995. *Food consumption and food policy in Papua New Guinea*. Port Moresby: Institute of National Affairs.

Giddens, Anthony. 1998. *Conversations with Anthony Giddens*. Stanford: Stanford University Press.

————. 2000. *Runaway world*. New York: Routledge.

Goddard, Michael. 1992. Big-Men, thief: The social organization of gangs in Port Moresby. *Canberra Anthropology* 154:20–34.

————. 1995. The rascal road. *Contemporary Pacific* 7:55–80.

Goffman, Erving. 1961. *Asylums*. Garden City, N.Y.: Doubleday-Anchor.

Goizueta, Roberto. 1989. Globalization: A soft drink perspective. *Vital Speeches of the Day*, April 1.

Gomez, Brian. 2001. PNG economy contracted last year. *National* (Port Moresby), November 8.

Gordon, Robert, and Mervyn Meggitt. 1985. *Law and order in the New Guinea Highlands*. Hanover: University Press of New England.

Gould, Steven Jay. 1980. *The panda's thumb*. New York: Norton.

Gourevitch, Philip. 1998. *We wish to inform you that tomorrow we will be killed with our families*. New York: Farrar, Straus and Giroux.

Gregory, C. A. 1982. *Gifts and commodities*. London: Academic Press.

Gregory, Derek, and John Urry. 1985. *Social relations and spatial structures*. New York: St. Martin's Press.

Griffin, James, ed. 1978. *Papua New Guinea portraits: The expatriate experience*. Canberra: Australian National University Press.

Guise, John. 1975. Proposed Sugar industry—Rigo Sub-District. Letter, Ministry for Agriculture, Port Moresby.

Hagelberg, G. B. 1974. *The Caribbean sugar industries: Constraints and opportunities*. New Haven: Antilles Research Program, Yale University.

Hanlon, David. 1998. *Remaking Micronesia*. Honolulu: University of Hawaii Press.

Hannah, A. C. 2000. The world sugar economy. Paper Presented at Ramu Sugar Limited's Sugar Seminar, Port Moresby, April 11.

Harrison, Simon. 1993. *The mask of war*. Manchester: University of Manchester Press.

Hart Nibbrig, Nand. 1992. Rascals in paradise. *Pacific Studies* 15:115–34.

Hasluck, Paul. 1977. *Mucking about*. Carlton: Melbourne University Press.

Health, garden, and home. 1985. *Sugar Valley News* 10:16–21.

Healy, J. P. 1953. Patrol report no. 8, 1952–53, Madang. National Archives, Port Moresby, Papua New Guinea.

Herman, Joseph. N.d. My two worlds. Manuscript.

Hermann, Elfriede. 1992a. The Yali movement in retrospect. *Oceania* 63:55–71.

————. 1992b. Kastom versus cargo cult. In *Cultural dynamics of religious change in Oceania*, ed. Ton Otto and Ad Borsboom, 87–102. Leiden: KITLV Press.

————. 1995. *Emotionen und Historizitat*. Berlin: Diertirch Reimer Verlag.

————. 2002. Yali. In *Australian dictionary of biography*, ed. John Ritchie, 601. Melbourne: Melbourne University Press.

Hirsch, Eric, and O'Hanlon, Michael, eds. 1995. *The anthropology of landscape*. Oxford: Clarendon Press.

Holzknecht, Hartmut. 1974. *Anthropological research and associated findings in the Markham Valley of Papua New Guinea*. Research Bulletin No. 15. Port Moresby: Department of Agriculture, Stock and Fisheries.

Holzknecht, Susanne. 1989. *The Markham languages of Papua New Guinea*. Canberra: Pacific Linguistics, Research School of Pacific Studies, Australian National University.

Huber, Mary. 1988. *The bishops' progress*. Washington, D.C.: Smithsonian Institution Press.

Hurney, A. P. 1975. Report on sugar cane growing in the Kemp Welch and Markham River Valleys, Papua New Guinea. Manuscript.

Imbun, Benedict. 2000. Mining workers or "opportunist" tribesmen. *Oceania* 71:129–49.

International Bank for Reconstruction and Development. 1965. *The economic development of the Territory of Papua New Guinea*. Baltimore: Johns Hopkins University Press.

International Monetary Fund. 1956. Domestic exchange rates for US dollars. *International Financial Statistics* 9:14.

Jarrett, F. G., and K. Anderson. 1989. *Growth, structural change, and economic policy in Papua New Guinea*. Pacific Policy Paper No. 5. Canberra: National Centre for Development Studies, Australian National University.

Jerry, Mungo. 1987. For love of bride-price. *Sugar Valley News* 16:13–14.

Keenan, G. R. 1960. Letter accompanying "Bundi patrol report no. 4." National Archives, Port Moresby, Papua New Guinea.

Keesing, Roger. 1992. *Custom and confrontation: The Kwaio struggle for cultural autonomy*. Chicago: University of Chicago Press.

Keesing, Roger, and Robert Tonkinson, eds. 1982. *Reinventing traditional culture*. Special issue, *Mankind* 13.

Kelly, John, and Martha Kaplan. 2001. *Represented communities*. Chicago: University of Chicago Press.

Kelly, Raymond. 2000. *Warless societies and the origin of war*. Ann Arbor: University of Michigan Press.

Kestner, Joseph. 1995. The Pre-Raphaelites and imperialism. *Journal of Pre-Raphaelite Studies* 4:49–66.

King, David. 1998. Elites, suburban commuters, and squatters. In *Modern Papua New Guinea*, ed. Laura Zimmer-Tamakoshi, 183–94. Kirksville, Mo.: Thomas Jefferson University Press.

King, Geoff. 1996. *Mapping reality*. New York: St. Martin's Press.

King, Peter, Wendy Lee, and Vincent Warakai, eds. 1985. *From rhetoric to reality?* Port Moresby: University of Papua New Guinea Press.

Knauft, Bruce. 2002. *Exchanging the past*. Chicago: University of Chicago Press.

Kulick, Don. 1991. Law and order in Papua New Guinea. *Anthropology Today* 7:21–22.

———. 1993. Heroes from hell. *Anthropology Today* 9:9–14.

Lacan, Jacques. 1981. *Speech and language in psychoanalysis*. Baltimore: Johns Hopkins University Press.

Lake, Larry. 2001. Missionary gardens: Food as a medium for cultural identity by expatriate missionaries. Paper presented at the Meeting of the Association for Social Anthropology in Oceania, February 2001, Miami.

Larson, Donald, and Brent Borrell. 2001. *Sugar policy and reform*. Policy Research Working Paper No. 2602. Washington, D.C.: World Bank.

Lattas, Andrew. 1992. Skin, personhood, and redemption. *Oceania* 63:27–54.

———. 1998. *Cultures of secrecy*. Madison: University of Wisconsin Press.

———. 2000. Telephones, cameras, and technology in West New Britain cargo cults. *Oceania* 4:325–44.

Lawrence, Peter. 1964. *Road belong cargo*. Melbourne: Melbourne University Press.

Lawrence, Peter, and Mervyn Meggitt. 1965. Introduction to *Gods, ghosts, and men in Melanesia*, ed. Peter Lawrence and Mervyn Meggitt, 1–26. Melbourne: Oxford University Press.

Layoun, Mary. 1992. Telling spaces: Palestinian women and the engendering of national narratives. In *Nationalisms and sexualities*, ed. Andrew Parker et al., 407–23. London: Routledge.

Lee, Dorothy. 1959. Codifications of reality: Lineal and nonlineal. In *Freedom and culture*, ed. Dorothy Lee 105–20. Englewood Cliffs, N.J.: Prentice-Hall.

Leenhardt, Maurice. [1947] 1979. *Do Kamo: Person and myth in the Melanesian world*. Chicago: University of Chicago Press.

Lefebvre, Henri. 1991. *The production of space*. Oxford: Blackwell.

Lévi-Strauss, Claude. 1962. *Totemism*. Boston: Beacon.

Lewis, D.C. 1996. *The plantation dream*. Canberra: Journal of Pacific History.

Lindstrom, Lamont. 1990. *Knowledge and power in a South Pacific society*. Washington: Smithsonian Press.

———. 1993. *Cargo cult*. Honolulu: University of Hawaii Press.

LiPuma, Edward. 1995. The formation of nation-states and national cultures in Oceania. In *Nation Making*, ed. Robert Foster, 33–68. Ann Arbor: University of Michigan Press.

———. 2000. *Encompassing others*. Ann Arbor: University of Michigan.

Lovick, G. Lee. 1984. The agronomy section. *Sugar Valley News* 4:9–10.

Lowndes, A. G., ed. 1956. *South Pacific enterprise: The Colonial Sugar Refining Company Limited*. Sydney: Angus and Robertson.

Lutz, Catherine A., and Jane L. Collins. 1993. *Reading National Geographic*. Chicago: University of Chicago Press.

MacGillivray, A.W. 1990. Message from the general manager. *Sugar Valley News* 21:3.

Macintyre, Martha. 1989. Better homes and gardens. In *Family and gender in the pacific*, ed. Margaret Jolly and Martha Macintyre, 156–69. Cambridge: Cambridge University Press.

Maino, Dessie, and Isabel Malein. 1988. Moba. *Sugar Valley News* 17:22–24.

Malinowski, Bronislaw. 1922. *Argonauts of the western Pacific*. London: Routledge and Kegan Paul.

Mandle, Jay. 1973. *The plantation economy*. Philadelphia: Temple University Press.

Mangru, Basdeo. 1996. *A history of East Indian resistance on the Guyana sugar estates, 1869–1948*. Lewiston, N.Y.: Edwin Mellon Press.

Manning, Michael. 2000. Foreword to *Reforming trade in Papua New Guinea and the Pacific islands*, ed. Malcolm Bosworth and Kym Anderson, vii–ix. Adelaide: Centre for International and Economic Studies; Port Moresby: Institute for National Affairs.

Marglin, Stephen, and Fredrique Marglin. 1990. *Dominating knowledge*. Oxford: Clarendon Press.

Marks, Stephen, and Keith Maskus. 1993. Introduction to *The economics and politics of world sugar prices*, ed. Stephen Marks and Keith Maskus, 1–14. Ann Arbor: University of Michigan Press.

Masirere, Johnny. 1987. Independence Day 1987—fighting. *Sugar Valley News* 16:25–26.

May, Patricia, and Margaret Tuckson. 2000. *The traditional pottery of Papua New Guinea*. Honolulu: University of Hawaii Press.

McCarthy, J. K. 1963. *Patrol into yesterday*. Melbourne: Cheshire Publishing.

McNamara, Neil. 1957. Bundi patrol report no. 3, 1956–57, Madang. National Archives, Port Moresby, Papua New Guinea.

McPherson, Naomi. 2001. "Wanted: Young man, must like adventure"—Ian McCallum Mack, patrol officer. In *In Colonial New Guinea*, ed. Naomi McPherson, 82–110. Pittsburgh: University of Pittsburgh Press.

Meggitt, Mervyn. 1972. System and subsystem. *Human Ecology* 1:111–23.

———. 1974. Pigs are our hearts. *Oceania* 44:165–203.

———. 1977. *Blood is their argument*. Palo Alto: Mayfield Press.

Miller, Daniel. 1997. *Capitalism: An ethnographic approach*. Oxford: Berg.

Mintz, Sidney. 1953. The culture history of a Puerto Rican sugar cane plantation, 1876–1949. *Hispanic American Historical Review* 33:224–51.

———. 1958. Labor and sugar in Puerto Rico and Jamaica. *Comparative Studies in Society and History* 1:273–83.

———. 1959. The plantation as a sociocultural type. In *Plantation systems of the new world*, 42–50. Social Science Monograph 7. Washington, D.C.: Pan American Union.

———. 1960. *Worker in the cane*. New Haven: Yale University Press.

———. 1977. The so-called world system: Local initiative and local response. *Dialectical Anthropology* 2:253–70.

———. 1985. *Sweetness and power*. New York: Penguin.

Morgan, Lewis Henry. [1877] 1969. *Ancient society*. Cleveland: Meridan Books.

Moulik, T. K. 1973. *Money, motivation, and cash cropping*. Boroko: New Guinea Research Unit.

Moulton, Philips, ed. 1971. *The journal and major essays of John Woolman*. Oxford: Oxford University Press.

Muhlhausler, Peter. 1981. Foreigner talk: Tok masta in New Guinea. *International Journal of the Sociology of Language* 28:93–113.

Myers, Fred. 1988. Locating ethnographic practice. *American Ethnologist* 15:609–24.

Naiko, Frank. 1990. Legend—why dogs cannot talk. *Sugar Valley News* 21:49–50.

Nash, Jill. 2001. Paternalism, progress, paranoia—patrol reports and colonial history in South Bougainville. In *In Colonial New Guinea*, ed. Naomi McPherson, 111–24. Pittsburgh: University of Pittsburgh Press.

Nelson, Hank. 1982. *Taim bilong masta*. Sydney: Australian Broadcasting Commission Publications.

Nester, William. 2000. "Haughty conquerors": Amherst and the Great Indian Uprising of 1768. Westport, Conn.: Praeger.

Neumann, Klaus. 1992. *Not the way it really was*. Honolulu: University of Hawaii Press.

———. 1997. Nostalgia for Rabaul. *Oceania* 67:177–93.

News around Ramu. 1983. *Sugar Valley News* 3:14–15.

Norton, J. E. 1951. Patrol report no. 7, 1950–51, Madang. National Archives, Port Moresby, Papua New Guinea.

O'Brien, J. G. 1960. Bundi patrol report no. 4, 1959–60, Madang. National Archives, Port Moresby, Papua New Guinea.

O'Hanlon, Michael. 1993. *Paradise*. London: British Museum Press.

———. 1995. Modernity and the "graphicalization" of meaning. *Journal of the Royal Anthropological Institute* 1:469–93.

Obeyesekere, Gananath. 1992. *The apotheosis of Captain Cook*. Princeton: Princeton University Press.

Papuan sugar: Big scheme afoot. 1931. *Pacific Islands Monthly*, October 23.

Papua New Guinea and Ramu Sugar Limited. 1979. Master Agreement. August 24, RSL, Papua New Guinea.

Pares, Richard. 1960. *Merchants and planters*. Cambridge: Economic History Society, Cambridge University Press.

Per, Zachery. 2000a. Landowners shut campus. *National* (Port Moresby), April 14–16, 1–2.

———. 2000b. Landowners to Get K5m compo. *National* (Port Moresby), April 17, 1–2.

Peter, Rufina. 1993. Evaluation of comparative advantage in producing sugar under the current industry structure in Papua New Guinea. M.A. thesis, University of New England, Armidale, New South Wales.

Pilato, Samson. 1984. Industrial training with Ramu Sugar. *Sugar Valley News* 4:7–8.

Polanyi, Karl. 1944. *The great transformation*. New York: Scribner.

Programmes and policies for the economic development of Papua New Guinea. 1968. Territory of Papua New Guinea, Port Moresby.

Ramu Sugar Limited. 1991. *Ramu Sugar reports and accounts*. Annual report, RSL, Papua New Guinea.

———. 1993. *Employees handbook: Grades 1 to 2*. Mimeographed pamphlet, RSL, Papua New Guinea.

Richter, Robert. 1985. *Hungry for profit*. Videorecording. Ho-Ho-Kus, N.J.: New Day Films.

Robbins, Joel, and David Akin, eds. 1999. *Money and modernity*. Pittsburgh: University of Pittsburgh Press.

Rodman, Margaret. 1992. Empowering place. *American Anthropologist* 94:640–56.

Rodrik, Dani. 2001. Trading in illusions. *Foreign Policy* March/April, 55–62.

Rosaldo, Renato. 1993 *Culture and truth*. Boston: Beacon.

Roscoe, Paul. 1996. War and society in Sepik New Guinea. *Journal of the Royal Anthropological Institute* 2:645–66.

———. 1999. Return of the ambush. *Oceania* 69:171–83.

RSL . . . manager arrested and tried at Ramu. 1987. *Sugar Valley News* 15:32

Sabel, Maureen. 1983a. Dear reader. *Sugar Valley News* 1:3.

———. 1983b. Pride in yourself is pride in your country. *Sugar Valley News* 2:8.

Sack, Peter, and Dymphna Clark. 1980. *Governor in New Guinea: Albert Hahl*. Canberra: Australian National University Press.

Sahlins, Marshall. 1976. *The use and abuse of biology*. Ann Arbor: University of Michigan Press.

———. 1985. *Islands of history*. Chicago: University of Chicago Press.

———. 1988. Cosmologies of capitalism: The trans-Pacific sector of "The World System." *Proceedings of the British Academy* 7:1–51.

———. 1992. The economics of develop-man in the Pacific. *Res* 21:13–25.

Salisbury, Richard. 1970. *Vunamami.* Berkeley and Los Angeles: University of California Press.

Scaglion, Richard. 1979. Formal and informal operations of a village court in Maprik. *Melanesian Law Journal* 7:116–29.

———. 1985. Kiaps as kings. In *History and ethno-history in New Guinea*, ed. Deborah Gewertz and Edward Schieffelin, 77–99. Sydney: Oceania Publications.

Scheper-Hughes, Nancy. 1992. *Death without weeping.* Berkeley and Los Angeles: University of California Press.

Schmid, Christin Kocher, and Stefanie Klappa. 1999. Profile of a leader, or The world according to Yulu Nuo. In *Expecting the day of wrath*, ed. Christin Kocher Schmid, 89–110. Port Moresby: National Research Institute.

Schmitz, Andrew, and Douglas Christian. 1993. The economics and politics of U.S. sugar policy. In *The economics and politics of world sugar policies*, ed. Stephen Marks and Keith Maskus, 49–78. Ann Arbor: University of Michigan Press.

Scott, James. 1998. *Seeing like a state.* New Haven: Yale University Press.

Shaner, Janet. 1989 *Mumias Sugar Company Limited: A success story.* Harvard Business School, Case Study 9-590-039, Cambridge, Mass.

Sharp, Lauriston. 1952. Steel axes for Stone-Age Australians. *Human Organization* 11:17–22.

Shaw, Barry. 1980. Integrated rural development projects in Papua New Guinea: Development by whom, for whom, of whom? Manuscript presented in the workshop "Integrated Rural Development: a Mostly Papua New Guinea Perspective," Australian National University, Research School of Pacific Studies.

———. 1982a. Food and nutrition policies for South Pacific countries: Determinants of government planning. Manuscript, Australian National University, Research School of Pacific Studies, Development Studies Centre.

———. 1982b. Options for feeding people in Papua New Guinea. In *Proceedings of the Second Papua New Guinea Food Crops Conference*, ed. R. M. Bourke and V. Kesavan, 13–33. Port Moresby: Department of Primary Industry.

———. 1985. *Agriculture in the Papua New Guinea economy.* Port Moresby: Institute of National Affairs.

Shearston, Trevor. 1979. *Something in the blood.* St. Lucia: University of Queensland Press.

Silverman, Eric. 1999. Art, tourism, and the crafting of identity in the Sepik River (Papua New Guinea). In *Unpacking Cultures*, R. Phillips and C. Steiner, 51–66. Berkeley and Los Angeles: University of California Press.

———. 2000. Tourism in the Sepik River of Papua New Guinea. *Pacific Tourism Review* 4:105–19.

Sinclair, James. 1995. *The money tree.* Bathurst: Crawford House Publishing.

Smith, Raymond T. 1962. *British Guiana.* London: Oxford University Press.

———. 1967. Social stratification, cultural pluralism, and integration in West Indian Societies. In *Caribbean integration*, ed. S. Lewis and T. G. Mathews, 226–58. Puerto Rico: Institute of Caribbean Studies.

Solomon, Sinclaire. 1979. Resign threat over sugar by Tago. *Post-Courier* (Port Moresby), October 1, 1.

Sontag, Susan. 1977. *On photography*. New York: Farrar, Straus and Giroux.

The Spirit of Ramu. 1996. Videorecording. Thame, England: Harvest Moon Productions

Steichen, Edward. 1955. *The family of man*. New York: Simon and Schuster.

———. 1983. *The family of man*. New York: Simon and Schuster.

Stirrat, R. L. 1992. "Good government" and "the market." In *Contesting markets*, ed. Roy Dilley, 203–13. Edinburgh: Edinburgh University Press.

St. Luke's Catholic Church. 1985. *Sugar Valley News* 11:41.

Stoler, Ann, and Frederick Cooper, eds. 1997. *Tensions of empire: Colonial cultures in a bourgeois world*. Berkeley and Los Angeles: University of California Press.

Storey, David. 1979. Ramu Sugar costs too much. *Post-Courier* (Port Moresby), November 27, 5.

Strathern, Marilyn. 1988. *The gender of the gift*. Berkeley and Los Angeles: University of California Press.

———. 1992. The decomposition of an event. *Cultural Anthropology* 7:244–54.

Street, Brian. 1992. British popular anthropology: Exhibiting and photographing the other. In *Anthropology and photography*, ed. Elizabeth Edwards, 122–31. New Haven: Yale University Press.

Strongman, Luke. 2002. *The Booker Prize and the legacy of empire*. Amsterdam: Rodopi.

Sturma, Michael. 1997. South Pacific. *History Today* 47:25–30.

Swatridge, Colin. 1985. *Delivering the goods: Education as cargo in Papua New Guinea*. Manchester: Manchester University Press.

Sykes, Karen. 1999. After the raskol feast. *Critique of Anthropology* 19:157–74.

Taylor, Jonathan. 1994. Lord Campbell of Eskan. Scotsman (Edinburgh), December 31, 14.

Thomas, Clive. 1984. *Plantations, peasants, and the state*. Los Angeles: Center for Afro-American Studies and the Institute of Social and Economic Research.

Thomas, Nicholas. 1991. *Entangled objects*. Cambridge: Harvard University Press.

———. 1992. Substantivization and anthropological discourse. In *History and tradition in Melanesian anthropology*, ed. James Carrier, 1–19. Berkeley and Los Angeles: University of California Press.

———. 1994. *Colonialism's culture*. Princeton: Princeton University Press.

Thompson, E. P. 1967. Time, work discipline, and industrial capitalism. *Past and Present* 38:56–97.

Toland, Donald, and Norma Toland. 1983. Customs and culture of the Rawa people. Manuscript, Summer Institute of Linguistics, Ukarumpa, Papua New Guinea.

Trouillot, Michel-Rolph. 1988. *Peasants and capital*. Baltimore: Johns Hopkins University Press.

Turkle, Sherry. 1992. *Psychoanalytic politics: Jacques Lacan and Freud's French Revolution*. New York: Guilford Press.

Unsworth, Barry. 1992. Sacred Hunger. New York: W.W. Norton and Co.

Upton, Sian. 1998. Expatriates in Papua New Guinea: Constructions of expatriates in Canadian oral narratives. M.A. thesis, University of British Columbia.

Van Heekeren, Deborah. N.d. Being Hula. Ph.D. diss., University of Newcastle, Newcastle, Australia.

Waldrop, Rosmarie. 1994. *A key into the language of America*. New York: New Directions.

Weber, Max. [1944] 1976. *The Protestant ethic and the spirit of capitalism*. New York: Rinehart and Co.

Welcome to Ted and Joan Kaines. 1985. *Sugar Valley News* 11:10.

Weller, Christian, Robert Scott, and Adam Hersh. 2001. The unremarkable record of liberalized trade. Briefing paper, Economic Policy Institute, Washington, D.C.

West, Francis. 1968. *Hubert Murray: The Australian pro-consul*. Melbourne: Oxford University Press.

Westermark, George. 1986. Court is an arrow: Legal pluralism in Papua New Guinea. *Ethnology* 25:131–49.

———. 1997. Clan claims: Land, law, and violence in the Papua New Guinea Eastern Highlands. *Oceania* 67:218–33.

———. 2001. Anthropology and administration—colonial ethnography in the Papua New Guinea Eastern Highlands. In *In colonial New Guinea*, ed. Naomi McPherson, 45–63. Pittsburgh: University of Pittsburgh Press.

Wolf, Eric. 1959. Specific aspects of plantation systems in the New World. In *Plantation systems of the New World*, ed. Vera Rubin, 136–46. Washington, D.C.: Pan American Union.

World Bank. 1991. *Papua New Guinea: Structural adjustment, growth, and human resource development*. World Bank Report No. 9396-PNG, Washington, D.C.

———. 1999. *Papua New Guinea: Improving governance and performance*. World Bank Report No. 19388-PNG, Washington, D.C.

Zimmer-Tamakoshi, Laura. 1998a. Introduction to *Modern Papua New Guinea*, Laura Zimmer-Tamakoshi, 1–16. Kirksville, Mo.: Thomas Jefferson University Press.

———. 1998b. Women in town. In *Modern Papua New Guinea*, ed. Laura Zimmer-Tamakoshi, 195–210. Kirksville, Mo.: Thomas Jefferson University Press.

Zorn, Jean. 1992. "Graun Bilong Mipela": Local land courts and the changing customary law of Papua New Guinea. *Pacific Studies* 15:1–38.

Index